INTRODUCTION TO

Operating Systems

A Survey Course

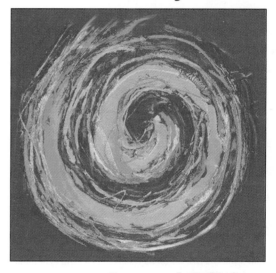

Second Edition

Mary S. Gorman
Cooper Career Institute
S. Todd Stubbs
Brigham Young University
CEP Inc.

THOMSON
COURSE TECHNOLOGY™

Australia • Canada • Mexico • Singapore • Spain • United Kingdom • United States

THOMSON
COURSE TECHNOLOGY

Introduction to Operating Systems, A Survey Course
by Mary S. Gorman, S. Todd Stubbs, John Anderson, and CEP Inc.

Managing Editor:
Chris Katsaropoulos

Senior Product Manager:
Dave Lafferty

Product Manager:
Robert Gaggin

Product Marketing Manager:
Kim Rytell

Associate Product Manager:
Jodi Dreissig

Development Editor:
Rose Marie Kuebbing
Custom Editorial Productions

Production Editor:
Megan Smith-Creed
Custom Editorial Productions

Cover Design:
Paul Vismara

Compositor:
GEX Publishing Services

Introducing our new
Survey Course on Operating Systems

Our operating systems texts provide a broad survey of topics for both the end user and administrator.

Introduction to Operating Systems, A Survey Course, 2ⁿᵈ edition
0-619-05529-4   Student Text (soft cover, perfect bound)
0-619-05531-6   IR (Instructor Resources)

Other available books include the following:

Introduction to Operating Systems, Comprehensive Course
0-619-05530-8   Student Text (soft cover, perfect bound)
0-619-05531-6   IR (Instructor Resources)

Microsoft Windows XP BASICS
0-619-05981-8   Student Text (soft cover, perfect bound)
0-619-05983-4   Review Pack (CD-ROM)
0-619-05982-6   IR (Instructor Resources)

Microsoft Windows 2000 Professional, Beginning Course
0-538-72418-8   Student Text (soft cover, perfect bound)
0-538-72417-X   Student Text (hardcover, spiral-bound)
0-538-72402-1   Review Pack (CD-ROM)
0-538-96856-7   IRK (Instructor Resource Kit CD-ROM)

Microsoft Windows 2000 Professional, Comprehensive Course
0-538-72401-3   Student Text (soft cover, perfect bound)
0-538-72402-1   Review Pack (CD-ROM)
0-538-96856-7   IRK (Instructor Resource Kit CD-ROM)

How to Use This Book

What makes a good computer instructional text? Sound pedagogy and the most current, complete materials. That is what you will find in *Introduction to Operating Systems, A Survey Course*. Not only will you find an inviting layout, but also many features to enhance learning.

Objectives— Objectives are listed at the beginning of each lesson, along with a suggested time for completion of the lesson. This allows you to look ahead to what you will be learning and to pace your work.

SCANS—(Secretary's Commission on Achieving Necessary Skills)—The U.S. Department of Labor has identified the school-to-careers competencies. The eight workplace competencies and foundation skills are identified in exercises where they apply. More information on SCANS can be found on the *Instructor Resource Kit* CD-ROM.

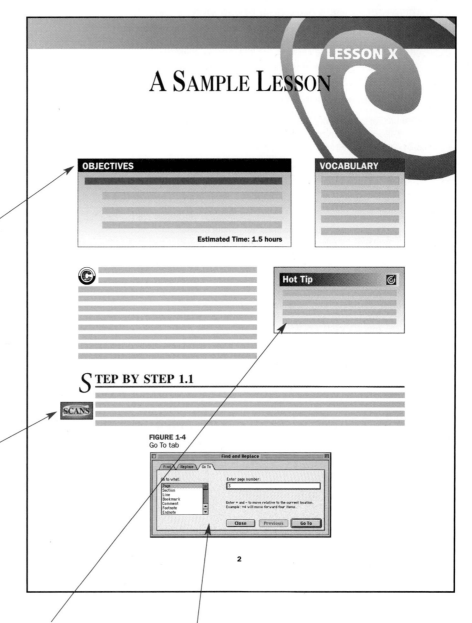

LESSON X

A SAMPLE LESSON

OBJECTIVES

Estimated Time: 1.5 hours

VOCABULARY

Hot Tip

STEP BY STEP 1.1

SCANS

FIGURE 1-4
Go To tab

2

Marginal Boxes— These boxes provide additional information for Hot Tips, fun facts (Did You Know?), Computer Concepts, the Internet, Extra Challenges activities, and Teamwork ideas.

Screen Shots—Screen shots come to life on each page with color and depth.

How to Use This Book

Summary—At the end of each lesson, you will find a summary to prepare you to complete the end-of-lesson activities.

Vocabulary Review—Review of important terms defined in each lesson reinforce the concepts learned.

Review Questions—Review material at the end of each lesson enables you to prepare for assessment of the content presented.

Lesson Projects—End-of-lesson hands-on application of what has been learned in the lesson allows you to actually apply the techniques covered.

Critical Thinking Activities—Each lesson gives you an opportunity to apply creative analysis and use the Help system to solve problems.

Lesson X Unit Sample

Intro Excel 3

SUMMARY

VOCABULARY*Review*

REVIEW*Questions*

PROJECTS

CRITICAL*Thinking*

PREFACE

You will find much helpful information in this introductory section. The *How to Use This Book* pages give you a visual summary of the information you will find in this text. Be sure to review the *Guide for Using This Book* to learn about the terminology and conventions used in preparing the pages and to find out what supporting materials are available for use with this book.

An Ideal Book for Anyone

Because computers are such an important subject for learners, instructors need the support of a well-designed, educationally sound textbook that is supported by strong ancillary materials. *Introduction to Operating Systems, A Survey Course* is just such a book.

The textbook includes features that make learning easy and enjoyable, yet challenging, for learners. It is also designed with many features that make teaching easy and enjoyable for you. Comprehensive, yet flexible, *Introduction to Operating Systems, A Survey Course* is adaptable for a wide variety of class-time schedules.

The text includes a wide range of learning experiences, from activities with one or two commands to projects that sharpen and challenge learners' problem-solving skills. This book is ideal for computer courses with learners who have varying abilities and previous computer experiences.

The lessons in this course contain the following features designed to promote learning:

- Objectives that specify goals students should achieve by the end of the lesson.

- Concept text that explores each new feature in detail.

- Screen captures that help illustrate the concept text.

- Step-by-Step exercises that help illustrate the concept text and allow students to practice using the features introduced.

- Summaries that review the concepts in the lessons.

- Review questions that test students on the concepts covered in the lesson.

- Projects that provide an opportunity for students to apply the concepts they have learned in the lesson.

- Critical Thinking activities that encourage students to use the knowledge gained in the lesson to solve specific problems.

About the Authors

Mary S. Gorman has a bachelor's degree from Edinboro University in Business Administration and Marketing. She is currently working to attain her Master's degree in computer science. Mary is a Microsoft Certified Professional in Windows 2000 Professional and Windows 2000 Server, an A+ certified technician, and holds all of the Microsoft Office User Specialist certifications in Office 2000. She teaches at Palm Beach Community College in West Palm Beach, FL.

S. Todd Stubbs has worked with microcomputers for over 18 years as an educator, programmer, writer, editor, and instructional technologist in higher education. His bachelor's degree from Brigham Young University is in English and he holds a master's degree in Instructional Technology from Utah State University. He is presently an instructional designer at Brigham Young University's Center for Instructional Design. He and his wife, Joy, are the proud parents of five beautiful children.

GUIDE FOR USING THIS BOOK

Please read this guide before starting work. The time you spend now will save you much more time later and will make your learning faster, easier, and more pleasant.

Conventions

The different type styles used in this book have special meanings. They will save you time because you will soon automatically recognize from the type style the nature of the text you are reading and what you will do.

WHAT YOU WILL DO	TYPE STYLE	EXAMPLE
Text you will key	**Bold**	Key **Don't litter** rapidly.
Individual keys you will press	**Bold**	Press **Enter** to insert a blank line.

WHAT YOU WILL SEE	TYPE STYLE	EXAMPLE
Glossary terms in book	***Bold and italics***	The ***menu bar*** contains menu titles.
Words on screen	*Italics*	Highlight the word *pencil* on the screen.
Menus and commands	**Bold**	Choose **Open** from the **File** menu.
Options/features with long names	*Italics*	Select **Normal** from the *Style for following paragraph* text box.

Instructor Resources CD-ROM

The *Instructor Resources* CD-ROM contains a wealth of instructional material you can use to prepare for teaching this course. The CD-ROM stores the following information:

- ExamView® tests for each lesson. ExamView is a powerful testing software package that allows instructors to create and administer printed, computer (LAN-based), and Internet exams. ExamView includes hundreds of questions that correspond to the topics covered in this text, enabling learners to generate detailed study guides that include page references for further review. The computer-based and Internet testing components allow learners to take exams at their computers, and also save the instructor time by grading each exam automatically.

- Electronic *Instructor's Manual* that includes lecture notes for each lesson and answers to the end-of-lesson Vocabulary Review and Review Questions.

- Instructor lesson plans as well as learner study guides that can help to guide students through the lesson text and exercises.

- Copies of the figures that appear in the student text, which can be used to prepare transparencies.

- Suggested schedules for teaching the lessons in this course.

- Additional instructional information about individual learning strategies, portfolios, and career planning, and a sample Internet contract.

- PowerPoint presentations that highlight the concepts covered in each lesson.

SCANS

The Secretary's Commission on Achieving Necessary Skills (SCANS) from the U.S. Department of Labor was asked to examine the demands of the workplace and whether new learners are capable of meeting those demands. Specifically, the Commission was directed to advise the Secretary on the level of skills required to enter employment.

SCANS workplace competencies and foundation skills have been integrated into *Introduction to Operating Systems, A Survey Course*. The workplace competencies are identified as 1) ability to use resources, 2) interpersonal skills, 3) ability to work with information, 4) understanding of systems, and 5) knowledge and understanding of technology. The foundation skills are identified as 1) basic communication skills, 2) thinking skills, and 3) personal qualities.

Exercises in which learners must use a number of these SCANS competencies and foundation skills are marked in the text with the SCANS icon.

TABLE OF CONTENTS

iv   How to Use This Book
vi   Preface
viii   Guide for Using This Book

1   Lesson 1: Introduction to Operating Systems

1   What Is an Operating System?
4   Hardware
8   Basic Functionalities of the Operating System
12   Evolution of Computing
20   Summary

25   Lesson 2: Disk Operating System: DOS

25   Introduction
26   Preparing for Installation
30   Installation of the Operating System
31   Basic Functionalities of the Operating System
44   Unique Features of DOS
49   Common DOS Error Messages
51   Summary

57   Lesson 3: Understanding Mac OS X

57   Mac OS X—A Whole New Operating System
58   Hardware Differences
62   The Three Faces of Mac OS X
64   Working in Aqua
70   Managing Files in Aqua
72   Managing Mac OS X's Options
79   Managing Networking and Users
85   Some Useful Utilities
89   Troubleshooting Mac OS X
91   Summary

97   Lesson 4: Microsoft Windows XP

97   Introduction
98   Installation of Windows XP
103   Basic Functions of Windows XP
117   File Management
131   Word Processing
137   Unique Features of Windows XP
147   Summary

153   Lesson 5: Windows 2000 Professional

153   Introduction
154   Differences between Windows 2000 and Previous Versions
155   Installation of Windows 2000
161   Basic Functions of Windows 2000
175   File Management
189   Word Processing
194   Unique Features of Windows 2000
206   Summary

211   Lesson 6: Windows NT Workstation

211   What Is Windows NT Workstation?
212   Installing Windows NT
215   Basic Functionality
225   Unique Features of Windows NT
236   Summary

241   Lesson 7: Novell Client

241   Introduction
247   Installing Novell Client
259   Basic Functions of Novell NetWare
262   Unique Features of NetWare
265   Summary

269   Lesson 8: Linux

269   Introduction
272   Installing Linux
289   Basic Functionalities
307   Unique Features
314   Shut Down the Linux System
316   Summary

Glossary-321   **Glossary**
Index-329   **Index**

Acknowledgments

The authors of this book would like to make the following dedications and acknowledgments:

Mary S. Gorman would like to thank her family for supporting her in all her endeavors. This book is dedicated to David Adiutori to thank him for sustaining her during this and many other of her goals in her life.

S. Todd Stubbs would like to thank Joy, Sarah, Marc, Elisabeth, Matthew, Manda, Sam, and Abby. He would also like to extend a special thank you to Stanford Stubbs, his father, for his example of generosity.

INTRODUCTION TO OPERATING SYSTEMS

OBJECTIVES

Upon completion of this lesson you should be able to:

■ Define the term "operating system."

■ Explain the three different types of user interfaces.

■ Identify the common physical components of your computer.

■ Understand how the operating system handles resources.

■ Understand how the operating system handles files.

■ Discuss the evolution of the microcomputer and different operating systems over time.

Estimated Time: 6 + hours

VOCABULARY

Basic input-output system (BIOS)

Command-line user interface

Central processing unit (CPU)

Graphical user interface (GUI)

Menu-based user interface

Operating system (OS)

User interface (UI)

What Is an Operating System?

Without software, a computer is just a pile of electronics that gives off heat. If the hardware is the heart of a computer, then the software is its soul. An *operating system* (OS) is a collection of system programs that allow the user to run program software (software that allows you to perform a task, such as play a game or write a letter). An operating system manages hardware and other programs; it provides very specific resources to the programs it manages. In the most basic terms, the operating system provides an intermediate interface between the hardware and the user(s). In a more general sense, it provides software and hardware management. For software, it loads, executes, and directs input to the program; displays output; and saves and unloads programs. For hardware, it boots the machine when turned on, provides a connection between the CPU and other hardware, manages memory, and allows for upgrades.

How an Operating System Works

The operating system software provides the look and feel of the system known as the **environment**. Most PCs can run one or more operating systems—and each one can have a very different look and feel. Most operating systems are made up of a number of functionally separate pieces that, together, comprise the operating system. The most basic and fundamental part is the kernel.

1

The kernel is responsible for managing all the other system programs; it can be thought of as upper management, which oversees the whole process of operating the computer system. The process involves the integration of the hardware and the software, so users can operate the machine effectively and efficiently to attain their goals.

In order to start understanding how an operating system works, let's look at a simple example. Consider what happens when you type the following command on a DOS machine:

```
C:\>dir
```

The command here is the directory command, which is used to display a list of files in a directory, the result is a listing of files on the hard drive in the current directory. See Figure 1-1.

FIGURE 1-1
Result of the dir command

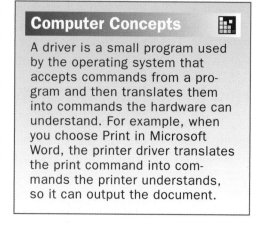

The shell is an environment designed to allow a user to manipulate the system. The shell also supplies cues so users know where they are and what is happening. C:\> is a prompt that the operating system shell displays. This prompt means that the system is waiting for the user to type some command. The keyboard driver enables the system to recognize what characters have been typed.

The keyboard driver passes the command to the shell, which processes it by looking for an executable command of the same name. It finds an appropriate match for the command, and the kernel reads the file containing instructions on how to perform that command. The dir command tells the file subsystem of the kernel to find out what files are available. The file system might make use of the file system information or use the disk device driver to read this information from the disk. The dir command then writes that information out and the video driver displays it on the screen. (It is not important that you understand the whole process just listed; just be aware that many things have to operate in concert in order for it to work.)

Computer Concepts

A driver is a small program used by the operating system that accepts commands from a program and then translates them into commands the hardware can understand. For example, when you choose Print in Microsoft Word, the printer driver translates the print command into commands the printer understands, so it can output the document.

Although this may seem rather complicated, it shows that even simple commands reveal that an operating system is a cooperating set of functions that work together to give you, the user, a coherent view of the system. Don't lose sight of the fact that the hardware is working in the background as well. Each program is responsible for managing a specific piece of hardware. The video card has a video driver, the keyboard has a keyboard driver, the hard drive has its own driver. The drivers can be thought of as middle management. Each driver controls a different part of the system. The kernel is still upper management, overseeing the whole process. The analogy can be extended further: If one of the managers is not doing its job correctly, it affects the whole system. When the drivers are correctly written, everything works perfectly.

Types of User Interfaces

Operating systems have both an inside and an outside—both a body and an engine. Because the instructions are built to work with the machine, human beings can barely read them. Therefore, the operating system must provide a way for humans to communicate with the machine. This part of an operating system (and all other programs) is called the human-computer interface (HCI) or, more often, the *user interface* (UI).

Because the UI is the part of the operating system that we see, we tend to categorize the operating system according to its user interface. User interfaces generally fall into one of three types: command-line, menu-based, and graphical.

Command-Line User Interfaces

Command-line user interfaces use the keyboard to communicate with the operating system and the computer. In the command-line UI, the user types in commands and the computer responds to them. The problem is that, because computers must receive their instructions in very precise ways, the user is required to type the commands in a very specific format (called syntax). Because this is true, a command-line UI requires the user to either remember a number of arcane commands, or have a book handy that reminds them what to type. Both Unix and DOS utilize a command-line user interface. See Figure 1-2.

FIGURE 1-2
A command-line user interface

```
C:\APPROACH>dir

 Volume in drive C has no label
 Volume Serial Number is 1103-0776
 Directory of C:\APPROACH

.               <DIR>        06-25-95   7:42p
..              <DIR>        06-25-95   7:42p
EXAMPLES        <DIR>        06-25-95   7:42p
TMPLATES        <DIR>        06-25-95   7:42p
ICONS           <DIR>        06-25-95   7:44p
IMGBMP   DIL          7,088 08-18-93  12:00a
IMGTGA   DIL          9,376 08-18-93  12:00a
IMGGIF   DIL          9,888 08-18-93  12:00a
README   WRI          9,984 08-18-93  12:00a
IMGPCX   DIL         15,920 08-18-93  12:00a
IMGEPSF  DIL         20,784 08-18-93  12:00a
IMGTIFF  DIL         38,496 08-18-93  12:00a
APPROACH HLP        215,152 08-18-93  12:00a
APPROACH EXE      1,205,504 08-18-93  12:00a
APPROACH V21              3 08-18-93  12:00a
        15 file(s)      1,532,195 bytes
                      139,026,432 bytes free

C:\APPROACH>
```

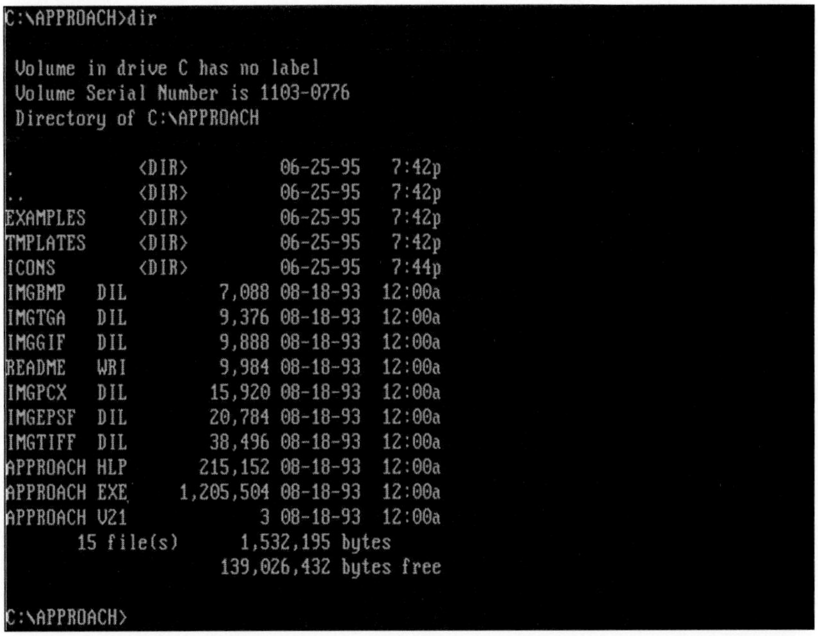

Menu-based Interfaces

Generally speaking, *menu-based user interfaces* are not common in operating systems. However, menus can simplify the use of a command-line UI by providing a list of commands from which to choose. The user selects the menu item by typing an identifier (a number or letter) or by clicking with a mouse, then the menu-based UI types the complete and correct syntax for the user. This makes it much easier for people with few computer skills to interact with a command-line UI.

Graphical User Interfaces

The *graphical user interface* (GUI, pronounced "gooey") is really a very sophisticated form of menu-based interface. However, instead of listing the commands, it represents them as a number of small pictures called icons. Windows and MacOS, two of the most popular GUIs, use icons to represent frequently-issued commands. By manipulating these graphic elements with a mouse, the user can open, close, move, and delete files.

Both menu-based interfaces and GUIs are simply facades for the command-line interface, which is hidden from the user. Early versions of Windows used this system, as do several of the GUIs for Unix. See Figure 1-3.

FIGURE 1-3
A graphical user interface

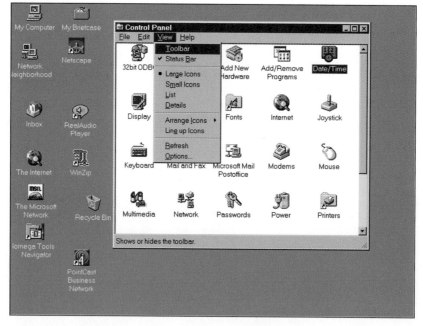

Hardware

Now that you have some idea of how the computer works, let's take a small tour of its hardware. The following hardware items are physical components you can find in almost any modern computer:

- CPU—the *central processing unit* is the brain of the computer. It performs all processing functions done by the computer.

- **RAM**—random access memory, which functions as the principal workspace of the computer. You change the contents of RAM as you work. However, because RAM chips require power to maintain their content, you must save your data to a disk before you turn off the computer.

- **ROM**—read-only memory, which is programmed once at the factory. You cannot change the contents of ROM. This type of memory is used to store specific control routines, such as the BIOS process described below. ROM instructions are non-volatile; that is, they retain information when you turn off the computer.

- **BIOS**—basic input-output system. This is a ROM chip that has been programmed with the instructions needed to begin the boot process. It contains the necessary code to enable the CPU to talk to the other hardware in the system.

- **Motherboard**—the main circuit board in the computer. On it reside the CPU, RAM, BIOS, and all the other chips your machine needs to run. It also contains empty "expansion" slots where upgrades or expansion cards can be added.

- **Keyboard**—the device used to input information for the computer's programs. It can also be used to manipulate the computer system through keyboard shortcuts that replace using the mouse to communicate with the operating system. For example, when using the Microsoft Word program, the user can click the Save icon on the toolbar with the mouse or press Ctrl + S on the keyboard to save.

- **Pointing Device**—Most commonly used are a mouse or a trackball. When the user moves the pointing device, a pointer (often in the form of an arrowhead) moves across the screen in a relative motion that corresponds to the motion of the user. The devices may have two or more buttons. By placing the pointer at different locations on the screen and then pressing the buttons (clicking), the user can run programs, use menus, and manipulate the system interface.

Classifications of Hardware Components

The hardware components attached to your computer fall into four categories: input, output processing and storage. Input components allow the user to communicate information to the computer. The output components allow the communication of information back to the user. The CPU is used to process information. Storage devices are used to permanently store information.

Input: Keyboard, Mouse, Scanner, and Voice Devices

Input devices such as the keyboard, mouse, scanner, and microphone devices are used to input different kinds of information. Each of these devices has an associated driver that oversees its operation. The driver takes the incoming data, translates it into a common form if needed, and directs it to the appropriate destination. Most input devices include some kind of feedback from an output device (usually the monitor) to let

Computer Concepts

QWERTY is the name of the keyboard layout. It is named QWERTY for the first six letters in the left corner of the first alphabetic row.

you know whether or not your efforts are working. In the case of the keyboard, your cursor shows you where you are on the screen, while the letters that you type appear on the screen. Other devices may provide feedback in a dialog box that pops up on the screen, or as a change in color or the shape of a symbol.

The keyboard is the most common input device. A keyboard is just a collection of spring-loaded switches—one for each letter of the alphabet, number, or symbol. Most keyboards are laid out in a traditional QWERTY pattern that must be learned. Once learned, however, a keyboard allows you to enter text very quickly and efficiently. Special keys on the keyboard, such as Backspace and Delete, allow you to make corrections. Others, such as the Alt or Option keys, can be used in combination with letter keys to display unusual characters. Still others (such as the Control or Command keys) can be used, in combination with letters, to send commands to the program.

As mentioned earlier, the mouse is a screen pointing device that helps you move quickly to a certain location on the screen. When you reach the location where you want to work, you use the mouse buttons to make something happen. For example, you might press the mouse button once and let it go; this is called clicking. Clicking twice in rapid succession is called double-clicking. When you hold the mouse button down as you move the pointer, it's called dragging. Each of these gestures produces an action by the computer. These will be discussed in detail for each of the operating systems that use the mouse. Drawing tablets, trackballs, lightpens, and touch-sensitive screens are all variations on the mouse idea. They perform the same function and their names are sometimes used interchangeably.

Another important input device is the scanner, which is a close relative of the digital (still) camera and digital movie camera. These devices allow you to capture pictures or other graphics and move them to the computer. Because the input process can be very complex, special programs with buttons and dialog boxes are used to interact with the device and let you know if it's working.

The ability of computers to understand and act on spoken commands was only a dream for many years, but it has become a reality. Analyzing human speech is an enormously complex process. As a human being, you perform speech recognition without even thinking about it—it's a tribute to the power of your human brain. Speech recognition requires several devices to work in cooperation: the soundcard, a voice-recognition program, a powerful CPU, and the operating system.

Output: Monitor and Printer Devices

Computers would be of no value if they could not report back to their human users. The devices for doing so are called output devices. The two most common are monitors and printers.

A monitor is little more than a fancy television set. However, most monitors lack a tuner for capturing transmitted programs; instead, they take their information directly from the computer. Circuitry inside the computer organizes the electronic signals so that they display properly. Some computers have the circuitry for more than one monitor, and can display more than one

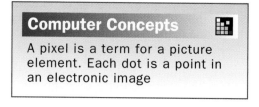

Computer Concepts

A pixel is a term for a picture element. Each dot is a point in an electronic image

screen at a time. Though this configuration is used mostly by professional designers, it gives them the ability to view twice as much information. Monitors that use technology other than the traditional cathode ray tube (CRT) displays are becoming more common, with liquid crystal displays (LCD) such as those used in digital watches and laptop monitors, and plasma displays also becoming popular. The popularity of LCDs and plasma displays lies in the fact that they are flatter (meaning they are only three to five inches from front to back, instead of the usual 15+ inches). They also consume less electricity and consequently run cooler. The downside is that they have a shorter lifespan than CRTs. Computer monitors traditionally have the same 4:3 aspect ratio as conventional television. This means that if you divide the number of pixels horizontally by 4 and the number of pixels vertically by 3, you get the same number. (For a small monitor, 640 3 480, the common denominator is 160.) Monitors range upward in size from 640 3 480. Some monitors are now appearing in other aspect ratios as well. The operating system (or its extensions) must know the size and type of monitor in order to transmit the correct signals to the monitor.

Early printers used actual metal type to print text onto paper. Modern printers use tiny dots of toner or ink to get the same effect and a whole lot more. Modern laser printers (which use lasers to sensitize paper and toner to form the ink) and ink jet printers (which spray tiny droplets of ink on the paper) can be used to print pictures as well as text. With either type of printer, the computer must have the ability to translate the desired output into a form that the printers can understand. Some printers require raw information—that is, information about what dot of ink goes where on the paper. Others can be sent more intelligent information, which then translates into print. Clearly the operating system must be able to speak the printer's language, or printing cannot take place.

Processing

As previously mentioned the CPU processes all information done by the computer. Data received by input devices goes to the CPU and output travels from the CPU to output devices. The CPU stores data and instructions on storage devices and performs calculations and other processing of data.

Storage Types: Tapes, Disks, and Hard Disks

The computer needs to be able to write data for safekeeping and also have a storage place for programs. Storage devices come in many shapes, sizes, formats, and speeds. One of the earliest devices was the diskette drive. On most systems today this is a 3.5-inch diskette that holds 1.44 million bytes (a byte is usually equal to one character; a million bytes is called a megabyte) of information. Hard drives are an advanced form of diskette drive. They hold much more (billions of bytes—gigabytes—instead of just over a megabyte), are faster, and are about the same physical size. The hard drive is a fixed storage device in the computer. It consists of several disks, called platters, that store data electronically. Saving data to the hard drive is like writing it down on a piece of paper. It won't change until you physically erase it.

On all IBM-compatible machines the first diskette drive is called A:\ and the second is called B:\. While it is possible to have more diskette drives, it almost never happens. If it did, the third diskette drive wouldn't be C:\, because this letter is reserved for the first hard drive on the system. A computer's hard drives start at C:\ and continue down the alphabet. CD-ROM drives start anywhere from drive letter D:\ and continue down the alphabet. On the machine editing this document there are seven hard drives, ranging from C:\ to I:\. There are also 11 CD-ROM drives, starting at drive letter M:\ and continuing to W:\. You will notice there is a gap between I:\ and M:\. This is because you often leave some letters free, so you can assign future drives to fit your needs.

There are several formats for storage media, each with their own advantages and disadvantages. Different types include tapes and magnetic disks (hard drives, diskettes, and zip drives). The advantage of tape is that it is potentially capable of holding large amounts of information; its disadvantage is that it is relatively slow. Disks, on the other hand, offer much faster storage and retrieval; however, their space is somewhat limited. Once a disk is full, you either have to add another drive or replace it. Table 1-1 summarizes the capacities of five types of floppies.

TABLE 1-1
Floppy disk types and capacities

TYPE	STORAGE CAPACITY
3 1/2-inch extra high density	2.88 MB
3 1/2-inch high density	1.44 MB
3 1/2-inch double density	720 K
5 1/4-inch high density	1.2 MB
5 1/4-inch double density	360 K

With tape you can just remove the full cartridge and insert a blank one. One solution is to make the disk removable (like diskettes) so that you can place a new disk in the machine when the old one is full. Removable disks cannot be designed to hold as much information as fixed hard disks, which are hermetically sealed inside the computer. CD-ROMs, which are removable, are a compromise between the two. They are faster than tape but slower than hard drives.

Basic Functionalities of the Operating System

Resource Management

Starting Up

Turning on a computer is much more complicated than turning on a light bulb or motor. Imagine the processes that are required to turn on a toaster, for example. After you put a piece of bread into the slot and press the lever, at least two other processes must begin: A switch must turn on power to the heating element so the bread can be toasted, and a timing mechanism must keep track of the time elapsed, automatically turn off the heating element at the correct time, and trigger a mechanism to eject the toast.

A computer, by contrast, runs a program, a set of detailed instructions on how to do something. The CPU can't load instructions until it knows how and from where to load them. And since nothing has been loaded, it doesn't know where to begin. The computer must find a way to start itself—or, to use the old phrase, "lift itself by its own bootstraps." (In fact, this is where the term booting a computer comes from.) To enable a computer to boot itself, designers decided to hard code a standard starting place into every computer. When the computer is turned on, it is set to look at the starting address for the *basic input-output system* (*BIOS*). It then reads the BIOS, the list of all the instructions it needs to get going. The last instruction in the BIOS is to start reading the operating system—first from the diskette drive, or if that is not available, from the hard drive. That way, if the hard drive ever fails, you can use a boot disk to start the computer. The computer just continues to read and execute programs off of the hard drive.

Remember that an operating system is nothing more than a program running on the computer. However, it is unique in that it must oversee all the other programs running on the computer. Part of its job is to make sure that all the parts of the computer are available to the programs that will run on top of the operating system. Modern computers can take considerable time (from five seconds to many minutes) to boot because of the many configurations and connections that must be made to allow for all the various parts of the computer to operate.

Shutting Down

When you drive a car, you don't drive to the general vicinity of the place you're going and just turn the key off and leave it in the middle of the road. A good driver finds a place to park where the car will be out of harm's way. As the driver, you set the car in a parking gear or set the parking brake, turn off the lights, and so forth. When everything is set, you turn off the key, unbuckle your seat belt, and get out. There is a well-defined procedure people go through to make sure no problems will occur.

A computer has the same needs. There are several processes that need to be finished before power is removed: Data needs to be put away, settings (such as dates and file sizes) need to be calculated and stored, connections with devices and the network need to be terminated, and so forth. The shutdown process accomplishes all of these. It's like putting your tools away after work so you know where they are the next time you want to use them.

If you forget to shut down your computer before turning it off, don't panic. Most operating systems provide for accidents by doing some of these things as you use the computer. If something is damaged by suddenly losing power, tools have been developed to help minimize the damage. If the computer is shut down without going through the entire shutdown cycle, it will take a little time to start up again, and you may notice that you have lost some of your settings when you restart. In most cases settings can be easily restored to their former values.

Multitasking and Allocating CPU cycles

Like minicomputers and mainframes, microcomputers have become powerful, complex machines. Unlike their larger cousins, PCs do not always have multiple users using them at the same time; however, they do have to accommodate several programs running simultaneously, as mentioned earlier. In many ways this is the same thing. For example, as I write this paragraph, I am typing into a word processing program while listening to music that is playing from the computer's CD-ROM drive. My computer allows me to type and play music at the same time. Many people add email and an Internet browser, and run other programs all at the same time. Each of these programs requires a part of the microprocessor's attention. The less time the CPU can spend working on a program, the more its performance suffers.

John Von Neumann, a computer scientist of many years ago, noted that computer processors can only do one thing at a time. Even though the machine editing this book has many things running—music, word processor, Internet connection, and network services—only one of the programs is running at any instance in time. In order for the brain of a computer, the microprocessor, to appear to do more than one thing at a time, it must share its attention in small portions among all the active tasks. This is called multitasking. The CPU counts the number of programs running and divides that number into one second; i.e., if ten programs are running, the computer spends 1/10 of a second on each program. Once all the programs have been serviced, it starts at the top of the list and begins again. This is how modern operating systems work.

Of course, it all happens faster than the eye can see. Think of it as watching a movie. The film on which the movie is recorded is composed of individual frames. Each frame is slightly different from the one before it. When all the frames are shown in rapid order, they appear to move. The computer does the same to your programs. It updates every program very quickly—so quickly that you don't notice the tiny pauses.

For example, neither the typing that I am doing nor the CD I am playing require much work by the CPU, so it can accommodate both activities at the same time, with CPU cycles to spare. No matter how fast I type, the music never skips.

However, if in addition to typing and listening to music I were running a complex mathematical formula that required several minutes to compute, the operating system might decide that the math program required more attention, and it might borrow cycles from my word processing program or CD player, or both. In that case, I might notice that letters don't reach the screen as fast as I type them, or the music might start skipping while the CPU was paying attention to the math program. It is usually the operating system's job to manage this.

Memory Management

Once the computer is up and running, the next job of the operating system is to allocate and manage memory. Modern PCs are capable of running several programs at the same time. Some RAM (random access memory) resources are used by the operating system, some by each of the programs running, and some are shared by two or more of the programs. It is the operating system's job to make sure all of these processes run in harmony without conflicting with each other.

Because computer processes can be so memory-intensive, the computer sometimes runs out of available RAM to run a process. The operating system can handle this in one of two ways: it can simply report to the user that it doesn't have enough memory and stop the process, or it can compensate. One of the ways that computers compensate is through a little trick called **virtual memory**. Virtual memory moves blocks of memory from the RAM to the computer's hard disk so that the process will have room to continue. The difference in speed between the two can be as much as 1000:1. This is why it is so important to have all the RAM your programs expect. This is why it is so important to keep all of the program in RAM so you don't waste time swapping chunks of code to the hard drive. Otherwise, the programs perform poorly and slow the computer down considerably.

File Management

Operating systems arose when it became necessary to connect to storage devices such as the disk drive. It is not enough to tell the computer to put a file away. The computer must know whether there is enough room for storage, must know precisely where the user wants to store the file, and must store the file in such a way that it can be retrieved later. Files sometimes need to be moved, duplicated, and have their names and other information changed. In addition, the operating system must provide a way to discard files that are no longer needed. These are all management functions the operating system performs for file storage.

File Types: Programs, Documents, and Containers

Regardless of the storage medium, the operating system usually distinguishes at least three types of files. They are programs, documents, and containers.

Programs, sometimes known as applications, are executable files. That is, they contain instructions to have the computer perform some tasks. Common types of programs include word processing programs, spreadsheets, Internet browsers, database programs, financial and tax programs, and many others.

Documents, on the other hand, generally contain human-intelligible information such as text, pictures, sounds, or movies. Most programs play and create documents.

Finally, there are containers. Strictly speaking, containers aren't files. They are really just a way to organize all the other files. In some operating systems they are called folders, in some directories. Basically they exist to organize the stored data into smaller groups of files.

Identifying Files and Types

Two principal methods are used to identify the file type. The simplest method, used by DOS and by some versions of Unix, is the addition of an extension to the filename. In DOS, for example, a rule known as the 8.3 convention specifies that filenames can only be eight characters long, followed by a period, then by a three-character extension to the name. This extension tells the operating system what kind of file it is. For example, a DOS file ending in .exe is an executable file—usually a program of some sort. A .txt ending indicates a text file.

Some files are identified by information that is hidden from the user, but which is used by the operating system to identify the file. The Mac operating system uses this method by attaching two four-letter codes to every file. The first tells what type of file it is (TEXT, PICT, etc.). The second tells what program created the file. In this way, when you open a document, the Macintosh is aware of what program was used to create that document and opens the appropriate program to deal with that document.

Navigating and Locating Files

When filing systems consisted of only one layer, navigating to locate files was pretty straightforward. As numbers of files grew, and as containers were used to classify and hold these numerous files, the situation grew more complicated.

Simply speaking, navigating is the ability to recognize a container and open it to see what is inside. Since containers can contain containers, and so forth, this can be very time-consuming if files are stored randomly. For this reason, people usually group files together into logical bunches. On my home computer, for example, there are three folders (containers) on the hard disk. One is for programs (it's called Applications), one is for documents (called Documents), and one is for the operating system (it's called System Folder). Inside the Documents folder are folders for each member of my family. Within each of those, each member of my family has created their own structure to keep track of their files. In this way, if I'm looking for my daughter's English paper, I can narrow down the search pretty quickly, unless it has been misfiled.

Occasionally files get misplaced. When this happens, the operating system provides a way to search for the file by name. The trick is you have to remember the name of the missing file. More sophisticated operating system searches will even search the content of the documents, so you can look for an unusual word or phrase.

Copying and Moving Files

One of the great strengths of operating systems is their ability to make copies of files and move them. To understand the need for this, imagine that you are taking an English course for which you know there will be two major papers required. You start out believing that, with only two files to keep track of, you do not need to separate these files. You keep them in a container called Homework. As the course begins, you realize that in each case the teacher requires a rough draft, a proof draft, and the final paper. You realize that it might be a good idea to keep a copy of the early drafts of papers just in case you want to locate something you wrote earlier, or in case the teacher loses your paper. Your two files have just multiplied to six, with four of them based on the other two.

Then you find out the English teacher is going to require a bibliography for each of these papers. You need a place to write down every source in rough order so you can clean it up later. There are at least two more files. How will you keep them all straight? Easy. Inside your Homework container, you create a new container called English. All the files associated with your English course will be moved into that container, where you will be able to find them easily.

Because documents are created by programs, the operating system must not only provide a way to find files directly through the operating system, it must also provide the program with a way to store and find files as well.

Removing Files

After the labor of creating those files, you may not think you will ever want to part with them. But as the semester ends, you may realize that if you don't do some housecleaning, you will run out of space on your hard disk. You may choose to back them up onto removable media (like a diskette) to keep them, or you may simply remove them from your hard disk. Either way, the operating system must have the ability to discard files that the user specifies.

Evolution of Computing

What is the earliest computer you can think of? If you watch movies, you might think of main-frames. These were huge computing devices that filled whole buildings. See Figure 1-4. The only resemblance they bear to today's computers is that, given the same problem, they would produce the same answer. Before digital computers, were computers that did not use a microprocessor.

FIGURE 1-4
Mainframe computer

Some Early Computers

Charles Babbage was an English mathematician and inventor, often referred to as the father of computing. See Figure 1-5. His work in mathematics led him to design a differential calculating machine that contained many of the processes still used today, including an arithmetic unit, a memory for storing numbers, and sequential control techniques.

FIGURE 1-5
Portrait of Charles Babbage

At approximately the same time (1810), the Jacquard weaving loom—an automated weaving loom controlled by a series of punched cards—was developed in France. See Figure 1-6. The punched cards contained a grid of rows and columns. Each column corresponded to the shuttle, a thread on the loom that does the actual weaving. Each row corresponded to one pass of the weaving thread. There were also a series of pins on the loom. As the cards passed across the pins, a pin would poke up through any square that was punched out, and hold up a thread for the next pass of the shuttle. The pattern formed by the holes in the card would thus be woven into the fabric. The great thing about this was that anyone could weave the exact same pattern in a very short time without years of training or without having to count all the threads. It was all handled automatically. This process was so efficient it wasn't abandoned until the 1970s.

FIGURE 1-6
Jacquard weaving loom

JACQUARD LOOM CARDS

These two devices paved the way for the modern computer. Think of the differential engine as a computing engine, i.e., a CPU. The punch cards on the weaving loom are a sort of storage device—a hard drive. Put them together and you have a computer.

Once people realized that these strange machines could save time and effort, computer development was limited only by existing technology. Until World War II, computing machines were so simple that the operating system wasn't part of the design. The user, who controlled how the machine reacted, was the operating system. With the outbreak of World War II, the U.S. War Department (now known as the Department of Defense) needed to know how to accurately place bombs in enemy territory during bombing raids. This is not something that can be done just by looking. It is a complex mathematical calculation that takes into account many factors: wind speed, difference in height between target and launcher, size/shape of the bomb, etc. A small error can mean the difference between a hit and a miss—a very expensive mistake. To calculate all these numbers, the DOD employed hundreds of women who ran through the pertinent calculations for most of the war. Their work was periodically updated in a series of tables used by bombardiers and gunnery crews. The difficulty of a problem was gauged by how many woman-hours it took to solve it. (Remember that even calculators hadn't been invented yet. Everything was done by hand.)

Even with many people working long and hard, the answers could not be produced fast enough for special problems. The answer came from an unlikely source: cryptography, or the art of breaking codes. Code breakers had a similar calculating problem. How do you break a code composed of millions of variations without a key?

Computer Concepts

A modern computer is just a collection of circuits, with electronics that make the calculation process faster than it used to be. But a computer can be defined as any device that accepts a valid input, rejects invalid input, and produces output. According to this definition, a soda machine is a type of computer. It accepts coins inserted into a slot, sorts the coins, and delivers a soda. If you insert the wrong coin, the machine won't work until you supply the correct coin.

It was never a question of *whether* it could be done, just *how fast*. People were working as fast as possible, but they needed a machine that could do the job faster. So work started on a machine that was based on differential gears similar to those used by Babbage. It was called project ULTRA (which referred to the intercepted message intelligence), and it could translate a coded message in a day, instead of the month it took to do it by hand. During the war, the Germans had invented a code machine named ENIGMA, which was stolen by the Poles, who gave a copy of it to the British. The device used rotor wheels to mechanically encode a message. Once the British were able to obtain the correct rotor wheels and the key codes, they could use the device to read German messages. The result was victory in the Battle of the Atlantic, which proved the value of computers beyond a doubt.

Although this was the first computer recognizable by today's standards, it still didn't have an operating system. It was completely run by a human administrator. Still, the machine had been a great success: It saved thousands of lives and helped shorten the war. This fact was not lost on the government, which immediately began to develop others that would be faster and solve more complex problems. The more complex the problem, the bigger the machines needed to solve it—and the harder it was to control the machine. Then someone came up with the idea of letting the machine control itself. All the user had to do was set certain operating parameters and the machine configured itself. This helped the situation, but there still wasn't an operating system.

Mainframes and Minicomputers

By the beginning of the silicon age in the 1960s, computers had became so large and complex that it was no longer possible for a human to control them. This was the birth of mainframes—giant computers designed solely to solve complex math problems. Think about it: If a machine has two million switches that need to be checked in order for a program to run correctly, even one switch out of order would prevent it from working. There are simply too many connections and switches to monitor. Some method had to be implemented to make the machine easier to use. This is the origin of the operating system.

> **Did You Know?**
>
> It is interesting to note that the term "debug" literally means to remove the insects from a program. In modern times it means to remove the programming mistakes from the computer code. The first credited use of the term is attributed to USN Rear Admiral Grace Hopper. A program was not working and the technicians were called in to check the switches and relays. The problem was found: A small white moth had lodged itself between the contacts of a relay. This small problem caused the whole program not to work. The technician who found the problem wrote in the maintenance logbook "Debugged program." It should also be noted that Grace is generally credited with starting the Y2K issue as well.

The earliest general-purpose electronic computers had only the barest of operating systems. Each machine was a unique creation, completely customized to the buyer's needs. Basically, the programmers wrote code directly to the computer hardware, so an operating system was unnecessary. As computers caught on, there began to be more than just one copy of a specific brand and model of computer in the world. Each one cost millions of dollars and had a large crew of PhDs who tended to its every need. Programs for these machines took years—and millions of dollars—to develop. Companies realized that they could cut their development cost/time by selling copies of their software to other companies. This worked wonderfully. One company could trade a copy of their program for others and suddenly their machine could do lots of new tricks. And so a brand new technology/market was born.

As the machines grew in sophistication there was a need for better software. Companies also needed a way to make the computers more economically viable. One way was to eliminate the teams of people needed to run them. As more software became available, there had to be some way of loading the code without having teams of engineers to oversee it. The operating system was devised to help handle this. Slowly it was extended to help with other tasks like writing programs. Shortly thereafter someone designed the first computer game. It is not recorded what that game was, but chances are it was tic-tac-toe.

Mainframe computers were so named because they were built on a frame or chassis—initially by hand. With the invention of the transistor, and later the microchip, computers became smaller in size and started to be manufactured rather than custom-built. These smaller, manufactured computers were known as minicomputers. They were still big by today's standards. The CPU alone was the size of a large refrigerator. A 16 KB RAM device was about the same size. When you add in all the hard drives, cooling, and communication equipment, the machines still took up a large conference room—instead of a football coliseum. See Figure 1-7.

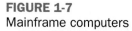

FIGURE 1-7
Mainframe computers

The smaller size and lower cost meant larger production runs of a model. The greater numbers of computers being built led to standardization and an assembly line production, which meant that software no longer needed to be unique to a given installation. Now general-purpose software could be created and sold separately from the computer and its support. Because different computers of the same model could exchange software, the need for an operating system became more apparent.

The operating system was responsible for starting up all the components of the computer and for managing the storage and communication devices connected to the computer. Most early operating systems were proprietary, meaning that they would only run on a certain brand and model of machine. Even today, operating systems will only run on certain hardware. For instance, you can't run Macintosh software on a PC.

One of the earliest operating systems was developed not for computers, but to solve phone switching problems. Like most milestones in computing, big solutions often come from unexpected places. During the 50's and 60's the phone company experienced huge growth. The problem was not to physically connect all the customers, but to make sure there were lines available for them all to use. One workaround involved the hassle of party lines. So AT&T commissioned a mathematical model of the phone system to be built. This enabled them to quickly test various solutions without investing heavily in hardware. The model was so complex a computer was needed to solve it. Also a new operating system was needed to handle the very complex model. Here again, the answer came from an unlikely source. The operating system designed for the first multiuser game, called SKY, was adopted and modified. The result is the most powerful and flexible operating system ever invented, called Unix. Unix became a popular operating system with engineers because of all it would do. The downside was that it was so expensive to buy the program and all the hardware it required, only governments or the top 20 companies in the world could afford it. It was also hard to learn.

For 25 years this one thing—cost—held back computer development more than anything else. There were also other issues. For example, how do you talk to a machine so it understands what you are saying, and how do you know what it is saying? In the early days people communicated with the computer by typing on a kind of typewriter that punched holes in cards. A stack of these cards was then fed into a special machine to be read by the computer. The results were printed on paper. Later, users could communicate directly with the computer by typing into a device called a dumb terminal. The first terminals used a printer to show the computer's response. Later computers used a television-like screen.

Because of the costs associated with computers, they were built to be multiuser systems. A multiuser system means that there is one computer and lots of people using it at the same time. This spread out the cost and made it cheaper per user. Each of the users was connected to the computer by a terminal. The operating system had to keep track of what everyone was doing, so computer operating systems became very adept at multitasking, that is, doing more than one thing at a time.

Early Microcomputers

While minicomputers were considerably less expensive than their big, mainframe cousins, they were still more than most individuals could afford. In the early and mid-70's there was a movement to bring less expensive computers to the masses. The advent of the microchip made it possible to create computers that individuals could afford. Most of the small computers of this period were experimental machines built by electronics hobbyists. Like their early mainframe cousins, these computers were so simple they hardly needed an operating system. They were usually built by hand and had few useful features.

The device credited with being the first mainstream microcomputer, the Altair 8800, was based on an early microprocessor (the Intel 4004). Its relationship to modern microcomputers is hard to see: It was a metal box with several switches and lights on the front; it had no keyboard, no monitor, only 256 bytes of RAM, and it was operated (programmed, really) by clicking the switches and watching the lights flicker. Still, a million of them were sold. Keyboards, monitors, and more memory were soon added to make the machine useful. When designers added a flexible, removable disk storage device (floppy disk drive), they needed a way to control and manage it. This was the reason for the invention of CP/M—the first really usable microcomputer operating system. CP/M used a command-line user interface.

One group of electronics hobbyists, the Home Brew Computer Club on the San Francisco peninsula, had a number of members—later to become famous—who were especially interested in building and showing off these new microcomputers. The idea of making prebuilt microcomputers that were genuinely useful (as opposed to a kit for hobbyists) belongs to two members of this club. Steve Wozniak, with his friend Steve Jobs, came up with the concept of a fully functional personal computer, which included a keyboard for input and a television screen for output. They called it the Apple II. Wozniak and Jobs sold enough Apple I computers (a hobbyist kit) to finance the Apple II. See Figure 1-8.

FIGURE 1-8
Wozniak and Jobs

Storage for the original Apple II used a connection to an audio cassette tape recorder. Later, when floppy disks became available, Apple added the ability to store programs and data on these 5¼-inch disks (like the Altair's). A program was needed to call and work with the contents of this disk drive, and that program was the real beginning of Apple's operating system.

When computer giant IBM saw the microcomputer concept taking hold, they decided to create a system of their own. IBM created its microcomputer from mostly generic parts. In a marketing coup, they called it the IBM Personal Computer—and the term PC was born. One of the parts they purchased for this computer was the operating system, which IBM licensed from a small startup called Microsoft, headed by a man named Bill Gates. The operating system was called MS-DOS, which stands for Microsoft Disk Operating System. This operating system had many similarities to Unix.

Because the new IBM PC was built with mostly commonly-available parts, and since IBM's arrangement with Microsoft was not exclusive, there was an opening for someone to create PCs without the IBM brand name on them. A critical part of the system called the BIOS (basic input-output system), which is the intermediary between the operating system and hardware, was the hardest part to replicate. But once it had been done, clones came into existence, and computers began to be common in businesses and homes. The open-ended design also encouraged other software companies—such as word-processing vendors like WordStar and WordPerfect, and financial software developers such as Lotus Development Corporation, whose 1-2-3 spreadsheet program was an early bestseller—to develop a wide range of programs for the PC.

As microcomputers became commonly available, MS-DOS (shortened to DOS) became the prevalent PC operating system, and slowly emerged as the standard system for businesses. Meanwhile, Apple II (and its successors) became dominant in schools.

Steve Jobs recognized the need to create a system to compete with IBM. While looking for ideas for a new computer, he visited Xerox's Palo Alto Research Center (PARC). A computer scientist named Doug Englebart had begun to experiment with a different kind of operating system, which used visual symbols and metaphors on the screen. They were manipulated using a screen pointing device called a mouse, which replaced the hard-to-remember file commands of DOS and the Apple II operating system. Englebart's idea was that computers should be easy to use.

Jobs brought the concept back to Apple and used it to create a computer called the Lisa. Lisa was an engineering and user interface marvel, but at over $15,000 each, nobody was buying them. Jobs and Apple worked to package the system in a more cost-conscious model, and the Macintosh was born. See Figure 1-9.

FIGURE 1-9
The first Macintosh design

From the beginning, the Macintosh was recognized as something distinctly different from an IBM PC. Software for the machine was scarce. Because it was so easy to use, thanks to its graphical user interface (GUI), it seemed more like a toy to many people than a serious computer. But even Microsoft took notice and began working to replicate its ease of use and functionality.

Their first attempts, Windows 1.0 and 2.0, were considered imitations of the Macintosh. This had as much to do with the relative power of the microprocessors in the two machines as it did with the operating systems themselves. Finally by the time Windows 3.0 and 3.1 were introduced, the PC microprocessor had become powerful enough to handle the complex graphics required. It brought the magic of a GUI to millions of PC users, and due to the open IBM PC-style computers (whose hardware and software could be produced by virtually anyone) rather than a closed system (like the single-vendor Macintosh), it was an immediate success.

Since that time, microprocessors have become ever more powerful, and both Microsoft and Apple have added capability and features to their operating systems. During a brief flirtation with open systems Apple called their operating system MacOS. But by then the equivalent version of Windows, called Windows 95, was more or less on par with MacOS in terms of features.

During the same time frame, users realized that having their own computer was great, but they were isolated from each other. Large computing mainframes were still very desirable despite their price tag because users could share their data and ideas across multiple computers also referred to as a network. A small computer company called Novell, in Provo, Utah, headed by their new president, Ray Noorda, decided to create a way to connect multiple computers together to share printers and hard disks. Novell created another kind of operating system, a network operating system called Netware. The network operating system allowed for the connection of two or more computers, which can share files and services (such as a printer) between them. Microsoft followed along years later and created their own version of the network operating system, called Windows NT.

Unix, the multiuser operating system for larger, more expensive minicomputers, had not been idle all this time. It had been gradually moving toward desktop computers that used a GUI. One of those moves was made by Stephen Jobs who, after he left Apple, created a Unix-based GUI operating system called Nextstep. Apple later acquired Jobs' company, Next, and Nextstep became the foundation of Apple's MacOS X.

Another, even more important, movement of Unix toward the desktop in recent years was the development of a version of Unix by a Finnish student named Linus Torvald. He lent the new Unix his name—Linux. One of Linux's most interesting features is that, unlike Windows and MacOS, it is free and open and legally situated to stay that way. In many ways, Linux has an advantage over other operating systems because it has millions of average, everyday computer users developing programs versus a few hundred for Apple or IBM PCs. The disadvantage of Linux is that it is much harder to learn initially.

You will continue to learn about operating systems throughout this book. Subsequent chapters will describe the various operating systems mentioned in this introduction. Each chapter will give a brief overview of the operating system, and describe its evolution into its present form. You will then walk through a typical installation and setup of the operating system. From there, the discussion will focus on the basic functionalities of the operating system—including resource management, memory management, and file management. Finally, the unique features of the operating system will be explained.

SUMMARY

In this lesson, you learned:

■ An operating system is a collection of system programs that allow the user to run program software (software that you allows you to perform a task, such as edit a document or play a game). An operating system manages hardware and other programs.

- There are three basic types of user interfaces (UI). Command-line user interfaces use the keyboard to communicate with the operating system and the computer. In a command-line user interface, the user types in commands and the computer responds to them. Menu-based user interfaces are often used to simplify the use of a command-line UI by giving the user a list of commands from which to choose. The graphical user interface (GUI) is a sophisticated form of menu-based interface. Instead of listing the commands, the GUI presents them as a series of small pictures called icons.

- Hardware includes the physical components of your machine. All modern computers have the following components: CPU—the central processing unit, at the heart of the computer. RAM—random access memory, the main memory of the computer, which is updated as you work, and which requires power to maintain information. ROM—read-only memory, which is programmed once at the factory and cannot be changed. BIOS—the basic input-output system, a ROM whose program contains the bare essentials to get the machine up and running. Motherboard—the main circuit board in the computer. Keyboard—a device used to input information to the computer's programs.

- An operating system manages resources in many ways. Its main functions are starting up, shutting down, multitasking and allocating CPU cycles, and changing the way it works by using extensions and managing memory.

- An operating system also manages files in many different ways. Its main functions are utilizing the different storage devices available, recognizing and using the different file types (programs, documents, and containers), navigating and finding files, and copying and moving files as needed.

- The evolution of the modern personal computer and its operating system has occurred over the past half-century and will continue into the future.

VOCABULARY *Review*

Define the following terms:

Basic input-output system (BIOS)	Central processing unit (CPU)	Operating system (OS)
	Graphical user interface (GUI)	User interface (UI)
Command-line user interface	Menu-based user interface	

REVIEW *Questions*

MULTIPLE CHOICE

Select the best response for the following statements.

1. Most keyboards are of this style:
    A. ANSI
    B. QWERTY
    C. American Typist Standard
    D. None of the above.

2. Which is an example of a pointing device?
    A. Mouse
    B. Tablet
    C. Touchpad
    D. None of the above.

3. Which is an example of a storage device?
    A. Printer
    B. Hard drive
    C. Scanner
    D. Modem

4. Which is an example of an input device?
    A. Scanner
    B. Tape drive
    C. Printer
    D. Sound card

5. Operating systems can be of these types. Circle all that apply:
    A. GUI
    B. Command-line
    C. Menu-driven
    D. Portable

FILL IN THE BLANK

Complete the following sentences by writing the correct word or words in the blanks provided.

1. OS stands for _____.

2. GUI stands for _____.

3. BIOS stands for _____.

4. CPU stands for _____.

5. RAM stands for _____.

CRITICAL*Thinking*

 ACTIVITY 1-1

Given what you know about computers and the operating systems that control them, discuss what new problems will have to be solved as more and more of the world becomes connected.

 ACTIVITY 1-2

How much should computers be allowed into our lives? Should restrictions be imposed on how far technology should go? Give reasons and examples.

 ACTIVITY 1-3

Discuss the implications of allowing computers to invade your daily life and privacy. What restrictions should be imposed, if any? Who gets to decide what is private and what isn't? How much information do you think is freely available about you?

DISK OPERATING SYSTEM: DOS

OBJECTIVES

Upon completion of this lesson you should be able to:

- Understand why DOS is important to Windows 3.1 and Windows 9x users.

- Prepare the hard disk drive for installation of DOS.

- Install DOS correctly on your personal computer.

- Create and use directories for file management.

- Create, view, print, copy, move, delete and rename files in DOS using the text editor.

- Recognize common error messages in DOS.

Estimated Time: 14+ hours

VOCABULARY

CD

COPY

DEL

DIR

FDISK

Format

MD

REN

Introduction

In this lesson, we will be discussing DOS (disk operating system). DOS was the first widely installed operating system in personal computers. The first version of DOS, called PC-DOS, was developed for IBM by Bill Gates of Microsoft Corporation. He retained the right to market a Microsoft version, called MS-DOS. PC-DOS and MS-DOS are almost identical, and most users have referred to either of them as just "DOS." DOS is a command-line operating system, with a relatively simple user interface. It uses verbal commands, the user keys them at the command prompt. A prompt to enter a command looks like this:

```
c:\>
```

DOS was once a major operating system and is the underlying layer of some Windows products. When using Windows 3.1 or Windows 9x it is important to understand DOS because:

1. DOS controls the flow of information between you and the computer (the translator).

2. DOS allows you to store information on your computer.

3. DOS allows you to retrieve information stored on your computer.

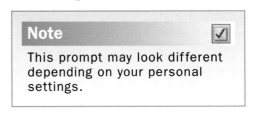

Note ☑

This prompt may look different depending on your personal settings.

4. DOS interprets and translates the software you have on your computer.

5. DOS gives you access to all its functions, such as saving, copying, and printing files.

6. DOS allows you to fix your system when Windows cannot load properly.

Preparing for Installation

Before you install any operating system, your system must be prepared. That means that your connections should all be secure and any internal components (hard drives, cables, sound card, modem, and so on) should be installed. The machine needs to be set up physically and you must have all the necessary tools available to construct the operating system to correctly operate your hardware. This means you have all the necessary drivers, settings, and documentation you will want to correctly set up your hardware to work with the operating system. Drivers tell DOS how to interact with hardware components such as a mouse. Driver objects can be obtained online from the manufacturer of the specific hardware device.

Preparation of the Hard Disk Drive

Once your hardware has been installed properly, your hard disk drive (HDD) needs to be prepared. In DOS, this is accomplished with the help of two external utilities: *FDISK* and *Format*. FDISK is a fixed disk utility; its purpose is to partition a hard disk drive. A partition is the structure DOS uses to designate usable space, just as we designate space in a building by giving it a name (room, closet, and so on) Once the hard disk drive is partitioned, it must be formatted (using the format utility) so that it may hold data. A formatted disk accepts and holds data in the same way that we build shelves and drawers to store our belongings. Once the disk is formatted, DOS can be installed.

Think of your hard drive/fixed disk as an empty dirt lot. When you partition the drive, you are pouring the foundation of the operating system. With that in place, you can format the drive and actually build a house to hold everything you need. Setup/Install then places all the finishing touches such as plumbing, wiring, and fixtures. Your house is ready for occupancy and your operating system is ready for use.

You need to begin with a formatted DOS system disk (often called a boot disk). This floppy disk contains special files that allow it to start DOS without the hard drive. This is usually Disk 1 of a DOS installation set. Once booted, it prompts you for the date and time. Most computers have an internal clock that will automatically set the date and time for you when you turn on the computer. However, if your computer does not have this feature, you will need to use the following steps to set the date and time.

S TEP-BY-STEP 2.1

1. At the C: prompt, key the date in this format: **mm-dd-yy**. For example, if today is January 16, 2000, you would key the date as **01-16-00**.

2. Press the **Enter** key on the keyboard.

STEP-BY-STEP 2.1 Continued

3. At the C: prompt, key the time in this format: **hh:mm**. For example, if the current time is 8:46, you would key it as **8:46**.

4. Press **Enter**.

Notice that the C:\> prompt appears.

FIGURE 2-1
Setting the system time

DOS marks the date and time on everything you do. It is important to periodically check the date and time to ensure that the system clock is correct. See Figure 2-1.

Check the Date and Time

DOS lets you check or change the date and time once it has been set. The procedure to check the date and time follows in Step-by-Step 2.2.

STEP-BY-STEP 2.2

1. Key **date** and press **Enter**.

2. If the correct date is displayed, simply press **Enter**. If the date is incorrect, key the correct date and press **Enter**.

3. Key **time** and press **Enter**.

4. If the correct time is displayed, simply press **Enter**. If the time is incorrect, key the correct time and press **Enter**.

Using FDISK

Now you'll use the FDISK utility to prepare the hard drive for formatting. To begin, key FDISK and press Enter. You are now presented with a menu. See Figure 2-2.

1.   Create DOS partition or Logical DOS Drive

2.   Set active partition

3.   Delete partition or Logical DOS Drive

4.   Display partition information

FIGURE 2-2
Setting the DOS partition

The first option, Create DOS Partition or Logical DOS Drive, is the most frequently used. You will press 1 and then Enter to create the DOS partition.

A submenu opens to offer three additional options.

TABLE 2-1
Options on FDISK submenu

OPTION	DESCRIPTION
Create Primary DOS Partition	Allows you to construct the first and main partition.
Create Extended DOS Partition	Allows you to create additional partitions. This is also how you set any partition that is secondary.
Create Logical DOS Drive(s) in the Extended DOS Partition	The primary partition automatically gets drive C; however, you must assign a drive letter to any other partitions so you can access them).

If you don't want to use the options in the submenu, you can press Escape to return to the main menu. Computers have a pecking order, or hierarchy, that they follow. In the case of FDISK, you must first create a primary partition, then you can create any additional partitions/drives or extensions of the primary partition.

Why not just keep everything in the primary partition and forget about the extended partitions? Until Windows 95 Service Release 2 (SR-2) was developed, the DOS file system's FAT-16 (16-bit File Allocation Tables) could only manage two gigabytes per partition. If your hard drive was larger than this, you had to create multiple partitions and logical drives to be able to use the entire memory space. Once Windows 95 SR-2 was released, FAT-32 (the 32-bit File Allocation Table, which has more capability) offered support for larger hard drives. Many rejoiced when the 2 GB barrier was shattered.

You must create the primary partition by pressing 1 and the Enter key. The DOS boot disk verifies the drive integrity to ensure it can hold the data, then it asks if you wish to use the maximum amount of space and set the partition active.

What is hard drive integrity? A hard drive stores information on a metallic disk that is surrounded by a magnetic field. If the magnetic field has weak spots, those locations may be unstable and unsafe for data. So the boot disk is basically verifying the magnetic field of the hard drive.

If you do not set an active partition, the hard drive cannot boot. To set an active partition, you press Y and Enter. The boot disk partitions the drive and prompts you to press Esc to continue. Now you must restart the computer for the changes to take effect. To do that, press Esc until you are back at the DOS prompt (A:\>), then restart the computer.

Computer Concepts

Just as the Dewey Decimal System categorizes the library, FATs categorize your hard drive and provide a table of contents so the computer can find the files. FATs are an internal component of the operating system and not viewable. One FAT is used by the operating system, and a second is kept as a back-up copy in case the first is corrupted.

Did You Know?

There are two ways to reboot. You can simply turn off the computer; this is known as a *hard boot*. Alternatively, you can press the Ctrl, Alt, and Del keys on the keyboard simultaneously; this is known as a *soft boot*.

Note

Using FDISK will destroy all data on a partition when that partition is removed. Do not do this on your machine until you are absolutely sure you no longer need any data on that partition.

S TEP-BY-STEP 2.3

1. Press **1** and **Enter**. A submenu opens with three additional options.

2. Press **1** to create the primary partition, then press **Enter**.

3. Press **Y** and then **Enter** to use the maximum amount of space and set the partition active.

4. Now press **Esc** to continue.

5. Press **Esc** until you are back at the DOS prompt (A:\>), then restart the computer by pressing **Ctrl+Alt+Del**.

Note

You may need to delete an existing partition bfore creating a new one.

Formatting the Hard Drive

Now the drive is ready for formatting. To start the process, you key Format C: and press Enter. The disk prompts you with a warning that all data will be lost, and asks if you wish to proceed. Press Y and Enter. The boot disk begins to format the drive while displaying the percentage of completion. Once it is completed by reaching 100%, it prompts you for a label, which is the name you choose to assign to that drive. This is optional: You can key a label and press Enter—or simply press Enter.

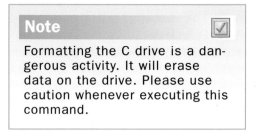

Note ✓

Formatting the C drive is a dangerous activity. It will erase data on the drive. Please use caution whenever executing this command.

The drive is now ready for installation of the operating system.

Installation of the Operating System

To start the installation process, you key Setup at the A:> prompt and press Enter. The installation menu will scan your system and then appear with a welcome message. This screen explains Setup, prepares MS-DOS to run on your system, and advises you to press F1 if you need additional help. You may also exit the setup program by pressing F3. As the screen indicates, you press Enter to continue the setup process.

Settings

Now you see a menu screen that contains the basic settings the computer will use: DATE/TIME, COUNTRY, KEYBOARD, and INSTALL TO. You can use the arrow keys on your keyboard to move up and down the menu. The DATE/TIME option allows you to set the correct system time. The COUNTRY option lets you enter your COUNTRY settings. The KEYBOARD option sets your keyboard to work with DOS, and the INSTALL TO option allows you to choose where you want to install the DOS operating system.

STEP-BY-STEP 2.4

1. Highlight **DATE/TIME** and press **Enter**. The menu highlights System Date.

2. If the date is incorrect, key the correct date and press **Enter**. System Time now highlights.

3. Key the correct time and press **Enter**. Now you are back at the original settings screen.

4. If you are in a country other than the USA, highlight **COUNTRY** and press **Enter**.

5. From the list of countries supported by DOS, select the appropriate country and press **Enter**. You are now back at the original settings screen.

6. Highlight **KEYBOARD** and press **Enter**.

7. From the list of supported keyboards, select the keyboard used with your system and press **Enter**. You are now back at the original settings screen.

STEP-BY-STEP 2.4 Continued

8. Highlight **INSTALL TO** and press **Enter**.

9. Select **Hard Disk** and press **Enter**.

10. If all settings are correct, highlight **'The settings are correct'** and press **Enter**.

Changing the Install Directory

The boot disk now prompts you to verify and change the install directory. The default is C:\DOS. If you want DOS to install to some other location, you may highlight the option to change the install directory and press Enter. This allows you to select a different directory to install to or leave C:\DOS as the default. Choose the option you want, then press Enter.

This screen also gives you an option to Run Shell on Startup. This is set to Yes by default, which means it will launch the MS-DOS shell overlay. This simply offers a fancier environment in which to communicate with the operating system, if you prefer. In this installation you will change that option to No, and then highlight 'The listed options are correct' and press Enter.

The screen now reports that MS-DOS is being set up; you should see a status bar that shows the percentage of completion. The operating system files are now copied to the hard drive from the installation set. If there are multiple disks in the set, you may be prompted to insert the additional disks. Simply remove the current disk, insert the requested disk, and press Enter. Once the files are copied, you are prompted to remove all disks and press Enter. The computer restarts and you are at the DOS Prompt [C:\>]. Installation is now complete.

Basic Functionalities of the Operating System

The Environment

The environment provided by DOS is not a pretty one. Its purpose is to give the user quick and direct access to the basic utility of the computer and little else—a carryover from the days when the abilities/limitations of the computer dictated how the user could interface with it. All tasks are accomplished by typing in commands at a command prompt (described in the following section). This is not to say, however, that a command prompt interface doesn't have its advantages. Once you learn the interface, it can offer advantages such as speed, efficiency, and reliability.

Usually, however, users or network administrators alter their system so that the user does not have to deal with this command-line interface. An example of this is Windows or other graphical user interface overlay programs. However, GUIs can prevent the beginner (or new) user from becoming comfortable with DOS itself.

Note ☑
An argument specifies exactly what a command is going to do. For example, if I wanted to copy the file mine.txt from C to A, the command would be as follows: copy mine.txt a:\. The filename itself and the directory it is being copied to are examples of arguments. They specify that the copy command should duplicate the file mine.txt to the A drive.

In DOS and other command-line interfaces, it is easy to become disoriented. Unlike your office, in which you know where you are because of the physical things you see and feel, the computer environment is organized around your work and your files. Therefore, any sense of "where you are" is going to be with respect to the files on your disk.

Many commands in the DOS environment follow a certain format. In order to tell DOS to perform a function, at the command prompt, you would key the command followed by *arguments*, which specify what you want DOS to do. For example:

```
C:\>COPY practice.txt a:
```

"COPY" is the command that you want DOS to perform. "practice.txt a:" is an example of an argument that specifies what will be affected by the command. In this case, DOS will copy the file practice.txt from the C: drive to the A: drive. Commands such as edit, del, and rename require arguments similar to the example listed above. You will see more examples of these arguments throughout this chapter.

The Command Prompt

When you look at the screen of a computer that's running DOS, you are likely to see a blank screen with only a few lines, at least one of which begins with a capital letter followed by a colon, a backslash, and a greater-than symbol (>). See Figure 2-3.

FIGURE 2-3
DOS command prompt

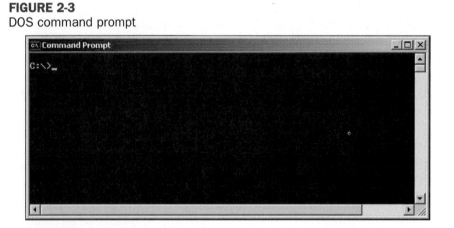

```
C:\>
```

Any line in DOS that begins like this is a command prompt. This prompt tells users where they are in DOS. Here is how:

The C: tells the user that he/she is working within the file space (disk storage) on the hard drive given the designation C. C is usually reserved for the main internal hard disk of a PC.

The *backslash* (\) represents a level in the hierarchy of the file structure. There is always at least one backslash because the first one represents the *root directory*—the very first level of your hard disk.

```
C:\DEMO\DOS&WIN\SAMPLES\SAMPLE.TXT
```

means that the file SAMPLE is on the internal hard disk, four levels deep (inside the directories DEMO, DOS&WIN, AND SAMPLES). The list of directories (\DEMO\DOS&WIN\SAMPLES\) is referred to as a pathname (following the path of directories will get you to the file). The name of the file itself (SAMPLE) is referred to as the filename. Think of a filing cabinet. If you had a folder called Purchase Orders, inside of which was a folder called Microsoft, and you submitted an order to purchase some new software from Microsoft, the order would be placed in the Microsoft subfolder. Directories work the same way. You have to follow the path of directories to end up eventually at your file.

Directory

If you need more help in orienting yourself, it sometimes helps to look at the files and directories available by using the *DIR* command (short for directory).

```
C:\>dir
```

The DIR command is like a table of contents in a book. This directory will list the following information:

■ File names

■ File extensions

■ Size of each file

■ Date and time the file was last updated.

This will give you a listing of all the files and directories contained in the current directory in addition to some information about the directory itself. See Figure 2-4. You will see the word "volume" in this information. Volume is simply another word for a disk that the computer has access to. Your hard disk is a volume, your floppy disk is a volume, a server disk (hard disk served over a network) is a volume. Now you know the fancy words for all the parts of the format DOS uses to represent a file.

FIGURE 2-4
Result of dir command

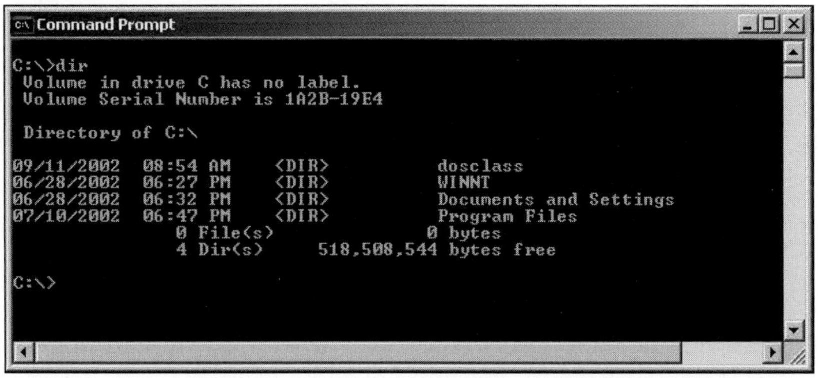

```
Command Prompt                                          _ □ ×

C:\>dir
 Volume in drive C has no label.
 Volume Serial Number is 1A2B-19E4

 Directory of C:\

09/11/2002  08:54 AM    <DIR>          dosclass
06/28/2002  06:27 PM    <DIR>          WINNT
06/28/2002  06:32 PM    <DIR>          Documents and Settings
07/10/2002  06:47 PM    <DIR>          Program Files
               0 File(s)              0 bytes
               4 Dir(s)     518,508,544 bytes free

C:\>
```

Volume: C:

Pathname:\DEMO\DOS&WIN\SAMPLES\

File name: SAMPLE

Here are some helpful extensions of the DIR command: (These are often called *switches*, and are just additional options to get more out the command.)

```
C:\>dir/p
```

(displays the directory one screen at a time with a <Press any key to continue> prompt. You use Ctrl-C to escape)

```
C:\>dir /w
```

(wide: displays the directory in columns across the screen)

```
C:\>dir /a
```

(all: displays the directory—including hidden files and directories)

You can print a list of the files in your directory by instructing DOS to send the information to your printer.

STEP-BY-STEP 2.5

1. Key **dir>prn** and press **Enter**.

2. Press **Enter**.

The > symbol stands for output. The PRN stands for printer.

Now that you have a grasp of where you are in DOS and how to find out, let's take a look at how to manage the files.

> **Note** ☑️
>
> You can print a wide listing of your files by typing dir/w>prn. LaserJet printers and other sheetfeeder printers will not eject the page after the dir>prn command. You must take the printer offline and press the form-feed button. Remember to press the online button when you are done, in order to continue using the printer.

File Management

Understanding how to manage files on your disk is not the same as being able to use them, though it's a start. If you've ever looked inside a folder of a freshly installed commercial package (such as WordPerfect), you'll have seen a large number of files with many different kinds of extensions. It can be rather daunting.

File Types

However, DOS (like most operating systems), recognizes only two kinds of files: binary files and text files (ASCII). Text files are quite easy to read or view. Binary files, on the other hand, are not easily viewed. In fact, most binary files are not to be viewed, but to be executed (like a full program such as WordPerfect or simple commands such as Copy). When you try to view these binary files (with a text editor, for example), your screen is filled with garbage and you may even hear beeps.

While there are only two types of files, it is often difficult to know which kind a particular file is, for files can have any extension. Fortunately, there is a small set of extensions that have standard meanings:

Text	Binary
.TXT	.EXE
.BAT	.COM

Executing Binary Files in DOS

Binary files ending in .EXE are usually "executed" in DOS by typing the file name as if it were a command. The following command would execute the WordPerfect application, which appears on the disk directory as WP.EXE:

```
C:\apps\wp51\wp.exe
```

Binary files ending in .COM often contain one or more commands for execution either through the command prompt or through some program.

Let's make sure we are at the root directory, the first directory on the hard drive. The root directory is where all the startup files must be located and from where all subdirectories stem.

Make a Directory

Now, let's make a couple of directories so we can put our files away in places that make sense to us. The DOS command for making a directory is *MD* (short for "make directory") and is followed by the name of the directory you want to make.

STEP-BY-STEP 2.6

1. At the C: prompt, key the command **md dosclass**. This creates a directory on C: called dosclass.

2. At the C: prompt, key the command **dir/w**. This will show a directory listing of C: with the new dosclass subdirectory.

3. At the C: prompt, key the command **cd dosclass**. This will move you into the dosclass subdirectory. At the C:\dosclass prompt, key the command **md samples**. This makes a subdirectory named samples inside of the dosclass directory.

4. At the C:\dosclass prompt, key the command **dir**. This will allow you to view the new directory samples in the dosclass directory.

As soon as you change the directory, (cd dosclass) the prompt changes to represent the new directory. See Figure 2-5.

FIGURE 2-5
Prompt changed to show new directory

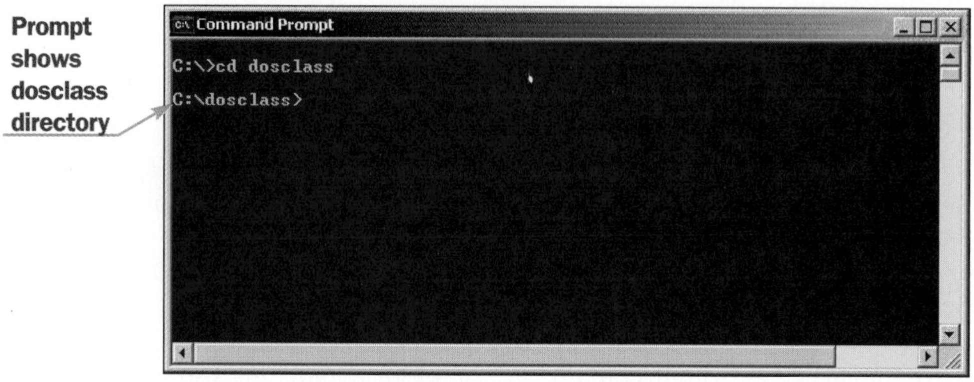

Prompt
shows
dosclass
directory

Remember that if you want to get your bearings, you can look at the command prompt or display a directory list of the current directory (dir).

Change Directory

To move to a different directory, use the command *CD* (for "change directory"), followed by the directory you want to move to. The backslash by itself always represents the root directory.

S TEP-BY-STEP 2.7

1. At the command prompt key **cd**. This will return you to the root directory.

2. At the command prompt key **cd dosclass**. This will change the directory from the root to dosclass.

Working with a Text Editor

Before we move on to creating files in DOS, let's take a look at the text editor provided with DOS. It is known simply as Edit. To load the editor, key Edit from a command prompt and press Enter. See Figure 2-6.

FIGURE 2-6
Working with a text editor

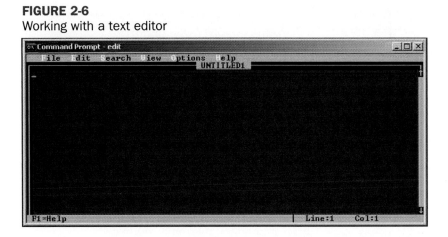

Figure 2-6 shows the screen you see when you open a new Edit window. Across the top are the menu bar and document title. On the right side is the scroll bar and on the bottom is the status bar. If your mouse driver is loaded you will also see a blinking square, which is the mouse cursor. On the menu bar, you have a number of options. You access them by moving the cursor over one of them and clicking, or you can press Alt and the first letter of the menu you want. For example, the key combination Alt-F opens the File menu. Table 2-2 displays the keyboard shortcuts used to display the editor's menus.

TABLE 2-2
Keyboard shortcuts to access menus

KEYBOARD COMBINATION	DISPLAYS
ALT-F	File menu
ALT-E	Edit menu
ALT-S	Search menu
ALT-V	View menu
ALT-O	Options menu
ALT-H	Help menu

Once you have accessed a menu, you can also use keyboard shortcuts to perform the functions available from those menus. See Table 2-3.

TABLE 2-3
Keyboard shortcuts to menu functions

KEYBOARD COMBINATION	FUNCTION LOCATED UNDER
ALT-N	File menu. Creates a new file
ALT-O	File menu. Opens a file
ALT-S	File menu. Saves a file
ALT-A	File menu. Opens the Save As dialog box, which allows you to save the file to a different storage device, different directory, or with a different file name.
ALT-C	File menu. Closes the file
ALT-P	File menu. Prints the contents of the file
ALT_X	File menu. Closes the editor
ALT-X	Edit menu. Cuts (removes) text
ALT-C	Edit menu. Copies text
ALT-V	Edit menu. Pastes (inserts) cut or copied text
DEL	Edit menu. Clears unwanted text

From the File menu you can start a new file, open an existing file, save your file, save your file under a different name, close the current file, or print your file. On the Edit menu, you may cut, copy, paste, and clear text. You can use the Search menu to find a certain set of characters or words, repeat your search, or replace one set of characters or words with a different set using the Replace option. The next menu available in a true DOS version of Edit is Options, where you can change the settings and colors. The final menu is Help. Here you can receive help with the text editor commands or find information about the editor.

Now let's create a file. At this point it is important to mention that DOS requires that file names be no longer than eight characters, with the option of a three-character extension for descriptive purposes. In addition, no spaces or slashes are acceptable.

S TEP-BY-STEP 2.8

1. First, make sure that you are in the root directory by looking at your C: prompt. If you are not, key **cd** and press **Enter**.

2. At the C:>\ prompt, key **edit practice.txt** and press **Enter**. This opens the editor to a screen where you can key your document.

3. Key your name or some other message.

STEP-BY-STEP 2.8 Continued

4. Press the **Alt** key, followed by the **F** key (make sure to keep pressing the Alt key when you press the F key) to display the File menu. (You may also use the mouse.)

5. Press the **S** key to save the file. To exit, press the **Alt** key, the F key, and then the **X** key.

If we look at the root directory, the PRACTICE.TXT file will be included. See Figure 2-7.

FIGURE 2-7
Directory listing showing the practice.txt file

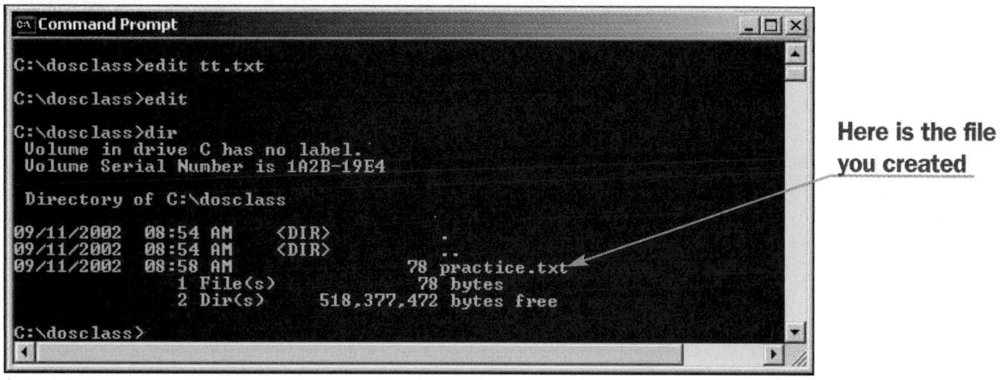

Viewing Text Files

You can quickly view text files by using the type command. See Figure 2-8.

FIGURE 2-8
Quick view of a file

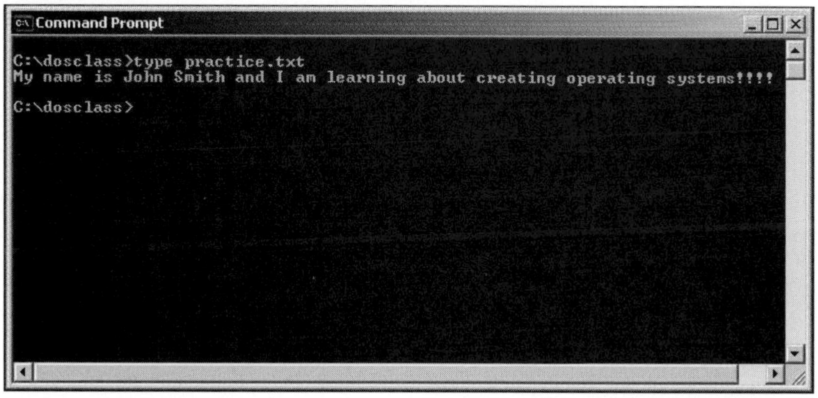

STEP-BY-STEP 2.9

1. At the command prompt key the command **type practice.txt | more**.

2. When you display a file with the type command, you are just viewing its contents and cannot make any changes to it.

Editing Text Files

Alternatively, you can view the file in the DOS text editor (just as you did when you first created practice.txt).

S TEP-BY-STEP 2.10

1. First, make sure that you are in the root directory by looking at your C: prompt. If you are not, key **cd** and press **Enter**.

2. At the C:>\ prompt, key e**dit practice.txt** and press **Enter**. This opens the editor to a screen where you can edit your document.

3. Key another line of text into to your practice file.

4. Then press the **Alt** key, followed by the **F** key (make sure to keep pressing the Alt key when you press the F key) to display the File menu. (You may also use the mouse if you installed the mouse driver.) Then press the **S** key to save the file.

5. To exit, press the **Alt** key, followed by the **F** key followed by the **X** key. Now quickly view the practice.txt file by typing at the command prompt **Type practice.txt**.

Printing Text Files

If you want to send a text file to the printer, you can use the print command.

S TEP-BY-STEP 2.11

1. At the command prompt, key the command **print practice.txt**.

2. When DOS prompts for the name of list device [PRN], key **lpt2**. If you want to print to a networked printer, usually lpt2 is the correct response. For a local printer (which is physically connected to the computer, as opposed to a network device), the correct response is usually lpt1.

Copying Files

The *COPY* command allows us to make a duplicate of a file. We can create a backup of the practice file created earlier by copying that to the SAMPLES directory which is inside the DOSCLASS directory.

To keep things simple, let's use the cd command to return to the root directory where the practice file is.

```
C:\>cd \
```

Now copy that file to the SAMPLES directory, which is inside the DOSCLASS directory. In order to copy something, you must first issue the command (copy), then identify the file to be copied (source), and then name the directory to which you want to copy the file (destination).

S TEP-BY-STEP 2.12

1. At the prompt, key the following command: **copy practice.txt dosclass\samples**.

2. This copies the practice file to the samples subdirectory in the dosclass directory.

3. At the command prompt key **CD dosclass\samples** to change to the samples subdirectory.

4. Check to make sure the practice file was copied to the samples subdirectory by keying in **dir** at the command prompt.

A somewhat unfriendly yet useful diagram of the command format would look something like this (where items in brackets are optional):

```
Copy [volume+pathname+]file name [volume+path name+]directory
```

This means you don't have to include the volume and pathname of the source file and the destination directory (we didn't in the first example). DOS assumes that any file name or directory included in the copy command is in the current directory (the one you're currently in.). Because you had moved to the root directory, both PRACTICE.TXT and DOSCLASS were in the current directory.

The command-line interface makes it possible for the user to use one command to copy any file anywhere to any other location; you don't have to be in the directory of the files you want to act on. From any directory (within volume C:), you could have used the following command to copy the same file to the same directory:

```
C:\DOSCLASS>copy \practice.txt \dosclass\samples
```

This tells the computer where to find the source file (since it wasn't in the current directory) by placing a backslash in front of the file names (which told the computer that the file was in the root directory). You use the same procedure to copy files between volumes. All you have to do is specify the volume:

```
Z:\ANYWHERE>copy c:\practice.txt c:\dosclass\samples
```

Another common and useful example is:

```
C:\>copy practice.txt a:\backup\dosclass
```

This command copies the file to a floppy disk in the PC's floppy drive (which already had the directories, BACKUP\DOSCLASS).

Copying a File from the Hard Drive to a Floppy Disk

Sometimes you may need to copy a file from the hard drive onto a floppy disk. This is helpful if you would like to have an extra copy of a certain file as a backup or to transport the copied file to another computer.

STEP-BY-STEP 2.13

1. At the command prompt key **copy Practice.txt a:** and press **Enter**.

2. Wait for a few seconds; notice the light on the floppy drive. Never attempt to remove a disk from the disk drive while this light is on.

3. To check to see if the file was copied, key **a:** at the C:\> prompt and press **Enter**.

4. Key **dir** and press **Enter**. If the file was copied correctly you should see listed here the file practice.txt.

> **Note** ☑
>
> Most floppy disks you buy today in the store are already formatted, meaning they are prepared to hold data.

Diskcopy Command

Sometimes you may need to copy all the files from one diskette to another. First you will need a blank formatted disk (refer to the section on formatting disks.)

STEP-BY-STEP 2.14

1. At the command prompt, key **diskcopy a: a:** and press **Enter**.

2. When asked to insert the source disk, insert the diskette that has the information you want to copy into drive A and press **Enter**.

3. Wait a few seconds. When asked to insert a target disk, remove the diskette from drive A, insert a blank diskette, and then press **Enter**.

4. When the process is complete, you will be asked if you want to write to another duplicate diskette (Y/N). Press **N**.

5. Then you will be asked if you want to copy another disk (Y/N)? Press **N**.

Moving Files

Move means to take a file from one location and place it in a new location. In order to move something, you must first issue the command (move), then identify the file to be moved (source), and then name the directory to which you want to move the file (destination).

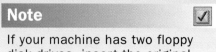

> **Note** ☑
>
> If your machine has two floppy disk drives, insert the original (source) disk into drive A and the blank (target) disk into drive B. Then key: DISKCOPY A: B:

STEP-BY-STEP 2.15

1. First change to the samples subdirectory. At the command prompt key **cd dosclass\ samples**.

2. Insert a floppy disk into the A drive.

3. At the prompt, key **move practice.txt a:**.This moves the practice file from the samples subdirectory to your floppy disk

4. If necessary press **Y** to confirm overwriting the existing file.

5. At the command prompt key **a:** to change to the floppy drive.

6. Check to make sure the practice file was moved by keying **dir** at the command prompt.

Delete

Now you discover you have a slight problem. The PRACTICE.TXT file was copied into the SAMPLES directory, but there is no reason to have two copies of PRACTICE.TXT. To delete a file, use the *DEL* command (short for "delete"), followed by the name of the file.

STEP-BY-STEP 2.16

1. At the C: prompt key **cd \dosclass\sample** to change to the samples subdirectory.

2. Then key **del practice.txt** to delete the file practice.txt from the samples subdirectory.

Again, you can delete the file from any directory by including the full pathname.

```
Z:\>del c:\practice.txt
```

Rename

The *REN* command allows the user to change the name of a file previously created. As with the DOS commands described earlier, you need not be in the same directory as the file you want to rename, provided you include the pathname of the file you wish to change. However, the second argument of this command, the new filename, will not accept a pathname designation. In other words, the second argument should just be a filename (with no pathname):

```
C:\>ren \dosclass\samples\practice.txt prac.txt
```

Use caution: if you do not include the extension (.TXT, .BAT, .DOC), some programs may not be able to open the file.

S TEP-BY-STEP 2.17

1. At the command prompt key **cd** to return to the root directory.

2. To rename the file practice.txt to prac.txt the command would be **ren practice.txt prac.txt**.

Unique Features of DOS

There are many commands that are unique to DOS. Earlier in the chapter you were introduced to the most popular commands of the DOS operating system. The following commands are also helpful when working in the DOS environment.

Command Functions

F3

The F3 function key can be a timesaver if you're prone to typographical errors. If you make a mistake when typing in a command and receive an error message, you can have DOS completely rekey the last command by pressing the F3 button. Pressing F1 will do this one character at a time.

Directory Commands

Parentdirectory(..)

If you wish to move up one level in the hierarchy of the file structure (for example, change to the parent directory), DOS provides a shortcut—two consecutive periods ("..").

```
C:\DOSCLASS\SAMPLES>cd ..
```

This works in a pathname as well:

```
C:\DOSCLASS\SAMPLES>ren ..\practice.txt prac.txt
```

If the file PRACTICE.TXT were in the directory above SAMPLES (the DOSCLASS directory), the above command would change it to PRAC.TXT.

Directory, Delete

Deltree removes the directory and all of its contents (meaning all files and subdirectories).

Key: **DELTREE [directory name]**

RD removes the directory only if it is empty (meaning that it contains no files or subdirectories).

Key: **RD [NAME OF DIRECTORY TO BE REMOVED]**

File Commands

Wildcards (*) and (?)

Another benefit of the command-prompt interface is the ability to use wildcard characters—special symbols that stand for other characters. The * wildcard character stands for any combination of characters. For example, dir*.doc means list every file with a .doc extension; dir training.* means list every file named training, regardless of its extension. The ? wildcard character is used when you can't recall one letter or if you need files that are similar. For example, to get all copies of the Windows registry, you would enter dir system.da? This would list System.daT and System.da0 (which is the backup copy).

For example, if you want to copy only files with the .txt extension, you would employ a wildcard character, as in the following command: **C:\>copy *.txt a:\backup\txtfiles**. This command would copy all of the files with the .txt extension onto a floppy disk inside the TXTFILES directory that is inside the BACKUP directory. However, to copy all files from the C drive to the A drive, you would enter C:\copy *.* a:.

The wildcard character is also used to retrieve a directory of similarly named files, as in **C:\>dir *.txt**. This command would display all files ending with the .txt extension. To list all files that begin with the letter g, you would key **C:\>dir g*.***.

Additionally, the ? can be used to substitute for individual letters as previously mentioned. If there are many similarly named files that end with the letters GOP but begin with letters A through G, then you can use the **C:\>dir ?gop.*** command to list those files. The following command would list all similar files beginning with the letters REP and ending with A: **C:\>dir rep?a.***.

Wildcard characters such as * and ? can be useful when you do not know the full name of a file or files and wish to list them separately from the main directory listing.

Batch Files

Batch files are text files that contain a series of DOS commands that will be executed in the order listed in the file. You can create batch files that will perform a variety of commands. These are commonly used for repetitive tasks. For example, if every day when you sit down at your PC, you check the date and time. Why not create a batch file to do this for you, instead of typing in two commands daily? To do this we would use the editor and inside have the commands for date and time. If you name the batch file morning.bat, when you sit at your PC everyday, you would only have to type in the command "morning," and the date and time commands would execute for you. These are time savers.

STEP-BY-STEP 2.18

1. Key **edit LS.BAT** and press **Enter**.

2. Key **dir | more**.

3. Then press the **Alt** key, then the **F** key to display the File menu. (You can also use the mouse.)

4. Then press the **S** key to save the file. To exit, press the **Alt** key, then the **F** key, then the **X** key.

STEP-BY-STEP 2.8 Continued

5. Now, when you press **[LS] + [ENTER]**, the operating system will run the LS.BAT batch file, which in turn will provide a page-by-page directory.

Data Protection and Integrity Commands

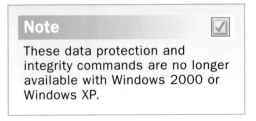

Note ✓

These data protection and integrity commands are no longer available with Windows 2000 or Windows XP.

To Create a Backup Disk

You should always back up data that is important to you. If the information is something that you cannot live without, the following command will create a backup disk for you.

MSBACKUP

Check Disk

This is useful when ScanDisk isn't available. It checks the file structure and informs you of errors. You can add /F to fix any errors that may be there.

CHKDSK [drive]:

Defragment Disk

This command organizes files so the computer can find and read them more easily.

DEFRAG

Diagnostics

This program will take a snapshot of the computer and run a series of diagnostic tests that examine the computer's condition and determine if all is well.

Enter **MSD** to display diagnostic information about your system.

FIGURE 2-9
Display of MSD examining the computer system

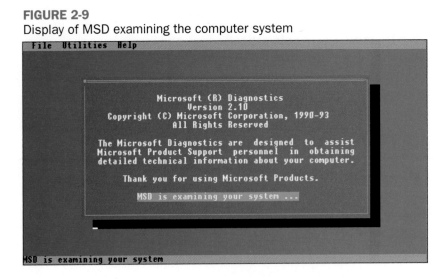

MSD will examine your system and then tell you what is in it. You can click any of the buttons or press a topic highlighted in red that you would like to see more about.

You can also use this handy tool to see a memory map, which graphically shows your memory usage. See Figure 2-10.

FIGURE 2-10(a)
System properties analyzed with MSD

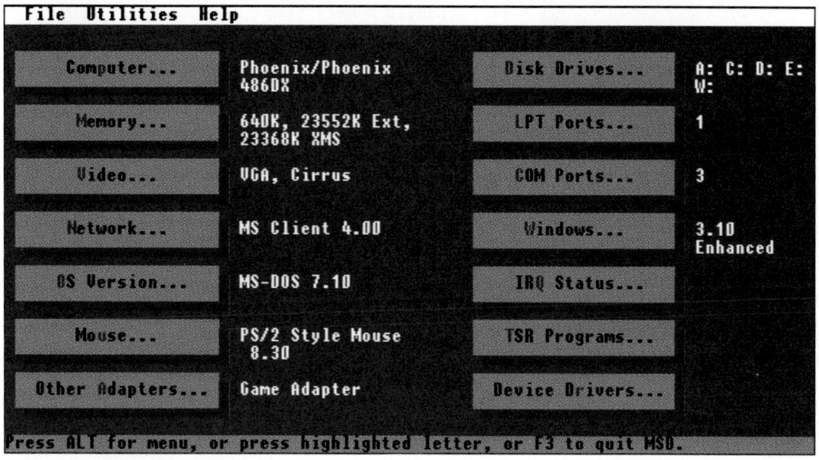

```
 File  Utilities  Help

   Computer...        Phoenix/Phoenix      Disk Drives...    A: C: D: E:
                      486DX                                  W:
   Memory...          640K, 23552K Ext,    LPT Ports...      1
                      23368K XMS
   Video...           VGA, Cirrus          COM Ports...      3

   Network...         MS Client 4.00       Windows...        3.10
                                                             Enhanced
   OS Version...      MS-DOS 7.10          IRQ Status...

   Mouse...           PS/2 Style Mouse     TSR Programs...
                      8.30
   Other Adapters...  Game Adapter         Device Drivers...

Press ALT for menu, or press highlighted letter, or F3 to quit MSD.
```

FIGURE 2-10(b)

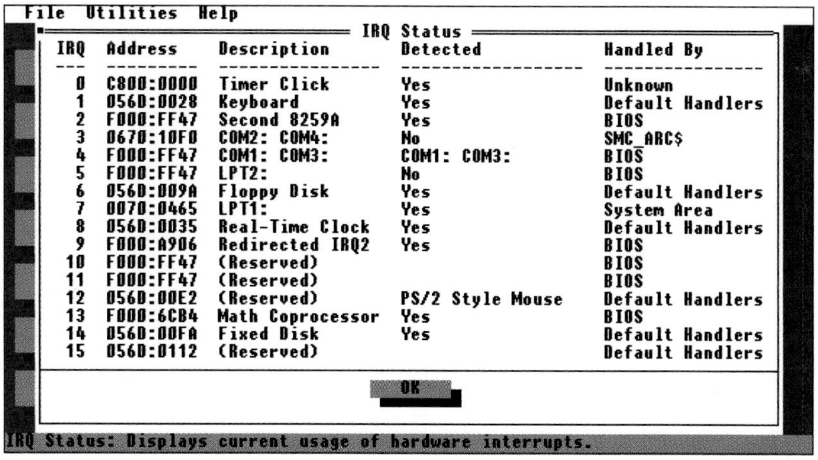

```
 File  Utilities  Help
 ================================ IRQ Status ================================
  IRQ  Address    Description       Detected            Handled By
  ---  ---------  ----------------  ------------------  ------------------
   0   C800:0000  Timer Click       Yes                 Unknown
   1   056D:0028  Keyboard          Yes                 Default Handlers
   2   F000:FF47  Second 8259A      Yes                 BIOS
   3   0670:10F0  COM2: COM4:       No                  SMC_ARC$
   4   F000:FF47  COM1: COM3:       COM1: COM3:         BIOS
   5   F000:FF47  LPT2:             No                  BIOS
   6   056D:009A  Floppy Disk       Yes                 Default Handlers
   7   0070:0465  LPT1:             Yes                 System Area
   8   056D:0035  Real-Time Clock   Yes                 Default Handlers
   9   F000:A906  Redirected IRQ2   Yes                 BIOS
  10   F000:FF47  (Reserved)                            BIOS
  11   F000:FF47  (Reserved)                            BIOS
  12   056D:00E2  (Reserved)        PS/2 Style Mouse    Default Handlers
  13   F000:6CB4  Math Coprocessor  Yes                 BIOS
  14   056D:00FA  Fixed Disk        Yes                 Default Handlers
  15   056D:0112  (Reserved)                            Default Handlers

                          OK

IRQ Status: Displays current usage of hardware interrupts.
```

FIGURE 2-10(c)

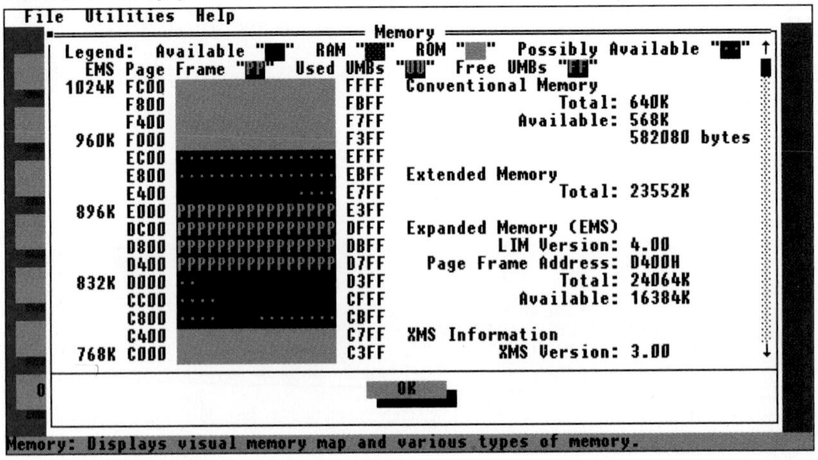

```
┌──────────────────────────────────────────────────────────┐
│ File  Utilities  Help                                      │
│╔══════════════════════ Memory ═══════════════════════════╗│
│ Legend:  Available "■"   RAM "■"   ROM "▒"  Possibly Available "■" ↑│
│    EMS Page Frame "■"  Used UMBs "UU"  Free UMBs "■"       │
│  1024K FC00                FFFF  Conventional Memory        │
│        F800                FBFF              Total:  640K    │
│        F400                F7FF          Available:  568K    │
│   960K F000                F3FF                 582080 bytes │
│        EC00 ............    EFFF                             │
│        E800 ............    EBFF  Extended Memory           │
│        E400          ....   E7FF              Total: 23552K  │
│   896K E000 PPPPPPPPPPPPPPP E3FF                            │
│        DC00 PPPPPPPPPPPPPPP DFFF  Expanded Memory (EMS)      │
│        D800 PPPPPPPPPPPPPPP DBFF          LIM Version:  4.00 │
│        D400 PPPPPPPPPPPPPPP D7FF  Page Frame Address: D400H │
│   832K D000 .               D3FF              Total: 24064K  │
│        CC00 ....            CFFF          Available: 16384K  │
│        C800 ....  ........  CBFF                            │
│        C400                C7FF  XMS Information            │
│   768K C000                C3FF          XMS Version:  3.00 ↓│
│                     ┌─────────┐                             │
│                     │   OK    │                             │
│                     └─────────┘                             │
│ Memory: Displays visual memory map and various types of memory.│
└──────────────────────────────────────────────────────────┘
```

ScanDisk

Replaces CHKDSK; adds functions such as the ability to do a surface scan of the hard drive to find problem areas of memory and mark them unusable.

SCANDISK

Other Commands

DOS Version

To display the version of DOS

VER

Format Disk

To prepare a disk to hold data, insert the disk in the drive:

FORMAT [drive letter]

Format Disk, Bootable

This creates the essential boot disk.

FORMAT [d]: **/S**

Unformat

Like UNDELETE, this command is available in case you accidentally format a floppy or hard drive and you need to unformat it.

UNFORMAT [drive:]

Help

HELP [command]

FASTHELP gives you a complete list of all DOS commands.

> **Note** ☑
>
> Be careful with this command. It will erase all of the information on the drive. If you accidentally run the FORMAT command on the C drive, it will erase your entire hard drive.

Label Disk

Insert the disk to be labeled in drive [d]: Use this command to give the drive a name. The main purpose of this command is to organize the contents of your drive(s). **LABEL [d]:**

Volume

To display volume label, which was created with the LABEL DISK command:
VOL

Common DOS Error Messages

Here is a listing that explains the DOS messages you may see on your screen.

Abort, Retry, Fail?

The computer cannot read the disk in the drive, or there is no disk in the drive.

Access denied

This usually means the file might have an attribute on it limiting the use of this file.

Bad command or file name

You may have miskeyed a command or entered a command DOS does not understand.

Bad or missing command interpreter

DOS cannot locate COMMAND.COM, an important file that enables the operating system to interpret commands. You will need to recopy it into your root directory. There is also a chance your computer could be infected with a virus.

Drive not ready error

Disk in the drive is not readable, or there is no disk in the drive.

Duplicate file name or file not found

When attempting to rename a file, the computer could not find the file to be renamed, or it has discovered an existing file with the designated name.

File cannot be copied onto itself

An attempt to copy a file could not be completed because the file already exists, or the source and destination are the same.

File creation error

Directory could be full because DOS limits the number of files allowed in one directory, or the file may already exist, or the file was not copied correctly.

File not found

The directory you searched does not contain the file named, or there are no files in the directory.

General failure

This message is displayed when DOS is uncertain of the specific problem. DOS could not read the specified drive. If the problem is a floppy disk, try using another disk. If it's the hard drive, you should try rebooting. Consult a repair person if the problem persists.

Insufficient disk space

The disk may be full or the file may be too big to fit on the disk.

Internal stack overflow

DOS's internal storage areas are full. You may need to go into your config.sys and increase the STACKS=0,0. For more information about the config.sys file, please refer to your MS-DOS manual. On most Windows systems you should set the increase to STACKS = 9,256.

Invalid directory

Directory does not exist or is not accessible from the current directory.

Invalid drive specification

Drive does not exist or cannot be found on the computer.

Invalid file name or file not found

DOS couldn't find the file specified in the current directory or the file has an invalid character in it.

Invalid media, track 0 bad or unusable

Format command cannot format the specified disk or the disk capacity is invalid, or bad disk.

Invalid number of parameters

The command was miskeyed, a necessary element was omitted, or an extra space was added.

Invalid parameter

The command specified an incorrect parameter, such as format /z.

Invalid switch

The wrong slash was keyed—such as cd/ instead of cd\.

Non-system disk or disk error

When booting the computer, this error often occurs when there is an unbootable floppy disk in the external drive slot. If there is no disk in the slot, this could be an indication of an unrecognized hard drive, unformatted hard drive, or a hard drive with missing system files.

Not ready, reading drive X

Attempted to read a disk that is not readable, or there is no disk in that drive.

Write fault error

Tried to reroute text to a device that is not connected, not valid, or not hooked up.

Write protect

Tried to write to a disk that is write-protected

SUMMARY

In this lesson, you learned:

- DOS controls the flow of information between you and the computer (translator); allows you to store information on your computer; allows you to retrieve information stored on your computer; interprets and translates the software you have on your computer; gives you access to all its functions (saving, copying, and printing files); and allows you to fix your system when Windows 3.1 or 9x cannot load properly.

- Your hard disk drive (HDD) needs to be prepared to hold data. You accomplish this in DOS by using two external utilities, FDISK and Format. FDISK, which stands for fixed disk utility, is used to partition a hard disk drive. DOS uses partitions to designate usable space—something like the rooms in a house. Once the hard disk drive is partitioned, it must be formatted (using the Format utility) so that it can hold data. Formatting it prepares it to accept and hold data.

- How to run through the installation program and follow the screen-by-screen instructions to install DOS correctly on your personal computer.

- You want to save files in an orderly fashion, organized like the file folders in a filing cabinet. The command MD allows you to create directories for file storage and the command CD allows you to move into these directories and work with the files located there.

- You can create files in DOS by using the EDIT command. This opens the text editor provided with DOS, where you create your file. To view a file's contents without having to open the text editor, use the VIEW command followed by the file name. You can print files in DOS by using the PRINT command. After you create files in DOS, you may later need to copy, rename, and delete them. The COPY command will create a duplicate of a file in another directory. The MOVE command will take a file from one place to another. The REN command will rename a file and the DEL command will remove a file from the directory when it is no longer needed.

- There are many commands in DOS that help you do more things with the operating system. You can change the actions of commands themselves, issue data-protection commands to prevent loss of data, and use file and directory commands to make your work more efficient.

■ The ability to recognize common errors in DOS will help when you are working with the operating system. Although errors will happen, your ability to decipher what the operating system is trying to tell you will save you time in the long run.

VOCABULARY *Review*

Define the following terms:		
CD	DIR	MD
COPY	FDISK	REN
DEL	Format	

REVIEW *Questions*

MULTIPLE CHOICE

Select the best response for the following statements.

1. Which command will display the current directory in a wide column format?
   A. dir/p
   B. dir/q
   C. dir/w
   D. dir|more

2. Which command will create a directory named Reports?
   A. rd reports
   B. md reports
   C. cd reports
   D. mkdir reports

3. Which command will copy the file report.txt from the hard drive to the floppy drive?
   A. copy C:\report.txt A:
   B. copy C:\report.txt B:
   C All of the above.
   D. None of the above.

4. Which command opens report.txt in the DOS text editor?
   A. Edit C:\report.txt
   B. Open C:\report.txt
   C. Spawn Edit Report
   D. Create C:\report.txt
   E. All of the above.
   F. None of the above.

5. Which command will rename the file myfile.txt to file.txt?
   A. Ren file.txt myfile.txt
   B. Ren myfile.txt file.txt
   C. Ren myfile.txt
   D. Rename myfile.txt file.txt

TRUE/FALSE

Circle T if the statement is true or F if the statement is false.

T   F   1. cd.. will always return you to the root directory.

T   F   2. Del *.* and Del ????????.??? will perform the same task.

T   F   3. Del homework will delete the homework directory.

T   F   4. DOS is considered a GUI-type operating system.

T   F   5. The commands CHKDSK and SCANDISK perform the same function.

FILL IN THE BLANK

Complete the following sentences by writing the correct word or words in the blanks provided.

1. The _____ command is used to change to another directory.

2. The _____ command is used to remove a directory.

3. The _____ command is used to make a directory.

4. The _____ command is used to duplicate a file.

5. The _____ command is used to delete a file.

PROJECTS

SCANS PROJECT 2-1

1. Put your disk into the floppy drive.

2. Change to the **A:** prompt.

3. Using the DOS editor, create two text files on drive A. Name one **junk.txt** and the other **garbage.txt**.

4. Create a directory on drive A named the **Schedule**.

5. Create two subdirectories in the **Schedule**, called **Work** and **Play**.

6. Create a subdirectory in the **Work** directory, named **School**.

7. Create two subdirectories in **Play**, named **Workout** and **Walk**.

8. Return to the root directory.

9. Create another directory on the root, named **Clean**.

10. Create two subdirectories in **Clean**, named **Room** and **House**.

11. Create two subdirectories in the **Room** directory, named **Makebed** and **Vacuum**.

12. Create two subdirectories in the **House** directory, named **Living** and **Kitchen**.

13. Return to the root directory.

14. Copy the **junk** file from the root to the **Clean** directory.

15. Copy the **junk** file from the **Clean** directory to the **Work** directory.

16. Rename the **junk** file in the **Work** directory to **myjunk.txt**.

17. Copy the **garbage** file from the root directory to the **Kitchen** directory.

18. Delete the **garbage** file from the root directory.

19. Rename the **garbage** file in the **Kitchen** directory to **mygarb.txt**.

20. Remove the **Living** directory.

21. Remove the entire **Schedule** directory tree.

22. Hand in your disk to your instructor for credit.

PROJECT 2-2

1. Create a batch file on your disk named **mybatch.bat**.

2. The batch file should perform the following actions:
   - Display the version of DOS that is being used.
   - Display the current date.
   - Display the current time.
   - Display a directory listing of A: in the wide format.

CRITICAL *Thinking*

ACTIVITY 2-1

Using the Internet, search the classifieds for jobs requiring DOS. Were there any jobs that require knowledge of this operating system? Were you surprised at the outcome? Why do you think knowledge of DOS could still be important in today's job market?

ACTIVITY 2-2

DOS has a COPYDISK command that allows you to duplicate the contents of one disk to another. Software that is copyrighted may not be copied legally, yet this practice of pirating software continues. Do you think that it is ethical to pirate software? What are the penalties for pirating software? How do you think the software companies could better prevent this practice?

UNDERSTANDING MAC OS X

OBJECTIVES

OBJECTIVES

Upon completion of this lesson, you should be able to:

- Explain how the Macintosh mouse and keyboard are different from those on a PC and know how to use them.

- Tell the difference between Aqua, Darwin, and Classic.

- Use the parts of Mac OS X's user interface (desktop, menu bar, windows, and the dock).

- Manage files using Mac OS X (get info, move, copy, rename, create, make aliases, and delete).

- Change system settings using System Preferences (especially Classic Preferences, ColorSync Preferences, Display Preferences, Dock Preferences, and Software Update Preferences).

- Explain the use of some system utilities to manage disks, find keystrokes, and manage printing.

- Do simple troubleshooting when a problem has occurred.

Estimated Time: 3.5 hours

VOCABULARY

Alias

Aqua

Classic

ColorSync

Command key

Darwin

Desktop

Dock

Finder

Get info

Icon view

List view

Option key

Panels view

System Preferences

Mac OS X—A Whole New Operating System

Mac OS X (pronounced Mack-Oh-Ess-Ten), from Apple Computer Inc., seems as easy to use as earlier Macintosh operating systems, leading you to think that Mac OS X is just the latest version of the same operating system that has been running on Macintosh systems for years—but it isn't. Mac OS X is a completely new and different operating system for the Macintosh, as different as Windows 3.0 was from Windows 95.

Macintosh has always been visually appealing. In fact, Mac OS X looks a lot like previous versions of Mac OS. But looks can be deceiving. Actually, it uses some of the best features from previous Macintosh operating systems, combined with features from Windows and Unix, to create a unique "best of class" interface. Underneath its skin, Mac OS X is really a form of BSD Unix—the operating system that drives much of the Internet.

The version of Mac OS X described in this lesson is designed for Macintosh workstations—not servers. (Using Macintosh as a server is dealt with in Lesson 10: Mac OS X Server.)

Hardware Differences

This lesson assumes you have some knowledge of Microsoft Windows-based systems so you can see the differences between those computers and a Macintosh.

Contrary to popular belief, there are really very few differences in the hardware between Windows-based computers and Macintosh computers. Of course on the inside of the computer they each have their own unique way of doing things, but the mouse, the keyboard, the monitor and other parts of the interface between you and the computer should be very familiar. This section will discuss some of those differences.

Monitor

Some Macintosh systems are built with the monitor and the CPU in the same all-in-one enclosure. The iMac and eMac are examples of this: the entire computer is found in the same case as the monitor. Whenever you use a Mac display, either an all-in-one or an Apple-brand monitor, you will find that the monitor has a special button on the front with a "sun" icon that brings up the Displays System Preferences panel when you press it. (System Preferences will be discussed in a later section.) Another button on the front may turn the computer on. This button is pictured in Figure 3-1. On some monitors, the on button will be white when the computer is on, and even glow and fade when the monitor is in sleep mode.

FIGURE 3-1
The on/off button of an Apple monitor

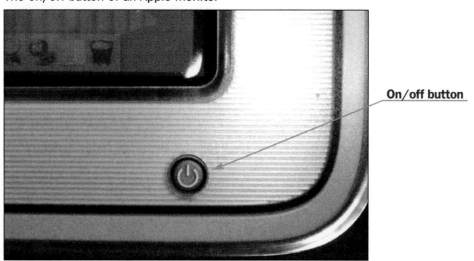

On/off button

Mouse

Most Macs come with a mouse that has a single button, like the one that is pictured in Figure 3-2. If you are not used to Macs, you may be more familiar with a mouse that has two or more buttons. Most software on Macs supports two-button mice. Pressing this second button is often called a right-click. On a Mac, this action is performed by pressing and holding the control button on the keyboard while clicking the mouse. Right-clicks are often used to access menus that hold item-specific options. For example, right-clicking an icon may bring up a menu that allows you to delete the icon, while right-clicking a link in a Web page may allow you to open the link in a new window.

FIGURE 3-2
An Apple optical mouse

Keyboard

The keyboard on a Mac contains the standard QWERTY format letter board, some function keys, and sometimes a number pad. In fact, with the exception of some keys found along the bottom row next to the spacebar (as in Figure 3-3), it is virtually identical to a PC keyboard. However, some of the keys in the first row are specific to a Mac. These keys are used to access certain commands and features in Mac OS X. To use them, you hold the key down while pressing another key—such as a shift key.

FIGURE 3-3
Keys unique to an Apple keyboard

Unique keys

Open-Apple or Command Key

Most keyboard functions are accessed by using the **command key**. The command key is found on the same row as the space bar and has both a clover symbol and an open apple symbol on it. (There may be two of these keys, one on either side of the spacebar.)

Although not all programs have the same keyboard commands, Table 3-1 lists some that are common to several applications as well as to the operating system.

TABLE 3-1
Command keystrokes and their actions

KEYSTROKES	ACTION
command+X	Cut
command+C	Copy
command+V	Paste
command+P	Print
command+O	Open
command+W	Close window
command+M	Minimize window
command+N	New
command+S	Save
command+A	Select all
command+Z	Undo
command+Q	Quit

Option Key

The *option key* allows the user to key other characters than those that appear on the faces of the keycaps. For example, you can key a copyright symbol (©) by pressing option+c; the "cent" (¢) symbol by pressing option+4; etc. Some symbols require you to press the shift key, option key, and another key at the same time. For example shift+option+8 will give you the degree symbol (as in 42°).

The option key is often used when you are keying characters with accents, as in some European languages. Table 3-2 provides a list of some option key combinations that result in accented characters.

TABLE 3-2
Option keystrokes and their results

KEYSTROKE	RESULTS	WHAT IT'S CALLED
Press **option+u**, then press **a**	ä	umlaut
Press **option+`**, then press **a**	à	grave
Press **option+e**, then press **a**	á	accent
Press **option+i**, then press **a**	â	caret
Press **option+n**, then press **a**	ã	enye
Press **option+a**	å	halo

Function Keys

The function keys (sometimes called F keys) are the keys on the top row of the keyboard. Depending on your particular keyboard, you will have anywhere from twelve to fifteen. These keys are included on the keyboard to allow software developers increased flexibility when making keyboard shortcuts to features. Complex applications like video editing or computer animation applications allow the F keys to access some of their vast numbers of commands. Despite the variety in their use, some F keys have common uses. The F1 key is usually used to open up extra help, and pressing the F12 key will eject a CD in the CD slot or open the CD drive tray.

S TEP-BY-STEP 3.1

1. Open the application **TextEdit**. This application is located in the Applications folder. You can get to the Applications folder by double-clicking the icon of the hard disk on your desktop, and then double-clicking the folder called **Applications**. Scroll down until you see the **TextEdit** application icon and double-click it to open it.

2. Once the TextEdit program has started, you should see a new window into which you can key. Using your knowledge of the option key, key the following items exactly as they appear:

   How to say Hello in nine different languages

   Apache: Dáazho

   Estonian: Jõudu tööle

   Finnish: Päivää

   German: Grüß dich

   Hungarian: Jó napot

   Icelandic: Sæll

   Norwegian: Hêia

   Romanian: Bunã

   Swedish: Hallå där

3. If you need help, use the following information:

   option + e, then a = á

   option + n, then o = õ

   option + u, then o = ö

   option + u, then a = ä

   option + u, then u = ü

   option + s = ß

   option + e, then o = ó

   option + ' = æ

   option + i, then e = ê

   option + n, then a = ã

   option + a = å

STEP-BY-STEP 3.1 Continued

4. Close the TextEdit application by choosing **Quit Textedit** from the **Textedit** menu or pressing **command+Q**. When asked whether you want to save changes before closing, click **Don't Save**.

The Three Faces of Mac OS X

Mac OS X can be described as having three faces. The first is an open-source operating system core called *Darwin*. It is based on a form of Unix called BSD, and like most Unix systems it is text based, not very pretty, but very powerful. The second face is the user interface that Apple has placed over Darwin to make it more useful. This user interface is called *Aqua*. Lastly, to accommodate programs written for the older Macintosh systems, a form of the old operating system will run in a kind of emulation mode called *Classic*, which is identical to Mac OS 9.

Darwin

Darwin, Apple's open-source version of BSD Unix, is invisible to the user. To see it you must open one of two programs. One, the Console program, lets you peek at the communication happening between programs in Darwin. It is text and may be rather obscure. The second, the Terminal program, allows you to talk to the Darwin kernel. The Terminal is pictured in Figure 3-4.

FIGURE 3-4
The Console and Terminal windows—a look at Darwin

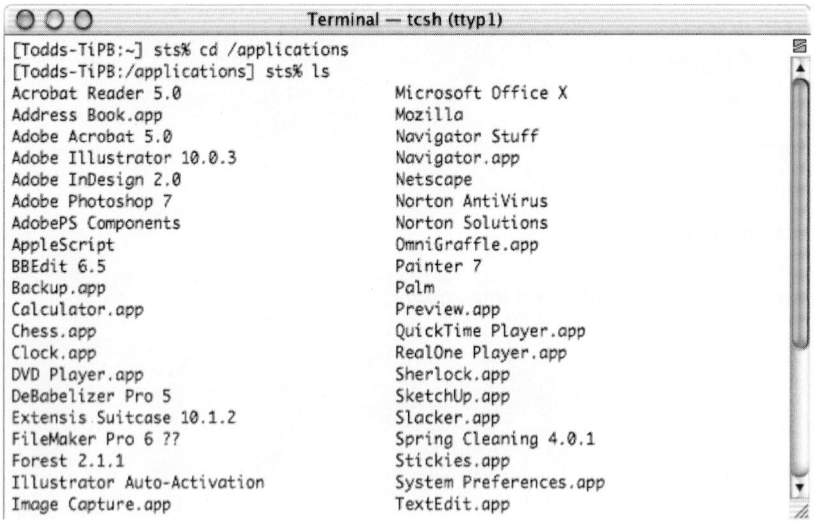

```
Terminal — tcsh (ttyp1)
[Todds-TiPB:~] sts% cd /applications
[Todds-TiPB:/applications] sts% ls
Acrobat Reader 5.0              Microsoft Office X
Address Book.app               Mozilla
Adobe Acrobat 5.0              Navigator Stuff
Adobe Illustrator 10.0.3       Navigator.app
Adobe InDesign 2.0             Netscape
Adobe Photoshop 7             Norton AntiVirus
AdobePS Components            Norton Solutions
AppleScript                   OmniGraffle.app
BBEdit 6.5                    Painter 7
Backup.app                    Palm
Calculator.app                Preview.app
Chess.app                     QuickTime Player.app
Clock.app                     RealOne Player.app
DVD Player.app                Sherlock.app
DeBabelizer Pro 5             SketchUp.app
Extensis Suitcase 10.1.2      Slacker.app
FileMaker Pro 6 ??            Spring Cleaning 4.0.1
Forest 2.1.1                  Stickies.app
Illustrator Auto-Activation   System Preferences.app
Image Capture.app             TextEdit.app
```

Aqua

The second face of Mac OS X is the set of visual objects that allow you to interact with your computer, sometimes called a graphical user interface (GUI, pronounced "gooey"). The GUI for Darwin is called Aqua. Aqua uses some of the technology that is used to view a PDF (an electronic document file format developed by Adobe). Aqua is easily recognized by its glassy translucent style and easy-to-use interface.

It's not hard to tell when you're in Aqua—this is the mode in which Mac OS X boots. The easiest way to tell if you are in Aqua is by looking in the menu bar at the top left corner of the screen. If you see a translucent blue apple, as shown in Figure 3-5, then you are in Aqua. In the remainder of this lesson we will use Aqua to do our activities.

FIGURE 3-5
The menu bar for Aqua

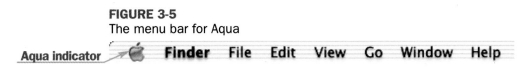

Aqua indicator

Classic

Even though Mac OS X is wildly different under the hood than earlier versions of the Mac OS, older applications will still run under OS X. Apple has included a version of the earlier system, called Classic, that runs all of your old software. It looks like and behaves just like Mac OS 9. Any application that runs within Classic mode is easily recognized by its older-looking interface distinguished by the rainbow-striped Apple icon in the Apple menu.

FIGURE 3-6
The menu bar in Classic

Classic mode indicator

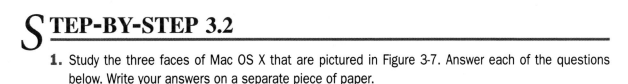

STEP-BY-STEP 3.2

1. Study the three faces of Mac OS X that are pictured in Figure 3-7. Answer each of the questions below. Write your answers on a separate piece of paper.

FIGURE 3-7
The three faces of Mac OS X

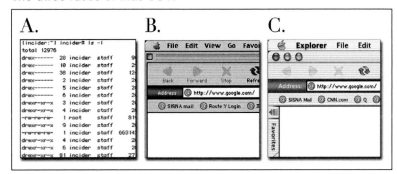

a. Which picture (A, B, or C) is an example of Aqua?

b. What makes you think it is Aqua?

c. Which picture (A, B, or C) is an example of Classic?

d. What makes you think it is Classic?

e. Which picture (A, B, or C) is an example of Darwin?

f. What makes you think it is Darwin?

Working in Aqua

Desktop

After the computer has finished starting up, you will see the ***desktop***. Here, you can see the different parts of the operating system (see Figure 3-8). At the top of the screen, you will find a menu bar that contains different options and features. The ***Dock*** is found on the bottom of the screen by default, but you can change its location. The Dock can contain application icons and folders, and always contains the Trash. You may find icons that represent the disks or other volumes on your computer (you may not always see the volumes because one option lets you remove them from the desktop).

FIGURE 3-8
Aqua desktop

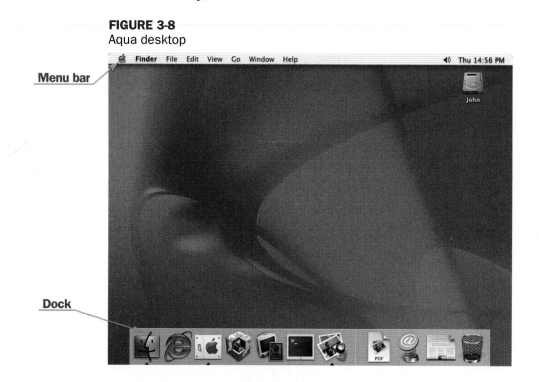

Menu Bar

The menu bar is always found across the top of the screen (this is different from Windows OS, where menu bars can sometimes be found across the top of individual windows). The only time the menu bar is not displayed is when your computer is displaying a program in full-screen mode.

When multiple programs are running, the menu bar shows the menu items for the currently active program (see Figure 3-9). When you switch to another program, the menu bar changes. The name of the active application always appears to the right of the apple icon on the menu bar.

FIGURE 3-9
A typical Aqua menu bar

The first few menus shown in this example of a menu bar are included in most programs: the Apple menu (represented by a small apple icon), an Application menu (which changes from application to application), the File menu, and the Edit menu. The Apple menu always contains a standard set of system commands that allow you to shut down, restart, log out, view system information, or force quit applications. The application's menu always contains the preferences for the program. (Preferences were often found in the Edit menu in previous versions of Mac OS). It also contains commands that allow to you find out more information about the program, hide the program, or quit. The File menu usually contains file commands like open, save, close, print, and quit. The Edit menu always contains editing commands like cut, copy, and paste. Commands that deal with searching are often found in the Edit menu as well.

Windows and the Finder

Mac OS X uses windows to show you the contents of files and folders. Mac OS X uses a program, called the *Finder*, to show you what is in a folder when you open it. The Finder is a program that is always running because it manages the volumes on your computer and allows you to navigate through your files. Mac OS X Finder window may contain icons for applications, files, and aliases. An example of a Finder window is shown in Figure 3-10.

FIGURE 3-10
A Finder window

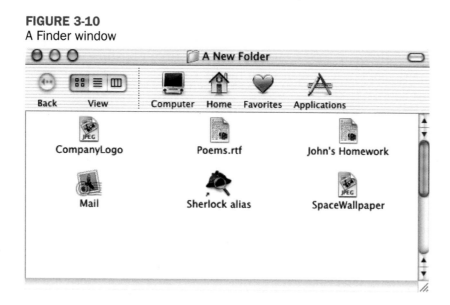

Icons

Each item on your computer is represented in the Finder by an icon. An icon is a small picture that represents, in some way, the contents of the item. There are five basic types of icons: documents, folders, applications, aliases, and volumes. A single example of each type is pictured in Figure 3-11.

FIGURE 3-11
Some enlarged sample icons in the Finder

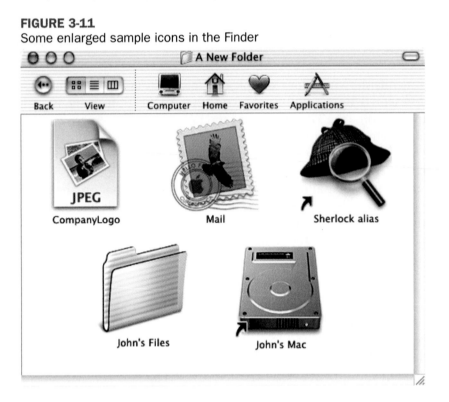

Document icons represent files that need to be opened by a specific program. Most document icons look like sheets of paper marked up with an application name or company logo. Double-clicking a document icon opens the file by running the application for that file, then opening the file.

As you would guess, a folder icon looks like a folder. Double-clicking a folder icon opens a new window that shows you the contents of the folder.

Application icons represent a specific program. Application icons vary greatly, but they usually do not look like documents or folders. They may contain the logo for the software, and are usually fancier visually than other icons.

Aliases are pointers to other files. They do not represent the file itself, but point to that file so that you can open the file. Alias icons look exactly like the original file icon, but they feature a small arrow in the bottom left-hand corner of the icon to show that they are an alias.

Volume icons usually look like the media they represent. A volume that represents your hard disk looks like a hard disk; the same applies to CDs and Zip® disks.

Title Bar

At the top of each window is a title bar. The title bar contains the name of the folder you opened, along with some buttons that control how the window looks and acts. The title bar also acts as a sort of handle; you can drag a window to a new position by the title bar. Notice the three colored buttons sitting on the title bar at the upper-left corner of the window. When you press the red button, the window will close. When you move the mouse pointer over this button you will either see an "X" or a dot. If you see an X, you will be able to close the window in a single click. Seeing a dot means that you will have to do something additional before the window will close (for example, an application may ask you if you want to save a document before you close the window).

The middle button will minimize the window in the Dock. When you click the minimize button, the window will slide into the Dock and you will see a miniature of the window in the dock. To view the window later, click its icon inside the Dock. You can also minimize a window by double-clicking its title bar. The green, right-most button will maximize the window, or resize it so it is as big as possible—or make it smaller, depending on the current state of the window. If you click the maximize button when the window has already been maximized, the window will shrink back to the size it was before you maximized it.

Scrolling

Occasionally, the contents of the window may be larger than the window itself. When this happens scrollbars will appear on the right side of the window. Scroll the contents of the window either by dragging the slider to the desired position, or by clicking the arrows that appear within the scrollbar.

Window Views

Mac OS X allows you to view the contents of folders in different ways. You can change the way a window is displayed by choosing an option from the view options panel. This panel is found just below the title bar in the upper left corner of the window, just to the right of the Back button.

There are three ways to view the contents of a folder: as icons (the left button in the panel), as a list (the middle button), and in panels (the right button).

When in *icon view*, items within the window will be represented by small pictures called icons. These icons can be moved around by dragging them. The *list view* still allows items to be represented as icons, though the icons are much smaller (and sometimes less detailed) with information to the right of the icon. You can see the difference by comparing

> **Note** ☑
>
> Mac OS allows multitasking. Multitasking means that more than one program can be running at the same time. When you have more than one program running, you will usually have more than one window in view. The last window you opened (whether it is a program window or a folder window) is called active. You can tell which application is active by looking at the name of the menu to the right of the Apple Menu in the upper-left corner of the screen. All other windows will become inactive once you open a new window. Inactive windows can be identified easily by their transparent title bars.

Figure 3-10 or 3-11 with Figure 3-12. Items are sorted into a list, usually by name. The titles of the columns within the list are found at the top of the window, below the toolbar. Clicking the title will cause the list to be sorted by that title. Repeated clicks change the sorting from ascending to descending. For example, if you wanted to find the largest file in the folder, you would view the window as a list, and click the Size title once.

FIGURE 3-12
An Aqua window's list view

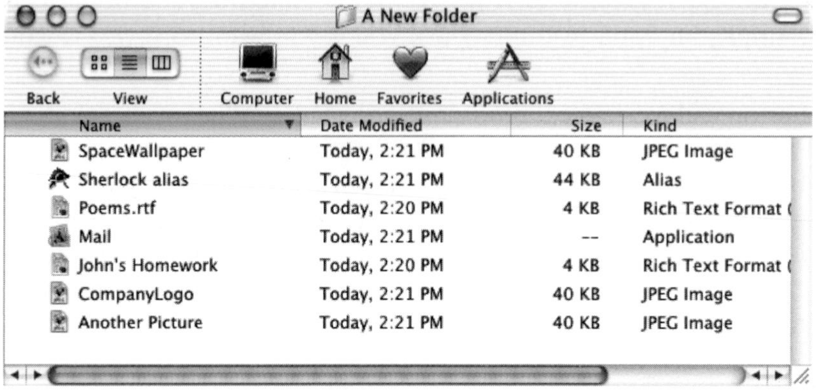

The *panels view* is a very clever way to navigate the files on your system. Figure 3-13 shows a Finder window in panels view. When you select the panels view, the window divides itself into columns. Each column represents the contents of a folder. Within those contents, you may find other folders—they are marked by small triangles to the right of their names. Each time you click a folder, its contents are shown in the panel to its immediate right. If a file other than a folder is clicked, the panel to its right shows an enlarged view of the icon, with some extra details about the file. Clicking certain types of files may even bring up a short preview of the contents of the file in the new panel.

FIGURE 3-13
An Aqua window's panels view

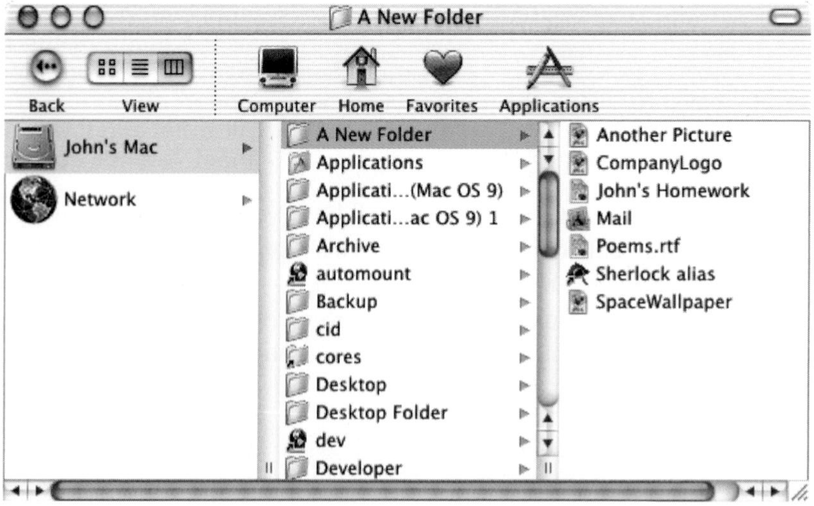

The Dock

The Dock, pictured in Figure 3-14, is found at the bottom of the screen on a newly installed Mac OS X system (you can also set it to appear on the left or right edge of your screen). It is split into two parts. The left side (or top) holds the icons of programs that are either currently open, or that the user starts often. To add a program icon to the Dock, drag its icon to the left side (or top) of the Dock and release. To remove a program icon, drag the icon off of the Dock when the program is not running and release the mouse button. (The icon will vanish in a small puff of smoke.) The right side (or bottom) can hold icons that point to folders or files on your computer. Add and remove icons to the right side (or bottom) in the same way you would to the left side (or top).

FIGURE 3-14
The Mac OS X Dock

Trash

The far right (or bottom) icon on the Dock is called the Trash. Using the Trash will help you do a number of things, but it is mostly used to delete things. When you wish to delete a file, simply drag it into the trash. Files remain in the Trash until you ask the computer to empty the Trash.

When you want to eject a disk, you also use the Trash. Do not worry: Dragging a disk to the Trash does not delete it. Once you have started to drag the volume's icon, the Trash icon will change to an eject icon. Release the disk icon over the eject icon to eject the disk.

S TEP-BY-STEP 3.3

1. Close any open applications if necessary so you can see the desktop.

2. Find the icon that represents your hard drive. If it hasn't been moved, it will appear in the top right-hand corner of the desktop.

3. Double-click your hard drive's icon.

4. A new window should appear. Move the window to a new position by dragging its title bar.

5. Change the view type to **Icon View** by clicking the left button of the View options button in the toolbar at the top of the window.

6. Change the view type to **List View**.

7. Drag the slider or click the arrows on the scrollbar to view the rest of the contents of the window.

8. Change the view type to **Panels View** by clicking the right-most part of the View Options button in the toolbar at the top of the window.

9. Minimize the window by clicking the yellow button on the title bar. Watch where the window slides into the Dock.

STEP-BY-STEP 3.3 Continued

10. Click your window (which now is in the Dock) to maximize it.

11. Close the window by pressing the red button on the title bar.

Managing Files in Aqua

One purpose of the Finder is to help you organize your files. By using a combination of keystrokes and mouse actions, the Finder will arrange your files in a number of ways.

Creating Folders

The easiest way to create a new folder is by selecting New Folder from the File menu when Finder is the current application (when the word Finder is the second menu from the left). The New Folder button is found to the left of the View Options. Another way to create a new folder is by selecting New Folder from the File menu in the Finder.

Copy

To copy a file, drag the file to its new location while pressing the option key. The option key does not need to be pressed if you are copying the file to a removable disk, such as a CDR or Zip disk.

Move

To move a file, drag it to its new location.

Rename

To rename a file, click the file once to select it, then click its name. The name of the file will be surrounded by a box and highlighted. Key the new name for the file and press Enter.

Make Alias

To make an alias, select the file by clicking it. Once selected, press command+L, or select Make Alias from the File menu in the Finder.

Get Info

You may want to know how big a file is, when it was created, or the access privileges for the file. This information is accessed by the *Get Info* command. Select the file by clicking it, then press command+I. A small window will open, showing you the information you need.

An example is found in Figure 3-15. If you wish to see the same set of information for a different file, all you need to do is select that file by clicking it. The Get Info window will remain open to show you information about every item you select until you close it.

FIGURE 3-15
The "Get Info" window for a JPEG file

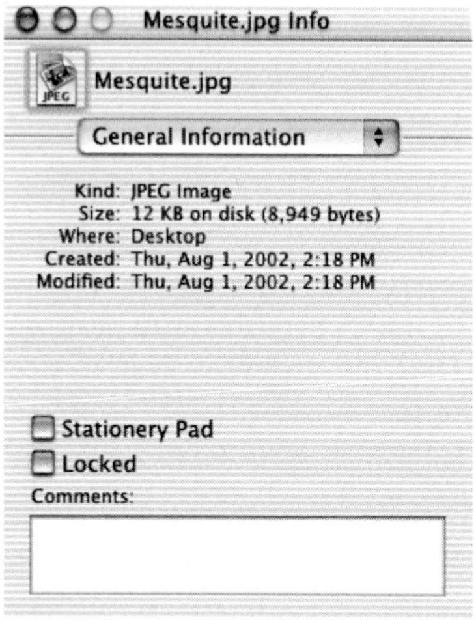

Delete

To delete a file, drag it to the Trash. To permanently delete the file, empty the Trash by selecting Empty Trash from the Finder application menu.

STEP-BY-STEP 3.4

1. Close any windows if necessary so you can see the desktop.

2. Create a new folder by selecting **New Folder** from the **File** menu.

3. Rename this folder by keying **Number One**.

4. Make a copy of your Number One folder by selecting it (by clicking it once) and then selecting **Duplicate** from the **File** menu or by pressing **command-D**.

5. Rename the copied folder **Number Two**.

6. Open your Number One folder by double-clicking it.

7. Move your Number Two folder into your Number One folder by dragging into the new window that appears.

8. Close your Number One folder by pressing the red button on its title bar.

9. Make an alias of your Number One folder by clicking it once and pressing **command+L**.

10. Double-click your new alias. You should see your Number Two folder inside!

STEP-BY-STEP 3.4 Continued

11. Close the folder window.

12. Delete both the folder and the alias by dragging their icons into the Trash.

Managing Mac OS X's Options

System Preferences

Control panels in Mac OS X are located in an application called *System Preferences*. To open this application, click its icon in the Dock or find and double-click its icon in the Applications folder. Once open, you will notice that the different system preferences have been organized into four categories for easier use (see Figure 3-16).

FIGURE 3-16
System Preferences application for Mac OS X

Most system preferences are easy and intuitive to use. Following is a list of system preferences that are not dealt with directly in this lesson. We explore some of these in the Step-by-Step below, but we also recommend that you take some time on your own to become acquainted with each of them.

- General
- International
- Keyboard

- Energy Saver
- Mouse
- Date & Time
- QuickTime
- Screen Saver
- Sound
- Speech
- Startup Disk

STEP-BY-STEP 3.5

1. Open System Preferences by clicking its icon in the Dock. (System Preferences can also be opened by selecting from the Apple menu.)

2. Click the **General** icon in the Personal category. Change the appearance and highlight color to different settings by clicking the list and selecting a new color. Watch to see what parts of OS X change color.

3. Click the **Show All** button in the top left-hand corner of the window.

4. Click the **Screen Saver** icon in the Personal category. Select a screen saver from the list at the left. Click the **Test** button. When the screen saver is running, move the mouse to stop it.

5. Click the **Show All** button.

6. Click the **Mouse** icon in the Hardware category. Change the tracking speed by moving the slider on the left. Move your mouse around the screen to see the difference after you change the setting.

7. Click the **Show All** button.

8. Click the **Sound** icon in the Hardware category. Click some of the alert sounds to hear them. Choose one you like best.

9. Click the **Show All** button and leave the System Preferences open for the next Step-by-Step.

The sections below discuss some of the more critical system preferences and those that are, perhaps, more important.

Computer Concepts

Many of the System Preferences display a small padlock icon at the bottom. If this icon is in the "locked" position, you will need to click on the icon and provide an administrative password before you will be able to make any changes.

Classic Preferences

The Classic system preference, as shown in Figure 3-17, allows you to configure the running of Mac OS 9.x on your OS X system. When you run an application in classic mode, you will notice the difference from OS X's smooth Aqua interface. In this system preference, you can start, restart, and force quit Classic. Because the Classic OS and OS X can reside either on the same or different disks, this panel also allows you to specify which disk Classic will call home. For increased performance and security, you should run Classic on a different disk from OS X.

FIGURE 3-17
The Classic system preference window

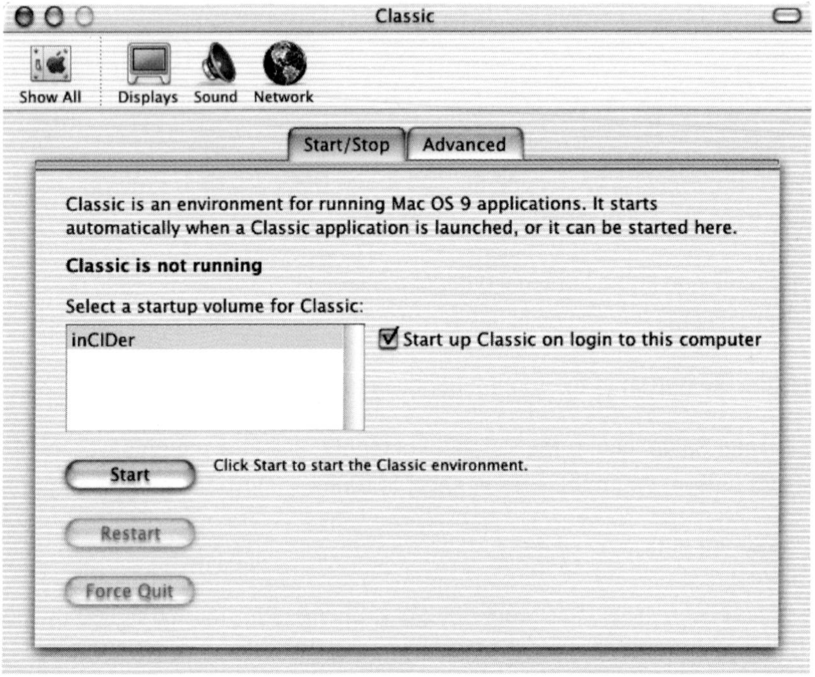

The Advanced tab contains functions that allow you to restart the system during problems, and set a time when Classic should run in sleep mode. It also allows you to rebuild the desktop, a process that optimizes the Classic application performance.

STEP-BY-STEP 3.6

1. If it is not already open, open System Preferences (see Step-by-Step 3.5, step 1).

2. Open the Classic system preferences by clicking its icon in the System category.

3. Click the **Start up Classic on login to this computer** option. Choosing this option starts the Classic environment every time you start up your computer.

4. Click the **Show All** button and leave the System Preferences window open for the next Step-by-Step.

ColorSync Preferences

ColorSync is Apple's system for making sure that colors match between devices. It uses a set of standardized profiles based on color space and intended input or output. For example, if you want your RGB color monitor and your CMYK color printer to work together, ColorSync ensures that the truest colors are shown on both devices. If you intend to use your Mac for visual art you will want to familiarize yourself with the ColorSync system preference.

When you are developing art for printed materials, you will want the screen colors to be as true as possible. That way, when the work is sent to press, your art will appear on paper just as it did when it was on your screen. An example of profile settings is shown in Figure 3-18.

FIGURE 3-18
The ColorSync preference window

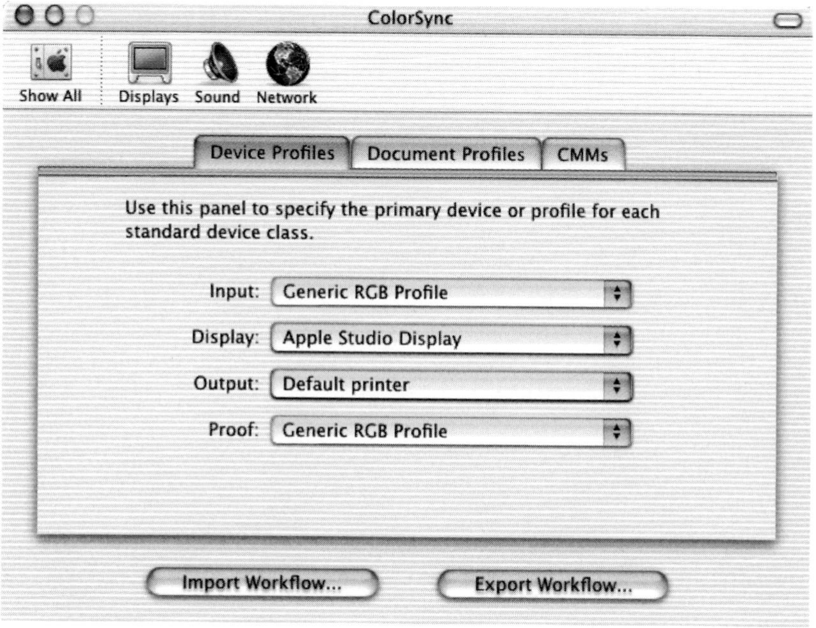

S TEP-BY-STEP 3.7

1. If it is not already open, open System Preferences.

2. Open the ColorSync system preference by clicking its icon in the Hardware category.

3. Notice what color profiles your computer is currently using to represent colors.

4. Record your settings and compare them with a neighbor and the settings pictured in Figure 3-18.

5. Click the **Show All** button and leave the System Preferences window open for the next Step-by-Step.

Displays Preferences

The Displays system preferences allow you to control the resolution, geometry, and color of your display.

The Display tab of this system preference window is shown in Figure 3-19. Here, you will be able to change the resolution, number of colors, contrast, and brightness. For best performance and compatibility, make sure the *Show modes recommended by display* box is checked before choosing any new settings.

FIGURE 3-19
The Display preferences window

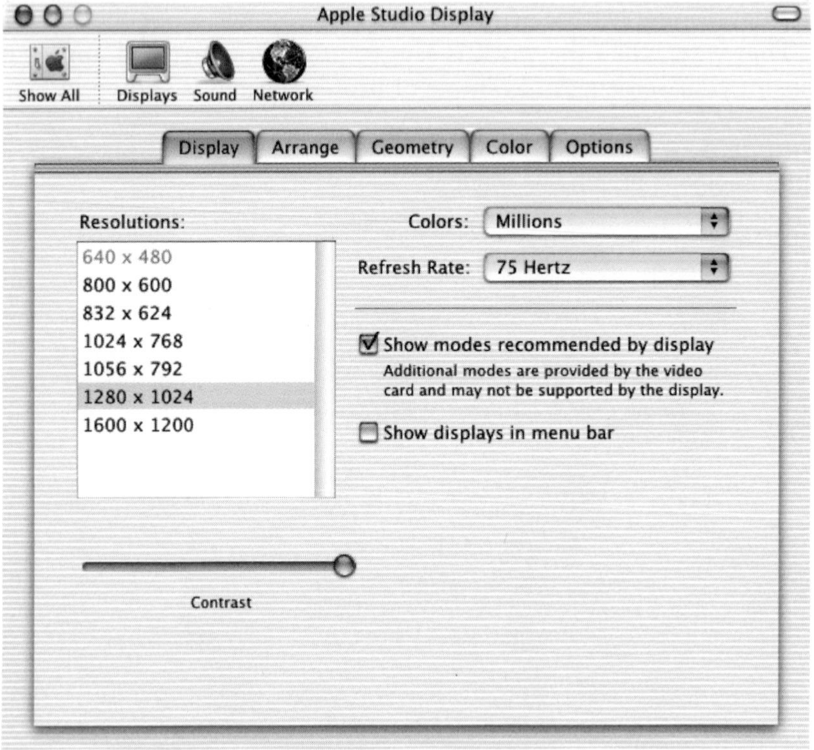

The Geometry tab allows you to change the way the screen image is projected against the front of your monitor. If your screen looks crooked or off center, you can adjust it using the controls within this tab.

The Color tab allows you to choose a generic color profile for your display. If you wish to fine-tune your color setup, see the ColorSync system preference mentioned above.

If you have more than one monitor connected to your Macintosh, the Arrange tab will appear. This allows you to make mouse and window movements reflect their relative positions.

S TEP-BY-STEP 3.8

1. If it is not already open, open System Preferences.

2. Open the **Displays** system preference by clicking its icon in the Hardware category.

3. Select one of the **Resolutions** settings in the list by clicking its title.

STEP-BY-STEP 3.8 Continued

4. When you press the mouse button, the computer screen should flicker and reappear with the new changes. Notice how different your new setting looks. You can return to the previous appearance setting by selecting it in the window. (Some settings may or may not work with a given computer. When this is the case, the computer displays a dialog box asking you to confirm whether to keep the new setting. If you don't respond within 15 seconds, the computer will reset your monitor back to its original setting.)

5. Scroll to the bottom of the list, and try the bottom setting just as you did in Steps 3 and 4.

6. Click the **Show All** button and leave the System Preferences window open for the next Step-by-Step.

Dock Preferences

The Dock in OS X can be changed in a variety of ways. When OS X is newly installed, the Dock appears at the bottom of the screen. If you want, you can change the appearance of the Dock from within System Preferences. Through the Dock preferences, you can change the size, magnification, and position of the Dock. You can also change how windows animate when they minimize into the Dock. These settings are shown in Figure 3-20.

FIGURE 3-20
The Dock preferences window

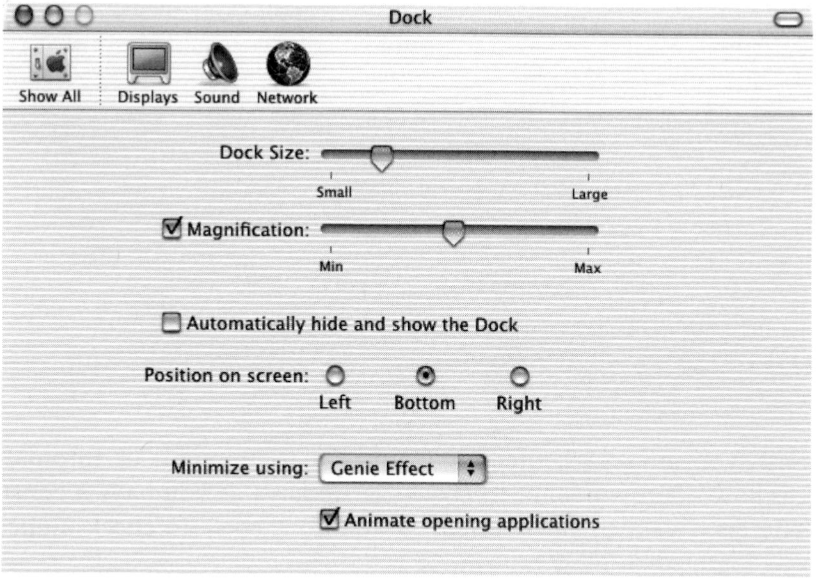

S TEP-BY-STEP 3.9

1. If it is not already open, open System Preferences.

2. Open the Dock system preference by clicking its icon in the Personal category.

3. Change the size of the Dock by dragging the slider near the top of the window by the label **Dock Size**. Notice how the Dock changes as you move the slider.

STEP-BY-STEP 3.9 Continued

4. Change the magnification of the Dock by dragging the other slider. (If necessary, select the Magnification check box to turn magnification on.) To see the change, move your mouse over the icons in the Dock after you change the position of the slider.

5. Move the Dock to different positions on the screen by pressing the **Left**, **Bottom**, and **Right** buttons. Decide which position you like best.

6. Click the **Show All** button and leave the System Preferences window open for the next Step-by-Step.

Software Update Preferences

OS X comes with a system preference that allows you to keep all of your software up to date. This preference allows you to connect to an Apple server to check and see if software updates are available. The Software Update system preference is shown in Figure 3-21.

FIGURE 3-21
The Software Update preferences window

In this preference you can set whether you would like to manually or automatically check for updates, as well as how often you want to check for updates. If you have a constant connection to the Internet, you may want to check often. In addition, you can check immediately for new updates by pressing the Update Now button.

STEP-BY-STEP 3.10

1. If it is not already open, open System Preferences.

2. Open the Software Update system preference by clicking its icon in the System category.

STEP-BY-STEP 3.10 Continued

3. Check the settings here to see how often your computer checks for software updates.

4. Check for any updates by clicking the **Update Now** button at the bottom of the window. Wait as the computer connects to the Internet and checks for any updates.

5. A new window may appear and show a list of the current updates. After Software Update shows you the list of current updates, close the window by pressing the red button on the title bar. Press the **Quit** button from the window that appears after you try to close the window.

6. Close the System Preferences.

Managing Networking and Users

Network System Preference

When you ran the Setup Assistant just after you installed, you probably already entered all the information needed by the Network system preference to set up your network. However, since all of the network settings for your server are managed in the Network system preference, double-checking the information listed in this system preference can solve many connection problems.

From the Network system preference, you can change the location information for your server. Unless you plan to move the server around, leave this option set to Automatic.

TCP/IP Tab

The active network port information is shown in the lower portion of the window. Select Active Network Ports from the Show list to view the different devices that allow you to connect to a network. If your server has been set up correctly, you will see Built-in Ethernet listed along with other network adapters (such as an internal modem or AirPort wireless). Select the Built-in Ethernet option from the Show list.

Net Business

A MOVING WORKSTATION?

If you use your workstation in multiple locations, the Network system preferences allow you to remember the settings for each location. Select the New Location option and enter in the name of your new location. When you move the server, create a new location once again, and the Network system preference will save the settings for the old location under the old location's name.

The lower part of the window should change to show you the network settings for Built-in Ethernet, as in Figure 3-22, which shows the different protocols. The first tab contains the network settings for TCP/IP (Transmission Control Protocol / Internet Protocol).

FIGURE 3-22
TCP/IP settings in the Network system preference

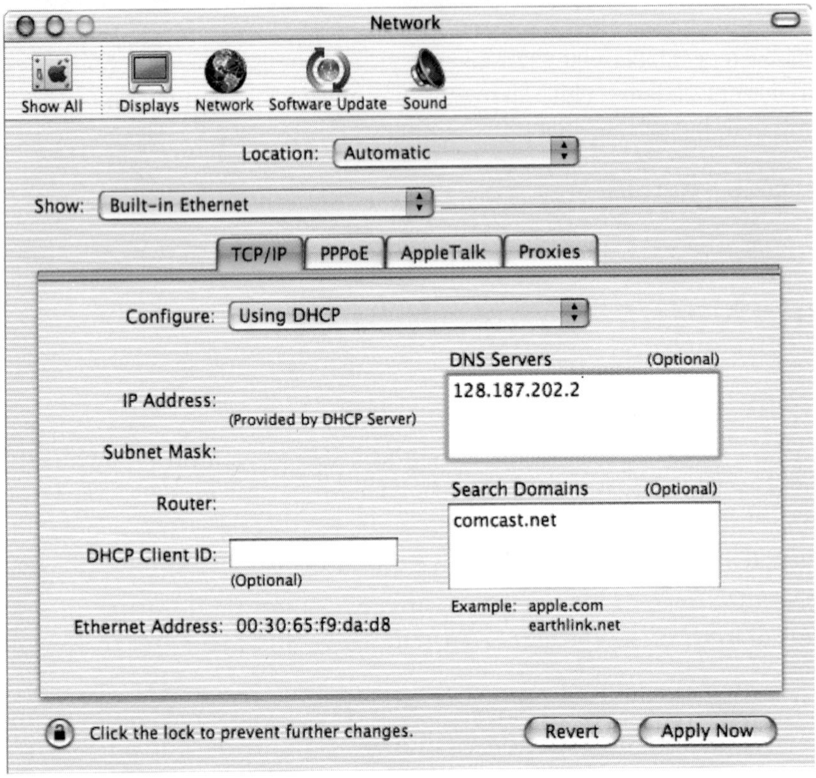

When you configure manually, remember you must also enter the correct subnet mask, router, and domain name server (DNS) information. An IP address is a set of four numbers, ranging from 0 to 255 (for example, 101.34.77.1). The subnet mask is information that allows the network administrator to divide and identify pieces of networks. The router is a device that connects networks together. Domain name servers help your computer look up other computers by using names instead of numbers. If you do not know the correct information, contact your Internet service provider (ISP) or network administrator.

The settings listed here can be automatically set by your ISP using a technology called DHCP (Dynamic Host Configuration Protocol). To use DHCP, set the Configure list option to Using DHCP or Manually using DHCP Router. When you select either of the DHCP options, some of the information below will be listed as (Provided by DHCP Server).

BootP (Bootstrap Protocol) is another technology used to automatically set network settings. BootP is slightly different because it also allows a computer to boot without requiring a hard or floppy disk drive. Basically, BootP not only fills in network settings, but it also fills in the operating system for the system using BootP.

A static (meaning permanent) IP address is needed if you plan to have other people access your computer over the Web. Every computer on the Internet has a unique IP address. DHCP or

BootP servers automatically assign this address, so it can change every time you connect (a dynamic IP address). It is really hard to find something when its address changes from day to day, so use a static IP for a Web server.

PPPoE Tab

The PPPoE tab allows you to enter Point-to-Point Protocol over Ethernet settings. PPPoE is often used if you plan to use a DSL Internet connection or if you wish to connect your Mac to the Internet wirelessly through an AirPort. Contact your ISP for the correct settings. Remember to check your TCP/IP settings once you enable PPPoE; they may change once PPPoE is enabled.

AppleTalk Tab

The AppleTalk tab contains the settings for your AppleTalk network. Here, you can activate AppleTalk and change your configuration settings. Try to let OS X configure the AppleTalk network automatically. If you have problems, try configuring manually. If you configure manually, your network administrator should be able to supply the correct information.

Proxies Tab

The Proxies tab lets you choose proxy servers for different Internet protocols. A proxy server is a server that operates between you and a real Web server. It intercepts every request and acts according to its own instructions. Proxies are set up to improve performance, increase security, and filter information. Enter the address of the proxy server in the correct blank to use a proxy server.

Internet System Preference

You open the Internet system preference window, shown in Figure 3-23, by clicking its icon in System Preferences.

FIGURE 3-23
The Email tab of the Internet system preference

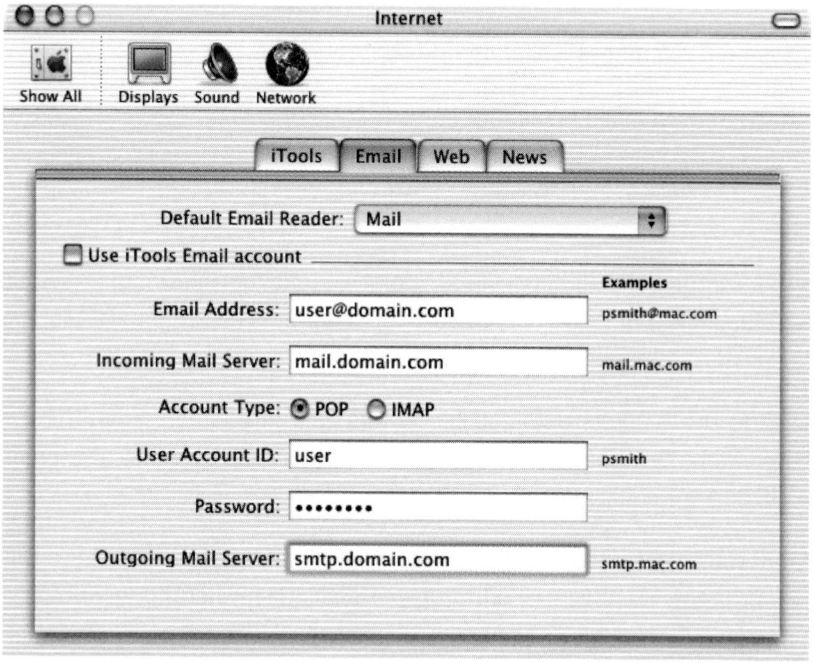

The iTools or .Mac Tab

The Internet system preference contains the options to change the settings for your iTools (now called .mac), e-mail, Web, and news accounts. Most applications on your server will look to the settings in this system preference to set up each of these accounts correctly.

You can change the settings for your iTools account. The iTools service is offered by Apple and includes services like Web hosting, e-mail, and sending electronic cards. For more information, see *http://www.mac.com*.

Email Tab

The Email tab contains e-mail settings. If this server doubles as a workstation, you can change what application you want to use to read your mail by selecting different options from the Default Email Reader: list. The rest of the settings are needed to connect to your e-mail server correctly. Your address, incoming server, account ID, password, and outgoing server can all be found by contacting your ISP.

Web Tab

The Web tab lets you specify your Web browsing preferences. You can choose your default Web browser, home page, and search page. By default the browser will download files to your desktop. If you would like files to end up in another folder, enter the path into the Download Files To text box.

News Tab

The last tab contains information about connecting to a news server. News servers let you browse a network of newsgroups that look very much like a bulletin board. Contact your Internet service provider for your news server address, your account ID, and password.

STEP-BY-STEP 3.11

1. Click the **System Preferences** icon in the Dock.

2. Click the **Network** icon found in the Internet & Network category.

3. Make sure that you are viewing the settings for your Built-in Ethernet, by choosing **Built-in Ethernet** from the Show box.

4. Suppose you want to set your server to reside at a static (nonchanging) IP address. On the TCP/IP tab, select **Manually** from the Configure box. You must then key an IP address, a Subnet Mask, and a Router address.

5. Notice how the DHCP server automatically enters your IP address. From this point, you can also enter Domain Name Servers by clicking the **Domain Name Servers** text box. Enter the address of a fictional DNS server (for example, 1.2.3.4).

6. Suppose that you also want to use a proxy server to filter your Web access (we will not be setting up a proxy server in this step; we will only tell your Macintosh where to look for a Web proxy server). Click the **Proxies** tab, and enter the address of a fictional Web proxy server: **2.3.4.5**.

STEP-BY-STEP 3.11 Continued

7. Now Mac OS X is set up to obtain its IP address from a DHCP server and use another server as a Web proxy. In order to keep the network settings that were originally on your computer, click the **Show All** icon in the top left corner of the window.

8. A new window will ask if you would like to save the configuration changes. Click the **Don't Save** button.

Accounts System Preference

The Accounts system preference (called Users in older versions of Mac OS X) lets you manage the user accounts (and their personal folders) on your server. When you open the Accounts system preference, the user accounts on the server are listed in a window to the left as shown in Figure 3-24. The buttons on the right allow you to create, edit, or delete user accounts.

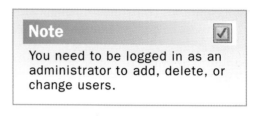

Note ☑

You need to be logged in as an administrator to add, delete, or change users.

FIGURE 3-24
The Users system preference

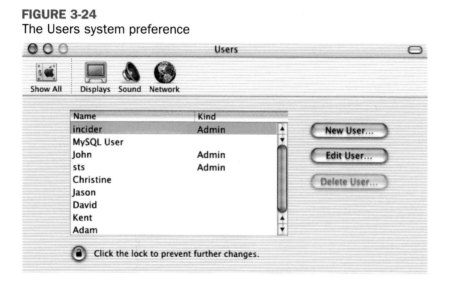

To add a new user, click on the New User button. Fill in the Name, the Short Name (an alternate name used by certain network services) and choose a picture to represent the user. Switch to the Password tab and enter the password and a password hint. The password hint is optional; if you decide to use it, make sure that it does not reveal the password easily. If you would like this new user to be able to act as a system administrator, click the *Allow user to administer this computer* option. Administrators are allowed to create new users, install software, and change computer settings. To add the new user, press the Save button.

Edit a user by selecting its name from the window to the left, then by pressing the Edit User button. The same information from the New User button is provided. Change the information as you need, then press OK.

If you want to delete a user, select its name from the window at the left. Press the Delete User button. A window will appear and ask if you are sure that you want to delete a user, along with its accompanying folders. Press the Delete button to delete the user and its folders.

Warning

User folders can contain important information. We recommend backing up or archiving before deleting a user!

Sharing System Preference

The Sharing system preference (shown in Figure 3-25) contains the basic controls for sharing files from your computer as a server. File sharing, Web sharing, and FTP sharing, among other things, are all controlled through the Sharing system preference. You can set whether you will allow users to log in remotely using terminal applications (like the secure shell, SSH—not Telnet which is not secure enough). This would allow you to log in from a remote location and act as if you were at your computer.

FIGURE 3-25
The Sharing system preference

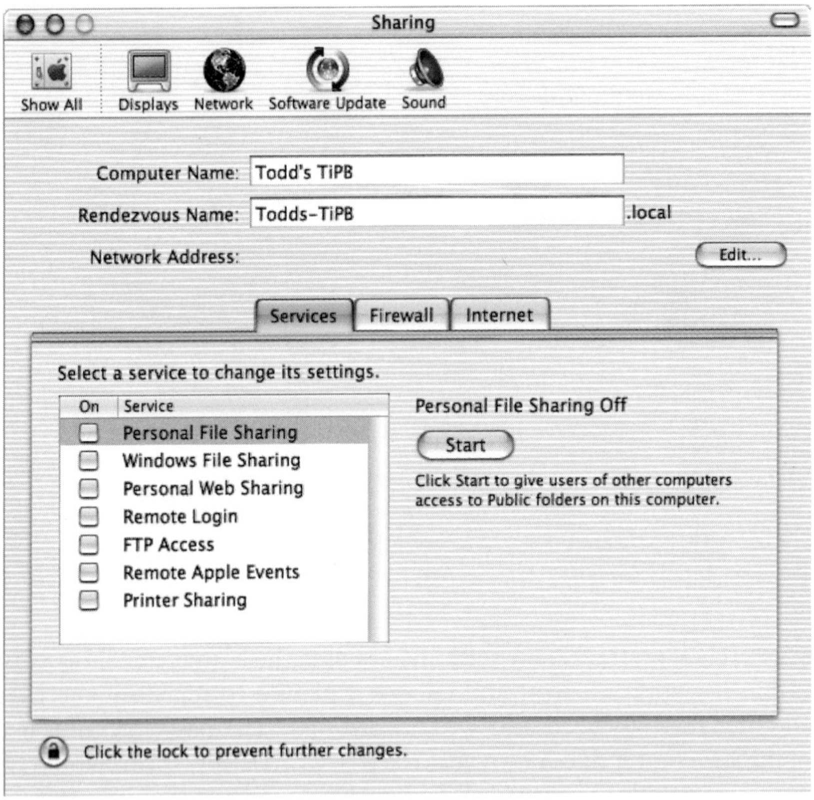

The Remote Apple events option changes how your computer interacts with other Macs on an AppleTalk network. If you want other Macs to be able to run scripts that interact with your computer, check this option. We recommend leaving this off for security reasons.

The upper portion of the window lets you change the computer's name. The computer name affects how other computers find your computer. The computer name also shows up as the first part of its Internet address when the address is displayed as a name (i.e., *computername.byu.edu*).

Because of the sophisticated changes the Sharing system preferences allows, we do not recommend making any changes until the services are needed.

STEP-BY-STEP 3.12

1. Click the **System Preferences** icon in the Dock.

2. Click the **Accounts** icon in the System category (choose **Users** on an older version of Mac OS X).

3. Click the **New User** button.

4. When the new window appears, enter **newuser** in the Name field, and **newuser** in the Short Name field. Choose a picture, if you wish.

5. Click the **Password** tab, and enter **1234** in the Password and Verify fields.

6. Click **Save**. You should now see your newly created user, "newuser," in the list on the left side of the window.

7. Click **newuser** and press the **Delete User** button.

8. A message window opens, asking you to confirm that you want to delete the user. Click **Delete**.

Some Useful Utilities

Mac OS X comes with a number of useful utilities. These programs are found within the Applications folder, inside another folder called Utilities. Never open these utilities unless you know how to use them. Misusing some applications within this folder can seriously damage your computer's setup—so proceed with caution.

Disk Utility

The Disk Utility allows you to manage the disks on your computer. A disk could mean your hard drive or a CD-ROM. When you open up the Disk Utility, you will be able to select a disk to manage from a listing on the left side of the window. To the right, on the Information tab, you will find another panel that will show information about your disk such as format, capacity, available and used storage, and the number of files and folders on the disk. An example set of this information is shown in Figure 3-26.

FIGURE 3-26
The Disk Utility window

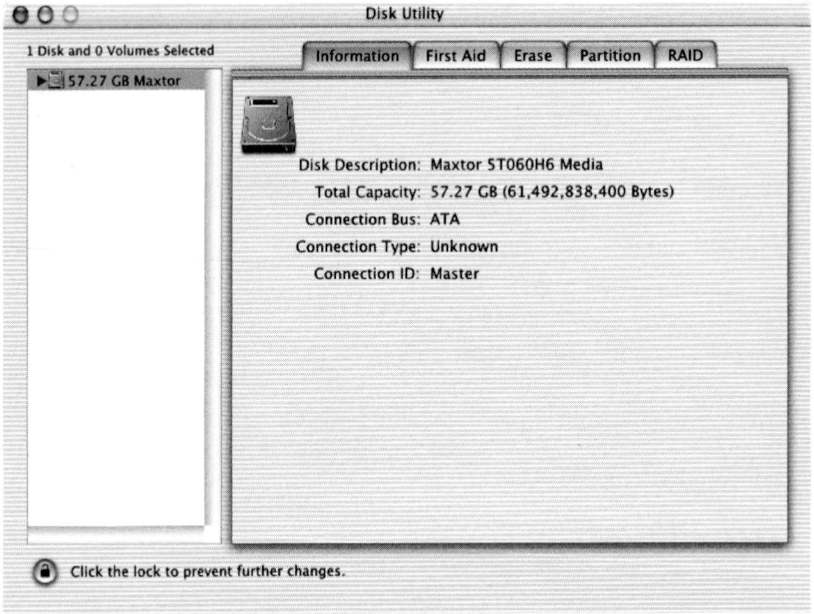

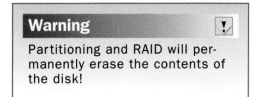

The First Aid tab allows you to detect and fix problems that may occur on a disk. The Erase tab allows you to erase a disk. This tab is especially useful when you want to erase the contents of an entire disk at once. This tab can also erase CD-RWs.

The Partition tab allows you to break up the disk into divisions. Partitioning a drive causes the computer to interpret it as two or more separate disks. The RAID tab is used to set up your disks in a RAID array. RAID is somewhat the opposite of partitioning. RAID is an acronym that stands for Redundant Array of Independent Disks. A RAID system allows you to have many disks act as one.

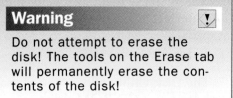

Warning

Do not attempt to erase the disk! The tools on the Erase tab will permanently erase the contents of the disk!

Warning

Partitioning and RAID will permanently erase the contents of the disk!

Key Caps

Key Caps is a simple utility that helps you understand which characters are keyed when you press certain key combinations on your keyboard. As shown in Figure 3-27, Key Caps displays an image of a keyboard inside the window. When you press a button on the keyboard (or click it with your mouse on the screen), the character will show in the character blank near the top of the window. When you press the option or command keys, new characters will be shown. To see the results in a different font, select a font from the Font menu.

FIGURE 3-27
The Key Caps utility window

Print Center

The Print Center is a utility that allows you to manage printers connected to your computer. When you start the Print Center for the first time (or if you have no printers installed), a window will appear asking you if you would like to add a new printer. The Add Printer window can also be found by pressing the Add Printer button at the bottom of the window or by selecting Add Printer from the Printers menu.

Once you start to add a new printer, you will need to select the type of printer you wish to add. The options on your particular system may vary, but the most common types of printers are LPR (using IP), AppleTalk, and USB.

The acronym LPR stands for Line Printer Requester, a default Unix printing protocol. When adding an LPR printer, you will need to enter the printer's IP address (i.e. 64.58.79.230) or DNS name (i.e. *www.myprinter.myschool.edu*). Once the address/name has been entered, select your printer from the Printer Model list.

AppleTalk printers will be listed when you select the AppleTalk option from the list. Select the printer you wish to add from the list that appears. Leave the Printer Model option at Auto Select unless you experience problems printing after adding the AppleTalk printer.

USB printers will be listed after you select the USB option from the list. Select your printer from the list and leave the Printer Model option at Auto Select unless you experience problems.

If you have more than one printer, like the list shown in Figure 3-28, you will need to select a printer to act as a default printer. Select the printer from the list by clicking it, then by selecting Make Default from the Printers menu. If you wish to see the print jobs that a printer is handling, double-click it. A new window will appear, showing the active jobs and options that allow you to delete, hold, or resume printing.

FIGURE 3-28
The Print Center window

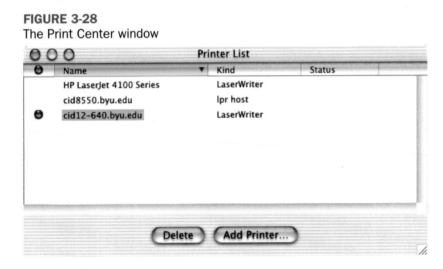

STEP-BY-STEP 3.13

1. Open the **Utilities** folder, located inside the Applications folder. You can get to the Applications folder by double-clicking the icon of the hard disk on your desktop, and then double-clicking the folder called **Applications**. Scroll down until you see the Utilities folder icon and double-click it.

2. Double-click the **Disk Utility** icon.

3. Select a disk from the window at the left by clicking it. Information about the disk will be shown in the window to the right.

4. Close the Disk Utility by clicking the red button on the title bar.

5. Double-click the **Key Caps** icon.

6. Experiment with Key Caps by keying on your keyboard by pressing the **option** key, the **shift** key, and both **option** and **shift** together, and notice which keys are highlighted in the window and what happens to the other keys.

7. Hold down the **option** key and press **e**, then release both keys and press **o**. An ó should appear in the top part of the window.

8. Close Key Caps.

9. Double-click the **Print Center** icon.

STEP-BY-STEP 3.13 Continued

10. Notice which printers are installed. If you have multiple printers installed, notice which one is the default.

11. Close the Printer List window, the Utilities window, and the Applications window if necessary.

Troubleshooting Mac OS X

What can you do when something goes wrong? Following are a few suggestions to try.

Macintosh Help

Mac Help is a great resource for finding answers to general questions about Mac OS X. When Mac Help starts up, it appears like the window shown in Figure 3-29. Ask Mac Help questions by keying them in the text box at the top of the window. Results will appear, and you can browse them by clicking on them. You can also go backward and forward by using the arrows in the bottom right-hand corner of the window.

FIGURE 3-29
The Macintosh Help center

Mac Help

Ask

Mac Help

Quick Clicks

What do I use the Finder for?

How do I change my computer settings?

What do I do to get connected?

Can I send email?

How do I print my documents?

What's new?

New features and improvements in Mac OS X v10.1

More

News

Info and updates, fresh from the Internet.

Go

Net Tip

The Apple Web site contains additional information. Select Support on Apple's Web site: *www.apple.com*.

STEP-BY-STEP 3.14

1. Close all windows so you can see the desktop. The Finder should be the active application. If it isn't, click anywhere on the desktop to make Finder the active application.

2. Choose **Mac Help** from the **Help** menu.

3. In the text box at the top of the window key, **How do I add a printer?** and press the **Ask** button.

4. Mac Help will display the answers, starting with ones that best match your question. Click the first listing to see the answer to your question.

5. Key a question of your own in the text box and press the **Ask** button.

6. Record the answer to your question on a separate piece of paper.

7. Close the Mac Help.

Manually Ejecting Disks

As we've explained before, you eject a disk by dragging its icon into the Trash icon (which turns into an eject icon). Sometimes you may not be able to use the Trash—either because the disk does not appear, or because the power is off. Each disk drive that is installed on a Mac has a manual eject access. Search around the drive opening for a small hole about the diameter of a paperclip wire. Unfold a paperclip and press it into the hole gently. The disk should be manually ejected as you press the paperclip into the hole.

Booting from a CD

When you are installing a new operating system or using a diagnostic tool, you may need to boot your Mac using a CD. When you use a CD to boot, the Mac looks to the CD for the system software instead of your hard drive. To do this, start up your computer while pressing the *c* key. Keep it pressed until you see the Mac OS X splash screen.

Force Quit

Occasionally a program will stop responding normally. When this happens, you can force an application to quit using the Force Quit function. This is either done by selecting Force Quit from the Apple menu, or by pressing command+option+esc. A new window will appear like the one shown in Figure 3-30. Select the "broken" application from the list and press the Force Quit button. Then press the Force Quit button again to confirm. The problem application should close, leaving the rest of the system running without any problem.

FIGURE 3-30
The Force Quit window

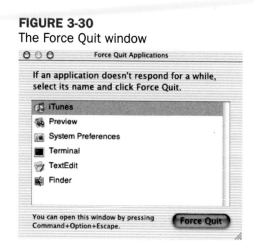

STEP-BY-STEP 3.15

1. Open the Force Quit window by pressing option+command+esc or by selecting **Force Quit** from the **Apple** menu.

2. Select an application from the list.

3. Press the **Force Quit** button. (If you selected the Finder in the last step, the button will read *Relaunch*.)

4. Click the **Cancel** button to avoid Force Quitting for now.

5. Close the Force Quit Applications window.

SUMMARY

In this lesson you learned:

■ How the Macintosh mouse and keyboard are different from those on a PC and how to use them.

■ To tell the difference between Aqua, Darwin, and Classic user interfaces.

■ To use the parts of Mac OS X's user interface (desktop, menu bar, windows, and the Dock).

■ To manage files using Mac OS X (get info, move, copy, rename, create, make aliases, and delete).

- To change system settings using System Preferences (especially Classic preferences, ColorSync preferences, Display preferences, Dock preferences, and Software Update preferences).

- How to use some system utilities to manage disks, find keystrokes, and manage printing.

- To do simple troubleshooting when a problem has occurred.

VOCABULARY *Review*

Define the following terms:

Alias	Darwin	Icon view
Aqua	Desktop	List view
Classic	Dock	Option key
ColorSync	Finder	Panels view
Command key	Get info	System Preferences

REVIEW *Questions*

MULTIPLE CHOICE

Select the best response for the following statements.

1. Mac OS X's user interface has borrowed elements from which of the following operating systems?
   A. Microsoft Windows
   B. PDP 11
   C. BSD Unix
   D. Apple Mac OS 9
   E. A, C, and D above.

2. Mac OS X's kernel (the core of the operating system) is based on which of the following operating systems?
   A. PDP 11
   B. Microsoft Windows
   C. Apple Mac OS 9
   D. BSD Unix
   E. A, B, and D above.

3. Because the Macintosh mouse has only one button, which of the following is the equivalent of right clicking?
   A. Holding down the shift key as you click.
   B. Turning the mouse sideways when you click.
   C. Holding down the control key as you click.
   D. Double-clicking.
   E. Holding down the *r* key as you click.

4. Holding down the open Apple key while pressing a letter of the alphabet usually results in what action?
   A. It issues a computer command.
   B. Nothing.
   C. It keys the letter of the alphabet you pressed.
   D. It keys an alternate character or symbol.
   E. It keys the capital form of the letter of the alphabet you pressed.

5. Holding down the option key while pressing a letter of the alphabet usually results in what action?
   A. It keys an alternate character or symbol.
   B. It keys the capital form of the letter of the alphabet you pressed.
   C. Nothing.
   D. It keys the letter of the alphabet you pressed.
   E. It issues a computer command.

6. In Mac OS X, the window bar is always found in what location?
   A. At the top of the screen.
   B. At the bottom of the screen.
   C. At the top of each window.
   D. At the bottom of each window.
   E. At either the top of the screen or the window depending on your settings.

7. Icons for which of the following may be found in the Dock?
   A. Applications
   B. Data files
   C. Open windows
   D. The Trash
   E. All of the above.

8. When you drag an icon from one window to another (on the same disk), what is the usual result?
   A. It copies the file to the new location.
   B. It moves the file to the new location.
   C. It makes an alias of the file in the new location.
   D. It turns the file into an alias and moves the original to the new location.
   E. None of the above.

9. What is an alias?
   A. What a file is named after you've changed its name.
   B. A file name containing illegal characters, such as a dollar sign.
   C. A file with more than one name.
   D. A pointer or short cut icon that directs you to the original file
   E. A and C above.

10. If you wanted to change the resolution of the screen, which System Preference would you use?
   A. Screen Saver preferences
   B. Display preferences
   C. General preferences
   D. ColorSync preferences
   E. Dock preferences

FILL IN THE BLANK

Complete the following sentences by writing the correct word or words in the blanks provided.

1. The three faces of Mac OS X are _____, _____, and _____.

2. To change system settings you use an application called _____.

3. _____, _____, and _____ are the three ways to view content in a Mac OS X window.

4. A quick way to find out how to key a particular symbol is to use the _____ utility.

5. If you hold down the *c* key while the Macintosh is booting, it will force the computer to boot from a system file on a(n) _____ if there is one.

PROJECTS

PROJECT 3-1

The main System Preferences window allows you to drag the icons of system preferences in and out of the shortcut panel at the top of the window. This allows you to place in that window the System Preferences you will access the most. For each of the following types of users, determine which System Preferences each would need to have shortcuts for. Justify your answers.

1. An artist or designer, working in an office.

2. A student or home user.

3. A programmer for an international company.

4. A salesman who travels a lot.

PROJECT 3-2

Using the utility Key Caps, find the key presses in the Helvetica font for the following symbols:

¶
◊
Æ
#
«
»

Extra credit.
ï
ñ
è

CRITICAL *Thinking*

ACTIVITY 3-1

Visual-content-oriented industries such as television production, graphic arts, advertising, and Web design often choose Macintosh computers. From what you have learned about Mac OS X, why do you think that would be so? On a separate paper write your answer to this question and support your answer with research from the Web or from your own experience.

ACTIVITY 3-2

In spite of the "X" proclaiming this to be the tenth version, Mac OS X is a relatively new operating system. As with most computer software, it will grow and add features as it matures. What additional capabilities and features do you anticipate Apple will want to add? On a separate paper write your answer to this question and support your answer with research from the Web or from your own experience.

MICROSOFT WINDOWS XP

VOCABULARY

Administrator

ClickLock

Context menu

Control Panel

Desktop

Folder

Format

My Computer

Partitions

Recycle Bin

Shortcut

Snap to

Subfolder

Taskbar

Title bar

Troubleshooter

Window

Introduction

Windows XP promises increased stability and improved device recognition over previous versions of the operating system. Several versions of Windows XP are currently available. Windows XP Home Edition targets users who historically purchased Windows Me or Windows 9x. Microsoft increased behind-the-scenes security for such users by adding an Internet connection firewall and a System Restore mode. XP Home Edition is more reliable for day-to-day use than Microsoft Windows 2000 Professional. XP Home Edition also contains the latest versions of Internet Explorer and increased support for video and audio file management.

Windows XP Professional includes the features of the Home Edition and adds support for up to 4 GB of RAM and two processors. XP Professional also promises increased support for wireless networks. In addition, system administrators have the option of having their systems revert to previous versions of device drivers, allowing administrators tighter control of third-party device driver installation.

Future editions of XP will support large computer networks and high volumes of data manipulation.

Installation of Windows XP

Installation is possible from a CD-ROM as with previous versions of Windows. The most direct method is to configure your BIOS to boot from CD-ROM. This procedure is usually simple, but is not covered in this text because it varies between models of motherboards. Consult your instructor or hardware documentation for specific instructions.

Preinstallation

When you install Windows XP, the Setup Wizard will ask you to provide information about how you want to install and configure the operating system. Preparation will help you avoid potential problems during the installation process. The following is a list of tasks you must perform in order to have a minimal amount of problems during installation.

- Identify the hardware requirements to install Windows XP Professional.
- Check to see if your hardware is on the HCL (Hardware Compatibility List).
- Determine how you want to partition the hard disk that will receive the installation of Windows 2000.
- Choose a file system for the installation partition.
- Decide whether you want to upgrade to Windows XP or do a clean installation.

Hardware Requirements

You must know the minimum hardware requirements before installing Windows XP. It is recommended that your hardware exceed these requirements to take full advantage of Windows XP as well as to be prepared for future upgrades. Table 4-1 lists the minimum hardware requirements.

TABLE 4-1
Windows XP hardware requirements

HARDWARE	REQUIREMENT
CPU	Pentium based
Memory	64 MB minimum
	256 MB recommended
Hard Disk Space	650 MB minimum
	4 GB recommended
Display	Monitor with VGA resolution or higher
Other	CD-ROM Drive, 12X or faster
	Keyboard
	Mouse or other pointing device
	Internet Access
	10/100 Ethernet Card (NIC)

The following guidelines will also be helpful.

- Look for the second or third fastest CPU in the store. The fastest model often costs the most without offering a proportional increase in performance.

- Leave room for future expansion without discarding the RAM that you have originally purchased.

- Look forward to adding another hard drive in the future.

Hardware Compatibility List

Prepare for installation by comparing your hardware against the Microsoft Hardware Compatibly List (HCL) at *http://www.microsoft.com/hcl/default.asp*. See Figure 4-1. Hundreds of vendors submit their products to Microsoft for possible inclusion on the HCL. Microsoft maintains an extensive laboratory to verify which products function effectively with XP and other Microsoft products.

FIGURE 4-1
The Microsoft Hardware Compatibly List (HCL)

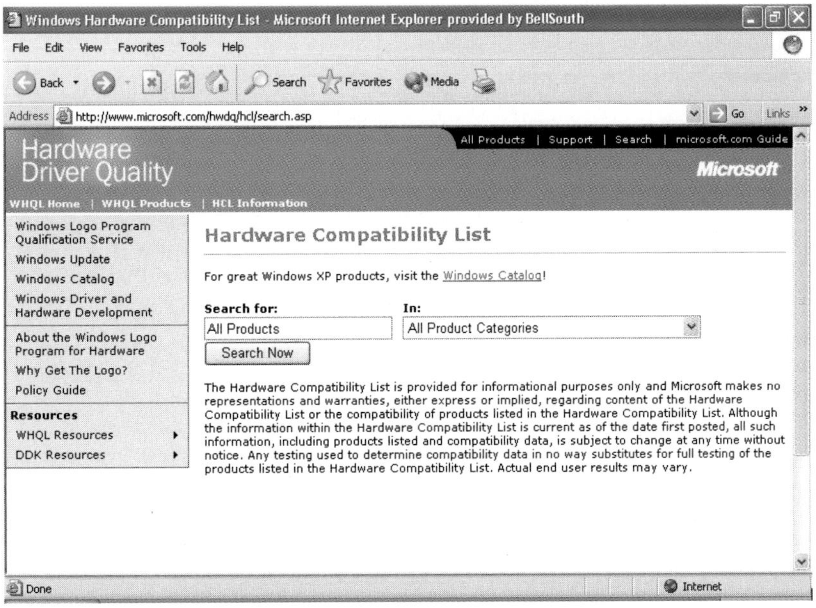

How important is it to follow the HCL? Even if your components do not appear on the list, you may never experience problems. Your supplier may or may not have submitted the hardware to Microsoft to test. However, you may have problems getting support from Microsoft if your hardware does not appear on the list.

Other compatibility issues deal with driver software. Many computer components require software programs called drivers to interface with the operating system. Many driver programs are on the Windows XP installation CD-ROM. If this is the case, Windows XP will identify the device during installation and automatically install the driver. A component that does not match an existing driver will require that you supply the driver manually. Look for driver programs on media included with the component or on the manufacturer's Web site. An example of such a site is shown in Figure 4-2.

FIGURE 4-2
Hewlett Packard and Compaq device drivers from the HP Web site

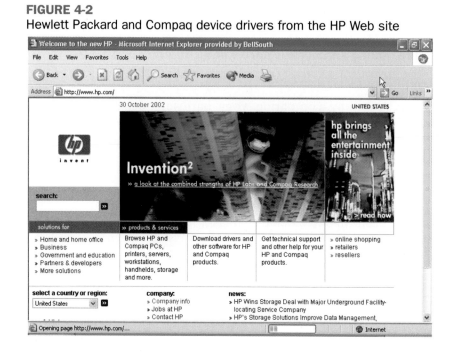

Partitions

Setup allows you to install Windows XP on an existing partition or to create a new partition. **Partitions** function as physically separate storage units on the same disk. Depending on the hard disk, you may choose one of the following options during installation:

■ If the hard disk is unpartitioned you must create the Windows XP partition.

■ If the hard disk is partitioned, you can use unpartitioned space to create the Windows XP partition.

■ If the hard disk is partitioned, you can delete existing partitions and then create a new one for the Windows XP partition.

■ You can create the Windows XP partition over an existing partition that is large enough.

It is recommended that you install Windows XP on a 1GB or larger partition. Using a larger partition provides some operating system flexibility later.

File Systems

One of the first choices you have to make when you install (or upgrade to) Windows XP is the file system. You must choose between FAT and NTFS. FAT stands for File Allocation Table. FAT is an older technology that offers no file and folder security. FAT is good for smaller operating systems (like MS-DOS) and when you need to have backward compatibility with an older operating system stored on the same hard drive. NTFS stands for New Technology File System. Microsoft created NTFS to compensate for the features it felt FAT was lacking. These features include increased fault tolerance and enhanced security.

This is really an easy choice. There is only one reason not to choose NTFS: if you need to have an operating system that cannot read NTFS (Win9x, MS-DOS, etc.) to be able to access the partition. This limitation only applies to the local machine. If you want to access an NTFS drive across a network, any OS can access the NTFS partition.

Upgrade versus Clean Install

During the setup process, you must also choose between upgrading or installing a new copy of Windows (performing a "clean install").

During an upgrade, the Windows XP Setup Wizard replaces existing Windows files but preserves your existing settings and applications. Some applications might not be compatible with Windows XP Professional and therefore might not function properly after an upgrade. You can upgrade to Windows XP Home Edition or Windows XP Professional from the following operating systems:

- Windows 98
- Windows 98 Second Edition
- Windows Millennium Edition

The following operating systems will only upgrade to Windows XP Professional:

- Windows NT 4.0 Workstation (Service Pack 6 and later)
- Windows 2000 Professional (including service packs)
- Windows XP Home Edition

If your computer is currently running an unsupported operating system, you cannot do an upgrade. The wizard installs Windows XP in a new folder. After the installation is complete, you will have to reinstall applications and reset your preferences.

If you have the time and spirit, it is recommended you choose to do a "clean install." The advantage is that this will get rid of many duplicate and leftover files that did not get deleted when you uninstalled the software.

If you choose to do a clean install, you need to make sure that you have all the disks and installation codes, or the downloaded files for your software, as you will have to reinstall all your applications.

STEP-BY-STEP 4.1

1. Power on the computer and immediately insert the Windows XP CD into the CD-ROM drive to boot from the CD-ROM.

2. Windows will automatically display the Welcome To Setup screen. Read the Welcome To Setup screen and press **Enter** to continue.

3. Read the licensing agreement and press the **F8** key to agree with the licensing terms.

4. Setup will prompt you to select an area of free space or an existing partition to install Windows XP. Press **Enter** to select the default of **C:**, usually labeled as Partition 1.

STEP-BY-STEP 4.1 Continued

5. The next screen may ask for confirmation to install the operating system on a partition that already contains an operating system. If you see this screen, confirm the step by pressing **Enter**.

6. Next the installation program will offer a choice of file systems for the target partition. Select **NTFS** if the option is available. If the partition was already formatted as NTFS, you may not see this screen. Confirm your intentions by pressing **Enter**.

7. The installation program will now warn you if a Windows folder already exists on the target partition. This occurs if you are upgrading from another version of windows. If necessary, confirm that you wish to delete the folder and recreate it by pressing **L**. The screen will update automatically as the installation program examines your hard disk and copies files to your hard drive. The computer will reboot. After rebooting, the computer will perform a disk check and initiate the conversion to NTFS if necessary. Another reboot will follow the conversion. (The computer will not reboot if updating from FAT to FAT32 or if you did a quick NTFS format.)

8. After rebooting the second time, the installation program will continue copying files and installing Windows XP until the Regional and Language options screen appears. Click **Next** to accept the installation defaults.

9. The next screen asks for your name and the organization name. Ask your instructor for the appropriate information to enter here. Click **Next** to continue.

10. The next screen will ask you to enter the serial number. Ask your instructor for the appropriate information to enter here. Click **Next** to continue.

11. Next, the system will ask you to key your computer name and administrator password. You may accept the default name and leave the administrator password blank right now. Click **Next** to continue.

12. If there is a modem present on the system, the modem dialing properties screen will appear. Ask your instructor for the appropriate information to enter here. Click **Next** to continue.

13. The Date and Time Settings screen will appear. Make adjustments as necessary and click **Next** to continue.

14. The Networking Settings screen will appear if there is a network adapter card present in the system. Verify that **Typical settings** is checked and click **Next** to continue.

15. The Workgroup or Computer Domain screen appears next. Ask your instructor for specific settings or accept the default workgroup name. Click **Next**.

16. The Welcome to Microsoft Windows screen appears. Click **Next** to continue.

17. The Internet Configuration screen will appear. You have two options here: Internet or No Internet. See your instructor for specific instructions or click **Skip** to move on to the next topic.

STEP-BY-STEP 4.1 Continued

18. The system now offers you the opportunity to create user accounts for the computer. You can create accounts at any time, but you must enter at least one name to continue to the next step. Enter your name in the field labeled **Your name** and click **Next** to continue.

19. At last the Thank you! screen appears confirming that installation is complete. Click **Finish** to close the screen.

Troubleshooting Setup

Hopefully your installation of Windows XP went smoothly without any major problems. Unfortunately, there are some issues that may occur. Table 4-2 gives some advice for resolving them.

TABLE 4-2
Troubleshooting tips

PROBLEM	RESOLUTION
Failure of Windows XP to install or start	Verify that Windows XP is detecting all of the hardware and that all of your hardware is listed on the hardware compatibility list (HCL) found on Microsoft's Web site.
Media Errors	Try another Windows XP Installation CD-ROM if this is your installation method.
CD-ROM drive isn't working	Replace the CD-ROM drive with one that is supported on the HCL.
	Try installing over the network and when finished running setup, install the driver for the CD-ROM drive.
Insufficient Disk Space	Delete partitions as needed and then create a partition large enough for installation.
Invalid CD Key Error message	Verify that you entered the proper product key properly.
	Verify that antivirus software is disabled.
	Try another installation CD-ROM.

Basic Functions of Windows XP

Logging on to the Computer

Before beginning to work with Windows XP, you must log on to the computer. Logging on to the computer allows you to use your account. You will point to and click on the icon for your user account and key your password in the text box that appears.

Desktop

Your *desktop* is your main workspace. Here you will find small pictures called icons as shown in Figure 4-3. Icons are used as an easy way to open programs and documents. You will also find application windows, desktop components, and the taskbar. You can customize your desktop by changing background colors, creating shortcuts to your favorite documents and programs, and adding and moving toolbars.

FIGURE 4-3
Desktop

Using Your Mouse

In XP, you use your mouse to navigate your desktop. Your mouse is the tool you will use to open files, programs, and menus. You use your mouse by sliding it around on your mouse pad. As you move your mouse across the mouse pad, you will see the arrow on your monitor move. A typical mouse has two buttons on the top. The left mouse button is used to select or open a file, program, or icon. By single-clicking the left mouse button you will select the item. By holding down the left mouse button you can move items around your desktop or drop them into folders on your desktop.

> **Hot Tip**
>
> You may encounter the welcome screen after leaving your computer idle for more than 12 minutes. You will have to log on to the computer again to gain access to it.

By double-clicking the left mouse button you can open a file or execute a program's icon. The right mouse button is used to activate ***context menus*** (shortcut menus), which display several tasks that are commonly performed with that item. Figure 4-4 is an example of a context menu.

FIGURE 4-4
A context menu

Open
Explore
Empty Recycle Bin
Create Shortcut
Properties

Configuring Your Mouse

To configure your mouse to work best for you, click the Start button, and then click Control Panel. The Control Panel window will open on your desktop. The ***Control Panel*** contains tools for configuring the operating system and hardware, such as the mouse. Click the Printers and Other Hardware link then click the Mouse icon in the Printers and Other Hardware window. See Figure 4-5.

FIGURE 4-5
Printers and Other Hardware

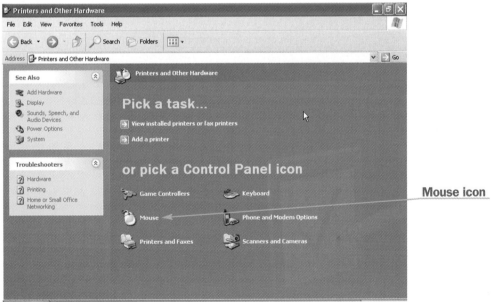

On the Buttons tab (shown in Figure 4-6) you can select to have a left-handed mouse button configuration or right-handed. You may also adjust the double-click speed here. You can move the double-click slider back and forth to increase or decrease the double-click speed. After adjusting the speed, test it by double-clicking in the test area. If you can double-click the test area quickly enough the folder will open. If not, you may need to reduce the double-click speed until you can do this easily. You may also choose to use the *ClickLock* feature of your mouse. This allows you to lock a mouse button to select text without continuously holding it down.

FIGURE 4-6
Buttons tab in Mouse Properties dialog box

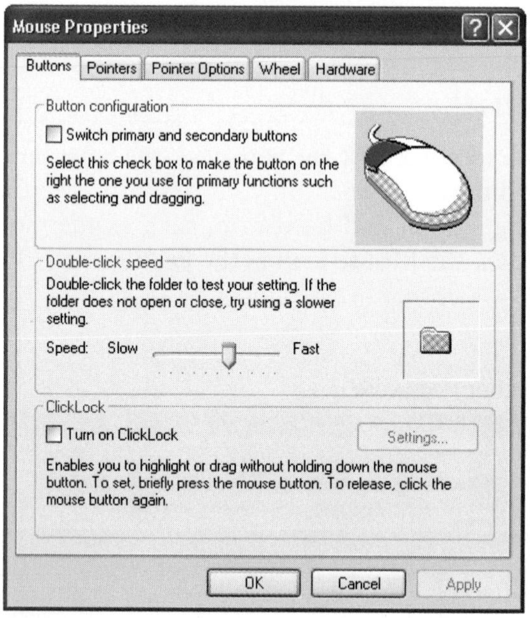

Click the Pointers tab to see the dialog box shown in Figure 4-7. From here you can change the size, color, and shape of the different pointers to make them easier to see and use or to meet your personal style. You can use the standard Windows scheme or choose another scheme from the drop-down list. To change your pointer, do the following:

■ Select the pointer you want to change.

■ Click the Browse button. A dialog box will appear with the available pointers. Choose one from the list.

■ Click Open if this is the pointer you want, or click Cancel.

■ If you change your pointer choose Save As to save your scheme.

■ Click the Apply button, and then click OK.

■ To return to your original pointers click the Use Default button.

FIGURE 4-7
Pointers tab in Mouse Properties dialog box

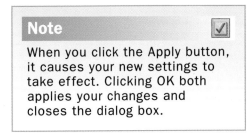

On the Pointer Options tab, you can adjust the pointer speed. This is the speed at which the mouse pointer moves when you move the mouse on a surface. To adjust the pointer speed, move the slider closer to fast or slow. On this tab, you may also choose to use the *Snap To* feature. This feature automatically snaps your mouse pointer to the default button in a dialog box. You can also set pointer trails, hide the pointer whenever you are typing, and show the pointer's location whenever you press the Ctrl key on the keyboard.

Note ✓

When you click the Apply button, it causes your new settings to take effect. Clicking OK both applies your changes and closes the dialog box.

STEP-BY-STEP 4.2

1. Point at any icon on your desktop and select it by clicking your left mouse button once. Notice how the icon highlights when it is selected.

2. Practice dragging your icons around the screen. To drag, point to the icon, click your left mouse button once and hold it down. Now slide your mouse across your mouse pad.

3. Right-click a blank space on your desktop. Point to **Arrange Icons By** and then **Name** and left-click once. Windows arranges your icons for you.

4. Right-click the **Recycle Bin** icon and view the shortcut menu. Click an empty area of your desktop to close the context menu.

5. Double-click the **Recycle Bin** icon to open its window. To close the window, click the **X** in the upper-right corner of the Recycle Bin window. Leave Windows running for the next Step-by-Step.

Taskbar

At the bottom of your desktop, you will see a rectangular bar like that shown in Figure 4-8. This is your *taskbar*.

FIGURE 4-8
Taskbar

The taskbar displays any programs that you have minimized, allowing for quick access between applications. It also can be customized with icons for easy access to your favorite programs. By right-clicking the taskbar, you can arrange open windows on your screen, tiling them horizontally or vertically, or cascading them.

To access taskbar options, you can right-click the taskbar and click Properties. There are several options you can choose from to customize your taskbar. Table 4-3 provides a brief description of the options you can choose.

TABLE 4-3
Toolbar options

TOOLBAR OPTION	DESCRIPTION
Lock the Taskbar	This keeps the taskbar located at the bottom of your desktop. By unchecking this option, you can move the taskbar to another location on your screen.
Autohide	When you check this box, the taskbar disappears when you click a window and activate it. This gives you more screen space. When you move your cursor to the very bottom of your screen the taskbar will reappear.
Keep the Taskbar on Top	When you check this box, your taskbar will be visible when any program is open. This will give you less screen space, but makes switching between windows easier.
Group Similar Taskbar Buttons	This will group multiple instances of the same program on one taskbar button.
Show Quick Launch	The Quick Launch toolbar is a customizable toolbar on the taskbar. It allows you to create shortcuts to commonly used programs here and start them with one click.
Show the Clock	When you check this box a small clock will appear at the bottom right of your taskbar.
Hide Inactive Icons	Keeps the taskbar notification area from displaying unused icons.

S TEP-BY-STEP 4.3

1. Practice moving your taskbar around the screen.

2. Point your mouse at the small icons on the right side (or bottom) of the taskbar. Little boxes called **Screen Tips** display and tell you what each icon is. Note what these icons are.

3. Point your mouse at the time on the right side (or bottom) of your taskbar. Double-click it with your left mouse button. A dialog box displays that allows you to change the time and date that appear on your taskbar. Click **Cancel**.

Start Button

On your taskbar, you will see a Start button as shown in Figure 4-9.

FIGURE 4-9
Start button

Start button

The Start button is one of the most useful items on your desktop. You can use the Start button to quickly find or open a document, start a program, access tools that help you customize and optimize your system, and shut down your computer.

When you click the Start button, you will see a menu similar to that shown in Figure 4-10.

FIGURE 4-10
Start menu

You can also open the Start menu by holding down the Ctrl+Esc keys on your keyboard or by pressing the Flying Windows button on a Microsoft compatible keyboard.

Most of the menu items on the Start menu contain submenus. If it contains a submenu, you will see a small black triangular shape next to the item. When you point to that item the submenu will appear. See Figure 4-11.

FIGURE 4-11
Submenu

You can click anywhere on your desktop to close the Start menu if you do not want to choose an item from the menus.

The Start menu is separated into two columns. The leftmost column contains your default Web browser program, your default e-mail program, and the six most frequently launched program icons.

The Start menu contains the following options:

■ **All Programs**—This is where you will find all of the software programs installed on your computer.

■ **My Documents**—This is where Windows stores shortcuts to the last ten documents you have opened.

■ **My Recent Documents**—Contains the last fifteen opened document files.

■ **Favorites**—This is where Windows stores links to favorite Web pages you have saved.

■ **My Pictures**—A storage area for photos.

■ **My Music**—Contains music files downloaded from the Internet.

■ **My Computer**—This gives you access to all of the storage devices attached to your computer.

■ **Control Panel**—This contains accessory programs that allow you to customize the Windows environment and your hardware.

■ **Connect To**—This is where you select your connection for the Internet to use.

■ **Printers and Faxes**—This is where you add, configure, and remove printers or fax machines.

- **Help and Support**—Here you can find a variety of Help topics from which to choose.

- **Search**—This option comes in handy when you know what you are looking for but do not know where you put it. The Search option allows you to search for folders, files, people, and computers.

- **Run**—This command enables you to run a program from a floppy disk, your hard disk, or a network drive.

- **Log Off**—Use this command to leave the computer on, but log off your user account.

- **Turn Off Computer**—This is where you shut down, restart, or hibernate your computer.

STEP-BY-STEP 4.4

1. Click the **Start** button on your taskbar.

2. With your mouse, point to **All Programs**. A submenu will appear.

3. Point to **Accessories**; another submenu will appear.

4. Point to the **Calculator** and left-click it. You have now opened the Calculator program.

5. To close the Calculator click the **X** in the upper-right corner of the window.

6. Click the **Start** button on your taskbar.

7. With your mouse pointer, point to **Turn Off Computer** and left-click. Here you are given the option to Shut Down the computer or Restart it.

8. Click **Cancel**. Leave Windows open for the next Step-by-Step.

Customizing the Start Menu

You can modify the appearance of the Start menu. You may add shortcuts to the Start menu, select a different menu style (XP or classic Windows), choose to display small or large icons in the menu, select more programs to display in the frequently used programs list, and select different programs as your default e-mail and Internet programs.

> **Important**
>
> You should always shut down when exiting Windows. Simply turning off the computer without shutting down properly could damage your programs. If your computer has a frozen screen and mouse, try pressing and holding down the Ctrl+Alt+Delete keys on the keyboard. This will open the Windows Security dialog box. From here you can click Task Manager and find out what programs are not responding. If this doesn't unfreeze the computer, try to choose the Shut Down option. As a last resort, you may need to power off the computer or press the Reset button on the front of your machine.

STEP-BY-STEP 4.5

1. Right-click the **Start** button and click **Properties** on the shortcut menu.

STEP-BY-STEP 4.5 Continued

2. Select the **Start Menu** tab and click **Customize**. The Customize Start Menu dialog box opens as shown in Figure 4-12.

FIGURE 4-12
Customizing the Start menu

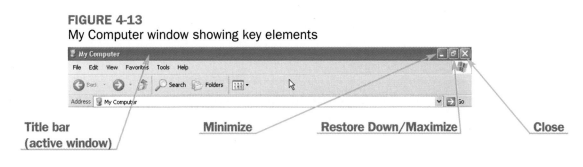

3. Click **Small icons** in the Select an icon size for programs area.

4. Adjust the Number of programs on Start menu to **10**.

5. Click **OK** twice and then click the **Start** button to view the changes you made. Leave Windows open for the next Step-by-Step.

Windows

A *window* is the area or workspace you see when you open a program or application. This defined workspace is movable and resizable. At the top of every window is the *title bar*. This bar displays at the top of the window and tells you the name of the application you are using and also contains the Minimize, Restore Down/Maximize, and Close buttons. If you have more than one application open on your desktop, you can tell which one is active by the color of its title bar. If it is dark, it is active; if it is light, it is inactive. See Figure 4-13. This could be different on your PC if you have customized the colors of your title bars.

FIGURE 4-13
My Computer window showing key elements

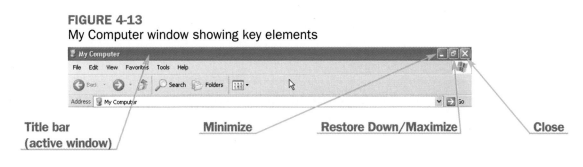

You can also move the window around the screen by left-clicking the title bar and dragging while holding down your mouse button. You can resize the window by pointing your mouse at the edge of the window. Your mouse pointer will change into a double-headed arrow. When it becomes a double-headed arrow, click your left mouse button and hold it while dragging your mouse in the direction you want to resize the window. Figure 4-14 shows what the double-headed arrows will look like in the default Windows pointer scheme.

FIGURE 4-14
Double-headed arrows

Vertical Resize	↕
Horizontal Resize	↔
Diagonal Resize 1	↘
Diagonal Resize 2	↗
Move	✛

In the top right of the title bar there are three control buttons. See Figure 4-13.

The left one is the Minimize button. Clicking this button keeps your window active, but reduces it to the taskbar. The middle button is the Restore Down/Maximize button. If you have a full screen window, it returns the window to a size that allows you to view the desktop in the background. If the window is already less than full size, the button returns it to the maximum size. The last button, the X on the right, is the Close button. Clicking that button closes the active window or program.

Scroll Bars

If you cannot see all the information in a window, use the scroll bars at the right or the bottom of the window to view the rest of the information. Figure 4-15 shows two vertical scroll bars.

FIGURE 4-15
Vertical scroll bars

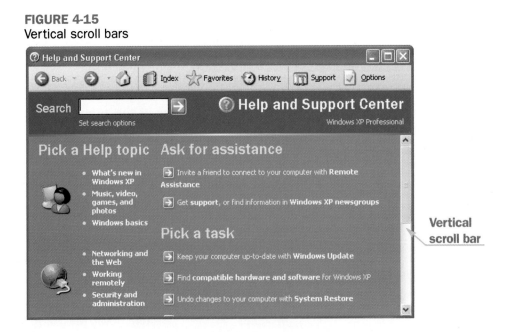

Vertical scroll bar

Click the up arrow on the vertical scroll bar to scroll up the contents of the window or click the down arrow to scroll down. To scroll from side to side, use the right or left arrows on the horizontal scroll bar at the bottom of the window. Instead of using the arrows, you can also click the scroll box between the scroll arrows and drag it left, right, up or down. Or you can click in the space above, below, to the left, or to the right of the scroll box to move one full screen in the direction selected.

> **Hot Tip**
>
> Scroll bars only appear when the window is not large enough to display all of the information. Therefore, not all windows contain scroll bars.

S TEP-BY-STEP 4.6

1. To open a window, click the **Start** button on your taskbar. Point to **All Programs**, point to **Accessories**, and then left-click **Notepad**. You will see an application window on your desktop.

2. Practice moving the window around your desktop.

3. Practice resizing the window.

4. Practice minimizing and maximizing the window.

5. Open a second application window. Click the **Start** button on your taskbar. Point to **All Programs**, point to **Accessories** and left-click **Paint**. You should now have two application windows open on your desktop.

6. Practice moving between the different windows by clicking their title bars. Minimize and maximize the windows. Notice how the applications appear on your taskbar when they are minimized.

7. Click the **Start** button and click **My Computer**. Practice resizing and moving the window.

8. Practice scrolling up and down your window and then from side to side. Move the icons around in the window by left-clicking on them once and dragging the icon with the mouse.

9. Double-click on the C: drive. Left-click the **View** menu below the title bar. Change your icon view by left-clicking, in turn, **Icons**, **Details**, and **List** choices. As you click each view, notice the changes that occur in the window.

10. Close the Paint and Notepad applications by left-clicking the **X** button on the title bar of each window. Leave the My Computer screen open for a later Step-by-Step.

Using Help

Windows XP Help and Support provides on-screen information about the program you are using. To access Help, click the Start button, and then left-click Help and Support. The Windows XP Help and Support utilizes all of the advantages of previous versions of Windows and adds the online help features of Microsoft's online help. See Figure 4-16.

FIGURE 4-16
Help and Support Center

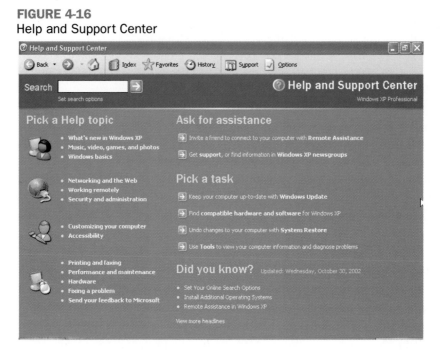

Contents

The *Pick a Help topic* section contains four categories from which to choose. Clicking one of these categories will display a list of subcategories under that topic area. The *Ask for assistance* section contains two subareas. The first one, Remote Assistance, allows another person to connect to your computer and troubleshoot from another location. The second one, Windows XP newsgroups, allows you to connect to a newsgroup and discuss your issues with other Windows XP users or locate a product expert to chat with about your issue. The *Pick a task* section contains four subcategories from which to choose. The first category, Windows Update, allows you to access Microsoft's Web site for a list of items that are needed to update Windows XP. The Compatible Hardware and Software category allows you to search the HCL for hardware and software that is compatible with Windows XP. The System Restore category allows you to store the current state of your system and restore your computer to that state without losing important information. The *Did you know?* section is updated daily with tips for using Windows XP.

S TEP-BY-STEP 4.7

1. Click the **Start** button and left-click **Help and Support**.

2. Under the *Pick a Help topic* section click the link for **Hardware**.

3. Click **Installing and configuring hardware** on the left side of the window.

STEP-BY-STEP 4.7 Continued

4. Click **Install a device**.

5. In the **Search** text box, key **Create a folder**. Uncheck the **Search only Hardware** check box and click the **Search** button.

6. Click **Create a new folder**.

7. Close Help and Support. Leave Windows open for the next Step-by-Step.

File Management

My Computer

The *My Computer* icon represents your computer with its hardware devices and two document folders. The My Computer window (shown in Figure 4-17) is divided into two panes: the left pane contains the System Tasks, Other Places, and Details areas, while the right pane contains three groups of icons.

FIGURE 4-17
My Computer

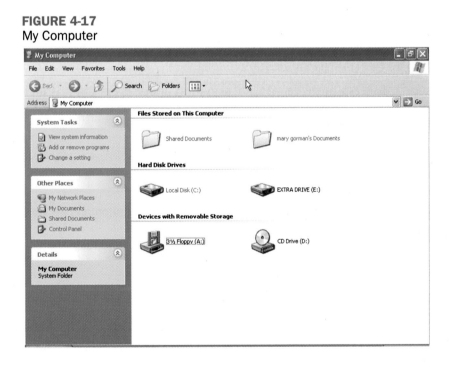

The *Files Stored on This Computer* group contains the Shared Documents folder, which allows you to share documents and folders with other users. The other document folder should be labeled [Your username] Documents folder and is your personal My Documents folder. The *Hard Disk Drives* group contains your local hard disk drive (C:) and other hard disk drives installed on the system. The *Devices with Removable Storage* area contains the 3½ floppy drive (A:) and the CD Drive (D:) and other removable storage devices on the system.

Customizing the My Computer Window

There are five different ways you can display your icons in the My Computer window: Thumbnails, Tiles, Icons, List, and Details. See Figure 4-18.

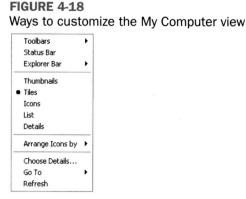

FIGURE 4-18
Ways to customize the My Computer view

- The Thumbnails view displays a small preview of the file. This only works when working with graphics files, so you can quickly see what picture the file contains.

- The Tiles view displays the icons in groups.

- The Icons view displays a large icon and the name of each file that the icon represents.

- The List view also displays a small icon and the name of each file that the icon represents. It takes up less screen space than the Large Icons view.

- The Details view displays more detailed information about every icon. It includes not only a small icon and the name, but the type of file it is, the size of the file, and the date it was last modified.

S TEP-BY-STEP 4.8

1. If necessary, open the **My Computer** window clicking the **Start** button and **My Computer**.

2. Double-click drive **C:**. There may be a warning message about browsing the C: drive. Click OK if necessary.

3. Click the **View** button and then click **Details**.

4. Repeat step 3 to see the **Icons**, **List**, and **Thumbnails** views. Return to the **Details** view when finished. Leave the My Computer window open for the next Step-by-Step.

You may also sort the files and folders in the My Computer window by **Name, Type, Size,** and **Modified.** See Figure 4-19.

FIGURE 4-19
Arranging Files and Folders in My Computer

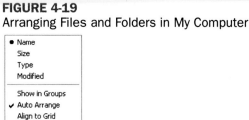

- The Name option arranges the files in order alphabetically.

- The Type option arranges the files by file type, alphabetically.

- The Size option arranges the files in order from smallest to largest.

- The Modified option arranges the files in order from most recent to oldest file created or modified.

STEP-BY-STEP 4.9

1. If necessary, open the **My Computer** window by double-clicking its icon on the desktop.

2. Double-click drive **C:**.

3. Click **View**, point to **Arrange Icons by**, and click **Name**.

4. Double-click the **Windows** folder to open it.

5. Repeat step 3 to arrange the files by **Type, Size,** and **Modified**. Return to the **Arrange Icons by Name** arrangement when finished. Leave the My Computer window open for the next Step-by-Step.

Formatting a Disk

Before you can save files on a floppy disk, you must *format* the disk. Formatting arranges the magnetic particles on a disk so that data can be stored on it.

Most of the disks that you purchase today are pre-formatted (ready to store data), but if you buy one that isn't formatted or want to erase everything off of an old disk it is important to know how to format a disk.

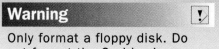

Warning

Only format a floppy disk. Do not format the C: drive because it will erase everything and render your computer useless.

To format a disk, insert a floppy disk into the A: drive. Open My Computer, right-click on the A: drive, and select Format from the shortcut menu.

Folders

Since there are so many files on your hard drive it is necessary to organize them. *Folders* are just a storage space for files, used for organizational purposes. See Figure 4-20.

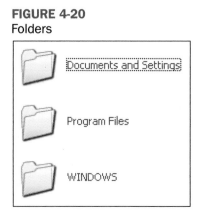

FIGURE 4-20
Folders

Think of a folder in a file cabinet and how it is used to organize paper files. Folders on your disk do the same thing. Sometimes, though, a folder has so many files in it, that it is necessary to organize it further using *subfolders*. The main folder that contains a subfolder is also referred to as a parent folder. All of these objects are represented in a hierarchical fashion that begins with the desktop and works its way down.

STEP-BY-STEP 4.10

1. If necessary, open the **My Computer** window by double-clicking its icon on the desktop.

2. Double-click the **My Documents** folder.

3. Click **Make a new folder** in the File and Folder Tasks area.

4. Key **My Stuff** as the name of the folder. Press **Enter**.

5. Double-click the **My Stuff** folder to view its contents.

6. Click **Make a new folder** in the File and Folder Tasks area.

7. Key your first name as the name of the folder. Press **Enter**.

8. Double-click your folder to view its contents.

9. Click **Make a new folder** in the File and Folder Tasks area.

10. Key your last name as the name of the folder. Press **Enter**. Leave the My Computer window open for the next Step-by-Step.

Changing Folder Options

You can change folders, windows, and the desktop by changing folder options. The Folder Options dialog box, shown in Figure 4-21, allows you to adjust the manner in which you open and work with icons, windows, files, and folders.

FIGURE 4-21
Folder Options dialog box

On the General tab of the Folder Options dialog box you can choose *Use Windows classic folders*, which changes the folder to appear and behave like previous versions of Windows. You can also select between opening each folder within the same window or in different windows. You may also choose to single-click or double-click to open items.

S TEP-BY-STEP 4.11

1. Open the **My Computer** window if it is not already open.

2. Click the **Tools** menu and click **Folder Options**.

3. If necessary, click on the **General** tab. Select all the opposites of what is currently set on your system and click **OK**.

4. Practice opening and closing items in My Computer and see how different the settings are now that you adjusted the folder options.

5. Click the **Tools** menu and click **Folder Options**.

6. Click the **Restore Defaults** button to return to the original factory settings of the folder options. Click **OK**. Leave My Computer open for the next Step-by-Step.

Moving Folders Around in the My Computer Window

The Standard toolbar, shown in Figure 4-22, contains buttons that allow you to navigate through your folders in My Computer.

FIGURE 4-22
Buttons in My Computer's Standard toolbar

Table 4-4 describes the first three, and most commonly used, buttons on the Standard toolbar.

TABLE 4-4
Commonly used buttons on the My Computer Standard toolbar

BUTTON	DESCRIPTION
Back	Takes you back to the folder or drive that you were viewing last.
Forward	Takes you forward to the folder or drive that you were viewing previously.
Up	Takes you up one level in the hierarchy.

STEP-BY-STEP 4.12

1. If necessary, open the **My Computer** window.

2. Open the **My Documents** folder.

3. Double-click the **My Stuff** folder.

4. Press the **Back** button once on the Standard toolbar to return to the drive A:.

5. Press the **Forward** button once on the Standard toolbar to return to your My Stuff folder.

6. Double-click on the folder with your first name.

7. Press the **Up** button once to return to your My Stuff folder.

8. Press the **Up** button again to return to drive A:.

9. Press the **Up** button again to return to My Computer. Leave My Computer open for a later Step-by-Step.

Files

Right now, there are no files in your My Stuff folder. A file is a collection of data that is named and stored on a permanent storage device. In the next several Step-by-Steps you will create, move, copy, rename, and delete files from your folder.

STEP-BY-STEP 4.13

1. Click the **Start** button, click **All Programs**, click **Accessories**, and then click **Notepad**.

2. Key a note to yourself in the Notepad window.

3. Click **File** on the menu bar and then click **Save As**.

4. Key **Note to Myself** in the File Name textbox and click **Save**.

5. Close Notepad.

Moving and Copying Files

If you want to place a file into another location you may either move or copy it. Cutting a file takes it from the original location and places it into a new one. Copying a file maintains the file in its original location and duplicates it in a new location.

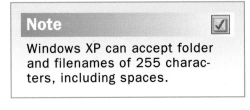

> **Note** ☑
>
> Windows XP can accept folder and filenames of 255 characters, including spaces.

One of the ways we move and copy files is through the commands Cut, Copy, and Paste. These commands can be found under the Edit menu (as shown in Figure 4-23), by right-clicking on an item and using keyboard shortcuts, or through the File and Folder Tasks pane.

FIGURE 4-23
Cut, Copy, and Paste commands on the Edit menu

The commands Cut and Copy place the file in a temporary location in memory called the Clipboard. An item will stay on the Clipboard as long as the computer is on and until you cut or copy something else. The Windows Clipboard can hold only one item at a time. The Paste command copies the item from the Clipboard and pastes it into its new location. The item remains on the Clipboard, however, in case you want to copy it somewhere else.

■ The Cut (Ctrl+X) command moves a file.

■ The Copy (Ctrl+C) command duplicates a file.

■ The Paste (Ctrl+V) command places a cut or copied file in its new location.

STEP-BY-STEP 4.14

1. Click the **Start** button and click **My Documents**.

2. Right-click the **Note to Myself** file and select **Copy** from the shortcut menu.

3. Right-click the **My Stuff** folder and select **Paste** from the shortcut menu.

4. Double-click the **My Stuff** folder. You should now see a duplicate of the *Note to Myself* file placed in this folder.

5. Right-click the **Note to Myself** file in the **My Stuff** folder and select **Cut** from the shortcut menu.

6. Right-click the folder with your first name and select **Paste** from the shortcut menu. The *Note to Myself* file should now be removed from *My Stuff* folder.

7. Double-click the folder with your first name. The *Note to Myself* file should be there now.

8. Right-click the **Note to Myself** file and select **Copy** from the shortcut menu.

9. Right-click the folder with your last name and select **Paste** from the shortcut menu. Leave My Documents and My Computer open for the next Step-by-Step.

Renaming a File

If you want to change the name of a file you can easily do this by using the Rename command. The command can be found under the File menu (as shown in Figure 4-24), when you right-click a file, or in the File and Folder Tasks pane.

FIGURE 4-24
Rename command on the File menu

STEP-BY-STEP 4.15

1. Open the **My Documents** folder if necessary.

2. Double-click the **My Stuff** folder.

3. Double-click the **First Name** folder.

STEP-BY-STEP 4.15 Continued

4. Right-click the **Note to Myself** file and select **Rename** from the shortcut menu.

5. Key the name **Note to Myself A** and press **Enter**.

6. Double-click the folder with your last name.

7. Right-click the **Note to Myself** file and select **Rename** from the shortcut menu.

8. Key the name **Note to Myself B** and press **Enter**. Leave My Computer open for the next Step-by-Step.

Deleting Files

It is good practice to delete the files that you no longer need or want so you can free up space on your storage devices. When you delete a folder you also delete all of its contents, so be careful that you do not need anything in that folder anymore. Thankfully, there is an area on your desktop called the *Recycle Bin*. The Recycle Bin is an area on the hard drive that holds files and folders deleted from your local hard drive(s) until you are absolutely sure you want to remove them. Be careful, though, because the Recycle Bin only stores files deleted from the local hard drive(s). When you delete from any other drive (such as the floppy drive or a network drive) the files are removed from the drive permanently.

You have several options for deleting files and folders.

■ Select the file or folder by single-clicking it and press the Delete key on your keyboard.

■ Right-click the file or folder and select Delete from the shortcut menu.

■ Select the file or folder and click the Delete this file option in the File and Folder Tasks pane. See Figure 4-25.

FIGURE 4-25
Delete this file option on the File and Folder Tasks pane

STEP-BY-STEP 4.16

1. If necessary, open the **My Documents** folder.

2. Double-click the **My Stuff** folder.

3. Double-click the **First Name** folder. Right-click the **Notes to Myself A** file and select **Delete** from the shortcut menu.

4. When Windows asks you if you are sure you want to delete this file click **Yes**.

5. Press the **Back** button until you are at the My Computer window.

<table>
<tr><td>

Hot Tip ◎

Pressing **Shift+Delete** when removing something from the C: drive will automatically skip the Recycle Bin and remove the item permanently. Only use this key combination when you are absolutely sure you want to remove the file or folder and will have no possible need to recover the file in the future.

</td></tr>
</table>

6. Double-click the **My Documents** folder.

7. Select the **Note to Myself** file by left-clicking it once.

8. Press **Delete** on your keyboard. When Windows asks you if you are sure you want to move the *Note to Myself* file to the Recycle Bin click **Yes**.

9. Minimize the My Computer window.

10. Double-click the **Recycle Bin** on your desktop.

11. To restore the *Note to Myself* file back to the C: drive, right-click it and select **Restore** from the shortcut menu. Minimize the Recycle Bin window.

12. Restore the My Computer window and view the contents of your My Documents folder.

13. Right-click the restored **Note to Myself** file and click **Delete** from the shortcut menu. Click **Yes** to confirm the deletion.

14. Restore the Recycle Bin window.

15. Click **File** and click **Empty Recycle Bin**. Click **Yes** to confirm.

16. Close the Recycle Bin window by clicking the **X** in the right-hand corner.

Copying a Floppy Disk

It is a good idea to make backup copies of all files that you have created. If the files are on a floppy disk you can copy and paste them to another location to back them up or use the copy disk command to copy the contents of one floppy disk to another. See Figure 4-26.

FIGURE 4-26
Copy disk command on the File menu

STEP-BY-STEP 4.17

1. If necessary, double-click on the **My Computer** icon on your desktop to open it. Make sure that you have a disk containing content you want to copy in the floppy drive.

2. Left-click drive **A:** to select it.

3. Click the **File** menu and click **Copy Disk**.

4. In the Copy Disk dialog box, click the **Start** button and then click **OK** to begin the copying process.

5. When prompted insert the floppy disk to which you want to copy the contents. Click the **OK** button.

6. When the copy has completed successfully click the **Close** button.

7. Remove your disk from the floppy drive. Leave the My Computer window open for the next Step-by-Step.

Finding Files

Sometimes it is necessary to search for an existing file. In Windows you can search for files by the filename, the date, the type of file, or by the file size. See Figure 4-27.

FIGURE 4-27
Searching for a file or folder

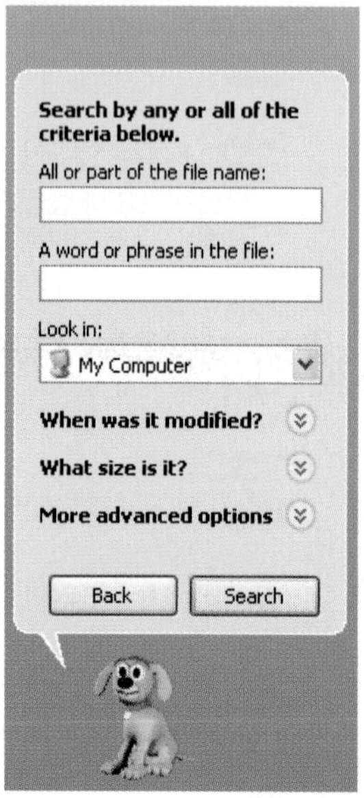

Search by any or all of the criteria below.

All or part of the file name:

A word or phrase in the file:

Look in:
My Computer

When was it modified?

What size is it?

More advanced options

Back   Search

STEP-BY-STEP 4.18

1. Click the **Search** button in the Standard toolbar.

2. Click the Documents (word processing, spreadsheet, etc.) link on the left-hand pane.

3. Key **setup** in the *All or part of the document name* textbox.

4. Click the **Search** button. Any matching files will appear in the Search Results pane. Leave My Computer open for the next Step-by-Step.

Windows Explorer

Windows Explorer is another method of viewing files and performing file management tasks like the ones we have already discussed (for example, copying, moving, renaming, and deleting files and folders). Figure 4-28 shows the My Computer folder as viewed through Windows Explorer.

FIGURE 4-28
Windows Explorer

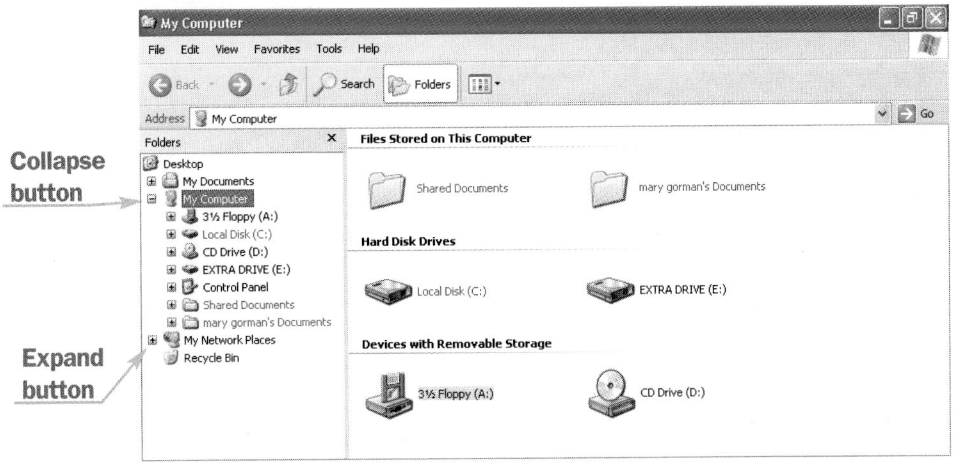

STEP-BY-STEP 4.19

1. Double-click the **My Computer** icon on your desktop if necessary.

2. Click on the **Folders** button on the Standard toolbar. The Folders pane will display in the My Computer window.

Using Windows Explorer

The Folders pane displays and allows you to view your storage devices in a hierarchical structure. The top level of the structure is the Desktop. All work in Windows originates from the Desktop. Below the desktop are the icons from My Computer, My Documents, My Network Places, and the Recycle Bin. To the left of the My Computer icon is a plus sign. If you click the plus sign, called the Expand button, it displays the folders within the drive or other objects. If an icon does not have a plus sign it means that the object contains no subfolders.

To display the contents of a drive or folder, you simply have to click on the object in the left pane and the contents of that object will display in the right pane. See Figure 4-29.

FIGURE 4-29
Displaying the contents of a drive or folder

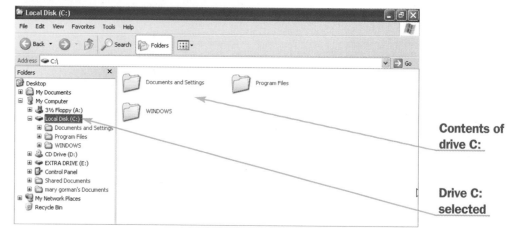

STEP-BY-STEP 4.20

1. Click the **+** sign next to **Local Disk (C:)** in the left-hand pane. All folders contained on the C: drive will now be expanded below it.

2. Click the **Local Disk (C:)** in the left-hand pane. All folders and files located on the C: drive will now be displayed in the right-hand pane.

3. Click the **My Documents** folder in the left-hand pane. All folders and files located in the My Documents folder will now be displayed in the right-hand pane.

Copying, Moving, Renaming, and Deleting Files and Folders

You can perform all of the file management techniques in Windows Explorer as you did in My Computer. In this section, however, we will demonstrate some other techniques for performing these same functions.

STEP-BY-STEP 4.21

1. Click the **Local Disk (C:)** in the left-hand pane. All folders and files located on the C: drive will now be displayed in the right-hand pane.

2. Click the **Windows** (or **WINNT**) folder in the left-hand pane. All folders and files located in the Windows/WINNT folder will now be displayed in the right-hand pane. Scroll down in the window until you see the file **Santa Fe Stucco**.

STEP-BY-STEP 4.21 Continued

3. Right-click and drag the **Santa Fe Stucco** file from the right-hand pane to the **My Documents** folder in the left-hand pane.

4. Click **Copy Here** from the shortcut menu.

5. Click the **My Documents** folder in the left-hand pane. All folders and files located in the My Documents folder will now be displayed in the right-hand pane. Scroll down in the window until you see the file **Santa Fe Stucco**.

6. Right-click and drag the **Santa Fe Stucco** file from the right-hand pane to the **Desktop** in the left-hand pane.

7. Click **Move Here** from the shortcut menu.

8. Click the **Desktop** in the left-hand pane. All folders and files located on the Desktop will now be displayed in the right-hand pane. Scroll down in the window until you see the file **Santa Fe Stucco**.

9. Right-click on the **Santa Fe Stucco** file in the right-hand pane and click **Rename**. Key **Stucco** as the new name of the file and press **Enter** on the keyboard.

10. Click and drag the **Stucco** file from the Desktop to the **Recycle Bin** in the left-hand pane. Click **Yes** to place the file in the Recycle Bin.

11. Right-click on the **Recycle Bin** icon in the left-hand pane. Click **Empty Recycle Bin** and click **Yes** to delete all files.

12. Close Windows Explorer. Leave Windows running for the next Step-by-Step.

Word Processing

Windows XP comes with a small word processing program called WordPad. This program will allow you to do basic word processing tasks such as keying and formatting text, saving a file, and printing.

The WordPad program, like all word processing programs, has a feature called word wrap. Word wrap automatically continues your text to the next line when you are keying. Therefore you only press Enter when you want a line to end manually. Otherwise you let the text word wrap so it will flow with the margins when you insert and delete text.

Inserting and removing text in WordPad is a simple process. In the window you will see a blinking line called the insertion point as shown Figure 4-30.

FIGURE 4-30
Insertion point in WordPad

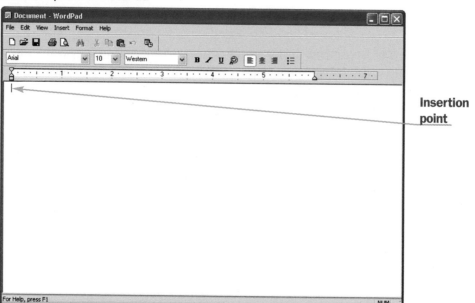

Insertion point

This line indicates where your text is going to appear when you begin to key. The insertion point will move as you key and your text will appear to the left of it. If you accidentally key something wrong you can remove it by using either the Backspace or Delete keys on your keyboard. The Backspace key removes text to the left of the insertion point. The Delete key removes text to the right of the insertion point.

STEP-BY-STEP 4.22

1. Click the **Start** button, point to **All Programs**, point to **Accessories** and click **WordPad**.

2. Key your first and last name. Press **Enter**.

3. Key your class name. Press **Enter**.

4. Key today's date. Press **Enter**.

5. Press **Enter** again to insert a blank line after the date and key in the following text:

   Vendors have refined the latest generation of antivirus software to catch viruses before they do serious damage. The products are easier to use, have better detection rates, and are cheaper than earlier virus scanners. Therefore, you have no excuse for failing to install a good virus scanner on your system.

   Leave WordPad open for the next Step-by-Step.

Selecting Text and Inserting Text

The default operating mode for WordPad is called insert mode. As you key the insertion point moves automatically. Sometimes, however, you may want to enter text in another location. To do this you will have to move the insertion point manually. You can move the insertion point either by using the arrow keys or by clicking the mouse in the text where you want it to appear.

Many formatting options can be performed on an entire block of text. Blocks of text can be selected by clicking and dragging the mouse over the text or by holding down the Shift key and using the arrows on the keyboard.

S TEP-BY-STEP 4.23

1. Press the **Up**, **Down**, **Left**, and **Right** keys on your keyboard to practice moving your insertion point around the document.

2. Use your mouse to click your insertion point around the document.

3. Move the insertion point to the left of the word *Therefore* in the last sentence.

4. Hold down the left mouse button and drag over the entire sentence.

5. Release the mouse button.

6. To deselect the text, click anywhere else in the document.

7. Move the insertion point to the left of your last name.

8. Key your middle name and press the spacebar.

9. Move the insertion point to the right of your middle name. Press the **Backspace** key until your middle name is removed. Press the **Delete** key until your last name is removed. Leave WordPad open for the next Step-by-Step.

Saving a File

When you are keying text, it is only temporarily being held in the computer's memory. If your computer lost power or froze up, the text would be gone. Therefore, it is very important to constantly save your work to prevent losing it accidentally. Figure 4-31 shows the Save As dialog box in which you can choose the location for a file, the name of a file, and the type of file.

FIGURE 4-31
Save As dialog box

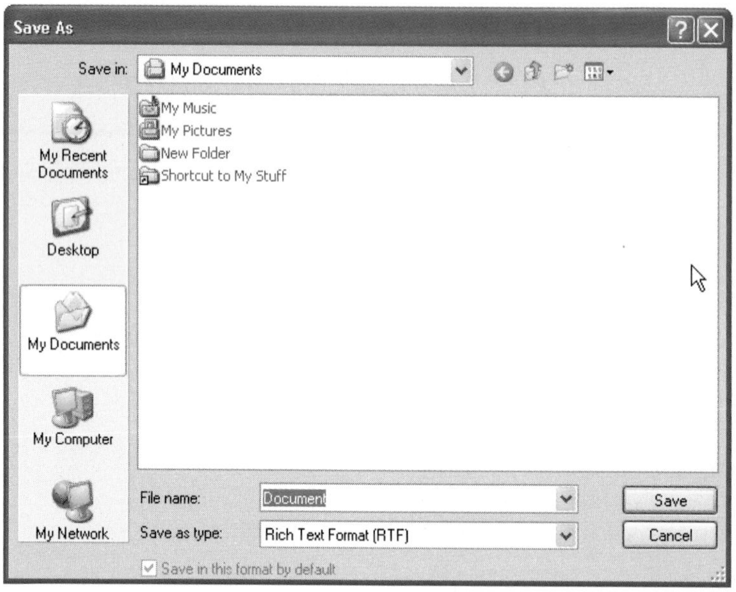

STEP-BY-STEP 4.24

1. Click the **File** menu and click **Save**. The Save As dialog box will open.

2. In the File name text box, key **Practice Word Processing**.

3. Click the **Save** button. Your file will now be saved in the My Documents folder with the name *Practice Word Processing*. Leave WordPad open for the next Step-by-Step.

Hot Tip

The Save As dialog box will open when you click Save or Save As on a file that has not been saved yet. This dialog box has you answer questions so WordPad can properly save the file for you. Once you have saved a file, the Save command will update its contents or the Save As command will allow you to specify a new location for the file or a different filename.

Printing a File

You can select from three ways to print your file. You can either send the file directly to the printer using the Print icon on the Standard toolbar, use the Print Preview icon on the Standard toolbar to first preview the file and then click Print, or open the Print dialog box shown in Figure 4-32 by selecting Print from the File menu. You can use the Print dialog box, shown in Figure 4-32, to change your default printer settings. Consult with your instructor about installing a printer if one has not been installed.

FIGURE 4-32
Print dialog box

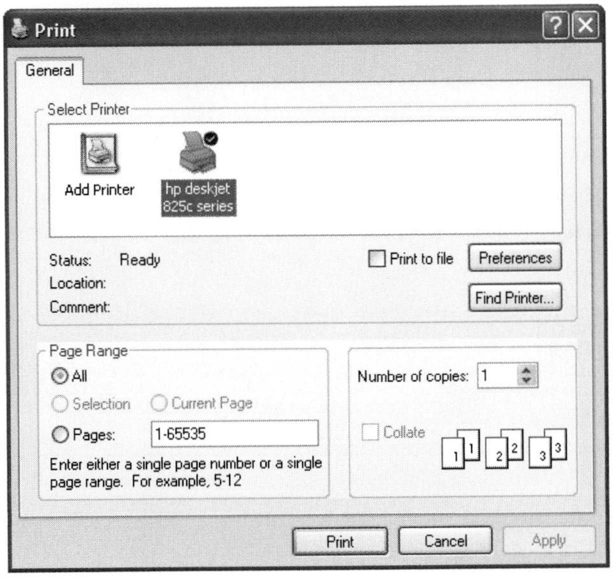

S TEP-BY-STEP 4.25

1. Click the **Print Preview** button on the toolbar. A preview of your page will appear.

2. Examine your document in the Print Preview window. Click **Close** in Print Preview to return to the normal document window.

> **Note** ☑
>
> These steps may not work if you do not have a printer installed. Ask your instructor for further instructions.

3. Click the **File** menu and click **Print**. The Print dialog box will open.

4. Click the **Cancel** button to exit the Print dialog box without printing the document.

5. Click the **Print** button on the Standard toolbar.

6. Close the document and WordPad by clicking the **X** in the right-hand corner. Leave Windows running for the next Step-by-Step.

Opening a File

You can open your file in two ways. You can either open the file from the folder it is in—which will automatically open WordPad—or from within WordPad. Figure 4-33 shows the Open dialog box.

FIGURE 4-33
Open dialog box

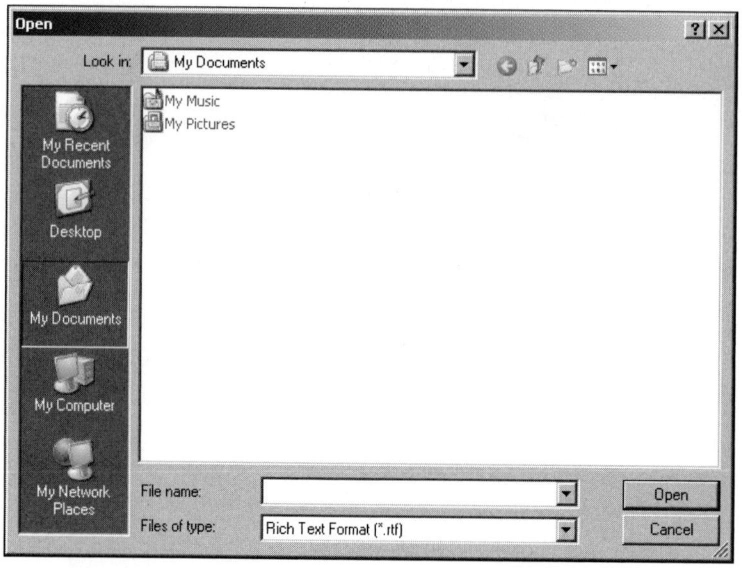

S TEP-BY-STEP 4.26

1. Click the **Start** button and click **My Documents**.

2. Double-click the **Practice Word Processing** file to open it.

3. Close WordPad and the document by clicking the **X** in the corner.

4. Start WordPad again by clicking **Start**, pointing to **All Programs**, **Accessories**, and clicking **WordPad**.

5. Click **File** and click **Open**.

6. Double-click the **Practice Word Processing** file to open it.

7. Close WordPad and the document by clicking the **X** in the corner. Leave Windows running for the next Step-by-Step.

Unique Features of Windows XP

Creating Shortcuts on the Desktop

Creating *shortcuts* is a very useful function of Windows XP. Shortcuts help save time and increase productivity by making your most commonly used programs and documents easily accessible from your desktop. A shortcut is simply a quick way to open a file or program without having to go to its original location. Shortcuts look like the original icons that they represent except they have small arrows at the bottom of them indicating they are shortcuts. Figure 4-34 is a shortcut to the Microsoft Word program.

FIGURE 4-34
Shortcut icon

There are several different ways to create a shortcut on the desktop. Among them are:

- Use the My Computer window to locate a file icon. Right-click the icon and select Copy from the shortcut menu. Move to the desktop, right-click an empty area and select Paste Shortcut from the menu.

- Use the My Computer window to locate a file icon. Right-click and drag the icon to the desktop. Choose Create Shortcuts Here when you release the mouse button.

S TEP-BY-STEP 4.27

1. Click the **Start** button and click **My Computer**.

2. Right-click drive **A:**. Hold the right-click and drag the icon to your desktop in the background.

3. Release the mouse button and select **Create Shortcuts Here** from the menu. Leave My Computer open for the next Step-by-Step.

Customizing the Start Menu

You can also customize the shortcuts in your Start menu. To place a shortcut in your Start menu, just drag the icon from the My Computer window and drop it on the Start button. To place a shortcut in one of the menus of your Start button, just drag it to the Start button and then drag and drop it on the menu where you want it to appear.

STEP-BY-STEP 4.28

1. Open the **My Documents** folder and click the **My Stuff** folder. Hold the click and drag the icon to your **Start** button. Release the mouse button.

2. To Remove the new shortcut from your Start menu, right-click the shortcut and choose **Remove from This List**. Leave Windows running for the next Step-by-Step.

Using the Control Panel

As mentioned earlier in this lesson, Windows has an area that allows you to configure the operating system exactly how you would like it to work. This area is called the Control Panel. Figure 4-35 shows the Control Panel window.

FIGURE 4-35
Control Panel window

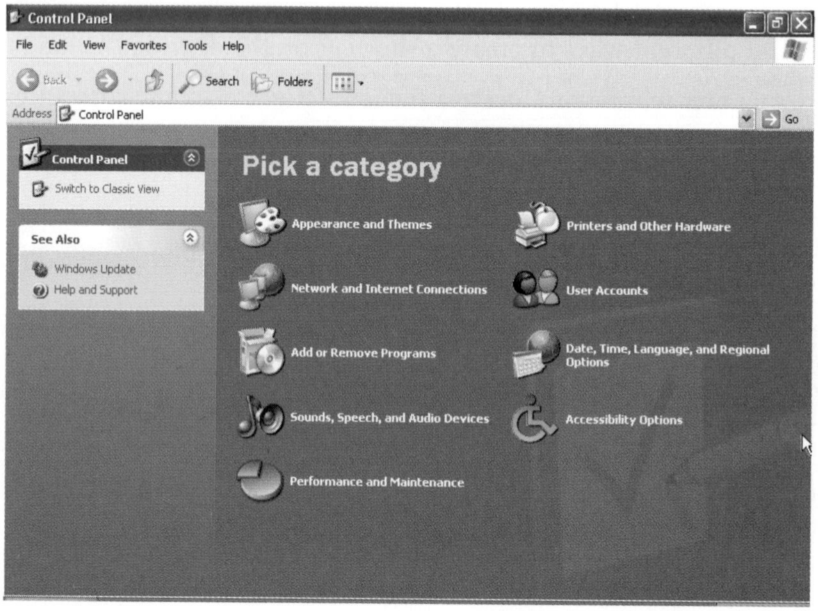

To open the Control Panel window, click the Start button and then click Control Panel. The Control Panel contains categories of options that allow you to customize the workings of Windows XP. Table 4-5 is a list of the categories in the Control Panel and their uses.

TABLE 4-5
Control Panel categories

NAME	DESCRIPTION
Appearance and Themes	Used to control properties of the display, such as wallpaper, the background, screen savers, etc.
Network and Internet Connections	Used to customize any network or Internet connections currently established or to create new ones.
Add or Remove Programs	Used to properly install and uninstall software programs on the system.
Sounds, Speech, and Audio Devices	Used to control the sounds made by your computer when certain events occur and to customize any audio devices installed on the computer.
Performance and Maintenance	Centralized location for maintenance tools on the system.
Printer and Other Hardware	Allows you to customize hardware devices currently installed and to add a new hardware device.
User Accounts	Allows you to create accounts for all users of the computer.
Date, Time, Language, and Regional Options	Allows you to adjust the date and time, languages and regional options for the system.
Accessibility Options	Used to customize the operating system for those with physical disabilities.

If you are used to working with a Classic View of the Control Panel as it was in Windows 95, 98, ME, or 2000 you can click the Switch to Classic View option in the left-hand side of the window. This will change the display to the way in which you are accustomed to working. When you are in the Classic View, the option in the task pane on the left will say Switch to Category View. Click on that option when you want to return to the XP View of the Control Panel.

STEP-BY-STEP 4.29

1. Click the **Start** button and click **Control Panel**.

2. Click the **Switch to Classic View** link.

3. To select wallpaper for your desktop, double-click the **Display** icon.

4. Make sure you are on the **Desktop** tab. Click **Ripple** in the Wallpaper list.

5. If necessary click the **Position** list and click **Tile** to display many copies of the image on the desktop.

6. Click **Apply** if you like the Ocean Wave or select a different picture.

STEP-BY-STEP 4.29 Continued

7. Click **OK**.

8. Click **Switch to Category View**.

9. Click **Sounds, Speech, and Audio Devices**.

10. Click **Change the sound scheme**.

11. Select the drop-down menu for the sound scheme and select **Windows Default**.

12. Click **Yes** to change the scheme and click **OK**.

13. Close the Control Panel window. Leave Windows running for the next Step-by-Step.

Using the Hardware Troubleshooters

Troubleshooters are available if you have problems with a hardware device. Among the problems that can be fixed are hardware problems and networking problems. You can also resolve issues with system setup, printing, and adding new hardware devices. As an example, assume that you are working in Microsoft Word and you press the Print button. A page prints but it is blank. What caused this issue? The troubleshooters included with XP can help you find a solution to this problem. Figure 4-36 shows the Help and Support Center's page for troubleshooting problems.

FIGURE 4-36
List of troubleshooters

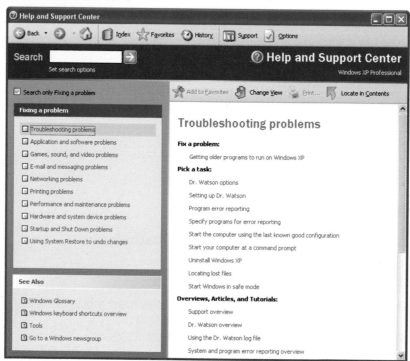

S TEP-BY-STEP 4.30

1. Click the **Start** button and click **Help and Support**.

2. Click the **Fixing a problem** link.

3. Click **Printing problems** in the left-hand pane.

4. Click **Fixing a printing problem**.

5. Click **Use the Printer Troubleshooter**.

6. Click **Step-by-step procedure**.

7. Select **My document doesn't print at all** and click **Next**.

8. Select **I cannot print any files, even in Notepad or WordPad** and click **Next**.

9. Ask your instructor whether to select **I am printing to a local printer (one that is attached directly to my computer) or I am printing to a network printer** and then click **Next**.

10. Work through as many steps as you would like in order to get the idea of how to use a troubleshooter and then close Help and Support. Leave Windows running for the next Step-by-Step.

System Maintenance

Windows has built-in tools to help you maintain and improve your system's performance. Your computer, like everything else, needs to be tuned up every once in a while to keep it running smoothly.

The most commonly used tools for maintaining your system are Disk Cleanup, Check Disk, and Disk Defragmenter.

Disk Cleanup

When you are doing work in Windows XP, unnecessary files accumulate in your hard drive. This slows down the system. The Disk Cleanup utility, shown in Figure 4-37, helps you remove unnecessary files safely from your machine.

FIGURE 4-37
Disk Cleanup dialog box

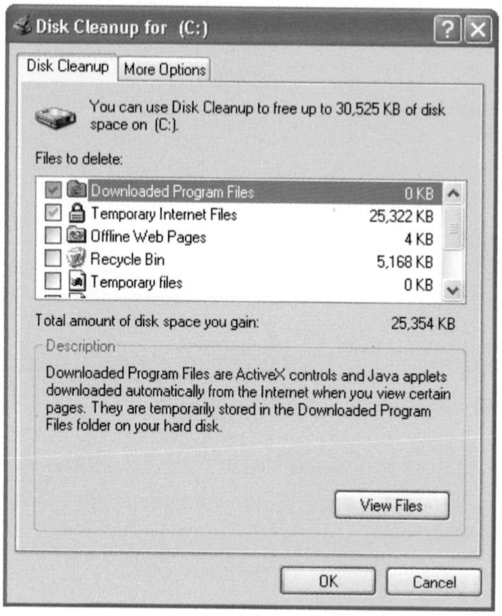

Table 4-6 contains the types of files Disk Cleanup may find on your machine that need to be removed.

TABLE 4-6
Disk Cleanup problem files

TYPE	DESCRIPTION
Downloaded Program Files	Program files that are downloaded automatically from the Internet on certain Web pages.
Old Scandisk files	Files created by the Scandisk utility when it finds bad data.
Recycle Bin	Files deleted from the hard disk.
Temporary Files	Files generated by programs to be used temporarily.
Temporary Internet Files	These files are stored on your hard disk so you can quickly view these Web pages later on.
Temporary Setup Files	These files are created when you install a program.
Windows XP Uninstall Information	Files from a previous version of Windows.

S TEP-BY-STEP 4.31

1. If necessary, close any open programs.

2. Click **Start**, point to **All Programs**, point to **Accessories**, point to **System Tools** and then click **Disk Cleanup**.

3. Click the **Drives** arrow and click **C:** if necessary. Click **OK**.

4. Check the boxes next to the files you want to delete.

5. Click **OK** and then click **Yes** to confirm you want to delete those files. Leave Windows running for the next Step-by-Step.

Check Disk

Sections of the disk surface may be damaged over time. Scanning the hard disk regularly for potential problems is a good way to avoid storing important data in a damaged area of the hard disk. The Windows XP Check Disk utility, shown in Figure 4-38, will locate problem areas of the hard disk, attempt to repair them and, if not repairable, mark them as bad, so that no data will be stored there in the future.

FIGURE 4-38
Check Disk utility

S TEP-BY-STEP 4.32

1. If necessary, close any open programs.

2. Open the **My Computer** window and right-click the **C:** icon.

3. Click **Properties** on the menu.

4. Click the **Tools** tab.

5. Click the **Check Now** button.

6. Check the *Scan for and attempt recovery of bad sectors* check box.

STEP-BY-STEP 4.32 Continued

7. Click the **Start** button to run the Check Disk program.

8. When complete, click the **OK** button twice to close the dialog boxes. Leave Windows running for the next Step-by-Step.

Disk Defragmenter

Once the surface of the hard disk is checked you can improve the performance of the drive by running the Disk Defragmenter utility shown in Figure 4-39. This utility will place pieces of files closer together so you can start and open files faster.

FIGURE 4-39
Disk Defragmenter

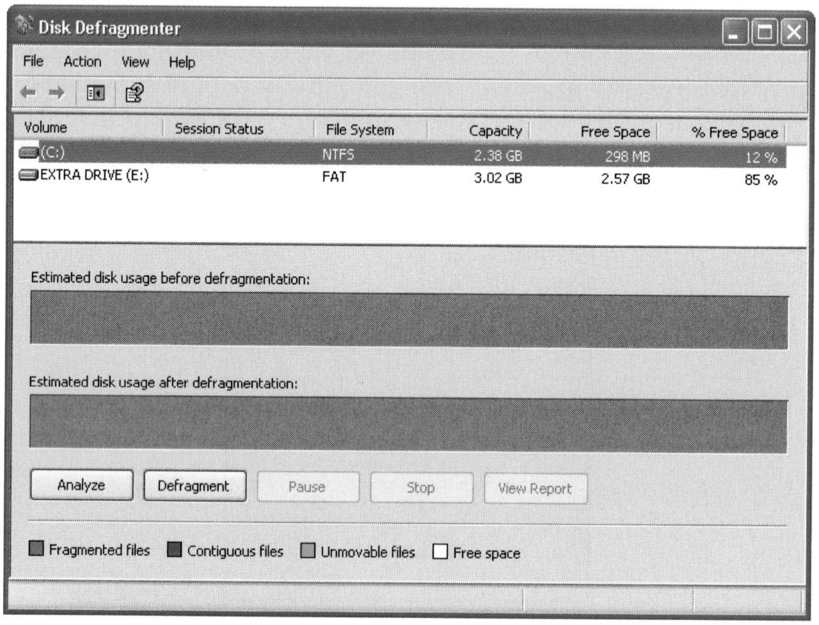

STEP-BY-STEP 4.33

1. If necessary, close any open programs.

2. Click **Start**, point to **All Programs**, point to **Accessories**, point to **System Tools,** and then click **Disk Defragmenter**.

3. In the Disk Defragmenter dialog box, select drive **C:**.

4. Click the **Defragment** button to begin defragmenting the drive.

5. Click **Close** when defragmentation is finished. Leave Windows running for the next Step-by-Step.

Scheduling Maintenance

The tasks listed above (Disk Cleanup, Check Disk, and Disk Defragmentation) must be performed regularly for your computer to run efficiently. Thankfully, you can schedule Windows XP to automatically run these tasks for you. This is accomplished through the Task Scheduler utility shown in Figure 4-40.

FIGURE 4-40
Task Scheduler

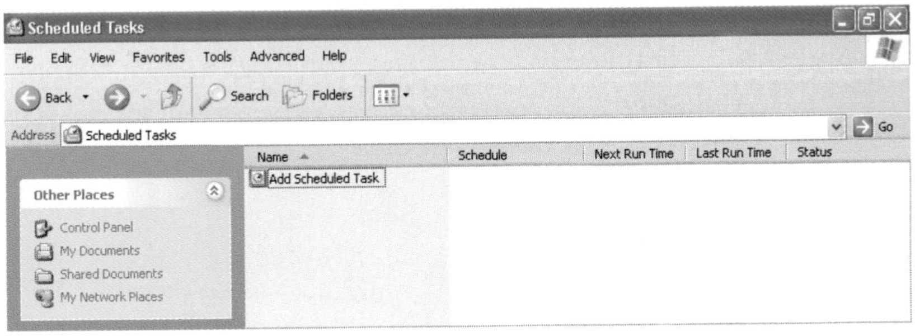

STEP-BY-STEP 4.34

1. If necessary, close any open programs.

2. Click **Start**, point to **All Programs**, point to **Accessories**, point to **System Tools**, and then click **Scheduled Tasks**.

3. Double-click the **Add Scheduled Task** icon.

4. Click the **Next** button.

5. Click **Disk Cleanup** in the list and then click **Next**.

6. Key **Clean Drive** in the task name box.

7. Click **Weekly** and then click **Next**.

8. Enter **8:00 PM** as the start time.

9. Check the **Friday** check box.

10. Click the **Next** button.

11. Enter your username and password if necessary. Click **Next**.

12. Click the **Finish** button. The Disk Cleanup utility will now run automatically at 8:00 P.M. on Fridays or it will run the next time your computer is turned on after that time.

13. Click the **Clean Drive** in Task Scheduler.

14. Press the **Delete** key and click **Yes** when asked if you want to delete the task.

15. Close the Scheduled Tasks window.

User Accounts

The *administrator* is the person who has all rights and privileges to the computer. This person can set up and manage other computers, create users, and apply permissions to other users. Figure 4-41 shows the User Accounts dialog box.

FIGURE 4-41
User Accounts

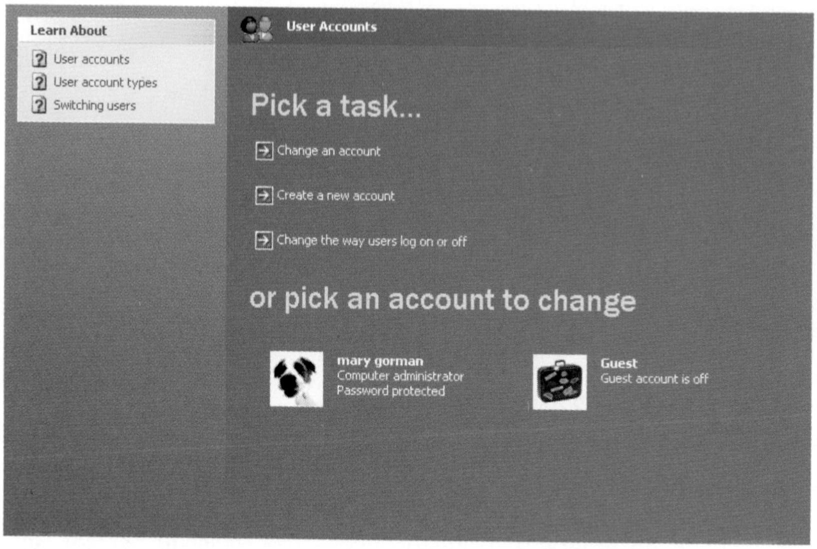

The administrator creates user accounts. A user account is a collection of information about a user. This information includes a user's username, password, rights, and permissions on the computer. Each user on a computer has certain permissions assigned by the administrator. The three types of Windows XP accounts are:

- Administrator—has permission to do any work on the machine.

- Limited—provides limited access to the computer.

- Guest—provides access to the computer for anyone who does not have an account currently set up.

STEP-BY-STEP 4.35

1. Click the **Start** button and click **Control Panel**.

2. Click **User Accounts** in the Control Panel.

3. Click on your username and click **Create password**.

4. In the *Type a new password* and *Type the new password again to confirm* textboxes key your new password.

STEP-BY-STEP 4.35 Continued

5. In the *Type a word or phrase to use as a password hint* key in something that will remind you of your password in case you forget it.

6. Click the **Create Password** button.

7. You may see a dialog box asking if you want to make their files and folders private. Click **NO**.

8. Click the **Change the picture** link.

9. Click whichever picture best represents you in the dialog box.

10. Click the **Change picture** button.

11. Close the User Accounts and Control Panel windows.

12. Click **Start** and **Log Off**.

13. Click **Log Off** again.

14. Click on your user account (see your new picture associated with your account) and log back on with your new password. Shut down Windows XP and your computer.

SUMMARY

In this lesson, you learned:

■ There are many improvements upon Windows XP Professional over earlier versions of the software including increased stability, improved device recognition, and increased security.

■ When you install Windows XP Professional, preparation will help you avoid potential problems during the installation process.

■ The desktop is your main workspace. It contains icons, which are used as an easy way to open programs and documents. You will also find application windows, desktop components, and the taskbar.

■ Your mouse is the tool you will use to open files, programs, and menus.

■ The taskbar displays any programs that you have minimized for quick access between applications. On your taskbar, you will see a Start button, which is used to quickly find or open a document, start a program, access tools to help you customize and optimize your system, and shut down your computer.

■ A window is the area or workspace you see when you open a program or application.

■ The My Computer window contains an icon for all of your disk drives (hard drive, floppy drive, CD-ROM drive, and possibly others). My Computer provides an access point to create folders, move, copy, delete, and rename files.

■ The Recycle Bin is an area on the hard drive that holds files and folders deleted from C: until you are absolutely sure you want to remove them.

- In Windows you can search for files by the filename, the date, the type of file, or by the file size. Windows Explorer is another method of viewing files and performing file management tasks such as copying, moving, renaming, and deleting files and folders.

- Windows XP comes with a small word processing program called WordPad. This program will allow you to do basic word processing tasks such as keying and formatting text, saving a file, and printing.

- A shortcut is simply a quick way to open a file or program without having to go to its original location.

- The Control Panel is an area that allows you to configure the operating system as you would like it to work.

- Windows has built-in tools to help you maintain and improve your system's performance. The most commonly used tools for maintaining your system are Disk Cleanup, Check Disk, and Disk Defragmenter.

- Windows XP has an area to create new user accounts. The administrator can create new accounts and assign permissions to those users. Limited users can change their passwords and pictures associated with their user accounts.

VOCABULARY *Review*

Define the following terms:

Administrator	Format	Subfolder
ClickLock	My Computer	Taskbar
Context menu	Partitions	Title bar
Control Panel	Recycle Bin	Troubleshooter
Desktop	Shortcut	Window
Folder	Snap to	

REVIEW *Questions*

MULTIPLE CHOICE

Select the best response to the following statements.

1. Windows XP supports which of the following file systems?
   A. NTFS
   B. FAT32
   C. Both A and B are correct.
   D. None of the above.

2. Which of the following is a good step to complete to ensure that your installation of Windows XP will avoid potential pitfalls?
    A. Identify the hardware requirements of Windows XP
    B. Check to see if your hardware is on the HCL
    C. Choose a file system with which to format the disk
    D. All of the above.

3. Which of the following is a hardware requirement of Windows XP?
    A. 64 MB of RAM
    B. 225 MB of hard disk space
    C. 14.4 Modem
    D. Trackball

4. Which of the following hardware devices is used to navigate the desktop?
    A. Printer
    B. Mouse
    C. Keyboard
    D. Modem

5. Which of the following options is located on the Start menu?
    A. All Programs
    B. Find
    C. Support from Microsoft
    D. Run Programs

6. Which of the following is a display mode in My Computer?
    A. Information
    B. Empty Screen
    C. Tiles
    D. Auto Display

7. To create a new folder click the _____ menu.
    A. Tools
    B. Edit
    C. Help
    D. File

8. To delete a file or folder
    A. right-click the file or folder and click Delete.
    B. select the file or folder and press Delete on the keyboard.
    C. select the file or folder, click the File menu, and click Delete.
    D. All of the above.

9. _____ is an area in Windows XP that allows you to customize the operating system.
    A. Control Panel
    B. Accessories
    C. My Computer
    D. Windows Explorer

10. Which of the following utilities can help you find information about Windows XP?
    A. Disk Cleanup
    B. Check Disk
    C. Disk Defragmenter
    D. Help and Support

FILL IN THE BLANK

Complete the following sentences by writing the correct word or words in the blanks provided.

1. The _____ _____ is the area that holds files deleted from the hard drive until you are absolutely sure you want to remove them.

2. _____ _____ is an area for file management that uses the same commands as My Computer to move, copy, rename, and delete files and folders.

3. The _____ has the ability to configure the operating system, create user accounts, and assign permissions.

4. _____ _____ is a utility that allows you to remove unnecessary files from the hard drive.

5. _____ in Windows XP will walk you through steps in order to resolve an issue or problem you are having.

PROJECTS

SCANS PROJECT 4-1

In this project, you will practice using Help and Support to resolve any issues you experience while working with Windows XP.

1. If necessary, log on to Windows XP.

2. Click the **Start** button and then click **Help and Support**.

3. Click **What's new in Windows XP** in the navigation pane.

4. Click **What's new with files and folders** in the topic pane.

5. Click the **Windows XP Articles** in the navigation pane and click the **What's new topics** link in the left pane.

6. Click **Walkthrough: Personalize your PC**.

7. List four ways in which your can personalize your PC.

8. Click the **Back** button and click **Walkthrough: Home networking**.

9. List four ways in which you can use Windows XP for home networking.

10. Return to the main page in Help and Support.

11. Use the Help Index feature to find help about the following four areas:
    A. What dialog box do you use to add a screen saver?
    B. How do you minimize all open windows?
    C. How do you use the Run command to start a program?
    D. How do you delete a shortcut from the desktop?

12. Close the Help and Support Center window. Leave Windows XP running for the next Project.

SCANS PROJECT 4-2

In this project, you will create a file and organize with a folder.

1. Open **WordPad**. Key a list of items you need to buy at the store this weekend. Save the document on your desktop and name it **Grocery List**.

2. Close WordPad.

3. Open **My Computer**. Open drive A:

4. Create a folder called **Tasks** on your floppy disk.

5. Move the file called **Grocery List** from the desktop into the **Tasks** folder.

6. Create another folder called **Tasks** in the **My Documents** folder on drive C:.

7. Copy the file called **Grocery List** from your floppy disk to the **My Documents** folder.

8. Move the **Grocery List** file from **My Documents** to the **Tasks** folder.

9. Delete the **Tasks** folder from your floppy disk.

10. Arrange the icons in the My Documents folder in alphabetical order and display it in Icons view. Show your instructor your results.

11. Close My Computer and shut down Windows XP and your computer.

CRITICAL *Thinking*

SCANS ACTIVITY 4-1

In this lesson, you learned about many of the advantages of using Windows XP. Use the Internet to search for three articles that are in support of upgrading to Windows XP. What advantages of Windows XP do the authors mention?

SCANS ACTIVITY 4-2

Windows XP contains many troubleshooters for users to help themselves when experiencing problems with XP. Name three troubleshooters in Windows XP and write down how this troubleshooter could benefit a user.

WINDOWS 2000 PROFESSIONAL

OBJECTIVES

Upon completion of this lesson, you should be able to:

- Describe the improvements of Windows 2000 Professional over earlier versions of the operating system.

- Install Windows 2000 Professional successfully from CD-ROM.

- Use the functions of the operating system.

- Manage folders and files.

- Use the Windows 2000 unique features to customize the use of your operating system.

Estimated time: 8 hours

VOCABULARY

Check Disk

Disk Cleanup

Disk Defragmenter

Domain

File

Format

Scroll bar

Shortcut

Task Scheduler

Workgroup

Introduction

There are many benefits to using Windows 2000 Professional. Table 5-1 outlines some of these benefits.

TABLE 5-1
Benefits of Windows 2000 Professional

BENEFIT	REASON
Security	Authenticates users before they gain access to network resources.
	Provides security for files, folders, printers, and other resources.
Internet integration	Integrates users with the Internet.
	Windows 2000 Professional has a personal Web server allowing users to create and host their own Web sites.
Performance	Supports multitasking for system processes and programs.
Administration tools	Able to create customized administration tools to manage computers.
Hardware	Supports USB (Universal Serial Bus) devices.
	Supports Plug and Play hardware. Plug and Play means that you can plug a device in and it will self-configure.

Differences between Windows 2000 and Previous Versions

This chapter will focus solely on Windows 2000 Professional. You will find many improvements over earlier versions of Windows you may have used, including ease of use, ease of file management, better security, and increased hardware compatibilities.

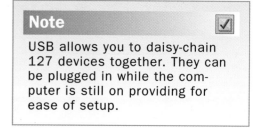

> **Note** ☑
>
> USB allows you to daisy-chain 127 devices together. They can be plugged in while the computer is still on providing for ease of setup.

Ease of Use

Changes made to Windows 2000 include cosmetic changes that make items such as the Start menu, the desktop, and windows easier to use. Enhancements that improve the usability of Windows 2000 include:

- **Start Menu**—The Start menu can now be customized, so that applications you use less frequently are hidden from view.

- **Tasks**—The Scheduler allows users to schedule programs to run at specific times.

- **Log on and Shut Down**—The dialog boxes are easier to use with fewer choices. This can be advantageous because many people could get confused as to what option to choose in the Shut Down dialog box.

File Management

Microsoft made significant changes to Windows 2000 file management capabilities. Included among them are:

- **NTFS (New Technology File System)**—NTFS supports file encryption. It supports per-user disk quotas to limit the amount of disk space each user is allowed. And it also allows for sharing of files and folders between Windows 2000 and Windows NT.

- **FAT32**—Supports the FAT32 file system. This allows for compatibility with Windows 95 and 98 systems.

- **Disk Defragmenter**—Utility that organizes files, applications, and free space on the drive so that programs and files run and open faster.

- **Backup**—Utility that allows you to schedule backups to occur automatically.

Security

Windows 2000 offers many security features. They include the following:

- **EFS (Encrypting File System)**—Encrypts files on the hard drive so that no one can access them without the proper password.

- **Internet Protocol Security**—Encrypts information sent over the Internet/intranet to secure all communications.

Hardware

Microsoft Windows 2000 supports over 7,000 hardware devices. Support is provided for various scanners, digital cameras, and other multimedia devices that previous versions of Windows did not support. Other benefits include:

- **Plug and Play Support**—Enhanced over previous versions of Windows.
- **Add/Remove Hardware Wizard**—Allows you to add, remove, and troubleshoot hardware.

Installation of Windows 2000

Preinstallation

When you install Windows 2000 Professional, the Setup Wizard will ask you to provide information about how you want to install and configure the operating system. Preparation will help you avoid potential problems during the installation process. The following is a list of tasks you must perform in order to have a minimal amount of problems during installation.

- Identify the hardware requirements to install Windows 2000 Professional.
- Check to see if your hardware is on the HCL (Hardware Compatibility List).
- Determine how you want to partition the hard disk that will receive the installation of Windows 2000.
- Choose a file system for the installation partition.
- Identify whether your computer will be in a domain or a workgroup.

Hardware Requirements

You must know the minimum hardware requirements before installing Windows 2000 Professional. Microsoft recommends that your hardware exceed these requirements to take full advantage of Windows 2000 as well as to be prepared for future upgrades. Table 5-2 lists the minimum hardware requirements.

TABLE 5-2
Windows 2000 hardware requirements

HARDWARE	REQUIREMENT
CPU	Pentium based
Memory	32 MB minimum 64 MB recommended
Hard Disk Space	650 MB minimum 2 GB recommended
Display	Monitor with VGA resolution or higher
Other	CD-ROM Drive, 12X or faster Keyboard Mouse or other pointing device

Hardware Compatibility List

Before you install Windows 2000, you must verify that your hardware is on the Hardware Compatibility List (HCL). Using hardware that is not on the list may cause problems during and after installation of the operating system. For a copy of the HCL, you will find the most recent version on the Microsoft Web site at *www.microsoft.com*. As an example, Figure 5-1 shows the hardware compatibility list for DVD-ROM drives.

FIGURE 5-1
Example hardware compatibility list

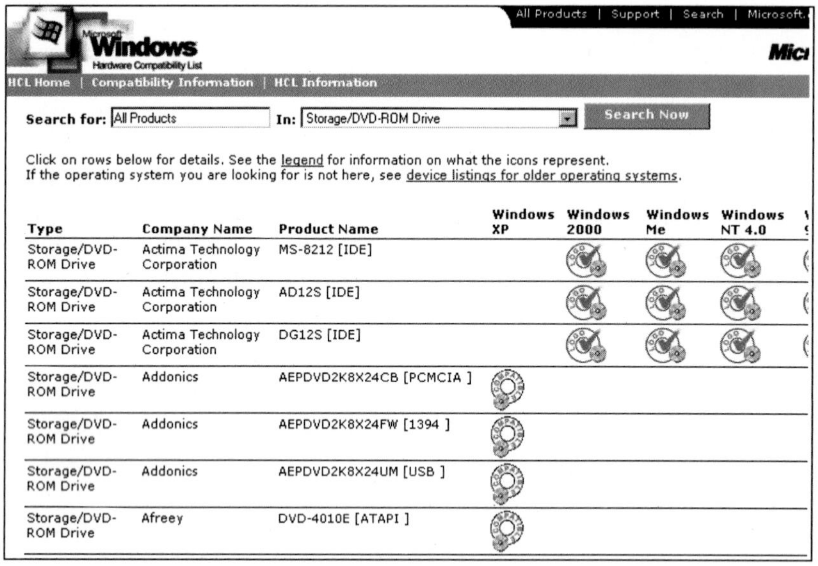

Disk Partitions

Setup allows you to install Windows 2000 on an existing partition or to create a new partition. Partitions function as physically separate storage units on the same disk. Depending on the hard disk, you may choose one of the following options during installation:

- If the hard disk is unpartitioned you must create the Windows 2000 partition.

- With a partitioned hard disk, you can use unpartitioned space to create the Windows 2000 partition.

- With a partitioned hard disk, you can delete existing partitions and then create a new one for the Windows 2000 partition.

- You can create the Windows 2000 partition over an existing partition that is large enough.

Microsoft recommends that you install Windows 2000 on a 1GB or larger partition. Using a larger partition provides some operating system flexibility later.

File Systems

After you create the partition, Setup asks you to select the file system you want to use on the partition. Windows 2000 supports NTFS, FAT32, and FAT. You should use the NTFS option when you want to have file and folder security, allow for disk compression, set disk quotas, and to allow for file encryption. FAT and FAT32 do not offer many of the features that NTFS does; therefore, you normally would not choose one of these options for the installation partition. The only time you would use FAT or FAT32 is when you want to set up the hard disk for dual booting, meaning that more than one operating system is installed on the same hard disk.

Domain or Workgroup

During installation, you must choose the type of group you want to join: domain or workgroup. A *domain* is a group of computers and devices on a network that are administered as a unit with common rules and procedures. A domain is found in server-based networks. A *workgroup* is a logical grouping of computers that share resources such as files and printers. A workgroup is called a peer-to-peer network because all computers act as equals.

> **Note** ☑
>
> NTFS has features to improve reliability, such as transaction logs to help recover from disk failures. To control access to files, you can set permissions for directories and/or individual files. NTFS files are not accessible from other operating systems such as DOS.

> **Hot Tip** ◎
>
> For large applications, NTFS supports spanning volumes, which means files and directories can be spread out across several physical disks.

Joining a Domain

In order to join a domain you must have the following information:

- **Domain name**—Ask the administrator for the domain you want to join. An example of a domain name is *tsbi.org*.

- **Computer Account**—A computer account must be created in the domain before a computer can join that domain. Ask your administrator to add you to the domain before installation or if you as a user already have privileges, you may join the domain during the installation process. If you choose to do this, you will be prompted for a username and password to authenticate that you have the rights to join this domain.

Joining a Workgroup

During installation, you can add your computer to an existing workgroup. When you join a workgroup during installation, you must give your computer a workgroup name. The workgroup name you give must be the name of an existing workgroup or it can be the name of a new workgroup you are going to create during installation.

Installing Windows 2000 from CD

There are four stages to installing Windows 2000. The four stages are:

- Running the Setup Program
- Running the Setup Wizard
- Installing Networking Components
- Completing the Setup Program

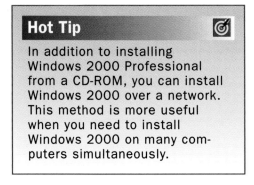

> **Hot Tip** ◎
>
> In addition to installing Windows 2000 Professional from a CD-ROM, you can install Windows 2000 over a network. This method is more useful when you need to install Windows 2000 on many computers simultaneously.

S TEP-BY-STEP 5.1

1. Insert the Windows 2000 Professional CD into the CD-ROM drive. Restart your computer and press any key to reboot from the CD.

2. Windows will then display the Welcome to Setup screen. Read the Welcome to Setup screen and press **Enter** to continue.

3. Read the licensing agreement and press the **F8** key to agree with the licensing terms.

4. Setup will prompt you to select an area of free space or an existing partition to install Windows 2000. Press **Enter** to select the default of C:.

5. Setup will now display a list of file system choices. Select **Format the Partition Using the NTFS File System** and press **Enter**.

6. Setup will now format the hard disk, examine it, and copy files to the Windows 2000 installation folders. This may take several minutes.

7. Setup will prompt you to restart the computer.

8. After you restart your computer, the Windows 2000 Setup Wizard will appear. Click **Next** to continue.

9. Setup will now detect and install all hardware devices. This might take several minutes. Setup will also configure NTFS file and folder permissions for the operating system files. Then all hardware devices supported by Windows 2000 will be detected and configured.

10. Setup then prompts you to customize Windows 2000 for your region of the world. Select the appropriate system locale, user locale, and keyboard layout. Ensure that they are correct for your language and location. Click **Next** to continue.

11. Setup then displays the Personalize Your Software Page. In the Name box, key your name. In the Organization box, key the name of your organization. Click **Next**.

12. You then must enter the 25-character product key that appears on the sticker on the back of your Windows 2000 Professional CD case, and then click **Next**.

13. The next screen sets up the Computer name and Administrator password. In the Computer Name box key **MINE1**. In the Administrator password box and in the Confirm password box, key **password** and then click **Next**.

STEP-BY-STEP 5.1 Continued

14. Ensure that the correct country and region are selected. If you have a modem, key in the correct area code. If you must dial a number for an outside line (for example, 9), key in the correct number. Ensure that the correct phone system is displayed. Click **Next**.

15. On the Date and Time Setting page, confirm that the Date and Time are correct and the Time Zone settings are correct for your location. Select Automatically Adjust Clock for Daylight Savings Time and then click **Next**.

16. The Networking Settings page will be displayed next. Ensure that the Typical settings option is selected and then click **Next**.

17. On the workgroup or domain page, select the option **No, this computer is not on or is on a network without a domain**. Ensure that **WORKGROUP** appears in the Workgroup or computer domain box. Click **Next**. Setup will now install components. Again, this may take several minutes.

18. The Completing Windows 2000 Setup screen will appear. Click **Finish**. The system will reboot.

19. To use the Welcome to the Network Identification Wizard, click **Next**.

20. The Users of This Computer Page appears. Select **Users must enter a user name and password to use this computer** and click **Next**.

21. Click **Finish**.

22. In the Log on to Windows dialog box, ensure that it says **Administrator** in the User Name box and in the password box, key **password**.

23. Click **OK**.

24. The Getting Started with Windows 2000 dialog box appears as shown in Figure 5-2. Clear the **Show this screen at startup** check box and click **Exit** to close this dialog box.

FIGURE 5-2
Getting Started with Windows 2000 dialog box

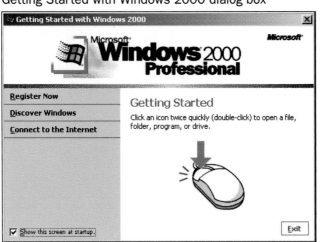

STEP-BY-STEP 5.1 Continued

25. Congratulations! You have now successfully installed Windows 2000 from the CD-ROM. Leave Windows running for the next Step-by-Step.

Troubleshooting Setup

Hopefully your installation of Windows 2000 Professional went smoothly without any major problems. Unfortunately, some issues may crop up during installation. Table 5-3 gives some advice for resolving some issues you may encounter.

TABLE 5-3
Troubleshooting tips

PROBLEM	RESOLUTION
Failure of Windows 2000 to install or start	Verify that Windows 2000 is detecting all of the hardware and that all of your hardware is listed on the hardware compatibility list (HCL) found on Microsoft's Web site.
Media Errors	Try another Windows 2000 professional Installation CD-ROM if this is your installation method.
CD-ROM drive isn't working	Replace the CD-ROM drive with one that is supported on the HCL. Try installing over the network and when finished running setup, install the driver for the CD-ROM drive.
Insufficient Disk Space	Delete partitions as needed and then create a partition large enough for installation.

> **Hot Tip**
>
> Be sure to remove the CD-ROM when finished installing Windows 2000 Professional. Otherwise when you reboot the machine, the setup program will start all over again. If this should happen, remove the CD-ROM and restart the computer. Do not go through the setup process again.

Basic Functions of Windows 2000

Your desktop is your main workspace. Here you will find small pictures called icons as shown in Figure 5-3. Icons provide an easy way to open programs and documents. You will also find application windows, desktop components, and the taskbar. You can customize your desktop by changing background colors, creating shortcuts to your favorite documents and programs, and adding and moving toolbars.

FIGURE 5-3
Desktop

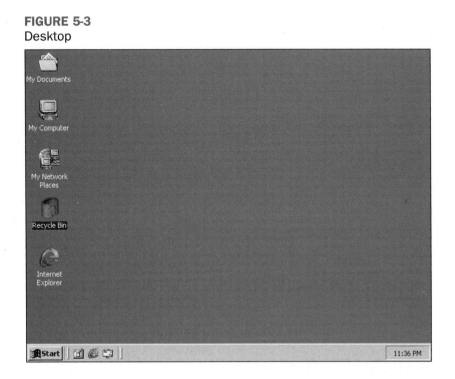

Using Your Mouse

In Windows, you use your mouse to navigate your desktop. Your mouse is the tool you will use to open files, programs, and menus. You use your mouse by sliding it around on your mouse pad. As you move your mouse across the mouse pad, you will see the arrow on your monitor move. A typical mouse has two buttons on the top. The left mouse button is used to select or open a file, program, or icon. By single-clicking the left mouse button you will select the item. By holding down the left mouse button you can move items around your desktop or drop them into folders on your desktop. By double-clicking the left mouse button you can open a file or execute a program's icon. The right mouse button is used to activate context menus (shortcut menus), which display several tasks that are commonly performed with that item. Figure 5-4 is an example of a context menu.

FIGURE 5-4
A context menu

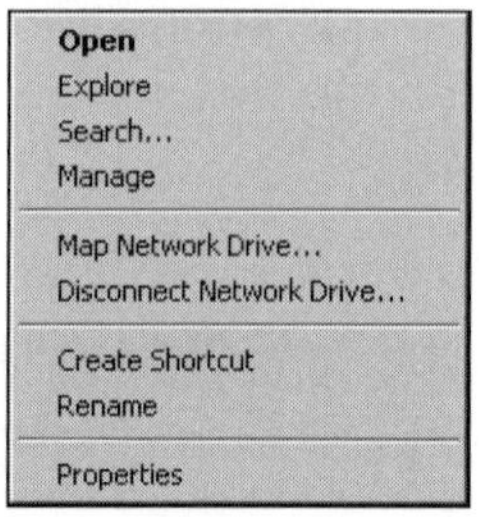

> **Open**
> Explore
> Search...
> Manage
>
> Map Network Drive...
> Disconnect Network Drive...
>
> Create Shortcut
> Rename
>
> Properties

Configuring Your Mouse

To configure your mouse to work best for you, click the Start button, click Settings, and then click Control Panel. The Control Panel window will open on your desktop as shown in Figure 5-5. Locate and double-click the Mouse icon. The Mouse Properties dialog box, as shown in Figure 5-6, opens. Click the Buttons tab if necessary. You can adjust the basic configuration of the mouse from right-handed to left-handed and vice versa. You can also check your double-click speed by double-clicking your mouse on the jack-in-the-box in the Test area. To adjust the double-click speed, move the slide arrow to the right or the left depending on whether you want your double-click speed faster or slower. Finally, you can change your mouse click options to single-clicking on items to open them and just hovering the mouse over an item to select it.

FIGURE 5-5
Mouse icon in Control Panel

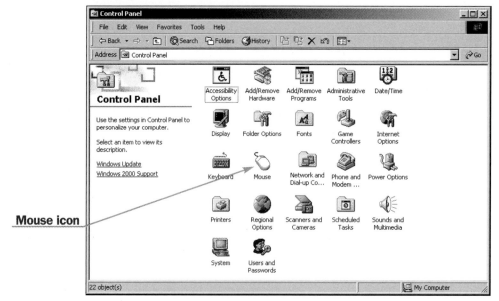

Mouse icon

FIGURE 5-6
Buttons tab in Mouse Properties dialog box

Mouse Properties

Buttons | Pointers | Motion | Hardware

Button configuration

⦿ Right-handed ◯ Left-handed

Left Button:
- Normal Select
- Normal Drag

Right Button:
- Context Menu
- Special Drag

Files and Folders

◯ Single-click to open an item (point to select)
⦿ Double-click to open an item (single-click to select)

Double-click speed

Slow ——————— Fast

Test area:

OK   Cancel   Apply

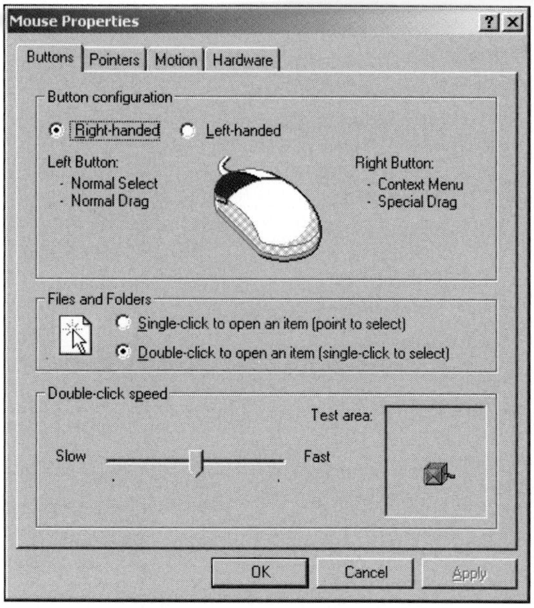

You can adjust the speed at which your pointer moves across your desktop by clicking the Motion tab, as shown in Figure 5-7, and choosing your most comfortable pointer speed. There is also a Snap to feature that will automatically snap your mouse to the default button in the dialog box.

FIGURE 5-7
Motion tab in Mouse Properties dialog box

Mouse Properties

Buttons | Pointers | Motion | Hardware

Speed

Adjust how fast your pointer moves

Slow ——————— Fast

Acceleration

Adjust how much your pointer accelerates as you move it faster

◯ None ⦿ Low ◯ Medium ◯ High

Snap to default

OK ☐ Move pointer to the default button in dialog boxes

OK   Cancel   Apply

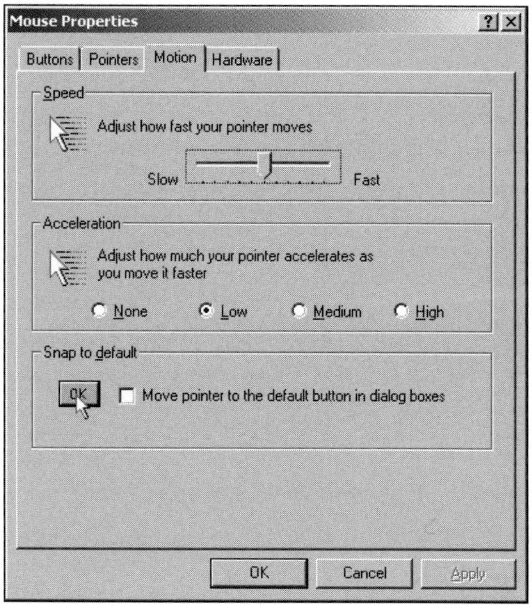

Click the Pointers tab. See Figure 5-8. From here, you can change the size, color, and shape of the different pointers to make them easier to see and use or to meet your personal style.

FIGURE 5-8
Pointers tab in Mouse Properties dialog box

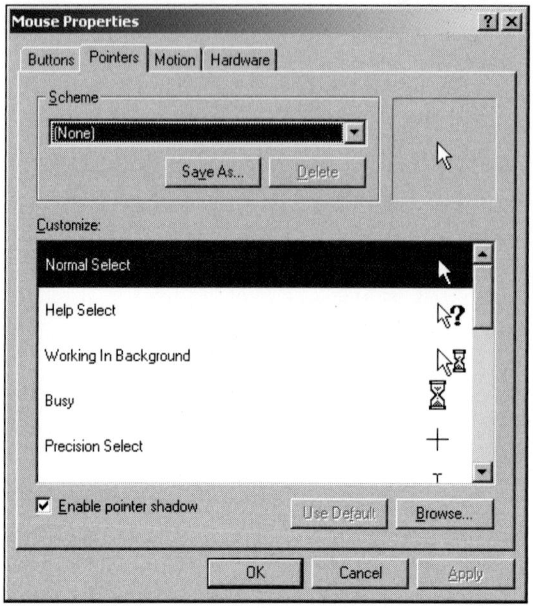

You can use the standard Windows scheme or choose another scheme from the drop-down list. To change your pointer, do the following:

- Select the pointer you want to change.

- Click the Browse button. A dialog box will appear with the available pointers. Choose one from the list.

- Click Open if this is the pointer you want, otherwise click Cancel.

- If you change your pointer scheme choose Save As to save your scheme. Enter a name in the Save Scheme dialog box and click OK.

- Click the Apply button, and then click OK.

- To return to your original pointers click the Use Default button.

> **Note** ☑
>
> When you click the Apply button, it causes your new settings to take effect. Clicking OK both applies your changes and closes the dialog box.

S TEP-BY-STEP 5.2

1. Point at any icon on your desktop and select it by clicking your left mouse button once. Notice how the selected icon is highlighted.

2. Practice dragging your icons around the screen. To drag, point to the icon, click your left mouse button once and hold it down. Now slide your mouse across your mouse pad then release the mouse button.

STEP-BY-STEP 5.2 Continued

3. Right-click a blank space on your desktop. Point to **Arrange Icons** and then to **by Name** and left-click once. Windows arranges your icons for you.

4. Right-click the **My Computer** icon and view the shortcut menu. Click an empty area of your desktop to close the context menu.

5. Double-click the **My Computer** icon to open its window.

6. To close the window click the **X** in the upper-right corner of the My Computer window. Leave Windows running for the next Step-by-Step.

Taskbar

At the bottom of your desktop, you will see a gray rectangular bar like that shown in Figure 5-9. This is your taskbar.

FIGURE 5-9
Taskbar

The taskbar displays any programs that you have minimized, allowing quick access between applications. You can also customize your taskbar with icons for easy access to your favorite programs. By default, your taskbar appears at the bottom of your desktop. You can move your taskbar to any side of your desktop by left-clicking the empty gray area, holding down your mouse button, and dragging it.

By right-clicking the taskbar, you can arrange open windows on your screen, tiling them horizontally or vertically, or cascading them. See Figure 5-10.

FIGURE 5-10
Right-clicking the taskbar

| Toolbars ▶ |
| **Adjust Date/Time** |
| Cascade Windows |
| Tile Windows Horizontally |
| Tile Windows Vertically |
| Minimize All Windows |
| Task Manager... |
| Properties |

To access taskbar options, you can click the Start button, choose Settings, and then choose Taskbar & Start Menu, or you can right-click the taskbar and click Properties. Several options are available to customize your taskbar. Following is a brief description of the options you can choose.

Hot Tip

If you hover your mouse briefly over any incomplete name in a minimized application, the entire name appears after a few seconds.

- **Always on Top**—When you check this box, your taskbar will be visible when any program is open. This will give you less screen space, but makes switching between windows easier.
- **Auto hide**—When you check this box, the taskbar disappears when you click any window and activate it. This gives you more screen space. When you move your cursor to the edge of the screen where the taskbar is located, it will reappear.
- **Show small icons in start menu**—When you check this box, it makes the icons on your Start menu smaller, leaving more room to add programs.
- **Show clock**—When you check this box a small clock will appear at the bottom right of your taskbar

On the right side of your taskbar, you will see the time and small icons to access programs that are automatically available when you turn on the computer. See Figure 5-11. These icons give you easy access to programs that manage system resources and let you access utilities that help to improve your computer's performance.

FIGURE 5-11
Small icons

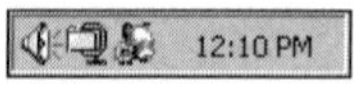

STEP-BY-STEP 5.3

1. Practice moving your taskbar around the screen.

2. Point your mouse at the small icons on the right side (or bottom) of the taskbar. Little boxes called **Screen Tips** display and tell you what each icon is. Note what these icons are.

3. Point your mouse at the time on the right side (or bottom) of your taskbar. Double-click it with your left mouse button. A dialog box displays that allows you to change the time and date that appear on your taskbar. Click **Cancel**.

4. Right-click the taskbar. Left-click **Properties**. Left-click the check box next to **Show small icons in the start menu** to put a check in the box. Click **OK**. Now click your **Start** button. Notice how the icons have changed.

5. Right-click the taskbar. Left-click **Properties**. Left-click the check box next to all of the properties to turn them all on. Click **OK**. Notice the changes.

STEP-BY-STEP 5.3 Continued

6. Right-click the taskbar. Left-click **Properties**. Left-click the check boxes next to the options again to turn them all off.

7. Click **OK**. Leave Windows running for the next Step-by-Step.

Start Button

On your taskbar, you will see a Start button as shown in Figure 5-12.

FIGURE 5-12
Start button

The Start button is one of the most useful items on your desktop. You can use the Start button to quickly find or open a document, start a program, access tools to help you customize and optimize your system, and shut down your computer.

When you click the Start button, you will see a menu similar to that shown in Figure 5-13.

FIGURE 5-13
Start menu

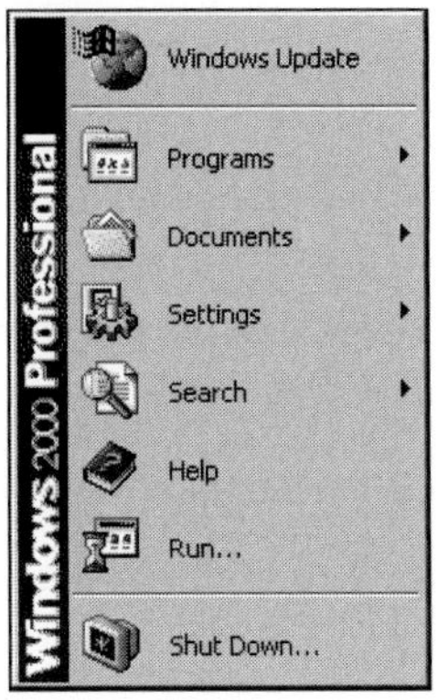

You can also open the Start menu by holding down the Ctrl+Esc keys on your keyboard or by pressing the flying windows button on a Microsoft compatible keyboard.

Most of the menu items on the Start menu contain submenus. If a menu item contains a submenu, you will see a small black triangular shape next to the item. When you point to that item the submenu will appear, as shown in Figure 5-14.

FIGURE 5-14
Submenus

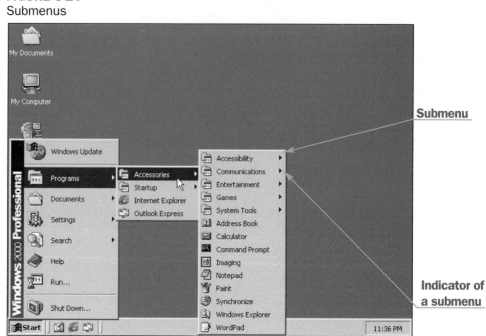

You can click anywhere on your desktop to close the Start menu if you do not want to choose an item from the menus.

Following is a description of the options found on the Start menu:

■ **Programs**—This is where you will find all of the software programs installed on your computer.

■ **Documents**—This is where Windows stores shortcuts to the last ten documents you have opened.

■ **Settings**—This is where you can access the Control Panel and your Printers folder. The Control Panel is where you can reconfigure the hardware (such as the mouse settings you adjusted earlier) and operating system settings, as well as add and remove software. The Printers folder is where you add, configure, and remove printers.

■ **Search**—This option comes in handy when you know what you are looking for but do not know where you put it. The Search option allows you to search for folders, files, people, and computers.

■ **Help**—Here you can find a variety of Help topics from which to choose.

■ **Run**—This command enables you to run a program from a floppy disk, your hard disk, or a network drive.

■ **Shut Down**—This is where you shut down, restart, or log off your computer.

STEP-BY-STEP 5.4

1. Click the **Start** button on your taskbar.

2. With your mouse, point to **Programs**. A submenu will appear.

3. Point to **Accessories**; another submenu will appear.

4. Point to the **Calculator** and left-click it. You have now opened the Calculator program.

5. To close the Calculator click the **X** in the upper-right corner of the window.

6. Click the **Start** button on your taskbar.

7. With your mouse pointer, point to **Shut Down** and left-click. Here you are given the option to Shut Down the computer, Restart it, or Log Off as Administrator.

8. Click **Cancel**. Leave Windows open for the next Step-by-Step.

> **Important**
>
> You should always shut down when exiting Windows. Simply turning off the computer without shutting down properly could damage your programs. If your computer has a frozen screen and mouse, try pressing and holding down the Ctrl+Alt+Delete keys on the keyboard. This will open the Windows Security dialog box. From here you can click Task Manager and find out what programs are not responding. If this doesn't unfreeze the computer, try to choose the Shut Down option. As a last resort, you may need to power off the computer or press the Reset button on the front of your machine.

Windows

A window is the area or workspace you see when you open a program or application. Figure 5-15 is an example of a window.

FIGURE 5-15
My Documents window

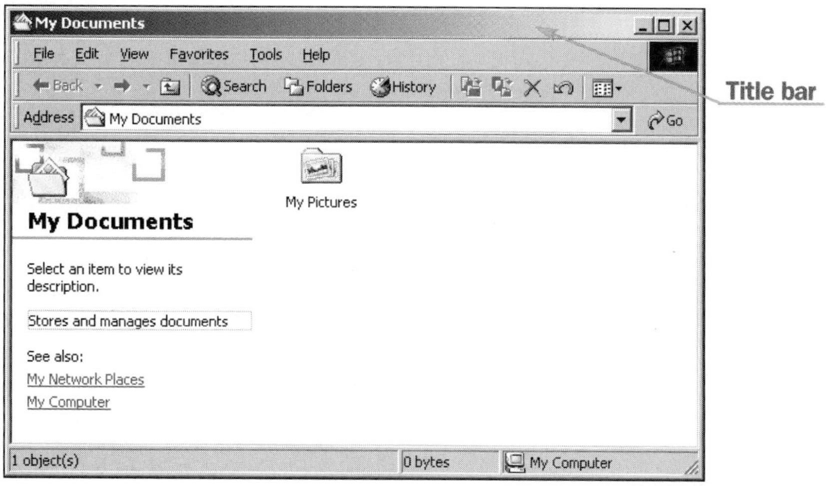

This defined workspace is movable and resizable. At the top of every window is the title bar. This bar displays at the top of the window, tells you the name of the application you are using, and contains the Minimize, Restore/Maximize, and Close buttons. If you have more than one application open on your desktop, you can tell which one is active by the color of its title bar. If it is dark, it is active; if it is light, it is inactive. This may be different if you have customized the title bars.

You can also move the window around the screen by left-clicking the title bar and dragging while holding down your mouse button. You can resize the window by pointing your mouse at the edge of the window. Your mouse pointer will change into a double-headed arrow. See Figure 5-16.

FIGURE 5-16
Double-headed arrows

Vertical Resize	↕
Horizontal Resize	↔
Diagonal Resize 1	↖
Diagonal Resize 2	↙

When it becomes a double-headed arrow, click your left mouse button and hold it while dragging your mouse in the direction you want to resize the window.

The top right of the title bar contains three control buttons. The left one is the Minimize button. Clicking this button keeps your window active, but reduces it to the taskbar. The middle button is the Restore/Maximize button. If you have a full screen window, it returns the window to a size that allows you to view the desktop in the background. If the window is already less than full size, the button returns it to the maximum size. The last button, the X on the right, is the Close button. Clicking that button closes the active window or program.

Scroll Bars

If you cannot see all the information in a window, use the *scroll bars* at the right or the bottom of the window to view the rest of the information. Figure 5-17 shows both a horizontal scroll bar and a vertical scroll bar.

FIGURE 5-17
Scroll bars

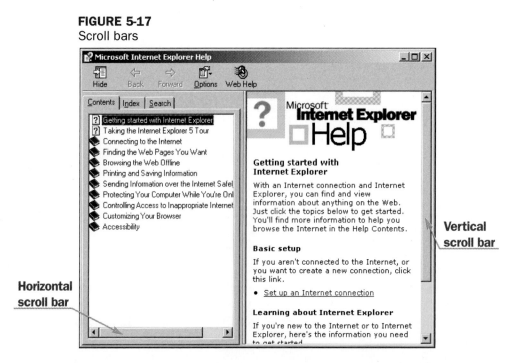

Click the up arrow on the vertical scroll bar to scroll up the contents of the window or click the down arrow to scroll down. To scroll from side to side, use the right or left arrows on the horizontal scroll bar at the bottom of the window. Instead of using the arrows, you can also click the scroll box between the scroll arrows and drag it left, right, up, or down. Alternatively, you can click in the space above, below, to the left, or to the right of the scroll box to move one full screen in the direction selected.

> **Hot Tip**
>
> Scroll bars only appear when the window is not large enough to display all of the information. Therefore, not all windows contain scroll bars.

STEP-BY-STEP 5.5

1. To open a window, click the **Start** button on your taskbar. Point to **Programs**, point to **Accessories**, and then left-click **Notepad**. You will see an application window on your desktop.

2. Practice moving the window around your desktop.

3. Practice resizing the window.

4. Practice minimizing and maximizing the window.

5. Open a second application window. Click the **Start** button on your taskbar. Point to **Programs**, point to **Accessories**, and left-click **Paint**. You should now have two application windows open on your desktop.

6. Practice moving between the different windows by clicking their title bars. Minimize and maximize the windows. Notice how the applications appear on your taskbar when minimized.

7. Double-click the **My Computer** icon on your desktop. Practice resizing and moving the window.

8. Practice scrolling up and down your window and then from side to side. Move the icons around in the window by left-clicking on them once and dragging the icon with the mouse. If you don't have scroll bars, resize the window down until they appear.

9. Left-click the **View** menu below the title bar. Change your icon view by left-clicking, in turn, **Large Icons**, **Small Icons**, and **List** choices. As you click each view, notice the changes that occur in the window.

10. Close your windows by left-clicking the **X** button on the title bar of each window. Leave Windows open for the next Step-by-Step.

Changing the Name of an Icon

To change the name of an icon, right-click the icon and choose Rename from the submenu. This will allow you to key a new name for the icon.

Using Help

Windows 2000 Help provides on-screen information about the program you are using. To access Help, click the Start button, then left-click Help. The Help Topics screen will appear. This screen has four tabs from which to choose: Contents, Index, Search, and Favorites. See Figure 5-18.

FIGURE 5-18
Windows 2000 Help

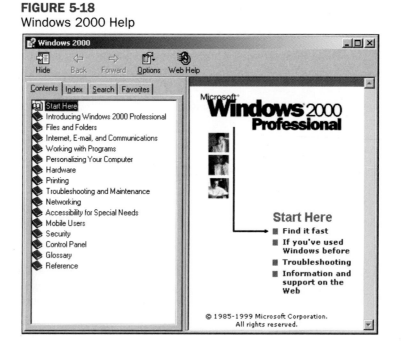

Contents

From the Contents tab, you can click the topic that you want to view. When you click a topic, subtopics appear. Clicking on a subtopic will display the Help information in the right windowpane. You can use the scroll bar to move up and down through the information.

To print a help topic, click Options on the menu bar and click Print.

Help Index and Search Features

From the Search tab, you can key a word related to the topic or information for which you are looking. Figure 5-19 shows a search for the word "save."

FIGURE 5-19
Help Search tab

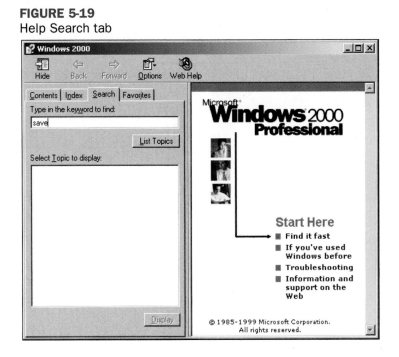

When you click the List Topics button, the related Help topics appear in the Topics window. Double-click the topic you want to read more about; Help will display the related text in the right windowpane. Note that you might see blue hyperlinks in the related text. Single-clicking these hyperlinks will provide you with more information about that particular word or phrase. You can use the scroll bars here as well to move up and down through the text.

The Index tab is shown in Figure 5-20.

FIGURE 5-20
Help Index tab

In the textbox on the Index tab, key the first letter of the topic for which you are looking. Help will jump to topics starting with that letter. You can then continue to key what you are looking for or scroll in that section to find the topic that you need. Click the topic that you want and then click the Display button. The related text will appear in the right-hand pane.

S TEP-BY-STEP 5.6

1. Click the **Start** button and left-click **Help**.

2. On the **Contents** tab, click the **Files and Folders** book icon. A list of topics will appear.

3. Click the **Save a file** topic. Information about saving a file will appear in the right-hand pane.

4. Click the **Index** tab.

5. Key **save**. Double-click the topic **saving information from the Web**. The information will appear in the right-hand pane.

6. Click any of the blue hyperlinks in the right-hand pane to display more information about the topic.

7. Click the **Options** button and left-click **Print** in the menu. Click **Print** in the Print dialog box to print the information about saving information from the Web.

8. Click the **Favorites** tab.

9. Click the **Add** button to add this to your list of favorite help topics.

10. Click the **Close** button to close the Help window. Leave Windows running for the next Step-by-Step.

File Management

My Computer

The My Computer icon represents your computer with its drives, printers, and other objects. The My Computer icon opens the My Computer window as shown in Figure 5-21, which contains an icon for all of your disk drives (hard drive, floppy drive, CD-ROM drive, and possibly others) and a special folder (called Control Panel) to control your printers and customize the operating system. You have already worked with the Control Panel to adjust your mouse settings. You will learn more about the other uses of the Control Panel later in this lesson.

FIGURE 5-21
My Computer

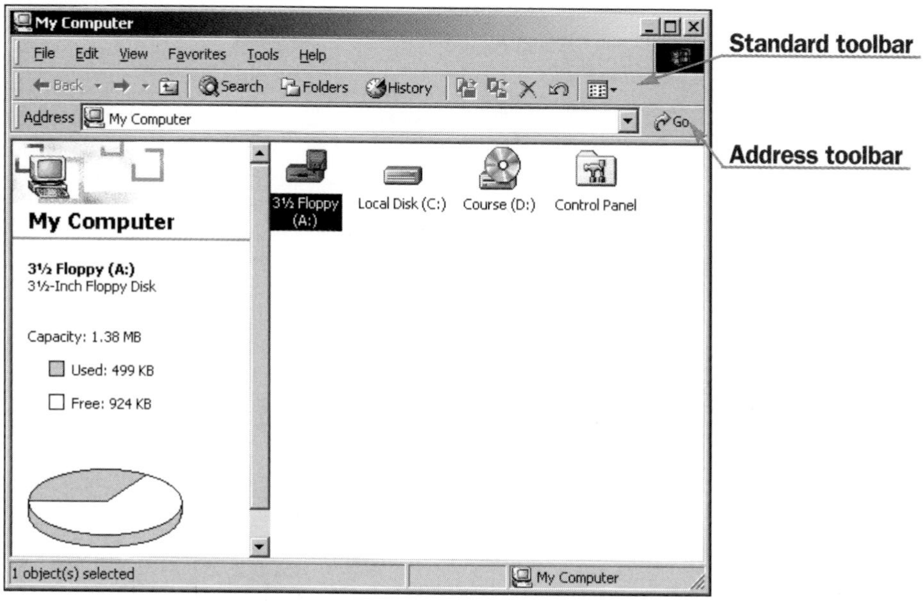

Your disk drives all have a letter associated with them. The floppy drive is generally designated as A:, the hard drive is generally designated as C:, and the CD-ROM drive as D:. Any other drives you have installed on your computer will have a letter designation.

Your computer can contain hundreds of thousands of files. My Computer provides an access point to move, copy, delete, and rename files as well as to create folders to help organize the files.

Customizing the My Computer Window

You can configure how your My Computer window looks in several ways. One of the first things you can do is control what toolbars display in the My Computer window. Toolbars contain shortcuts to commonly performed commands in a window. The My Computer window gives you four toolbars to display: Standard, Address, Links, and Radio. See Figure 5-22.

FIGURE 5-22
Toolbars in My Computer

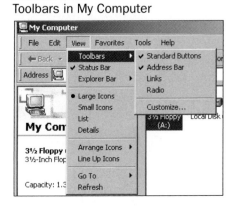

- The Standard toolbar contains buttons for commonly performed tasks in the My Computer window.

- The Address toolbar allows you to select an area in the My Computer window to open (such as the A: or C: drive) as well as to quickly access the Web.

- The Links toolbar contains favorite addresses on the Internet. It also allows another point from which you can access the Web quickly.

- The Radio toolbar is only available when your Windows Media Player is installed on your computer. This allows you to listen to the radio while working on your computer.

TEP-BY-STEP 5.7

1. Open the **My Computer** window by double-clicking its icon on the desktop.

2. Click **View**, point to **Toolbars**, and then look at the Toolbars submenu. The Standard toolbar and Address toolbar should have check marks next to them.

3. If the Standard and Address bars are not checked, click them to select them. You will have to repeat step 2 if both toolbars need to be opened.

4. If the Links or Radio toolbars are checked, repeat step 2 and click to deselect (close) them. Leave the My Computer window open for the next Step-by-Step.

Changing the Display

There are four different ways to display your icons—Large Icons, Small Icons, List, and Details. See Figure 5-23.

FIGURE 5-23
View options in My Computer

- The Large Icons view displays a large icon and the name of each file that the icon represents.

- The Small Icons view displays a small icon and the name of each file that the icon represents. It takes up less screen space than the Large Icons view.

- The List view also displays a small icon and the name of each file that the icon represents. It takes up less screen space than the Large Icons view.

- The Details view displays more detailed information about every icon. It includes not only a small icon and the name, but also the size of the file, the type of file it is, and the date it was last modified.

S TEP-BY-STEP 5.8

1. If necessary, open the **My Computer** window by double-clicking its icon on the desktop.

2. Double-click drive **C:**.

3. Click **View** and then click **Details**.

4. Repeat step 3 to view **Large Icons**, **Small Icons**, and **List**. Return to the **Details** view when finished. Leave the My Computer window open for the next Step-by-Step.

You may also sort the folders and files in the My Computer window by Name, Type, Size, and Date. See Figure 5-24.

FIGURE 5-24
File and Folder arrangement options in My Computer

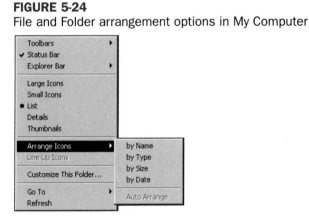

- The Name option arranges the files in order alphabetically.

- The Type option arranges the files by file type, alphabetically.

- The Size option arranges the files in order from smallest to largest.

- The Date option arranges the files in order from most recent to oldest file created or modified.

STEP-BY-STEP 5.9

1. If necessary, open the **My Computer** window by double-clicking its icon on the desktop.

2. Double-click drive **C:**.

3. Click **View**, point to **Arrange Icons**, and click **by Name**.

4. Repeat step 3 to arrange the files **by Type**, **by Size** and **by Date**. Return to the **by Name** arrangement when finished. Leave the My Computer window open for the next Step-by-Step.

Formatting a Disk

Before you can save files on a floppy disk, you must *format* the disk. Formatting arranges the magnetic particles on a disk so that data can be stored on it.

Most of the disks that you purchase today are pre-formatted (ready to store data), but if you buy one that isn't formatted or want to erase everything off of an old disk it is important to know how to format a disk.

Warning

Only format a floppy disk. Do not format the C: drive because it will erase everything and render your computer useless.

S TEP-BY-STEP 5.10

1. Insert a disk that does not contain important information into the floppy drive. It goes in label side up with the metal end going in first.

2. Double-click the **My Computer** icon on your desktop.

3. Right-click the **3½ Floppy (A:)** icon. Click **Format** from the shortcut menu. See Figure 5-25.

FIGURE 5-25
Format command

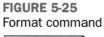

4. Your dialog box should look like Figure 5-26.

FIGURE 5-26
Format dialog box

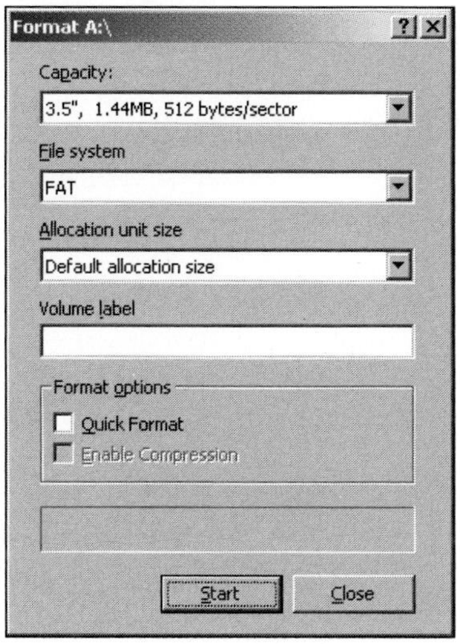

5. Click the **Start** button to begin formatting the disk.

6. Click **OK** to confirm that you want to format the disk.

7. Click **OK** when the format is complete.

8. Click the **Close** button to close the Format dialog box. Leave the floppy disk in the drive and the My Computer window open for the next Step-by-Step.

Folders

Since there are so many files on your hard drive, it is necessary to organize them. Folders are just a storage space for files, used for organizational purposes. Think of a folder in a file cabinet used to organize paper files. Folders on your disk do the same thing. Sometimes, though, a folder has so many files in it that it is necessary to organize it further using subfolders. The main folder that contains subfolders is referred to as a parent folder. All of these objects are represented in a hierarchical fashion that begins with the desktop and works its way down.

STEP-BY-STEP 5.11

1. If necessary, insert a floppy disk into drive **A:**.

2. If necessary, open the **My Computer** window by double-clicking its icon on the desktop.

3. Double-click drive **A:**.

4. Click **File** and point to **New**. See Figure 5-27. Click **Folder** from the submenu. A folder will appear with the label *New Folder*.

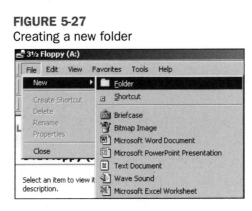

FIGURE 5-27
Creating a new folder

5. Key **Student** as the name of the folder. Press **Enter**.

6. Double-click the **Student** folder to view its contents.

7. Click **File** and point to **New**. Click **Folder** from the submenu. A folder will appear with the label *New Folder*.

8. Key **Your First Name** as the name of the folder. Press **Enter**.

9. Double-click the **Your First Name** folder to view its contents.

10. Click **File** and point to **New**. Click **Folder** from the submenu. A folder will appear with the label *New Folder*.

11. Key **Your Last Name** as the name of the folder. Press **Enter**. Leave the floppy disk in drive A: and the My Computer window open for the next Step-by-Step.

Moving Folders around in the My Computer Window

The Standard toolbar, shown in Figure 5-28, contains buttons that allow you to navigate through your folders in My Computer.

FIGURE 5-28
Standard toolbar

Table 5-4 describes the first three, and most commonly used, buttons on the Standard toolbar.

TABLE 5-4
Commonly used buttons on the My Computer Standard toolbar

BUTTON	DESCRIPTION
Back	Takes you back to the folder or drive that you were viewing last.
Forward	Takes you forward to the folder or drive that you were viewing previously.
Up	Takes you up one level in the hierarchy.

STEP-BY-STEP 5.12

1. If necessary, insert a floppy disk into the A: drive.

2. If necessary, open the **My Computer** window by double-clicking its icon on the desktop.

3. Double-click drive **A:**.

4. Double-click the **Student** folder.

5. Press the **Back** button once on the Standard toolbar to return to drive A:.

6. Press the **Forward** button once on the Standard toolbar to return to your Student folder.

7. Double-click the **Your First Name** folder.

8. Press the **Up** button once to return to your Student folder.

9. Press the **Up** button again to return to drive A:.

10. Press the **Up** button again to return to My Computer. Leave the floppy disk in drive A: and the My Computer window open for the next Step-by-Step.

Files

Right now, there are no files in your Student folder. A *file* is just a named collection of data that is stored in a specific location. In the next several Step-by-Steps you will create, move, copy, rename, and delete files from your folder.

S TEP-BY-STEP 5.13

1. Double-click drive **A:**.

2. Double-click the **Student** folder.

3. Click **File**, point to **New**, and click **Text Document** on the submenu as shown in Figure 5-29. A new file will appear with the name *New Text Document*.

FIGURE 5-29
Creating a file

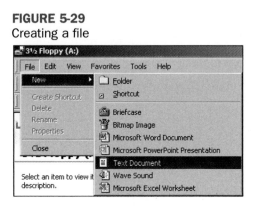

4. Key **Lab Five** as the name of the new file. Press **Enter**. Leave the floppy disk in drive A: and the My Computer window open for the next Step-by-Step.

Moving and Copying Files

If you want to place a file into another location, you may either move or copy it. Moving a file takes it from its original location and places it into a new one. Copying a file maintains the file in its original location and duplicates it in a new location.

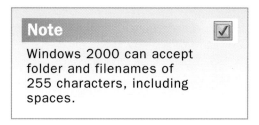

Note

Windows 2000 can accept folder and filenames of 255 characters, including spaces.

One of the ways we move and copy files is through the commands Cut, Copy, and Paste. These commands can be found under the Edit menu, or by right-clicking on an item and using keyboard shortcuts as shown in Figure 5-30.

FIGURE 5-30
A shortcut menu

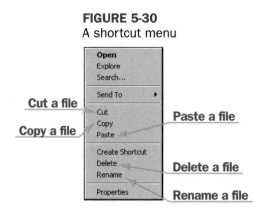

The commands Cut and Copy place the file in a temporary location in memory called the Clipboard. An item will stay on the Clipboard as long as the computer is on and until you cut or copy something else. The Windows Clipboard can only hold one item at a time. The Paste command copies the item from the Clipboard and pastes it into its new location.

- The Cut (Ctrl+X) command moves a file.

- The Copy (Ctrl+C) command duplicates a file.

- The Paste (Ctrl+V) command places a cut or copied file in its new location.

STEP-BY-STEP 5.14

1. Double-click drive **A:**.

2. Double-click the **Student** folder.

3. Right-click the **Lab Five** file and select **Copy** from the shortcut menu.

4. Right-click the **Your First Name** folder and select **Paste** from the shortcut menu.

5. Double-click the **Your First Name** folder. You should now see a duplicate of the *Lab Five* file placed in this folder.

6. Right-click the **Lab Five** file and select **Cut** from the shortcut menu.

7. Right-click the **Your Last Name** folder and select **Paste** from the shortcut menu. The *Lab Five* file should now be gone from the Your First Name folder.

8. Double-click the **Your Last Name** folder. The *Lab Five* file should be in there now.

9. Right-click the **Lab Five** file and select **Copy** from the shortcut menu.

10. Click the **Back** button until you get back to the My Computer window.

11. Double-click drive **C:**.

12. Right-click an empty area and select **Paste** from the shortcut menu. You should see the *Lab Five* file there now. Leave the My Computer window open for the next Step-by-Step.

Renaming a File

If you want to change the name of a file, you can easily do this by using the Rename command. The command can be found under the File menu or when you right-click a file and access the shortcut menu.

STEP-BY-STEP 5.15

1. Double-click drive **A:**.

2. Double-click the **Student** folder.

3. Right-click the **Lab Five** file and select **Rename** from the shortcut menu.

4. Key in the name **Lab Five A** and press **Enter**.

5. Double-click the **Your First Name** folder.

6. Double-click the **Your Last Name** folder.

7. Right-click the **Lab Five** file and select **Rename** from the shortcut menu.

8. Key in the name **Lab Five B** and press **Enter**. Leave My Computer open for the next Step-by-Step.

Deleting Files

It is good practice to free up space on your storage devices by deleting the files that you no longer need. When you delete a folder you also delete all of its contents, so be careful that you no longer need anything in that folder. Thankfully, there is an area on your desktop called the Recycle Bin. The Recycle Bin is an area on the hard drive that holds files and folders deleted from your local hard drive(s): until you are absolutely sure you want to remove them. Be careful, though, because the Recycle Bin only stores files deleted from the local hard drive(s). When you delete from any other drive (for example the floppy drive or a network drive) the files are removed from the drive permanently.

You have several options for deleting files and folders:

■ Select the file or folder by single-clicking it and pressing the Delete key on your keyboard.

■ Right-click the file or folder and select Delete from the shortcut menu.

■ Select the file or folder and click the Delete icon on your toolbar.

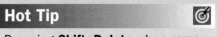

Hot Tip

Pressing **Shift+Delete** when removing something from the C: drive will automatically skip the Recycle Bin and remove the item permanently. Only use this key combination when you are absolutely sure you want to remove the file or folder and will have no possible need to recover the file in the future.

STEP-BY-STEP 5.16

1. Double-click drive **A:**.

2. Double-click the **Student** folder.

3. Right-click the **Lab Five A** file and select **Delete** from the shortcut menu.

4. When Windows asks you if you are sure you want to delete this file click **Yes**.

STEP-BY-STEP 5.16 Continued

5. Hit the **Back** button until you are at the My Computer window.

6. Double-click drive **C:**.

7. Select the **Lab Five** file by left-clicking it once.

8. Press **Delete** on your keyboard. When Windows asks you if you are sure you want to move the *Lab Five* file to the Recycle Bin click **Yes**.

9. Minimize the My Computer window.

10. Double-click the **Recycle Bin** on your desktop.

11. To restore the *Lab Five* file back to drive C:, right-click it and select **Restore** from the shortcut menu as shown in Figure 5-31. Minimize the Recycle Bin window.

FIGURE 5-31
Restore command

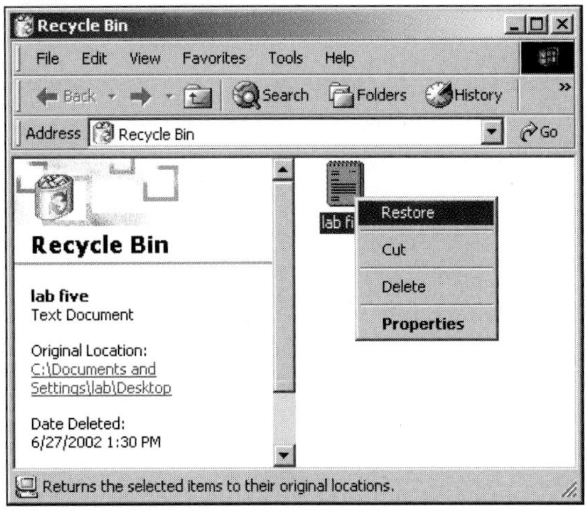

12. Restore the My Computer window and view the contents of drive C:.

13. Right-click the restored **Lab Five** file and click **Delete** from the shortcut menu. Click **Yes** to confirm the deletion.

14. Close the My Computer window by clicking the **X** in the right-hand corner.

15. Restore the Recycle Bin window.

STEP-BY-STEP 5.16 Continued

16. Click **File** and click **Empty Recycle Bin** as shown in Figure 5-32. Click **Yes** to confirm.

FIGURE 5-32
Empty Recycle Bin

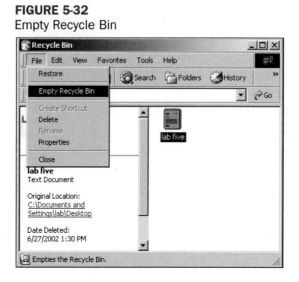

17. Close the Recycle Bin window by clicking the **X** in the right-hand corner. Leave Windows running for the next Step-by-Step.

Copying a Floppy Disk

It is a good idea to make backup copies of all files that you create. If the files are on a floppy disk, you can copy and paste them to another location to back them up or use the copy disk command to copy the contents of one floppy disk to another.

STEP-BY-STEP 5.17

1. Double-click the **My Computer** icon on your desktop. Make sure that you have a disk containing content you want to copy in the floppy disk drive.

2. Right-click drive **A:** and click **Copy Disk**.

3. In the Copy Disk dialog box shown in Figure 5-33, click the **Start** button and then click **OK** to begin the copying process.

FIGURE 5-33
Copy Disk dialog box

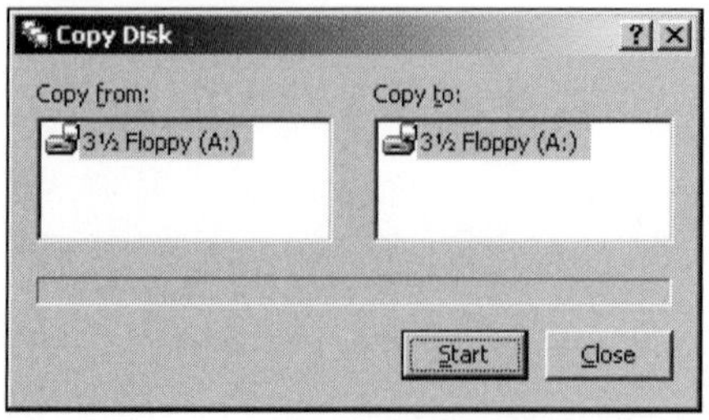

STEP-BY-STEP 5.17 Continued

4. When prompted insert the floppy disk to which you want to copy the contents. Click the **OK** button.

5. When the copy has completed successfully click the **Close** button.

6. Close the **My Computer** window.

7. Remove your disk from the floppy drive. Leave Windows running for the next Step-by-Step.

Finding Files

Sometimes it is necessary to search for an existing file. In Windows, you can search for files by the filename, the date, the type of file, or by the file size.

STEP-BY-STEP 5.18

1. Click the **Start** button, point to **Search**, and click **For Files or Folders**. The Search Results dialog box appears as shown in Figure 5-34.

FIGURE 5-34
Search Results dialog box

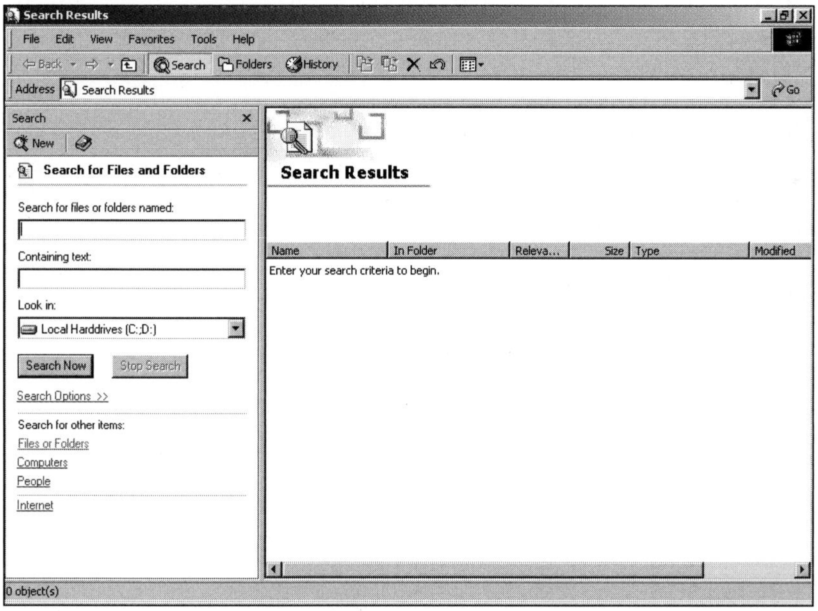

2. To search for a file that contains the text string *word* in the name, key **word** in the *Search for files or folders named* text box.

STEP-BY-STEP 5.18 Continued

3. Click **Look In** and select **Local Hardrives (C:)**.

4. Click the **Search Now** button. Any matching files are displayed in the Search Results pane.

5. Click the **New** button to start a new search.

6. Click the **Search Options** link and check **Date**.

7. Click the **between** option button and select 1/1/2001 from the calendar as the start date and select 12/25/2002 from the calendar as the end date.

8. Click the **Search Now** button. Any matching files will appear in the Search Results pane.

9. Click the **New** button again to start a new search.

10. If necessary, click the **Search Options** link and check **Type**.

11. Click the arrow next to **Type** and scroll down to find Text Document. Click **Text Document**.

12. Click the **Search Now** button. Any matching files will appear in the Search Results pane.

13. Click the **New** button again to start a new search.

14. If necessary, click the **Search Options** link and check **Size**.

15. Enter **125** in the KB box.

16. Click the **Search Now** button. Any matching files will appear in the Search Results pane.

17. Close the Search dialog box by clicking the **X** in the right-hand corner. Leave Windows open for the next Step-by-Step.

Word Processing

Windows 2000 comes with a small word processing program called WordPad, which is shown in Figure 5-35.

FIGURE 5-35
WordPad

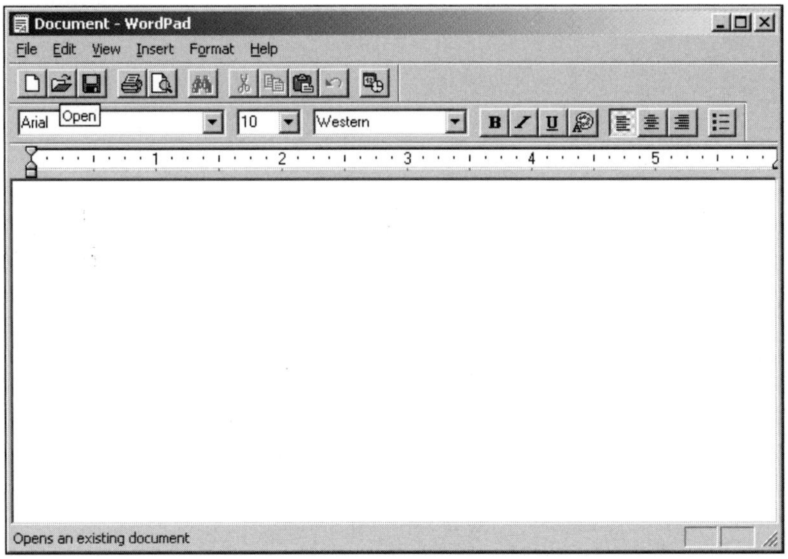

This program will allow you to do basic word processing tasks such as keying and formatting text, saving a file, and printing.

The WordPad program, like all word processing programs, has a feature called word wrap. Word wrap automatically continues your text to the next line when you are keying. Therefore, you only press Enter when you want a line to end manually. Otherwise you let the text word wrap so it will flow with the margins when you insert and delete text.

Inserting and removing text in WordPad is a simple process. In the window, you will see a blinking line called the insertion point. This line indicates where your text is going to appear when you begin to key. The insertion point will move as you key and your text will appear to the left of it. If you accidentally key something wrong, you can remove it by either using the Backspace or Delete keys on your keyboard. The Backspace key removes text to the left of the insertion point. The Delete key removes text to the right of the insertion point.

S TEP-BY-STEP 5.19

1. Click the **Start** button, point to **Programs**, point to **Accessories**, and click **WordPad**.

2. Key your first and last name. Press **Enter**.

3. Key your class name. Press **Enter**.

4. Key today's date. Press **Enter**.

STEP-BY-STEP 5.19 Continued

5. Press **Enter** again to insert a blank line after the date and key the following text:
Vendors have refined the latest generation of antivirus software to catch viruses before they do serious damage. The products are easier to use, have better detection rates, and are cheaper than earlier virus scanners. Therefore, you have no excuse for failing to install a good virus scanner on your system.

Leave WordPad open for the next Step-by-Step.

Keying and Inserting Text

The default operating mode for WordPad is called insert mode. When you key in a document, all characters to the right of the insertion point are pushed over to make room for the new characters.

Sometimes, however, you may want to enter text in another location. To do this you will have to move the insertion point manually. You can move the insertion point either by using the arrow keys or by clicking the mouse in the text where you want it to appear.

Many formatting options are performed on an entire block of text. Select blocks of text by clicking and dragging the mouse over the text or by holding down the Shift key and using the arrows on the keyboard.

STEP-BY-STEP 5.20

1. Press the **Up**, **Down**, **Left**, and **Right** keys on your keyboard to practice moving your insertion point around the document.

2. Use your mouse to click your insertion point around the document.

3. Move the insertion point to the left of the word *Therefore* in the last sentence.

4. Hold down the left mouse button and drag over the entire sentence.

5. Release the mouse button.

6. To deselect the text, click anywhere else in the document.

7. Move the insertion point to the left of your last name.

8. Key your middle name and press the spacebar.

9. Move the insertion point to the right of your middle name. Press the **Backspace** key until your middle name is removed. Press the **Delete** key until your last name is removed. Leave WordPad open for the next Step-by-Step.

Saving a File

When you are keying text, it is held only temporarily in the computer's memory. If your computer lost power or froze up the text would be gone. Therefore, it is very important to constantly save your work to prevent losing it accidentally.

Hot Tip

The Save As dialog box will open when you click Save or Save As on a file that has not been saved yet. This dialog box has you answer questions so WordPad can properly save the file for you. Once you have saved a file, the Save command will update its contents or the Save As command will allow you to specify a new location for the file or a different filename.

S TEP-BY-STEP 5.21

1. Click the **File** menu and click **Save** as shown in Figure 5-36. The Save As dialog box will open.

FIGURE 5-36
Save command

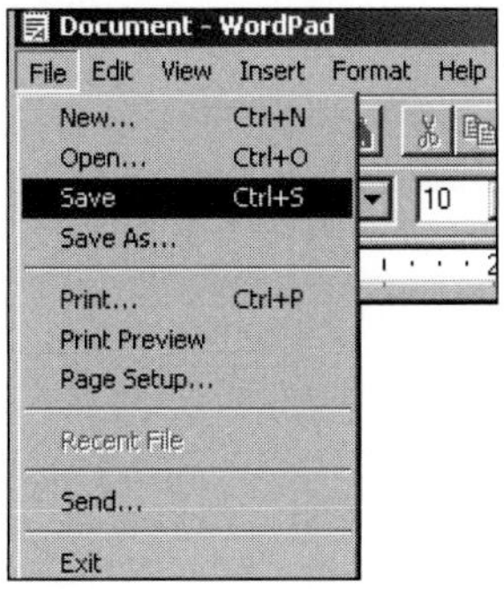

2. If necessary, click the **My Documents** folder on the **Save in** bar to specify where you want to save this file. See Figure 5-37.

FIGURE 5-37
Save As dialog box

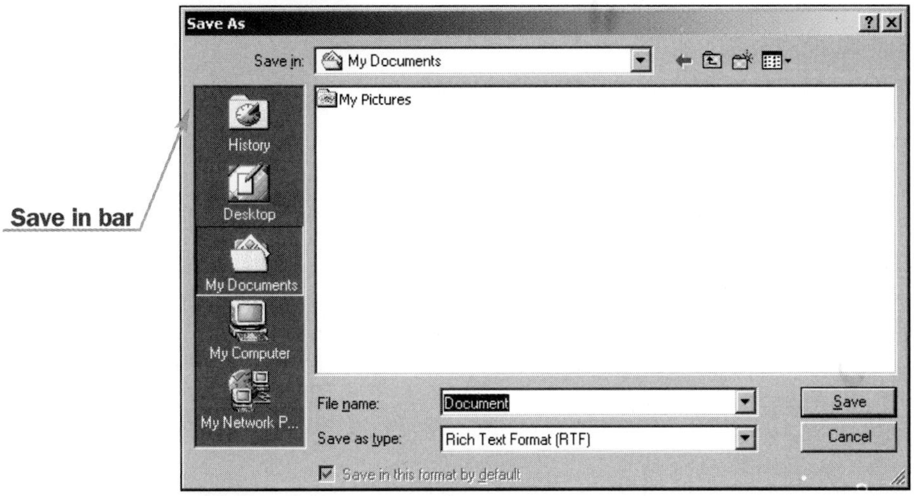

STEP-BY-STEP 5.21 Continued

3. In the File name text box, key **Practice Word Processing**.

4. Click the **Save** button. Your file is saved in the My Documents folder with the name *Practice Word Processing*. Leave WordPad open for the next Step-by-Step.

Printing a File

You can select from three ways to print your file. You can send the file directly to the printer, use the Print Preview button to first preview the file and then click Print, or open the Print dialog box to change your default printer settings. You can only complete these steps if a printer is installed. Consult your instructor about doing this if necessary.

STEP-BY-STEP 5.22

1. Click the **Print Preview** button on the toolbar. A preview of your page will appear as shown in Figure 5-38.

FIGURE 5-38
Print Preview

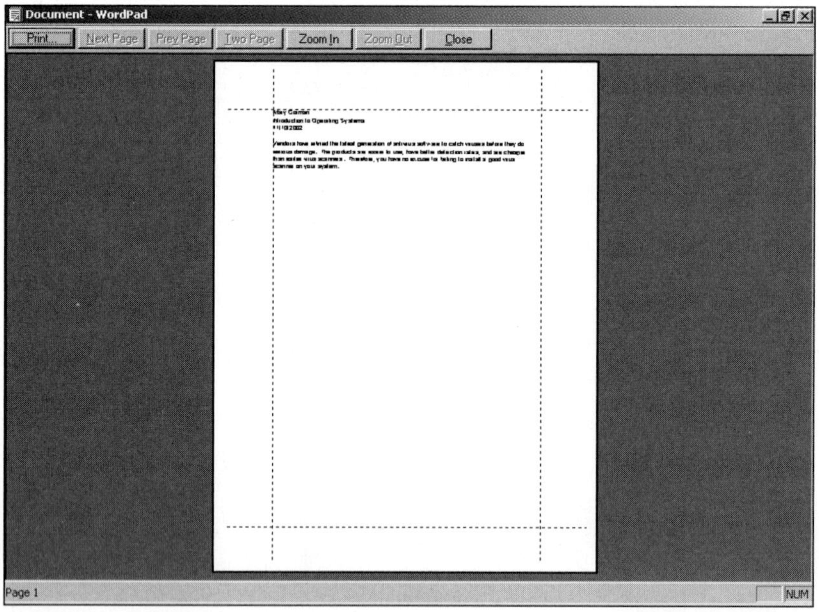

2. Click **Close** in Print Preview to return to the normal document window.

STEP-BY-STEP 5.22 Continued

3. Click the **File** menu and click **Print**. The Print dialog box will open as shown in Figure 5-39.

FIGURE 5-39
Print dialog box

4. Click the **Cancel** button to exit the Print dialog box without printing the document.

5. Click the **Print** button on the standard toolbar.

6. Close the document and WordPad by clicking the **X** in the right-hand corner. Leave Windows running for the next Step-by-Step.

Opening a File

You can open your file in two ways. You can either open the file from the folder it is in—which will automatically open WordPad—or from within WordPad.

STEP-BY-STEP 5.23

1. Double-click the **My Documents** icon on your desktop.

2. Double-click the **Practice Word Processing** file to open it.

3. Close WordPad and the document by clicking the **X** in the upper right-hand corner.

4. Start WordPad again by clicking **Start**, pointing to **Programs**, **Accessories**, and clicking **WordPad**.

5. Click **File** and click **Open**.

6. On the **Places** bar click **My Documents**.

STEP-BY-STEP 5.23 Continued

7. Double-click the **Practice Word Processing** file to open it.

8. Close WordPad and the document by clicking the **X** in the upper right-hand corner. Leave Windows running for the next Step-by-Step.

Unique Features of Windows 2000

Creating Shortcuts on the Desktop

Creating *shortcuts* is a very useful function of Windows 2000. Shortcuts help save time and productivity by making your most commonly used programs and documents easily accessible from your desktop. A shortcut is simply a quick way to open a file or program without having to go to its original location. Shortcuts look like the original icons that they represent except they have small arrows at the bottom indicating they are shortcuts.

There are several different ways to create a shortcut on the desktop. Among them are:

■ Use the My Computer window to locate a file icon. Right-click the icon and select Copy from the shortcut menu. Move to the desktop, right-click an empty area, and select Paste Shortcut from the menu.

■ Use the My Computer window to locate a file icon. Right-click and drag the icon to the desktop. Choose Create Shortcut(s) Here when you release the mouse button.

STEP-BY-STEP 5.24

1. Double-click the **My Computer** icon on your desktop.

2. Right-click drive **A:**. Hold the right-click and drag the icon to your desktop in the background.

STEP-BY-STEP 5.24 Continued

3. Release the mouse button and select **Create Shortcut(s) Here** from the menu as shown in Figure 5-40. Leave My Computer open for the next Step-by-Step.

FIGURE 5-40
Create Shortcut(s) Here

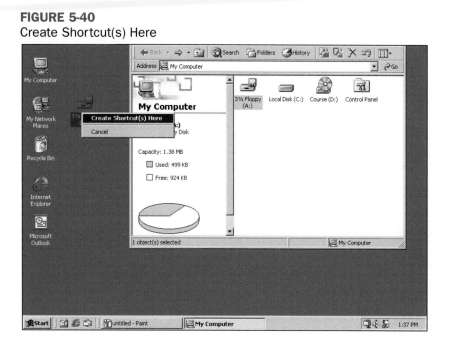

Customizing the Start Menu

You can also customize the shortcuts in your Start menu. To place a shortcut in your Start menu, just drag the icon from the My Computer window and drop it on the Start button. To place a shortcut in one of the menus of your Start button, just drag it to the Start button and then drag and drop it on the menu where you want it to appear.

STEP-BY-STEP 5.25

1. In the My Computer window, click drive **A:**. Hold the click and drag the icon to your **Start** button. Release the mouse button on your **Programs** submenu. Click **Yes** in the shortcut dialog box that appears. See Figure 5-41.

FIGURE 5-41
Creating a shortcut on the Programs menu

STEP-BY-STEP 5.25 Continued

2. To remove the new shortcut from your Programs menu, right-click the shortcut and choose **Delete**. See Figure 5-42. Click **Yes** to confirm the deletion. Leave Windows running for the next Step-by-Step.

FIGURE 5-42
Deleting a shortcut

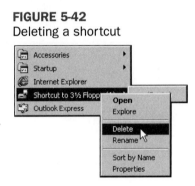

Using the Control Panel

As mentioned earlier in this Lesson, Windows has an area that allows you to configure the operating system exactly how you would like it to work. This area is called the Control Panel. Figure 5-43 shows the contents of the Control Panel.

FIGURE 5-43
Control Panel

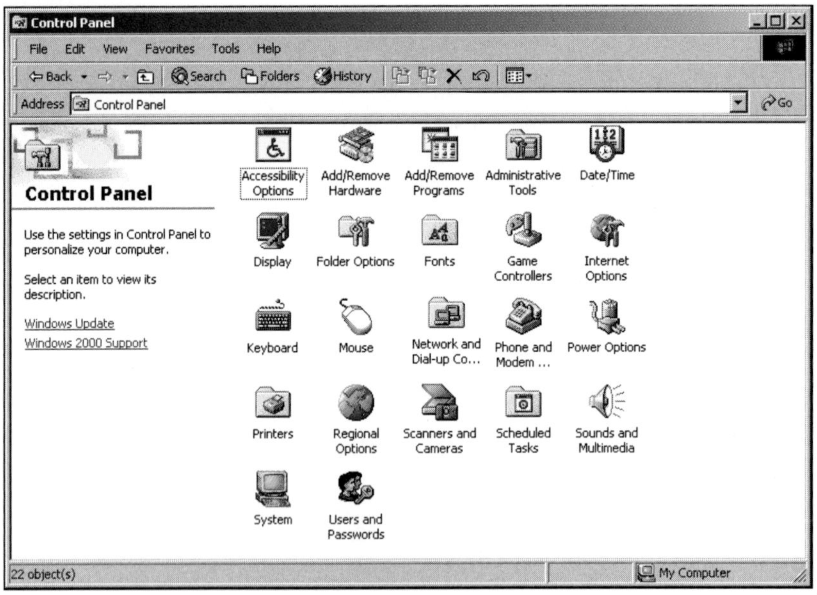

Table 5-5 is a list of the most commonly used icons in the Control Panel and their uses.

TABLE 5-5
Commonly used Control Panel icons

NAME	DESCRIPTION
Add/Remove Hardware	Used for adding and removing hardware on the system.
Add/Remove Programs	Used to properly install and uninstall software programs on the system.
Date/Time	Used to adjust the current date and time as well as the time zone in which you are living.
Display	Used to control properties of the display, such as wallpaper, the background, screen savers, etc.
Folder Options	Used to customize how you interact with files and folders on the system.
Keyboard	Used to control the workings of the keyboard.
Mouse	Used to control the workings of the mouse.
Printers	Used to add a new printer as well as control the workings of any installed printers.
Sounds and Multimedia	Used to control the sounds made by your computer when certain events occur.

S TEP-BY-STEP 5.26

1. Click the **Start** button, point to **Settings**, and then click **Control Panel**.

2. To select wallpaper for your desktop, double-click the **Display** icon.

3. Make sure you are on the **Background** tab. Click **Ocean Wave** in the Wallpaper list.

STEP-BY-STEP 5.26 Continued

4. If necessary click the **Picture Display** drop-down menu and click **Center** to display many copies of the image on the desktop. Your Display Properties dialog box should look like Figure 5-44.

FIGURE 5-44
Display Properties dialog box

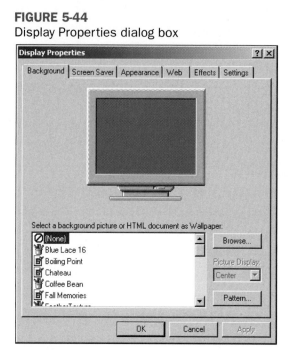

5. Click **Apply** if you like the Ocean Wave wallpaper or select a different picture. Click **Yes** in the Internet Explorer window to enable the Active Desktop.

6. Click **OK**.

7. Close the Control Panel window. Leave Windows running for the next Step-by-Step.

System Maintenance

Windows has built-in tools to help you maintain and improve your system's performance. Your computer, like everything else, needs to be tuned up every once in a while to keep it running smoothly.

The most commonly used tools for maintaining your system are Disk Cleanup, Check Disk, and Disk Defragmenter.

Disk Cleanup

When you are doing work in Windows 2000, unnecessary files accumulate on your hard drive. This slows down the system. The *Disk Cleanup* utility, shown in Figure 5-45, helps you remove unnecessary files safely from your machine.

FIGURE 5-45
Disk Cleanup

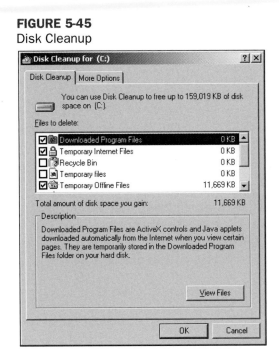

Table 5-6 contains the types of files Disk Cleanup may find on your machine that need to be removed.

TABLE 5-6
Disk Cleanup problem files

TYPE	DESCRIPTION
Downloaded Program Files	Program files downloaded automatically from the Internet on certain Web pages.
Old Scandisk files	Files created by the Scandisk utility when it finds bad data.
Recycle Bin	Files deleted from the hard disk.
Temporary Files	Files generated by programs to be used temporarily.
Temporary Internet Files	These files are stored on your hard disk so you can quickly view these Web pages later on.
Temporary Setup Files	Files created when you install a program.
Windows 2000 Uninstall Information	Files from a previous version of Windows.

STEP-BY-STEP 5.27

1. Close all open programs, if necessary.

2. Click **Start**, point to **Programs**, point to **Accessories**, point to **System Tools**, and then click **Disk Cleanup**.

3. Click the **Drives** arrow and click **C:** if necessary. Click **OK**.

4. Check the boxes next to the files you want to delete.

5. Click **OK** and then click **Yes** to confirm you want to delete those files. Leave Windows running for the next Step-by-Step.

Check Disk

Sections of the disk surface may be damaged over time. Scanning the hard disk regularly for potential problems is a good way to avoid storing important data in a damaged area of the hard disk. The Windows 2000 *Check Disk* utility will locate problem areas of the hard disk, attempt to repair them, and, if not repairable, mark them as bad so that no data will be stored there in the future.

STEP-BY-STEP 5.28

1. Close all open programs, if necessary.

2. Open the **My Computer** window and right-click the **C:** icon.

3. Click **Properties** on the menu.

4. Click the **Tools** tab as shown in Figure 5-46.

FIGURE 5-46
Check Disk

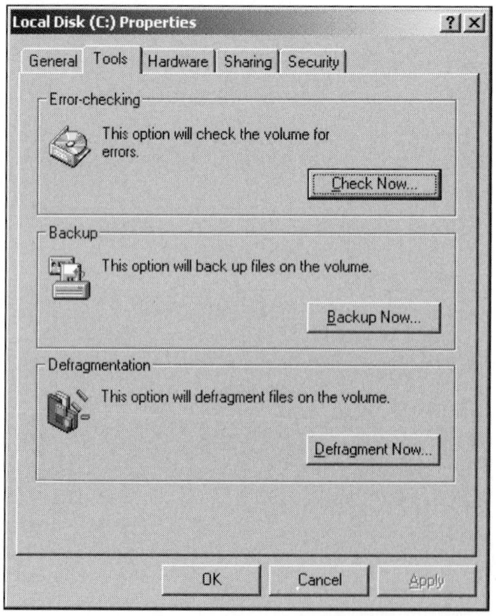

STEP-BY-STEP 5.28 Continued

5. Click the **Check Now** button.

6. Check the *Scan for and attempt recovery of bad sectors* check box as shown in Figure 5-47.

FIGURE 5-47
Scan for and attempt recovery of bad sectors check box

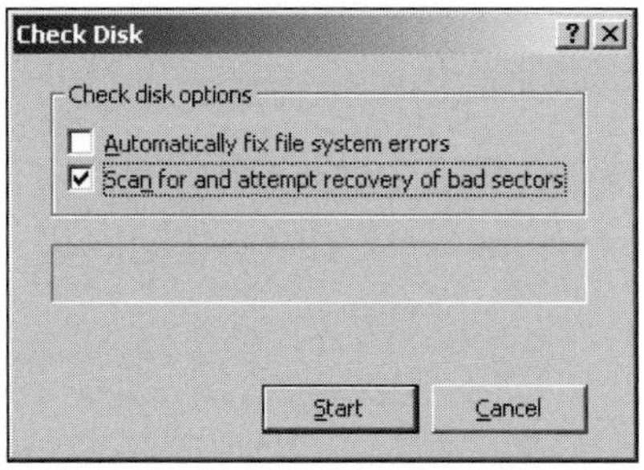

7. Click the **Start** button to run the Check Disk program. When complete, click the **OK** button twice to close the dialog boxes. Leave Windows running for the next Step-by-Step.

Disk Defragmenter

Once the surface of the hard disk is checked you can improve the performance of the drive by running the *Disk Defragmenter* utility. This utility will place pieces of files closer together so you can start and open files faster.

STEP-BY-STEP 5.29

1. Close all open programs if necessary.

2. Click **Start**, point to **Programs**, point to **Accessories**, point to **System Tools**, and then click **Disk Defragmenter**.

STEP-BY-STEP 5.29 Continued

3. In the Disk Defragmenter dialog box, select drive **C:** as shown in Figure 5-48.

FIGURE 5-48
Disk Defragmenter dialog box

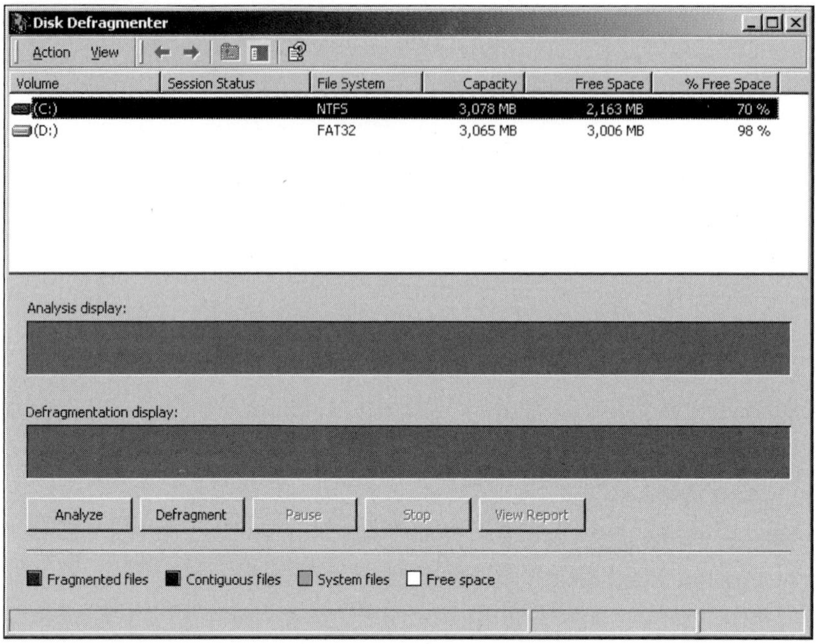

4. Click the **Defragment** button to begin defragmenting the drive.

5. Click **Close** when defragmentation is finished. Close the Defragmenter window.

Scheduling Maintenance

These tasks listed above (Disk Cleanup, Check Disk, and Disk Defragmentation) must be performed regularly for your computer to run efficiently. Thankfully, you can schedule Windows 2000 to automatically run these tasks for you. This is accomplished through the *Task Scheduler* utility.

S TEP-BY-STEP 5.30

1. Close all open programs if necessary.

2. Click **Start**, point to **Programs**, point to **Accessories**, point to **System Tools**, and then click **Scheduled Tasks**. The Scheduled Tasks dialog box appears as shown in Figure 5-49.

FIGURE 5-49
Scheduled Tasks dialog box

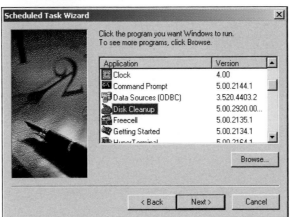

3. Click the **Add Scheduled Task** icon and then press **Enter**.

4. Click the **Next** button.

5. Click **Disk Cleanup** in the list (as shown in Figure 5-50) and then click **Next**.

FIGURE 5-50
Scheduled Task Wizard

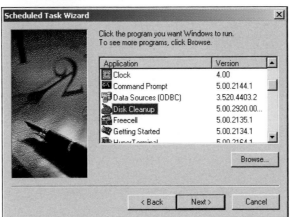

6. Key **Clean Drive** in the task name box.

STEP-BY-STEP 5.30 Continued

7. Click **Weekly**. Your screen should appear like that shown in Figure 5-51. Click **Next**.

FIGURE 5-51
Scheduled Task Wizard

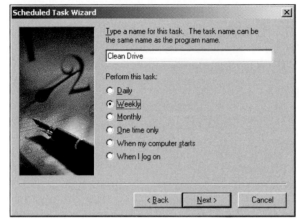

8. Enter **8:00 PM** as the start time.

9. Check the **Friday** check box. Your screen should appear like Figure 5-52.

FIGURE 5-52
Scheduled Task Wizard

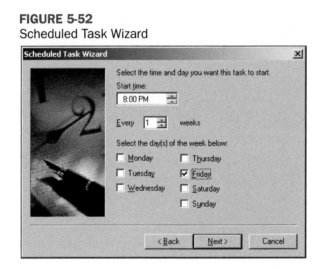

10. Click the **Next** button.

STEP-BY-STEP 5.30 Continued

11. Enter your user name and password if necessary. See Figure 5-53. Click **Next**.

FIGURE 5-53
Scheduled Task Wizard

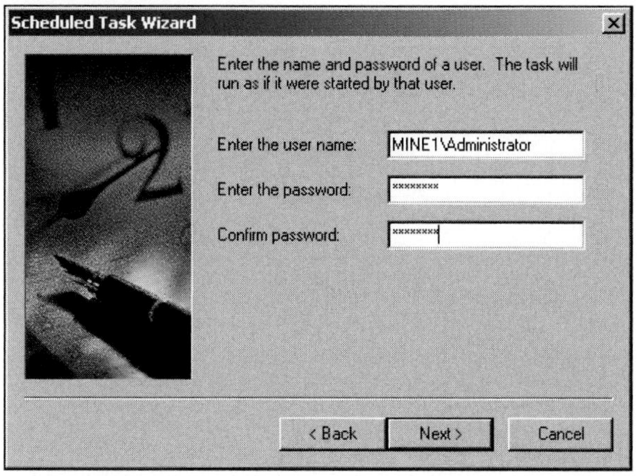

12. Click the **Finish** button. The Disk Cleanup utility will now run automatically at 8:00 p.m. on Fridays or it will run the next time your computer is turned on after that time.

13. Right-click the **Clean Drive** icon in the Scheduled Tasks dialog box. See Figure 5-54.

FIGURE 5-54
Deleting a Scheduled Task

14. Click **Delete** and click **Yes** when asked if you want to delete the task.

15. Close the Scheduled Tasks window. Shut down Windows and your computer.

SUMMARY

In this lesson, you learned:

- Windows 2000 Professional has many improvements over earlier versions of Windows you may have used including ease of use, ease of file management, better security, and increased hardware compatibility.

- When you install Windows 2000 Professional, preparation will help you avoid potential problems during the installation process. One of the most important preinstallation tasks is to verify that all hardware is on the HCL and if it is not listed, to be sure to have the driver disks from the manufacturer so you can manually install the hardware device later.

- The desktop is your main workspace. It contains small pictures called icons, which are used as an easy way to open programs and documents. You will also find application windows, desktop components, and the taskbar.

- Your mouse is the tool you will use to open files, programs, and menus.

- The taskbar displays any programs that you have minimized for quick access between applications. It also has a Start button that is used to quickly find or open a document, start a program, access tools to help you customize and optimize your system, and shut down your computer.

- A window is the area or workspace you see when you open a program or application.

- The My Computer window contains an icon for all of your disk drives (hard drive, floppy drive, CD-ROM drive, and possibly others) and a special folder to control your printers and to access the Control Panel.

- Windows 2000 comes with a small word processing program called WordPad. This program will allow you to do basic word processing tasks like keying and formatting text, saving a file, and printing.

- A shortcut is simply a quick way to open a file or program without having to go to its original location. You can customize the shortcuts in your Start menu or on your desktop.

- Windows has built-in tools to help you maintain and improve your system's performance. The most commonly used tools for maintaining your system are Disk Cleanup, Check Disk, and Disk Defragmenter.

VOCABULARY *Review*

Define the following terms:

Check Disk	File	Shortcut
Disk Cleanup	Format	Task Scheduler
Disk Defragmenter	Scroll bar	Workgroup
Domain		

REVIEW *Questions*

MULTIPLE CHOICE

Select the best response to the following statements.

1. Windows 2000 supports which of the following file systems?
   A. NTFS
   B. FAT32
   C. Both A and B are correct.
   D. None of the above.

2. Which of the following is a good preinstallation step to complete to ensure that your installation of Windows 2000 will avoid potential pitfalls?
   A. Identify the hardware requirements of Windows 2000
   B. Check to see if your hardware is on the HCL
   C. Choose a file system to format the disk with
   D. All of the above.

3. Which of the following is a recommended hardware requirement of Windows 2000?
   A. 32 MB of RAM
   B. 650 MB of hard disk space
   C. Monitor with VGA resolution
   D. QWERTY Keyboard

4. Which of the following hardware devices is used to navigate the desktop?
   A. Printer
   B. Mouse
   C. Keyboard
   D. Modem

5. You can open the Start menu by pressing which key combination?
   A. CTRL+ALT+DEL
   B. ALT+ESC
   C. CTRL+SHIFT
   D. CTRL+ESC

6. Which of the following is a display mode in My Computer?
   A. Large Icons
   B. Information
   C. Empty Screen
   D. Auto Display

7. A _____ folder is the main folder that contains subfolders.
   A. Root
   B. Parent
   C. Top
   D. Main

8. The _____ is an area on the hard drive that holds files and folders deleted from drive C:.
   A. Trash Can
   B. Trash Bin
   C. Recycle Bin
   D. Recycle Can

9. _____ is a feature in WordPad that automatically moves you to the next line when keying.
   A. Word wrap
   B. Word control
   C. Line wrap
   D. Line control

10. Which of the following is a utility to help maintain the performance of your system?
   A. Disk Cleanup
   B. Check Disk
   C. Disk Defragmenter
   D. All of the above.

FILL IN THE BLANK

Complete the following sentences by writing the correct word or words in the blanks provided.

1. A(n) _____ is a peer-to-peer network where all computers act as equals.

2. A(n) _____ is a quick way to open a file without having to go to its original location to do so.

3. The _____ command arranges the magnetic particles on a disk so data can be stored on it.

4. A(n) _____ is a group of computers on a network that are administered with common rules and procedures.

5. A(n) _____ allows you to move the information in a window up, down, right, and left.

PROJECTS

PROJECT 5-1

In this project, you will practice creating documents on the desktop and printing them.

1. Create a shortcut on the desktop to the printer you use in class.

2. Open **WordPad** and create a new document on your desktop called **My Stuff**. Key a list of things you need to do today.

3. Drag the **My Stuff** document icon to the printer icon. It will begin printing.

4. Delete both icons from the desktop.

5. Open **My Computer** and open drive **A:**.

6. Create a new folder on your disk called **Win2000**.

7. Start WordPad and create a document called **MyStuff**. Save it on your **A:** drive in the **Win2000** folder.

8. Right click and drag the **Win2000** folder from the My Computer window and drop it on your desktop to create a shortcut.

9. Rename the new shortcut **Windows 2000 Class**.

10. Test the new shortcut by opening it and opening the document you created earlier.

11. Close the document and delete the shortcut.

SCANS PROJECT 5-2

In this project, you will create files and folders.

1. Open WordPad. Write a one-page letter to a friend. Save the document on your floppy disk and name it **Letter**. Print the letter and sign it.

2. Close the *Letter* document and start a new document.

3. Write your school expenses for the year. Save the document as **Expenses** on your floppy disk. Print the document.

4. Open **My Computer**. Open drive **A:**.

5. Create a folder called **Documents** on your floppy disk.

6. Move the file called **Letter** into the **Documents** folder.

7. Create a folder called **Budget** on your floppy disk.

8. Copy the file called **Expenses** into the **Budget** folder.

9. Delete the **Expenses** file from the floppy disk (not the Budget folder).

10. Sort your floppy disk **by Name** and switch to details view. Show the instructor the results of your work.

CRITICAL*Thinking*

SCANS ACTIVITY 5-1

In this lesson, you learned how to copy data to a floppy disk. To protect yourself from losing data on your computer, you want to back up the C: drive. Your C: drive is 100 MB, so it would take many 1.44 MB floppy disks to accomplish this. Is copying all data to floppy disks a good method for backing up the computer? Why or Why not? If you answered "no," use the Internet to research a better method. What is it and how much does it cost?

SCANS ACTIVITY 5-2

Windows 2000 allows many options for users to customize their working environments. Name three different ways users can customize Windows 2000. If necessary, use Help to determine the different ways and to provide the steps to accomplish this.

WINDOWS NT WORKSTATION

What Is Windows NT Workstation?

Windows NT is Microsoft's version of Windows for the multiuser server platform. In 1993 when Windows 3.x was the version used on stand-alone PCs, Microsoft created a networked version called Windows NT 3.1 (which stands for New Technology). A network is a system of computers that are interconnected by telephone wires or other means in order to share information.

Windows NT is not designed for use by individual users. Rather, it was aimed at corporate users working on networked computers. Unfortunately, the market did not readily accept Windows NT 3.1. The second version of NT, 3.5—even though it still had the look and feel of Windows 3.x—began to challenge Novell NetWare in terms of networking market share. NT Version 3.5 was the first to offer two separate versions: Workstation and Server. Advances in Windows 95/98, with its overhaul of the graphical user interface, were incorporated into the next version of Windows NT, 4.0, which became a big hit. Because many users were already familiar with the Windows 95/98 interface, no retraining was needed to learn the NT interface. Now NT posed a real threat to Novell's networking market share.

As mentioned earlier, there are two different classifications of Windows NT: Workstation and Server. This chapter will concentrate on the Workstation implementation of NT, but it is important that you understand the difference between the two. By offering a combination of Workstation and Server software, Microsoft's goal is to provide a total client/server solution for businesses.

Workstation is designed for use on every desktop PC in the network, with Server as the back-end product used for sharing resources and security. Workstation generally serves as a desktop operating system, whereas Server is mainly used if your machine is a source for files, applications, or print services. Workstation can also handle this function, but only at the most basic level: It can only handle ten inbound client sessions at a time. This means that only ten computers (called workstations) can simultaneously access shared resources (such as a printer or files) from a machine that has NT Workstation on it, whereas Server can handle unlimited inbound client sessions. If you constantly reach the limit of ten inbound client sessions, then the purpose of sharing resources is defeated. In this case, Server is the better option. Also, if a business solution includes remote access (where users will be accessing shared resources through a modem), Workstation is limited to one remote access session at a time, whereas Server can sustain 256 remote access sessions at a time.

Installing Windows NT

Before you Begin

Before installing Windows NT Workstation, you need to address several issues to ensure that your installation process is as smooth as possible. Specifically, you must make sure that you meet the minimum recommended hardware requirements, that your hardware is on Microsoft's hardware compatibility list, and that your partition scheme is compatible with Windows NT.

Minimum Recommended Hardware Requirement

The advance of technology means that there are minimum hardware requirements for today's networking software, and NT Workstation is no exception to this rule. The minimum requirements for NT Workstation are as follows:

- Intel processor 486/33 or higher

- 12 MB of RAM (although 16 to 32 MB is preferable)

- 120 MB of free hard drive space

- CD-ROM drive or access to a network CD-ROM or share

- VGA or higher resolution graphics card

- Microsoft mouse or compatible device

Note ☑

Remember that these are the minimum requirements for Windows NT. If you are running many applications, it is recommended that you exceed the minimum requirements in order to obtain the most productivity from Windows NT Workstation.

In addition, the following hardware is recommended in order to get the most out of Windows NT Workstation:

- Intel Pentium, Pentium Pro, Pentium II, Pentium III Processor

- 32 to 48 MB of RAM

- 2 GB of free hard drive space

- CD-ROM drive

- SVGA or higher resolution and a 3-D graphics card

- Microsoft mouse

- Internet connectivity

Hardware Compatibility List

Before selecting Windows NT Workstation, you want to make sure that your hardware is listed on the *hardware compatibity list* (HCL) provided by Microsoft. In order for a manufacturer's hardware device to appear on the HCL, it must pass tests given by Microsoft that ensure no conflicts will occur when Windows NT Workstation is installed. To find the most current HCL, check out Microsoft's website (*www.microsoft.com*). This information is updated periodically by Microsoft to ensure that your installation of NT is as smooth as possible.

Once you have found out that your hardware is on the HCL and compatible with NT Workstation, you should make sure that you have the required device driver handy. Earlier, you learned that a device driver is a small program used to enable communication between the operating system and the device itself. Unlike Windows 98, Windows NT is not Plug-and-Play enabled, which means that you cannot just plug a new hardware device into a PC running Windows NT Workstation and expect the device to work. During installation, Windows NT Workstation will try to recognize all of your hardware devices, but if it does make a mistake, you will be required to install the correct driver for the device.

Partitioning the Hard Drive

A *partition* is a logical division of a disk drive. It is common to partition a drive before installing Windows NT Workstation. Once you partition the drive, you will need to decide which partition will be the active one (the partition from which the operating system will boot) and which will be the system partition. Once you finish partitioning the drive, it is ready for formatting.

There are two major types of file systems: *file allocation table* (FAT) and *new technology file system* (NTFS). The newest version of FAT, called FAT32, is used primarily for MS-DOS as well as Windows 3.x and 95. The FAT file system is good for smaller hard disks (2 GB or less), but does not provide any file or directory security. The FAT file system also requires that your filenames follow the original DOS 8-character limit, followed by a three-letter extension (commonly termed the 8.3 filename convention). It also does not provide for the security features in Windows NT Workstation. A disk formatted with the FAT32 file system cannot have Windows NT Workstation installed on it (Windows 2000 does support the FAT32 file system with some limitations).

The NTFS file system is the best choice for Windows NT Workstation. It allows the user to take advantage of the features that make NT so popular, such as Windows NT security, when using the NTFS file system. NTFS allows the user to specify access levels to files and directories on the network and on one PC. NTFS also supports filenames of up to 255 characters.

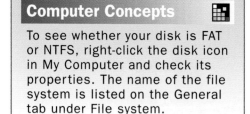

Computer Concepts

To see whether your disk is FAT or NTFS, right-click the disk icon in My Computer and check its properties. The name of the file system is listed on the General tab under File system.

Installation

Now that you have prepared to install the Windows NT Workstation operating system, there are many installation options from which to choose. You can install from the hard drive of the local computer, from a CD-ROM drive, or from the network. In this discussion, we cover only one of the installation options: installing from a CD-ROM.

STEP-BY-STEP 6.1

1. Place the CD-ROM into the drive.

2. At the command prompt, change to your CD-ROM drive by keying **D:** (If this does not work, try keying **E:** at the command prompt).

3. Key the command **cd I386** and then press **Enter** to change to the I386 directory.

4. Key the command **WINNT32.EXE /B** to begin the setup utility.

The setup program copies the actual files to your local hard drive. (Installation is quicker if the files are accessed from the hard drive rather than the CD-ROM.) When the files are copied, the text portion of setup begins to ask you questions about setting up Windows NT Workstation and tries to identify all of your hardware. The installation program tries to locate your processor type, motherboard type, file system, hard disk, the amount of free space on your hard disk, and the amount of memory for your system. If NT Workstation does not recognize all your hardware and you do not install the correct drivers when asked to do so, this almost guarantees that your installation of NT will fail.

The next stage of the installation is the partition selection. Here you select on which partition you want to install Windows NT Workstation. It is wise to install on an NTFS partition to take full advantage of NT's security features. You should partition the disk before beginning installation; otherwise it is a tedious and difficult process.

In the next stage, the installation program examines the hard disk to make sure that it has no physical problems. Finally, the graphical portion of the setup begins. A wizard walks you through this stage of the setup process.

STEP-BY-STEP 6.2

1. Select **Typical** as your configuration option and then click **Next**.

2. Enter your name and your organization name and click **Next**.

3. Enter the default administrator password and confirm it when prompted. DO NOT FORGET THIS PASSWORD.

4. Select **Yes** to create an Emergency Repair Disk.

5. Select **Install the Most Common Components** and click **Next**.

6. Select **Wired to Network** and click **Next** to continue. Windows NT should find your network adapter card if your card is on the hardware compatibility list.

7. Select **TCP/IP and DHCP** and click **Next**.

8. Select **Workgroup** and click **Next**.

9. Click **Finish**.

10. Enter the correct time zone and date/time properties and then click **OK**.

STEP-BY-STEP 6.2 Continued

11. Insert a blank disk to create the Emergency Repair Disk. When the disk is complete, remove it from the drive.

12. The sytem should reboot and then log in to Windows NT using the administrator setting you created in step 3.

Basic Functionality

The Basic Boot Process

Windows NT Workstation has a number of tasks to perform before it is ready to process information. When power is applied, the computer looks at a special chip on the motherboard called the BIOS, where it finds all the instructions it needs to start. Then the computer makes sure all the hardware required to boot is actually attached to the computer.

The next step is to start loading the operating system (OS) from the hard drive. If everything works correctly, your PC begins loading the rest of NT at this point. Before you can open a file or run a program, though, you'll have to log in.

Logging In

Logging in is the process of identifying yourself to the computer. You do this by entering a unique user name and password combination. To do this, press the Ctrl, Alt, and Del keys simultaneously. This brings up the login screen, and opens a dialog box where you type your user name and password. If you don't have a user name, you will need to obtain one from your network administrator. Your administrator can also explain how to set your password.

At this point NT performs user verification. It attempts to match your login name and password with a known list of users. If it makes a match, your personalized startup files load now. Windows keeps track of everything you've asked it to do, including what color you want the background to be and where you want all your icons to sit.

Once the computer has verified that you are allowed to use the machine, it also sets some rights. Rights are merely rules, such as what file access you have, what network access you have, and to which printers you can print. NT administrators specify just what the user can and cannot access. These are not the only rights you can have; you can be assigned additional rights at any time.

The reason for logging in is simple: NT acts like a security guard. You have to show your identification, and then NT has to check the list of names to make sure it's OK for you to come in. The password, which only you should know, is as good as a photo ID. When the system administrator first created an account for you, he or she added your name to the list of authorized users and gave you a password. Once you log in, NT will run for a minute and then drop you onto the desktop where all the work actually takes place.

If you have forgotten your password, just ask your administrator to help you set a new one. This will allow you to regain access to your account.

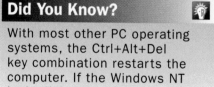

Did You Know?

With most other PC operating systems, the Ctrl+Alt+Del key combination restarts the computer. If the Windows NT login dialog box appears when you press these keys, you can be certain that Windows NT is running.

Changing Your Password

For security's sake it is best if you change your password every two or three months. This decreases the likelihood that someone will be able to access your system. It also makes you more aware of what is going on in your system. To change your password, press Ctrl+Alt+Del to display the login dialog box. Then click the change password option (remember, unless you are told otherwise, you always click with the left mouse button). You will be asked to enter your old password for verification and then you must type the new password twice. Make sure to write it down.

Here are some rules for protecting your password.

- Make the password long enough (at least 8 letters) to prevent random guessing by a stranger.

- Avoid the obvious: Don't use your birthday or your Social Security number or the names of your kids as a password.

- Mix numbers, letters, and symbols; nonsensical combinations are much harder to guess.

- If you must use a real word, use something that you won't forget and no one else could possibly guess, like the name of the sled you had when you were a child. You might try putting the capital letter somewhere other than the first letter—i.e., RosebUD.

- Change your password regularly, at least as often as you change the oil in your car. Your system administrator may require that you change passwords every six weeks or so.

- Don't forget: A good lock is sometimes more effective than a password. Use the keyboard lockout on the front of many machines. Someone can hack into your system if he or she can use the keyboard.

- To change your password, you first have to enter your old one. Then type the new one, and type it again to make sure you didn't make a mistake the first time.

What do you do if you can't change your password? Your system administrator may have placed additional restrictions on your account. For example, the administrator may have told NT that your password has to be at least 10 characters, or that you can't reuse any of the last four passwords you've used. If you have trouble, ask your system administrator whether any of these restrictions apply to you.

The Graphical User Interface

When you first log in to Windows NT Workstation, you will feel like you are using Windows 95. The desktop contains the familiar icons, My Computer, and the Recycle Bin. The taskbar is at the bottom of the desktop with the Windows Start button at the left end and the system tray icons at the right end. When you open a window, you'll see the close, minimize, and maximize buttons at the right end of the title bar. See Figure 6-1.

FIGURE 6-1
The Windows NT desktop

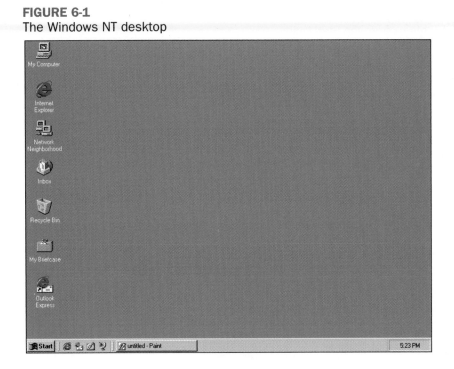

This is done on purpose to make new users familiar with the interface. If you are comfortable using Windows 95/98, you will be comfortable using Windows NT Workstation. All of the objectives discussed in Chapter 4 about maneuvering in the Windows 98 operating system hold true. However, there are some major changes under the hood, which will be discussed later in this chapter.

The Start Button

By default NT places a horizontal bar, called the taskbar, across the bottom of your screen. This bar displays the icons for the applications that are running. It enables you to quickly switch to a new application by clicking its icons instead of minimizing windows. On the right end of the taskbar you will see a clock and possibly a few other small icons; this area is called the system tray. On the left end of the taskbar you will see the Start button. See Figure 6-2.

FIGURE 6-2
The Start button

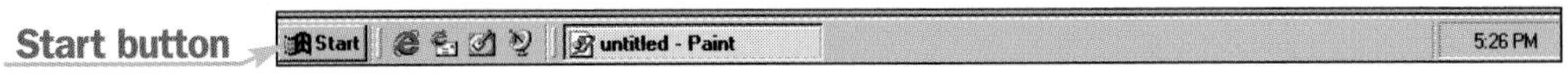

Start button → [🏁 Start] [icons] [untitled - Paint] [5:26 PM]

Place your mouse pointer (the on-screen arrow) over the Start button and click. This opens a menu that contains several options. To open the Programs submenu, hold your mouse pointer over Programs until the submenu opens. Or you can click the Programs option to open the Programs submenu immediately. Try it both ways. Until you learn some shortcuts, this is where you will select all your programs. Try opening a few. As you install new programs, the list will become longer. Don't be afraid to play around; there isn't anything you can break. If you find yourself in unfamiliar territory, just close the window and start again.

S TEP-BY-STEP 6.3

1. Click the **Start** button in your taskbar.

2. Click **Programs** from the Start menu.

3. Click **Accessories** from the submenu.

4. Open the **Paint** accessory program, then close it.

5. Repeat steps 2 through 4, except this time open and close the **Notepad** accessory program.

The My Computer Icon

When you open the My Computer window, you see icons for each of the disks in your system, as well as a number of folders. See Figure 6-3.

FIGURE 6-3
The My Computer window

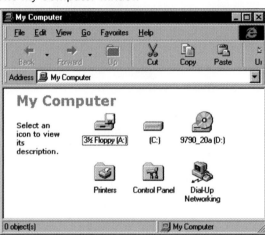

Hold your mouse pointer over one of the folders and notice that a message box, called a ScreenTip, pops up to show how you can use the folder.

Folders and files are stored on disks, which act just like file cabinets (and seem to fill up just as quickly). How much free space is left on your hard disk? To find out, open the My Computer window, click the Control Panel icon, click the System icon, then click the Performance tab. You'll see a listing of your system specs, including its free resources.

You can also use My Computer to ask Windows to attach an electronic label to your disks. To name a floppy disk, you would insert a disk into drive A, click the A: drive icon, choose Properties from the File menu, and type the name for the disk into the Label: field. Now the next time you insert the floppy disk you'll know it contains budget data before you even open it.

Finally, My Computer is one of many places in Windows where you can find, copy, or delete a file. In fact, many of the functions of My Computer are the same as those available in Windows Explorer.

Your office equipment claims a few icons here as well. For example, printers and modems get special icons that let you adjust their settings. Imagine how awkward life would be if you had to lug your monitor down the hall every time you wanted to show someone this quarter's budget spreadsheet. That's why printers are the most important pieces of computer hardware, next to your PC, and that's why they get their own folder in the My Computer window.

STEP-BY-STEP 6.4

1. Insert a floppy disk into drive A.

2. Double-click the **My Computer** icon to open it.

3. Double-click the drive **A:** icon to view the contents of your floppy disk. How many folders are on your disk? How many files on your disk?

4. Click the drive **A:** icon to highlight it.

5. Click the **File** menu in the menu bar, then click **Properties**.

6. In the label area of the dialog box, add a label to your floppy disk that describes its contents.

The Five Basic Icon Types

NT uses five types of icons to represent everything in your computer. The icons give you important clues about the type of object with which you are working.

■ *Folder*: Folders represent special files that are capable of holding documents and programs. Use them the same way you would with real file folders. You can even "nest" folders inside other folders in an unlimited series.

■ *Document*: A document might consist of a simple note, or it might be a complex combination of graphics, links, and text. Electronic documents are similar in many ways to documents in the real world.

■ *Program*: Programs (also called applications) are the parts of NT that actually do the work. They can be spreadsheets, word processors, games, and so on. Programs usually have custom-designed icons.

■ *Device*: Device icons provide links to the hardware of your computer—the mouse, keyboard, monitor, and so forth. The icons link to special utilities that allow you to configure the hardware.

■ *Shortcut:* Shortcuts are special links. They are really just a set of instructions telling the computer where the program actually exists. Every time you click a shortcut, the icon redirects the computer to the program. The purpose of shortcuts is to provide convenient access routes to a program from various places on your computer (from your desktop, for instance). You can identify shortcut icons by the little arrow in the lower-left corner of the icon. Shortcuts are available in Windows 95 and up. Once you learn how convenient they are, you'll find yourself using them everywhere.

> **Did You Know?**
>
> To quickly change an icon's label, select the icon, press the F2 key, and then start typing the new name.

Using Shortcuts

Consider this scenario: You, Mr./Ms. Sales Manager, have three customers who place large orders frequently. You keep each customer's sales records in a separate manila folder. You also have a product catalog the size of a phone book that you use, no matter which customer you're working with. If you make three copies of that catalog and put one in each client folder, you've created a big problem the next time you revise your catalog. You have to remember to put the latest copy in all three client folders, or you might wind up sending the wrong merchandise or charging the wrong price.

The solution is to store the catalog in its own folder, then store a note in each client folder that tells you where to find the catalog. That's how shortcuts work. They act like little notes that tell NT to find something stored elsewhere on the disk (or even on another computer) and open it up. Shortcuts use only a small amount of disk space, and they can point to just about anything: programs, documents, printers, and drives—even a location on the Microsoft Network.

Creating Shortcuts

One of the most useful places to create a shortcut is right on the Windows NT desktop. For a program you use every day, like the Windows Calculator, why should you have to rummage through the Start menu? You don't want to move the program out of its home in the Windows folder, but you would like to be able to start it up by just double-clicking an icon. Here's how: If you already know where the program is stored, just open its folder or highlight it in Windows Explorer. Drag the icon using the right mouse button, and then drop it onto the desktop, choosing Create Shortcut(s) from the menu that pops up.

Another way to create a shortcut to an item is to use the Create Shortcut dialog box. See Figure 6-4. Right-click your desktop and from the menu choose New and then Shortcut. In the dialog box, click the browse button to locate the program you want to create a shortcut to. In the final step, type the name you want to give the shortcut.

> **Note** ☑
>
> When you drag and drop a program to create a shortcut, NT calls the new icon Shortcut to .. [the program's original name]. You can delete the two extra words if you like, or even completely rename the shortcut. Calling it Word, for example, uses less screen space than calling it Shortcut to Microsoft Word for Windows.

FIGURE 6-4
The Create Shortcut dialog box

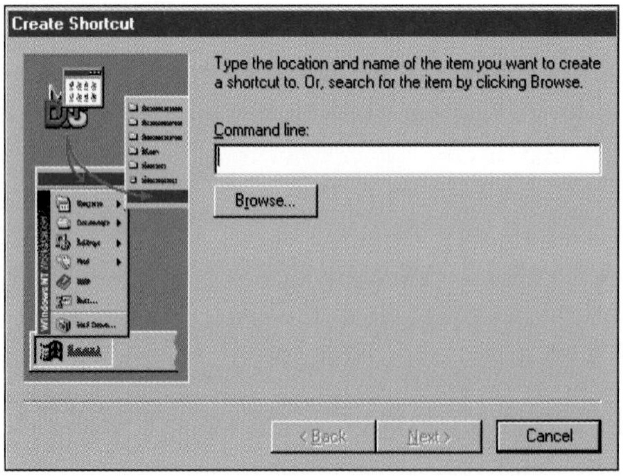

STEP-BY-STEP 6.5

1. Right-click the desktop.

2. Click **New** and click **Shortcut**.

3. Click **Browse** in the dialog box.

4. Double-click the **Windows** folder in the Browse dialog box.

5. Double-click the file **Calc.exe**.

6. Click **Next**.

7. Rename the shortcut **Calculator**.

8. Click **Finish**.

File Management

Windows NT has an update to the file system. You no longer need to have all those cryptic filenames. You can now have names up to 255 characters long. This means you can have filenames like "thank you letter to Bob 06201999.doc". This name has more meaning. But don't use the longer filenames as an excuse to get sloppy. You still need to develop a filing system to keep things orderly and easy to find.

You should be aware of one thing when dealing with longer filenames. If the file is copied to an older machine that doesn't support long names, the older machine will truncate the filename. (Don't worry; if the file is copied back to a newer machine that supports long filenames it will have the longer name again.) Truncating follows a rule. The machine preserves the first six characters, then adds a tilde ("~") the number 1, and then the extension. For example, our thank you letter to Bob would truncate to "thank y~1.doc". If you need to type in the filename on a machine that does not support long filenames, just type it in the way you see it, not the long version. It will work fine.

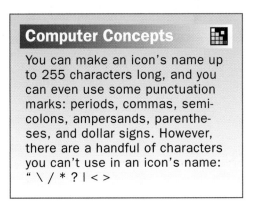

Computer Concepts

You can make an icon's name up to 255 characters long, and you can even use some punctuation marks: periods, commas, semicolons, ampersands, parentheses, and dollar signs. However, there are a handful of characters you can't use in an icon's name: " \ / * ? | < >

Windows NT still uses the file extensions you used to see in DOS and Windows 3.x. For the most part the usage is the same. However, NT does not normally display the extensions. People used to check the extension to know what type of file it was. Now different file types have different icons, so an extension would be duplicate information. If you wish, you can use Windows Explorer options to ask NT to display the extensions.

Storage Devices

Files go in folders, and folders go on drives. As the number of files on your computer builds up, you'll be glad to have a logical filing system that lets you find documents when you need them. If you expect Windows NT to help you organize your work, you need to understand two of its most important building blocks: drives and folders.

Working with Hard Disks

Your disk drives work just like filing cabinets. To keep your files organized you use the computer equivalent of manila folders. But just like the filing cabinets in your office, you have to do a little prep work before you place your data into folders. The challenge is to make sure there's enough free space on the disk and that the files are organized properly.

Checking Free Space on a Storage Device

Every time you save a file to a hard disk, it gobbles some of the empty space on that disk (which is measured in megabytes, or millions of bytes); sooner or later you'll fill up most of that space. As the disk reaches its capacity you will notice your computer starts running slowly, and eventually you won't be able to open or save new documents. That's why you should keep an eye on free disk space. It's especially important to check how much space is left on a disk when you're planning to install a new program.

> **Hot Tip**
>
> You can choose from four different ways to arrange the drives in the My Computer window. Pull down the View menu and choose Arrange Icons. Now you can sort the entries in the window by drive letter, type, size, or amount of available free space.

STEP-BY-STEP 6.6

1. Double-click the **My Computer** icon on your desktop to open My Computer.

2. Click the drive **C:** icon. The total disk capacity and free space appear in the status bar at the bottom of the My Computer window. (If the status bar isn't visible, pull down the **View** menu and click **Status Bar**.)

3. Close the window.

4. To see a graphical display of free disk space, right-click the hard drive icon, then choose **Properties** from the pop-up menu. Above the pie chart, you can see exactly how many free megabytes are left, as well as the total megabytes on your hard disk. See Figure 6-5.

FIGURE 6-5
Graphical display of free disk space

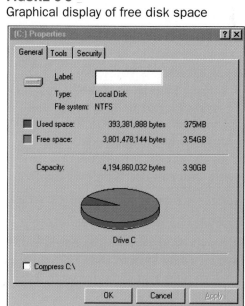

Out of Room

One of the realities of owning a computer is that sooner or later, you'll have more files than your hard disk can hold. If you've been checking your free disk space regularly, you'll get some advance warning. Otherwise, you'll just get an error message when you try to save a file. At that point you have three choices:

- *Clean some files off your hard disk.* The cheapest solution to an overstuffed hard disk is to delete the files you don't need. Try emptying your Recycle Bin first. There are disk utility programs you can purchase that will also clean up some of the other files that cause your hard drive to be cluttered.

- *Get a new hard disk.* You'll need a few hundred dollars to purchase this and you'll also need to find someone who'll install it for you. If you replace your hard disk, you will have to reinstall all your software, including NT.

- *Software compression of your files.* You can tell NT to pack one or more files, a folder, or even an entire drive so that they take up less space. This option is to be used at your own risk. Compression is such a risky affair, it is not recommended at all. Use it only under dire emergencies. There are two reasons. First, if you do this and something goes wrong, none of the data will be retrievable. The "key" used to compress/uncompress the files is stored on the hard drive along with the rest of your data; if something happens to your data, chances are it will damage the "key" as well. Second, if you are running out of space, you should solve the problem correctly, by adding a second hard drive or upgrading to a bigger hard drive. Compression is only a temporary bandage that buys you a little time. Even with compression you will soon run out of space.

Did You Know?
A byte is one character, and mega means million. So a megabyte is a million characters, right? Not exactly. Your PC can only count by powers of 2, so a megabyte is actually 2 to the 20th power, or 1,048,576 bytes. Of course, not all the storage space is used for data. Some of it is used by your system to keep track of the files and some special attributes. So it's practical to "round off" a megabyte of storage at an even million.

How Compression Works

Compression replaces small file containers with one big container that holds all your files. It separates each file from the one before it and after it with a special character. The result is that there is almost no wasted space. The tradeoff is that in order to find anything NT needs to start at the beginning of the file container and read through each file until it reaches the one it wants. This results in a huge slowdown. It can be as much as 100:1 when compared to the noncompressed method. So you are trading off speed and a little bit of wasted space for no wasted space and slower performance.

Hot Tip
You might have more free disk space than you think. Check the Recycle Bin first. If it's filled with files, simply emptying it might clear enough room to let you finish whatever you're doing. (To empty it, just right-click the Recycle Bin icon and select Empty Recycle Bin from the shortcut menu.)

DOS in Windows NT

If you learned to use a PC running MS-DOS, you might not initially know your way around a Windows environment. But once you learn a few landmarks, you will be off and running. Later, if something should go wrong with NT, you will be able to use DOS to fix it. For this reason, it's always handy to know a little DOS in order to use NT effectively.

Whenever you want to use DOS in a Windows environment, you have a choice of two command lines. Both are accessible from the NT Start menu. The first looks like the familiar DOS prompt. To reach it, click the Start button, then click Programs and choose MS-DOS Prompt from the menu. The C:\ prompt in this window does everything a DOS user would expect, and then some. See Figure 6-6. Unlike old-fashioned DOS, which fills your entire screen, the Windows NT Command Prompt displays in a window that you can resize and move around your screen. You can type the name of any program at the command prompt, and the program will start right up. You can even run some of your older DOS programs, although some of them won't work properly with Windows NT.

FIGURE 6-6
MS-DOS screen in Windows NT

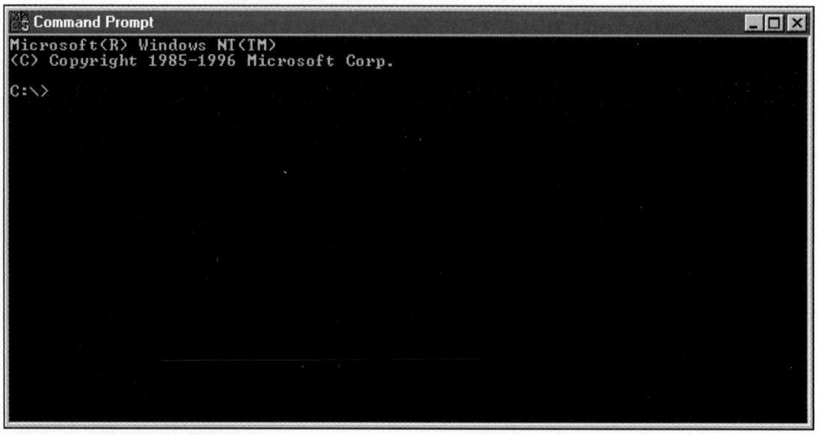

STEP-BY-STEP 6.7

1. Click the **Start** button.

2. Click **Programs** and then **MS-DOS Prompt**.

3. At the command prompt, key **NOTEPAD**. The program should start just as if you selected it using the Windows Start button.

4. Close Notepad and return to MS-DOS.

5. At the command prompt, key **EXIT** to return to NT.

Shutting Down Your Computer in NT

To turn off your computer, first click the Start button, then choose Shut Down from the menu. NT will start to terminate all applications that are still running. If you have any data that hasn't ot; Windows NT Workstation | 225

been saved, you will be asked to save it. Once all processes have stopped, NT will display a message that it is OK to turn off your computer. If you turn off the power without doing a shutdown, you may lose vital data or damage the system. If you aren't sure whether the computer can be turned off, ask someone.

Unique Features of Windows NT

The Control Panel

The Windows NT Workstation Control Panel is where most of the configuration of your operating system takes place. Configuration is the process of adjusting the settings to make the operating system perform as you want it to. If you have used Windows 95 or 98, you will find that many of the icons in the Control Panel are unchanged. See Figure 6-7. However, NT offers a few new ones, including Tape Devices and Servers. This discussion will describe the icons.

FIGURE 6-7
The Control Panel window

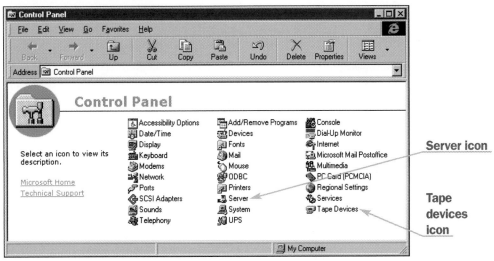

STEP-BY-STEP 6.8

1. Click the **Start** menu, click the **Settings** option, and then click **Control Panel**.

2. Or click the **My Computer** icon on the desktop, then click the **Control Panel** icon.

Tape Devices Icon

In order to use the built-in backup capabilities of Windows NT Workstation, you need to have a tape device installed on the sytem. When you click the Tape Devices icon, you will be ready to install and configure your device to back up information. See Figure 6-8.

Computer Concepts

It is common to find other icons in the Control Panel besides the ones with which you are familiar. Sometimes when you install new hardware or software, it will create an icon in the Control Panel for you. The idea is to centralize all of your configuration options into one location.

FIGURE 6-8
The Tape Devices icon

STEP-BY-STEP 6.9

1. Open the **Control Panel**.

2. Double-click the **Tape Devices** icon in the Control Panel to open it.

3. Click the **Drivers Tab** and then click **Add**.

4. Select your tape device from the list of manufacturers and models available.

5. If your device is not listed, make sure you have the driver disk that came with the device and click **Have disk** to install the appropriate drivers.

6. Click **OK**.

7. Restart the machine so the new changes will take effect.

The Server Icon

The Server icon in the Control Panel is needed if you are making shared resources (also called shares), such as a printer, accessible to users at other machines. This gives you an idea of what shares are available to users and who is currently accessing the shares. Because you have resources that others are using, it is completely legitimate for you to know who is accessing them and how many times they have accessed them. The Usage Summary dialog box gives you the following information (see Figure 6-9):

- *Sessions* are the number of users currently connected to your machine.

- *File Locks* are the number of files locked in use by users.

- *Open Files* are the number of open files and their users.

- *Named Pipes* allow one process to communicate with another.

FIGURE 6-9
The Usage Summary dialog box

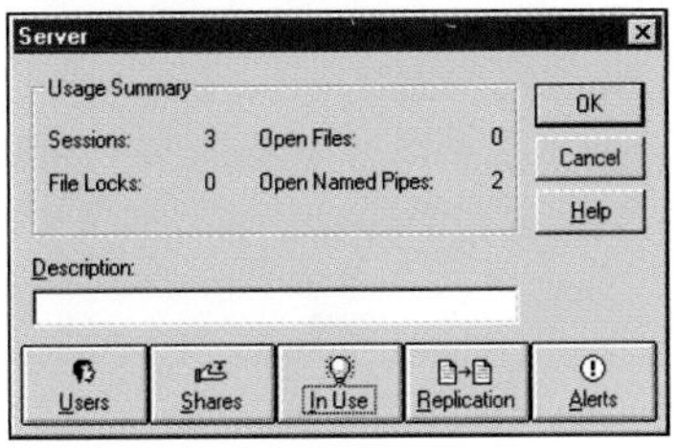

The Shares button displays all of the shares that are currently available and the number of users connected to each share. You can also see how long a user has been using a shared resource. If there are users connected that you no longer want connected, you can highlight the user name and click the Disconnect button.

The Windows Registry

While you are configuring your operating system using the Control Panel, a system file called the Windows *registry* is keeping track of these changes. The registry stores your software and hardware configuration settings. However, a new user can be overwhelmed by the registry and it is extremely easy to corrupt your system if you change things you do not understand. For the work in this chapter, use the Control Panel to make any system changes, but understand that all changes you make via the Control Panel are stored as command lines in the registry file. See Figure 6-10.

FIGURE 6-10
The registry

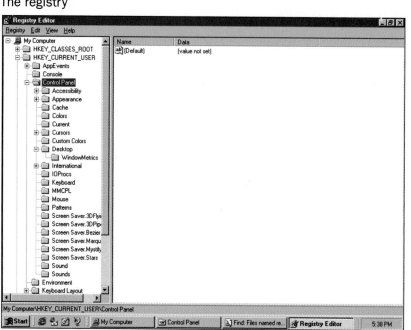

Managing Users

A Windows NT computer requires that all users have an account. Each user account is created with a unique user name and password.

Different Types of Users

Windows NT includes the following predefined groups (chances are, you already belong to one of them).

- *Administrators* includes everyone who has the right to log on and act as an administrator. Some administrators keep two accounts—one in this group, which they can use when they need to do system maintenance, and another account, for everyday use, that has more restricted user rights.

- *Everyone* has the fewest amount of rights of any group. Typically, users in this group get the right to log in at a specific machine and shut it down, and that's all.

- *Users* have restricted rights, not because they're not trusted, but because administrators want to keep them from accidentally deleting important files or stumbling into areas where they don't belong.

> **Did You Know?**
>
> Don't be surprised if your system has more than one administrator. In most companies, several people have the right to act as administrator on a given PC; that way, someone's always available to help with a problem, even if the regular system administrator is out sick or on vacation.

■ *Power users* are assumed to be more experienced and are allowed to share files and folders with other users, and to create new user accounts on their own computers.

■ *Guests*, as the name implies, are allowed to log in at a machine and use it temporarily. A guest account might be created to allow visitors to log in and use a few programs and a shared printer, storing their files in a special folder not shared by anyone else.

■ *Backup operators* are allowed to get around file and folder security, but only for the purpose of making backup copies of important data files.

Creating Users

One of the responsibilities of the administrator is to decide upon a unique naming scheme for the user names he or she creates. One common scheme is to use someone's first initial of the first name, followed by their full last name. For example the user name for Joe Smith would be JSmith. Whatever the administrator decides to do, it should be simple and consistent.

User Manager is the tool employed to create new users. See Figure 6-11.

FIGURE 6-11
User Manager dialog box

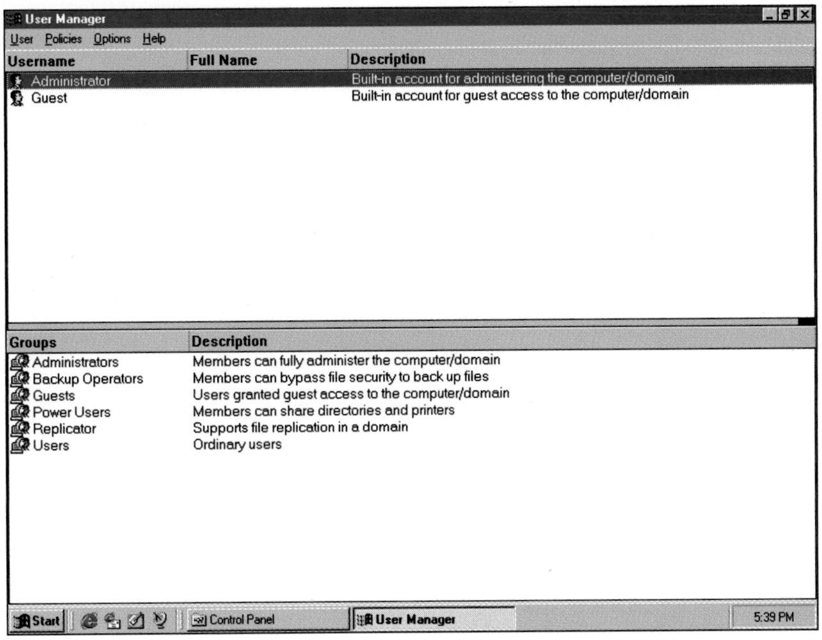

When creating a new account the administrator must enter information specific to that account. See Figure 6-12. Each account is assigned an ID by Windows NT. This security ID is unique to every account and this is part of the access token when the user logs in. To start User Manager, click the Start button, click Programs, and then click Administrative Tools and User Manager. Table 6-1 describes what you see in the User Manager dialog box.

FIGURE 6-12
Adding a new user

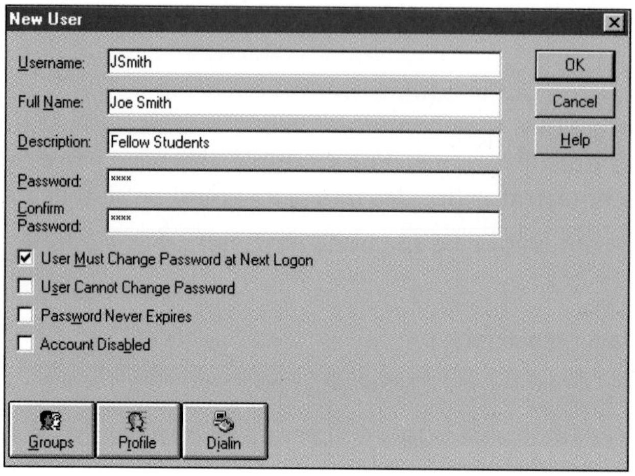

TABLE 6-1
Options in User Manager dialog box

BOX	DESCRIPTION
Username	A unique name up to 20 characters in length
Full Name	The name of the user
Description	A brief description of the user's account
Password	Passwords are case-sensitive and cannot be more than 14 characters in length
Confirm Password	Re-enter the password to make sure it is correct
User Must Change Password at Next Logon	Forces the user to change the password the next time they log in. This option is turned off once the user changes their password
User Cannot Change Password	Keeps the user from changing the password
Password Never Expires	Keeps the password from ever needing to be changed
Account Disabled	Prevents anyone from using the account

S TEP-BY-STEP 6.10

1. Click the **Start** button and select **Programs**, **Administrative Tools** and **User Manager**.

2. Click the **User** menu and select **New User**.

STEP-BY-STEP 6.10 Continued

3. In the Username field key **JSMITH**.

4. In the Full Name field key **Joe Smith**.

5. In the Description field, key **Fellow Student**.

6. Leave the Password field blank.

7. Click **OK**.

8. You have just created a new user.

9. Log off your NT machine and log back in as user name JSMITH and no password.

10. NT will prompt you to change JSMITH's password. Make it **JOE**.

Windows NT Security

Security is a main element of a network. One advantage of using Windows NT Workstation over Windows 95/98 in a networked environment is NT's security capabilities.

Windows NT security has four main parts:

■ *Logon process* is the way in which the user gets initial access to the system.

■ *Local Security Authority* creates security access tokens, authenticates users, and manages the security policy.

■ *SAM database* manages all users accounts. When a user logs in, the information is validated by comparing it to the SAM database.

■ *Security Reference Monitor* verifies that a user has access to a requested object, such as a folder or file.

When a user presses Ctrl+Alt+Del to log in, the security process begins. The user is prompted for a user name and password. This information is passed to the Local Security Authority, which verifies this information against the SAM database. If the user is verified, the Local Security Authority creates an access token which acts as the user's ID badge. Once the user presents an ID, it is no longer needed to gain access to the system.

Accessing Objects

Now that you are logged in to the system, how does NT know what you can and cannot access? If you choose to use the NTFS file system then the administrator can grant file and folder *permissions*. With NTFS the following permissions can be set to folders:

■ *No Access* does not allow users any access to this file.

■ *List* allows users to view the files and subfolders in the folder, but they cannot use anything within.

■ *Read* allows users to read files in the folder, but they cannot save any changes to the file.

■ *Add* allows users to add new files to the folder, but they cannot view any existing files or folder.

- *Add & Read* allows users to list, read, and write new files to the folder. However, they cannot save changes to any existing files.

- *Change* allows users to read, change, modify, and delete the existing files in the folder.

- *Full Control* allows users all of the rights allowed with Change, as well as the ability to change permissions and take ownership of the files and folders.

To set permissions on a file or folder, you can use Windows Explorer. See Figure 6-13.

FIGURE 6-13
Setting permissions in Windows Explorer

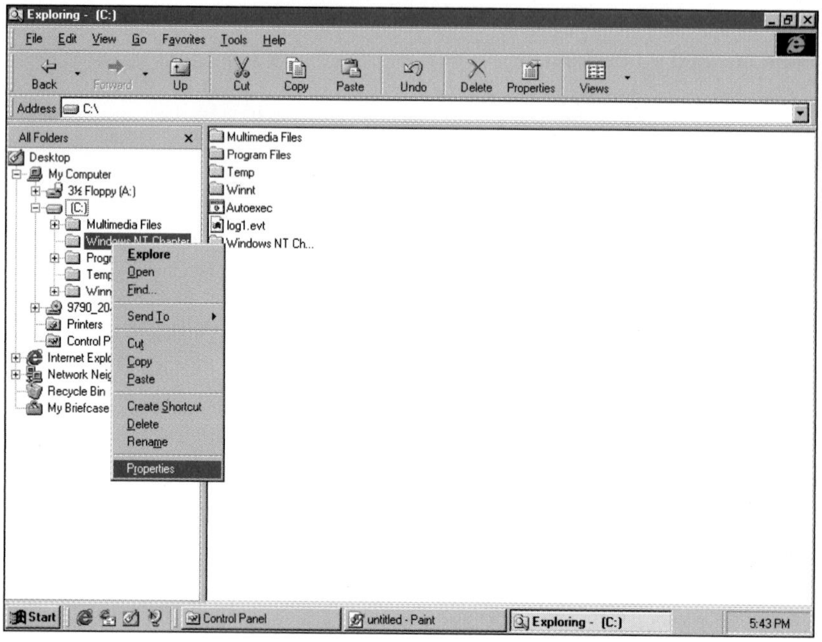

STEP-BY-STEP 6.11

1. Open **Windows Explorer**.

2. Double-click **C:** in the **All Folders** pane of Windows Explorer to view the contents of your hard drive.

3. Right-click the **Contents** pane and choose **New, Folder** from the menu.

4. Name the new folder **Windows NT Class**.

5. Right-click the **Windows NT Class** folder and choose **Properties**.

STEP-BY-STEP 6.11 Continued

6. Select the **Security** tab and then click the **Permissions** button. See Figure 6-14.

FIGURE 6-14
Setting permissions

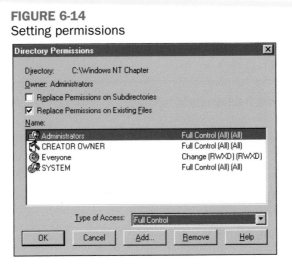

7. Click **Everyone** and then click the **Remove** button.

8. Click the **Show Users** button; select your user name from the list and click the **Add** button.

9. On the **Type of Access** drop-down menu, select **No Access**.

10. Return to Windows Explorer and try to access the folder. What happens?

11. Return to **Properties** and explore what happens when you choose the other types of access to the Windows NT Class folder. Do you notice the differences between the types of access?

Network Neighborhood

Most NT computers are connected to a network. In an office environment this allows fellow employees to share information and resources. You can even share with people in different offices in other parts of the world. If you double-click the Network Neighborhood icon on your desktop, you'll see a list of all the computers that you are allowed to access. See Figure 6-15.

FIGURE 6-15
Example of Network Neighborhood icon

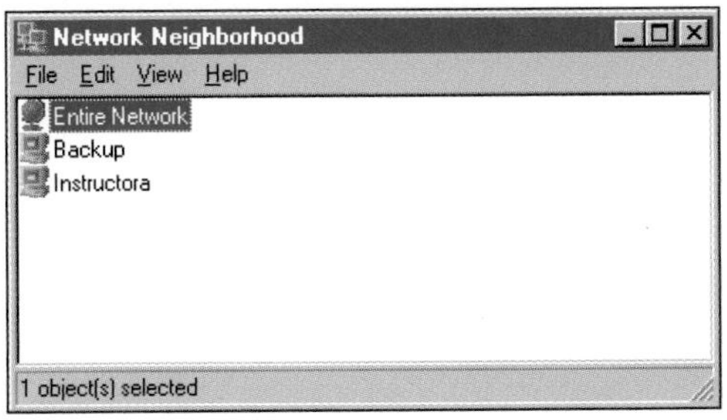

Computers may be arranged in groups of "like" departments. For instance, the engineering and finance departments may have separate groups. This helps filter out information you really don't need. It also helps with security. You may not want anyone outside of the engineering department to view a new product design until you release it. At the same time, a departmental listing makes it easier to locate a particular machine, because you'll have a shorter list to look through.

S TEP-BY-STEP 6.12

1. Double-click the **Network Neighborhood** icon.

2. You should see a listing of all the machines on the network.

3. Ask your instructor which machine is yours.

4. Double-click the icon for your machine. Is there anything inside it?

Network sharing is a multifaceted process. You can work with others' files, and share your own files, hard drive, and printer with others as well. You can tell if your printer or hard drive has sharing enabled. If it is shared, you'll see a hand beneath the printer or hard drive icon instead of the normal printer and hard drive icons. It should look as though the hand is holding the device. See Figure 6-16. If it isn't shared, you can quickly share it by right-clicking the device and selecting Properties from the menu. Select the Sharing tab at the top of the pop-up window. You can enable sharing and even password protection for the information, so only certain people can access it. You may also want to specify a name to use for the shared device. For instance, you can call one computer on your network "Walrus", another "Thing2", and a printer "Big Al". Some people have commented that network administrators name their machines as though they were pets. There is a very good reason for this: It's much easier to remember a name like "Walrus" than "ad1256f".

FIGURE 6-16
Icon of a shared printer

Mapping a Shared Network Drive

To map a shared network drive to a drive letter, just look in the Network Neighborhood. Double-click a computer icon and, when the list appears, select the name of the share you want to connect to. Then choose Map Network Drive from the shortcut menu. See Figure 6-17. When the dialog box appears, just pick any free drive letter from the list and click OK.

FIGURE 6-17
Mapping a network drive

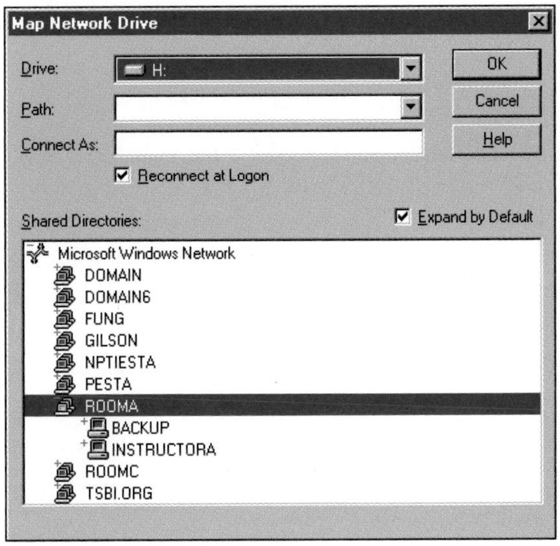

Let's say you want to map a drive to drive D on your boss's computer, Excalibur. You would look in Network Neighborhood for Excalibur, and browse to its drive D. Then pick any free drive name (say, J:) and map that drive name to D: on Excalibur. From now on, you can click drive J to get to D: on Excalibur. To tell NT that you want to continue to use this mapped drive letter every time you log in to your computer, check the Reconnect at Logon box.

S TEP-BY-STEP 6.13

1. Open the **Network Neighborhood** icon.

2. Find the name for your neighbor's computer.

3. Double-click the computer name to open it.

4. Right-click the icon for the CD-ROM drive (most likely D:) and click **Map Network Drive**.

5. On your computer, click the drive letter that you would like to use to represent your neighbor's CD-ROM drive.

6. Check the **Reconnect at Logon** option and then click **OK**.

7. Open Windows Explorer.

8. In the All Folders pane, you should see the mapped drive that you just created.

Extra Challenge

As you work with NT, ask yourself what you need to accomplish, then look for ways NT can help you do it. You might also ask others what they have done to solve a particular problem. Some of the obvious things NT can help you with are the routine tasks of the everyday office. Word processing, email, faxing, music, spreadsheets, contact lists, and even games are made easier. There's almost no end to what you can do. Jump in and explore a bit.

To disconnect a drive mapping, right-click My Computer, select the mapped drive and right-click it, then choose Disconnect from the shortcut menu.

SUMMARY

In this lesson, you learned:

■ To install Windows NT: First you need to make sure you have a working hard drive and CD-ROM. Remember that you should know all the system resources beforehand, if possible. Make a list to keep track. Check the hardware compatibility list to ensure your hardware is compatible with NT. Partition your hard disk to the NTFS file system, so you can fully utilize the power of NT security. With the CD-ROM in, key WINNT32.EXE /B to begin the setup utility. Answer the questions to complete the setup of your particular machine. When the system reboots, you can now log in for the first time as the Administrator.

■ NT uses many of the same functions you learned in Windows 98. You move around the operating system using your mouse and your keyboard. The main workspace is the desktop, where you work with windows and dialog boxes to perform tasks. As in Windows 98, you use My Computer and Windows Explorer to manage your files by cutting, copying, pasting, and deleting them.

■ The Control Panel contains most of the icons you learned in the Windows 98 chapter as well as a couple of new ones, including the Tape Devices and Server icons. The Tape Devices icon allows you to install a tape device on your system, in order to back up your information on the PC. The Server icon tells you what shared resources are available to other users and who is accessing the shares.

■ There are six different types of NT users: Administrators, Everyone, Users, Power Users, Guests, and Backup Operators. The User Manager utility allows the administrator to create new users for the system.

■ Security is a key element of Windows NT Workstation. The four main processes associated with NT security are the logon process, the Local Security Authority, the SAM database, and the Security Reference Monitor. When a disk is formatted with the NTFS file system you can set folder and file permissions. The permissions available for folders are: No Access, List, Read, Add, Add and Read, Change, and Full Control. User access to a folder depends upon the permission assigned to the folder.

■ The Network Neighborhood icon shows the computers you have access to. Here you can create maps to drives on other computers you would like access to. Right-click on a share in Network Neighborhood and choose Map Network Drive from the menu to access the resources on that drive.

VOCABULARY *Review*

Define the following terms:

Compression
File allocation table (FAT)
Hardware compatibility
  list (HCL)

New technology
  file system (NTFS)
Partition
Permissions

Registry
User Manager

REVIEW *Questions*

MULTIPLE CHOICE

Select the best response for the following statements.

1. The two different classifications of Windows NT are:
   A. User and Administrator.
   B. Server and Workstation.
   C. MS-DOS and PC.
   D. Workstation and Playstation.

2. One of the recommended hardware requirements is:
   A. a 486 processor.
   B. 12 MB of RAM.
   C. 120 MB of free hard disk space.
   D. 32–48 MB of RAM.

3. The NTFS file system is the best choice for Windows NT because:
   A. It follows the limitations of the 8.3 file naming convention.
   B. It takes advantage of NT's security features.
   C. It is good for smaller hard disks.
   D. You can have Windows 95/98 loaded on the machine.

4. Which one of the following is a good reason not to compress your hard drive?
   A. It will make the computer run faster.
   B. It will free up some space on the hard disk.
   C. It will make the computer run slower.
   D. You can back up files that are compressed.

5. When assigning the permission list to a folder, the user has what permissions?
   A. The user can view the files and folders within the folder, but cannot access any of them.
   B. The user has no access to the folder.
   C. The user can list, read, and write new files to the folder.
   D. The user can add new files to the folder, but cannot access any existing files.

FILL IN THE BLANK

Complete the following sentences by writing the correct word or words in the blanks provided.

1. A _____ is a logical division of a disk drive.

2. The two major file systems are _____ and _____.

3. _____ icons are special links pointing to the original location of a program.

4. Filenames can be _____ characters long.

5. The _____ keeps track of operating system changes made in the control panel.

PROJECTS

PROJECT 6-1

1. Create a folder on your floppy disk named **Windows NT Section**.

2. Open the **Notepad** accessory program.

3. Write a short memo to your instructor describing what you have learned in the past few weeks about operating systems.

4. Save the file as **Operating System** in your Windows NT folder on drive A.

5. Close Notepad.

6. Open **My Computer** and view the contents of A:.

7. Create a shortcut on the desktop to your **Windows NT Section** folder.

8. Open Windows Explorer.

9. Create a Read permission to the **Windows NT Section** folder.

10. Can you access the **Operating System** file? Can you save any changes to the **Operating System** file?

11. Change the permission on the **Windows NT Section** folder to List.

12. Can you access the **Operating System** file now?

PROJECT 6-2

1. Open the **My Computer** window. Under the Help menu, choose **About Windows NT**.
   - To whom is NT licensed?
   - How much physical memory is available?
   - What percentage of system resources is free?

2. What does that tell you about the operating system?

3. Work with a partner (who is on a separate computer); both of you create a folder on drive C called **I Love Windows NT**.

4. Using **Network Neighborhood**, map a drive to that folder on your partner's computer. Label the drive with whatever letter you wish. Make sure you can locate the folder at login.

CRITICAL *Thinking*

ACTIVITY 6-1

As always in the information world, software companies are improving their technology and introducing better operating systems. What are the improvements of more recent releases of Windows over NT?

ACTIVITY 6-2

New versions of Windows have been released since NT. Use the Internet to research jobs requiring knowledge of Windows NT. Why do you think so many companies still use Windows NT when newer and better versions of Windows are available?

NOVELL CLIENT

OBJECTIVES

Upon completion of this lesson, you should be able to:

- Understand the niche market addressed by Novell's operating system.

- Define local area network and wide area network.

- Install Novell Client to be used with a variety of other operating systems.

- Understand how Novell manages resources on the network.

- Install a shared printer.

Estimated Time: 10+ hours

VOCABULARY

Cabling

Container objects

Drivers

Ethernet

FDDI

Gateway

Local area network (LAN)

Leaf objects

NDS

NDS tree

Network

Network board

Packets

Printer server

Protocol

Rights

Router

Token

Token ring

Wide area network (WAN)

Introduction

Over time, desktop computers became popular because they were easier to use than mainframes. Their cost savings and productivity increases could not be ignored. However, even though they provided a cheaper solution than mainframes, they had comparatively limited computing power. In 1983, a new player named Novell entered the market and realized the potential of connecting all those computing resources and sharing them. This was the beginning of the *local area network (LAN)*. A LAN is a network of interconnected workstations sharing the resources of a single processor or server within a relatively small geographic area.

In the beginning only large computer mainframes had been networked. A network was very expensive to purchase and maintain. The technology was complicated, and training was difficult and limited. This helped fuel a standoff between users and administrators. Users felt that the system was too cumbersome to use and had too many restrictions. Administrators countered that the users abused and destroyed parts of the system. This "us" versus "them" mentality wasted time and resources.

Novell's idea was to connect all those cheaper PCs to the mainframe. The users would get to use the simpler interface and all the data could be passed back to the mainframe for processing. The user was relieved of the usage issues and the administrators could tell the work was getting done. The idea appealed to both camps, so they looked for a way to make it happen.

In the early days, the fact that the DOS operating system had no native network capabilities was a big obstacle. How would you enable it to print to a remote printer, access/save remote files, and communicate among the various hosts on the network? To solve this problem, engineers decided not to re-invent the wheel: They turned back to the mainframes and looked at how they did it. In fact, since the system had to be compatible with the mainframes, why not use the same system?

Mainframe communications had two components: software and hardware. The software took the form of *drivers*—programs that told the computer how to access the network. A driver is configured for use between the host computer and network card. At the other end, a sort of universal connector is created between the network card and the network. This is an optimum solution. Programs could be designed to use this universal connector. This kept the hardware design as simple as possible, which improved its reliability and ease of installation.

To enable DOS to use the communications hardware of a mainframe was fairly easy. In its initial conception, the PC had been loosely based on the mainframe. The peripherals just had to use a different physical connector to plug into the computer. Making the software work was more difficult. This is where Novell got clever. They figured out a way to install certain programs into DOS and make up for its deficiencies. These programs are referred to as extensions to the OS. The first couple of versions weren't very friendly by today's standards, but they worked well enough. The programs allowed smaller companies to implement low-cost networks and enhance their productivity. This in turn enabled them to spend more money on networking devices—which allowed them to save money and increase productivity. The self-sustaining cycle is responsible for much of the networking world as we know it. It also changed the way networks are defined. As networking became more prevalent, it went from one local area network (LAN) to groups of networks, and then to networks of networks (called wide area networks, or *WANs*). Throughout this evolution, the software has gone through many revisions, while the hardware has stayed relatively the same.

Customers

The following list of some Novell customers shows how popular the idea of networking is with large corporations.

■ *Automotive*: Allied Signal, Daimler Chrysler, Ford, General Motors, Michelin, Nissan, TRW Automotive, Volvo

■ *Banking and Finance*: ABN Amro Bank, American Express, Banc One Corp., Bankers Trust, California Federal Bank, Chase Manhattan, Citicorp, Deutsche Financial Services, First Union, J.P. Morgan, NationsBanc, PostBank, ReliaStar Financial Services, State Street, UBS Switzerland

■ *Consumer Products and Retail*: American Home Products, Blockbuster-Australia, Colgate-Palmolive, Domino's Pizza, Eddie Bauer, Hallmark Cards, Jenny Craig International, LensCrafters, Nintendo, Pepsico, Safeway Stores, Wal-Mart

- *Education*: Duke University, Loyola University, Minnesota Department of State Colleges and Universities, Purdue University, New York University, University of California at San Francisco, University of Southern California

- *Electronic Systems and Engineering*: Andover Controls, Fluor Daniel, Raytheon

- *Energy*: Aramco, Mobil Oil, Occidental Petroleum, Pemmex Oil

- *Government*: California Department of Transportation, Environmental Protection Agency, German Ministry of Education, States of Arizona, California, Michigan, North Carolina, Ohio, and Texas, U.S. Census Bureau, U.S. Postal Service, U.S. Department of Defense, U.S. Department of Justice

- *Healthcare and Pharmaceuticals*: Bristol-Myers Squibb, Foundation Health, Helix Health, Kaiser Permanente, Pfizer, United Healthcare

- *Industrial*: BASF Corporation, Hoechst Celanese, Litton/Solar Turbines, Whirlpool Corporation

- *Semiconductors*: National Semiconductor Corporation, SGS Thomson Microelectronics

- *Services*: EDS, KPMG Peat Marwick, Saatchi & Saatchi, Young and Rubicam

- *Telecommunications*: 3Com, Air Touch Cellular, ALLTEL, AT&T, British Telecommunications PLC, Nortel, Telecom Italia, WorldCom

- *Transportation and Shipping*: American Airlines, FedEx, Lufthansa SA, Southwest Airlines, United Airlines, United Parcel Service, and Virgin Atlantic

What Is a Network?

Simply stated, a ***network*** is a group of computers (or workstations—sometimes called hosts) that can communicate with each other, share hardware resources (such as hard disks or printers), and access remote computers or other networks. With Novell software there is also a server involved. (Some types of networks do not require a server. In peer-to-peer networking, all workstations act as the client and server at the same time.)

A basic Novell NetWare network consists of a server, client workstations, and printer(s). Each is connected to the network with cabling and a network board. More complex networks might include routers, hubs, switches, and gateways. See Figure 7-1.

FIGURE 7-1
A typical network

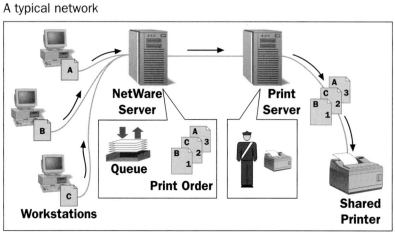

The actual communication between the different devices is done by first translating the data into a common protocol and then sending it across the network card into the network for use. A *protocol* is the set of rules that govern transmission between two machines or pieces of software, which lets them coordinate without ambiguity. Every device on the network does not natively speak the common protocol. This is because the protocols can be changed by the network engineers to fit their purposes or improve security. (For instance, if hackers can't talk to the network, they can't hack it.) The drivers that are loaded into each machine have instructions on how to encode the information into the protocols and then translate back again.

As stated earlier, today's PC networks are based on the networks developed for mainframes. Their protocol, called IP for Internet protocol, is the same protocol used by the Internet. NetWare's transport protocol is IPX—an extension of the IP protocol (IPX stands for Internet protocol extension). This means that it has certain extensions that allow the IPX protocol to do things not planned for in the IP protocol. The IP and IPX protocols are not compatible, but they can be run at the same time on a network without interfering with each other.

Each time a machine needs to send/request information, the data is translated into the protocol and sent across the network in small chunks called *packets*. This is very similar to sending a multipage letter one page at a time. The network doesn't send larger chunks because the machine with the largest chunk would tie up the network. Sending the data in uniform packets gives other machines a chance to send their data. This means the network resources are shared more equally.

- *Server.* The server manages the communication on the network. Because many users will access and use the server, a NetWare server should contain a fast processor and large amounts of disk space (usually over 20 GB) and memory.

- *Client Workstations.* Client workstations are computers running operating systems such as DOS, Windows, or Mac. To connect to the network, each client workstation requires Novell Client software and a network board, as described below.

■ *Printers*. Because many users need access to printers, placing printers on the network is cost-effective. Printers connect to the network with a network board or through a dedicated print server.

Network boards (also called LAN cards, network adapters, and network interface cards or NICs) provide the connection between the computing device and the network. Each device on the network must have a network board. Network boards are designed for specific network architectures such as FDDI, token ring, or Ethernet. The following paragraphs describe each of these architectures.

FDDI, or fiber distributed data interface, uses fiber-optic cable in two concentric rings. See Figure 7-2. If one ring is broken, all communications fall back on the unbroken ring. Data flows clockwise in one ring and counter-clockwise in the other ring. This means that data has a maximum distance of only half the ring to travel. This high-speed (128 MB/sec) network is used almost exclusively as a backbone to connect separate networks into a wide area network (WAN). FDDI allows data to be transmitted a much greater distance than other technologies allow. Distance is measured in kilometers, versus 300 meters for Ethernet. FDDI is based on earlier token ring networks and uses a token to pass information.

FIGURE 7-2
Fiber distributed data interface, or FDDI

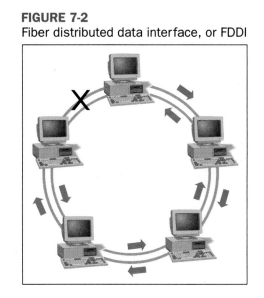

A *token ring* is a type of network that connects all machines on the network. See Figure 7-3. They are connected in a ring, similar to holding hands in a circle. It comes in two speeds, 4- and 16-megabit. In both cases, traffic is controlled by means of a *token*. The token is not a physical object, but a special bit configuration. When the network starts, the server has the token. No other machine is allowed to do anything until it receives the token. First the server looks at the token for any information addressed to it. If there isn't any, the server attaches any messages it may want to send and passes the token to the first workstation. The first workstation repeats the process. It looks at the token for any messages addressed to the first workstation. It removes these from the token and attaches any messages it wants to send. It then passes the token to the next machine. The process repeats until the server gets the token back. This technology has an extreme amount of overhead to manage. But information can flow very rapidly—almost as fast as newer technologies—because the traffic is controlled better. Usually speeds are approximately 86% of the maximum possible speed, even on large networks. The downside to this technology is that the whole network stops working if one machine fails.

FIGURE 7-3
Token ring

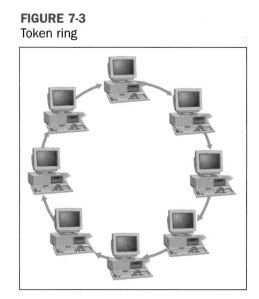

Ethernet technology comes in different types: 10Base2, 10Base-T, 100Base-T, and 5base-T (ThickNet). The parts of the name refer to the speed at which data is transmitted across the media and the types of media used. The number at the beginning of the name indicates the data speed: For instance, 10 means ten megabits/sec, and 5 means five megabits/sec. The number at the end of the name refers to the type of connection. For example, 2 refers to a coaxial cable (similar to cable TV) used to connect the hosts; T refers to connection made to a backbone, through an 8-conductor cable that looks physically like the letter "T." Ethernet technology is extremely fault-tolerant. If one machine stops working, the rest of the network continues to work without problems. The downside is that it has almost no traffic management. As a result, the network usually only performs at 20% of maximum possible speed. However, because it is cheap and easy to implement and maintain, it is still the dominant network technology today.

Cabling connects each device on the network. The cable can be coaxial, twisted-pair, or fiber-optic, depending on the network architecture (physical layout and technology used). For certain network types, you need cable both for the main network trunk and also for attaching individual computing devices to that trunk. The attachment cable is often called a drop, patch, adapter, or transceiver cable. Generically, the cabling is referred to as the transmission media.

A *router* provides a path from a device on one network to a device on another network. Multiprotocol routers can handle several protocols at the same time. Routers can filter different packet types and restrict certain network addresses from reaching other networks.

A *gateway* is a computer dedicated to providing a network with access to a different type of network or computing environment. A gateway computer needs at least one network board, plus software to provide the conversion and translation services to communicate with the other network. Gateway computers need a considerable amount of disk storage and memory.

A *print server* is a computer that does nothing but pass print requests from the network to a printer attached to the computer. The computer is capable of handling multiple printers at one time. Many times it is not financially feasible for the company to dedicate a computer to this task. A small, dedicated box has been developed that accomplishes the same task at a much lower cost. The downside is that it will not do anything else. This is considered acceptable because even a cheap new computer is about $1000 with monitor and software, but a print server device starts at about $100 complete.

A WAN, or wide area network, is where two or more networks are connected to create a larger network. See Figure 7-4. Generally you will see this in large companies that want to connect their regional offices to the corporate office.

FIGURE 7-4
Wide area network or WAN

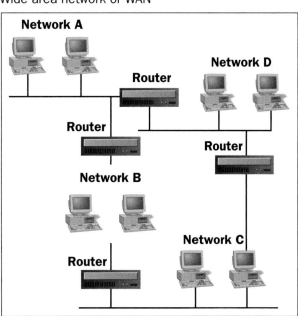

Installing Novell Client

Understanding What a User Might See

If this is a new client software installation or an upgrade from older client software, the software is installed or upgraded when a user logs in. The new software is copied to the client machines. The workstation must be restarted to make the changes active. Users might see system messages set up by the administrator as their workstations are upgraded, depending on how you set up the installation.

If workstations already have current client software, the client login runs as usual. For the most part the client software is invisible to the user. The difference between a client machine and a non client machine is that the file menus of a client machine may have extra options. The client machine may also show hard drives and printers that are not physically attached to the computer.

Before installing the client software, make sure the client workstation has sufficient resources and the required software. If not, the installation won't finish. The complete hardware and software setup for client workstations might require you to complete one or more of the following tasks:

■ Check server protocols and requirements.

■ Check for a valid network connection.

■ Check client workstation requirements.

Checking Server Protocols and Requirements

You must prepare your servers to work with the Novell Client software. You must know what protocols you use on the server and make sure that the servers are configured to support long filenames. NetWare 5 or later automatically supports long filenames.

You can install Novell Client with one of the following protocol options:

■ **IP Only (NetWare 5 or later):** Installs the IP protocol stack, which allows the client to run in IP-only networks; the workstation cannot communicate with IPX servers.

■ **IP with IPX Compatibility Mode (NetWare 5 or later):** Installs IP and includes Compatibility mode, which allows IPX applications to run in IP-only networks by converting IPX packets into IP packets. IPX Compatibility mode allows the client to communicate with services in IPX-only networks if the Migration Agent is installed on any NetWare 5 or later servers.

Checking for a Valid Network Connection

S TEP-BY-STEP 7.1

1. Open **Network Neighborhood**.

2. Check that the networks you expect to see actually appear in the Network Neighborhood window.

3. If you have never installed a client or created a network connection, you may not have access to Network Neighborhood. Therefore, you must install the client software from a CD-ROM. See Installing Clients from CD-ROM further on in this chapter.

Preparing Client Workstations

Certain client workstation requirements must be met before installing or upgrading Novell Client software. See Table 7-1 for these requirements.

TABLE 7-1

OPERATING SYSTEM	HARDWARE REQUIREMENTS
Windows 95/98	486 processor or better Minimum 28 MB free disk space
Windows NT/2000/XP	Must meet the minimum requirements for Windows NT/2000/XP
Windows 3.1x and DOS	A memory manager Minimum 15 MB free disk space Minimum 8 MB RAM

The Network Board

Novell Client for Windows NT and Novell Client for Windows 95/98 support Network Driver Interface Specification (NDIS) drivers. This is a set of standards set forth by Novell to ensure that all products capable of running Novell software are compatible. For specific information about installing the network board, refer to the board manufacturer's instructions.

Novell Client for DOS and Windows 3.1x supports ODI drivers. For information about installing the network board, refer to the board manufacturer's instructions.

Checking for Incompatibilities

Windows 95/98

The following network components are not compatible with Novell Client for Windows 95/98:

- Microsoft Client for NetWare networks

- Microsoft file and printer sharing for NetWare networks

- Microsoft Service for Novell Directory Services (NDS) software

- Novell NetWare workstation shell 3.x (NETX)

- Novell NetWare workstation shell 4.0 and later (VLM) clients

- Novell Internetwork Packet Exchange (IPX) ODI protocol (the 16-bit module for the NETX and VLM clients)

> **Important**
>
> Open Data-Link Interface (ODI) drivers are not installed on Windows 95/98 or Windows NT. ODI drivers are an early/primitive form of network driver. They have been upgraded to the newer and more powerful NDIS drivers. If you are upgrading an older version of the client and you have ODI drivers currently installed, these drivers are still supported. If you are installing for the first time, NDIS drivers will not be installed. If you do not already have the necessary NDIS driver, you might need to obtain it from the Windows 95/98 CD-ROM or from the network board manufacturer.

These network components conflict with Novell Client for Windows 95/98. If any of these network components are installed, the client installation program detects the conflict and removes the conflicting network components.

Windows NT/2000/XP

Novell Client cannot be installed on Windows 2000 or Windows XP if the Local Area Connection Properties Page is open. Close this page before running the Novell Client install.

IPX Compatibility and Novell NetWare/IP Adapter will not be upgraded from Windows NT to Windows 2000.

Some Windows NT 4.0 printer drivers are incompatible with Windows 2000 and XP and will not install.

DOS and Windows 3.1x

There are no known incompatibilities.

Installing Clients from CD-ROM

If you plan to install the Novell Client software on a small number of workstations, or if the workstations are not yet connected to a network, installing from the Novell Client CD-ROM works best.

If you plan to install the Novell Client on several workstations on the network, consider using one of several network installation options. A network installation can upgrade existing client software or install new client software. The Novell Client Setup utility helps you install Novell Client software on Windows-based workstations. When you use this utility, you can select the client you want to install from a list of available clients. Administrative options are also available.

STEP-BY-STEP 7.2

1. Insert the Novell Client CD-ROM. If the Client Setup utility does not start automatically launch **setupnw.exe** from the root of the CD-ROM.

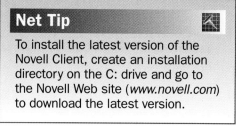

Net Tip

To install the latest version of the Novell Client, create an installation directory on the C: drive and go to the Novell Web site (*www.novell.com*) to download the latest version.

STEP-BY-STEP 7.2 Continued

2. Click **YES** to accept the license agreement. See Figure 7-5.

FIGURE 7-5
License agreement

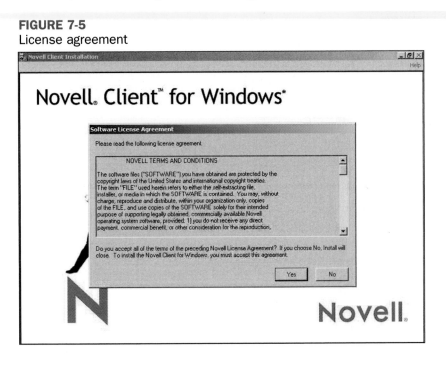

STEP-BY-STEP 7.2 Continued

3. Select **Typical Installation** and click **Install**. See Figures 7-6 and 7-7.

FIGURE 7-6
Installation window

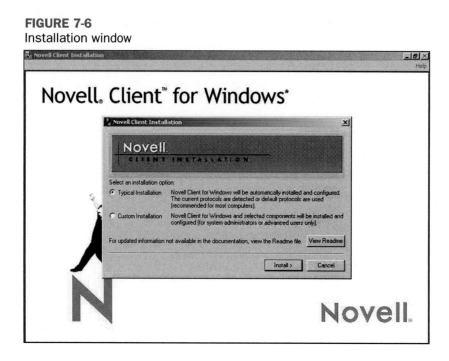

FIGURE 7-7
Installing the client

4. For help during the installation, refer to the online documentation that accompanies the software or contact your network administrator.

5. Click **Reboot**.

Configuring Network Protocols

After you install Novell Client, make sure that it is configured correctly for your network.

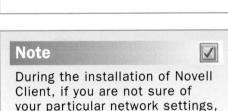

Warning ⚠

Before you configure network protocols, make sure you have the correct information and any addresses needed. If you configure protocols incorrectly, the workstation will not be able to connect to the network, or it might conflict with other workstations using the same address.

STEP-BY-STEP **7.3**

Do one of the following for your platform.

Windows 95/98 and Windows NT:

1. Right-click **Network Neighborhood** and click **Properties**.

2. Select the protocol that you want to configure, and then click **Properties**.

3. Configure the protocol options in each tab, then click **OK**.

4. Click **OK** to make the changes.

Windows 2000 and XP:

1. Right-click **My Network Places** and click **Properties**.

2. Right-click **Local Area Connection**.

3. Select the protocol that you want to configure, and then click **Properties**.

4. Configure the protocol options in each tab, then click **OK**.

5. Click **OK** to make the changes.

Note ✓

You might be prompted to supply the Windows operating system CD. If you do not have access to the correct files, you might not be able to create a network connection.

Installing Clients from DOS

The DOS-based installation installs the necessary files for Novell Client for DOS and Windows 3.1x files and allows you to select from several optional utilities.

If you previously installed the client software in Windows and you are using multiple location profiles, you should update using the Windows installation. Location profiles maintain information about your working environment for each workstation you work in, or for each networking environment in a location.

The DOS installation does not support Novell dial-up services or locations and it disables previously installed versions of the Locations Manager.

Note ✓

During the installation of Novell Client, if you are not sure of your particular network settings, see your instructor or network administrator for the necessary information.

S TEP-BY-STEP 7.4

1. Insert the Novell Client CD-ROM.

2. From a DOS prompt, switch to the drive where the Novell Client CD-ROM is located.

3. Change to the **PRODUCTS\DOSWIN32** directory, and then key **INSTALL**.

4. Press **Enter** to accept the license agreement.

5. Select the options you want to install on the workstation.

6. Press **F10** to continue.

7. If you want to return to the previous screen or cancel the installation, press Esc at any time before the program begins copying files.

8. Configure the options you are installing.

   a. Depending on the options you have chosen, various configuration screens appear. Use the arrow keys to move to a new field and press **Enter** to edit the field.

   b. Press **F10** to save your changes and continue.

   c. Depending on the type of network board you have installed in the workstation, select the 16-bit or 32-bit LAN driver type. DOS and Windows 3.1 will use the 16-bit drivers. Windows 95/98 can use either, but better performance and reliability are obtained with 32-bit drivers. Windows NT, Linux, and Macintosh must use the 32-bit drivers.

   d. Review the Installation Configuration Summary. To make necessary changes, use the arrow keys to move to a new field and press **Enter** to edit the field.

9. Press **F10** to continue. The program copies the appropriate files to your workstation and sets up the workstation to run the Novell Client software.

10. To exit Install, press **Enter** to return to DOS or press **Ctrl+Alt+Del** to reboot the workstation.

The Novell Client for DOS and Windows 3.1x software does not load until the workstation restarts.

Installing Clients from the Network

If you plan to install the Novell Client software on multiple workstations, you can install from the network by copying files to the server and modifying the login script. The login script is a pre-defined set of instructions the network uses to connect to the various printers and hard drives. This installation is sometimes called the Automatic Client upgrade. It also sets user access, based on rights set by the administrator. One network installation method is explained here. There are additional network installation options that might better suit your networking environment. You should evaluate these methods before deciding which is best for you.

Even if your network has workstations on multiple platforms (this generally refers to the OS being used; i.e., a machine running Windows is referred to as a Windows platform), you can install and upgrade the client software on all platforms when users log in. The process requires five tasks:

■ Create a folder on the NetWare server.

■ Copy Novell Client files and other required files to this folder (workstations can then read the files during login).

■ Grant rights to the new folder.

■ Create or update the appropriate configuration file (INSTALL.CFG, SETUP.INI, NWSETUP.INI, or UNTENDED.TXT) for each platform-specific client. These files are on the installation CD-ROM.

■ Create or modify the appropriate login script.

Let users know in advance about the upgrade so they understand what is happening and why their work environment is changing.

Creating a Folder

Log in to a server as Admin or log in as a user with Admin equivalence. You need rights to copy files to a network folder that all users can access. You also need rights to modify login scripts. Create a folder that will hold the client files; for example, create a client folder in the SYS:\PUBLIC network folder, which has the name SYS:\PUBLIC\CLIENT.

Copying Files

There are several subdirectories that need to be copied from the PRODUCTS directory on the Novell Client CD-ROM to the client system. Copy the WINNT and WIN95 directories to a new folder on your hard drive. The files in these directories will be used by the setup program to install the client and various services.

If you are installing the client in only one language or if your network does not have enough space to accommodate multiple language directories, you can delete the language directories you do not need from the NLS directory under each client directory. To ensure that you have all necessary files, copy the entire client directory and then delete only the extra language directories. Some steps in the installation process are conditional, meaning they only occur in certain circumstances. Any time a step in the process is labeled conditional, you only have to do it if you meet that condition.

■ (Conditional) If you are installing Novell Client for Windows 95/98, copy Windows 95 .CAB files to the Win95 directory. The files are on the Microsoft Windows 95/98 CD (and Upgrade CD) in the Win95 folder.

■ (Conditional) If you are installing Novell Client for DOS and Windows 3.1x and you will be using the DOS installation utility (INSTALL.EXE), create a LOG directory in the new folder.

The login script executes commands that create a LOG file in the LOG directory. The LOG file indicates whether the client update was successful. It is also useful in tracking down problems because it is a record of what happened and when.

Assigning Rights

Rights are the network's way of controlling who has access to what. For instance, you would never give anyone outside of the payroll department rights to view salary information. Rights also guarantee that new users automatically get the basic utilities they need to do their jobs. Rights are an impartial system of controlling access, which are assigned by the system administrator, then managed by the network.

Notice that only the administrator or someone with equal status can assign rights. As a general user you will not be able to do this. The exception is in your own private directory. Here is an example of the process an administrator might follow.

- Create a Group object called Client in the NDS tree.

- Place into that group users whose workstations need to be installed or upgraded.

- Make sure that the group has Read and File Scan rights to the new folder you created.

- If you created the new folder in SYS:\PUBLIC, the new folder should have Read and File Scan rights already associated with it, but you should make sure that these rights have not been changed.

Administrators assign rights by using NetWare Administrator—a utility to which only they have access. It allows the administrator to define and shape the network as needed. For an in-depth discussion on the topic, you can read the user manuals on the Novell Client installation CD-ROM.

Updating Configuration Files

If you are using the default settings to install the clients, you do not have to create or modify the configuration files. You can bypass this process and proceed to Creating or Modifying the Login Script.

Each platform-specific installation utility reads a configuration file in order to get information such as where to copy drivers during installation and what is the most recent version number. This file must be placed in the same directory as the installation utility. See Table 7-2 to determine what configuration file to use with your system.

TABLE 7-2

PLATFORM	CONFIGURATION FILE
Windows 95/98	NWSETUP.INI and a Novell Install Manager-generated text file
Windows NT/2000/XP	Novell Install Manager-generated text file
Windows 3.1x	SETUP.INI
DOS	INSTALL.CFG

Updating Windows 95/98 and Windows NT/2000/XP Configuration Files

You can use Novell Client Install Manager, a GUI-based utility, to configure the client properties. This method eliminates the need to configure each workstation manually. After you have created the configuration file with Install Manager, use the /U command-line parameter in the login script to call the configuration file and set the properties.

STEP-BY-STEP 7.5

1. Start the Novell Client Install Manager (NCIMAN.EXE).

   a. For Windows 95/98, the Install Manager is located in the SYS:\PUBLIC\CLIENT\WIN95\ IBM_LANGUAGE \ADMIN directory you copied to the server.

   b. For Windows NT/2000/XP, the Install Manager is located in the SYS:\PUBLIC\CLIENT\WINNT\ IS386\ADMIN directory you copied to the server.

2. Do one of the following:

   a. For Windows 95/98, click **File > New File > Windows 95** to create a new file.

   b. For Windows NT/2000/XP, click **File > New File > Windows NT** to create a new file.

3. Modify the installation options as needed.

   a. In the Configuration options list box, double-click the configuration option you want to modify.

   b. In the Property pages, set the parameters and then click **OK**. The values you set appear in the right list box.

   c. (Conditional) If you change properties for Novell Client for Windows NT/2000/XP or Windows 95/98 and intend to use the configuration file created with Novell Client Install Manager to upgrade existing client software, you must change the major or minor version parameter. If you are installing for the first time, proceed to Step 4.

   d. The client is updated only if the version numbers have changed. If the version numbers have not changed, even if parameters in the configuration file have been changed, the client and the new properties will not change.

      i. For Novell Client for Windows 95/98, you must change the version number in the NWSETUP.INI file. Open NWSETUP.INI and search for the Client Version section. The version number consists of four numbers, each separated by a decimal point (for example, 2.5.0.0). The third number is the major version number; the fourth number is the minor version number. Increase either number by one to install a new version.

      ii. For Novell Client for Windows NT/2000/XP, change the version number with Novell Client Install Manager by clicking **Installation > Client** and increasing the major or minor parameter by one or more.

4. Click **File > Save**. You can save the file with any filename you want to use. For example, you could rename the file **UNATT_95.TXT**.

5. Copy this file to one of the following directories:

   a. SYS:PUBLIC\CLIENT\WIN95\IBM_LANGUAGE directory (for Windows 95/98)

   b. SYS:PUBLIC\CLIENT\WINNT\I386 directory (for Windows NT/2000/XP)

This file is then used with the /U command-line parameter in the login script to call the configuration file and set the properties during installation.

Updating DOS and Windows 3.1x Configuration Files

You can control the Windows-based install program (SETUP.EXE) by modifying the SETUP.INI FILE, and you can control the DOS-based install program (INSTALL.EXE) by modifying the INSTALL.CFG file. However, the defaults work fine for most installations.

Evaluating Other Network Installation Options

There are additional network installation options that might better suit your networking environment. You should evaluate these methods before deciding which is best for you. The following section gives a brief overview of the other network installation methods and information on where to find complete documentation about them.

Using Other Windows 95/98 Installation Options

You can use the following methods to install Novell Client for Windows 95/98 software:

■ *MSBATCH*: Use this option to install and configure Novell Client for Windows 95/98 without your having to be present. This is called an unattended installation. The administrator has created a file with a listing of all options to install on the system. The installation program uses this file to know how to install the client. This process saves a great deal of time, especially if you need to install the software on multiple workstations. This is usually how it is done in the real world. An administrator creates one disk that works the way he wants and then makes many copies (for example, let's say 20 copies). He will then take a row of 21 machines and start at one end. He will stick a disk in the first machine. While the first machine is booting he will move onto the next machine, repeating his actions. He continues down the row until all 21 machines have been booted. Hopefully, by the time he reaches the last machine the first one is complete and ready for use. He then collects the disks and repeats the process on another row. Think of it as a sort of assembly line.

■ *Automatic Client Upgrade (ACU)*: Use this option to automatically upgrade multiple workstations from the Microsoft Client for NetWare Networks to Novell Client for Windows 95/98.

Using Other Windows NT/2000/XP Installation Options

You can use any of the following methods to install Novell Client for Windows NT/2000/XP software:

■ *Unattended install*: Use this option to install and configure Novell Client for Windows NT/2000/XP without having to be present. This feature saves a great deal of time, especially if you need to install the software on multiple workstations. By preconfiguring installation options with Novell Client Install Manager, you can install both Windows NT and Novell Client for Windows NT/2000/XP, or Novell Client for Windows NT/2000/XP by itself, on one or more workstations over the network.

■ *Automatic Client Upgrade*: Use this option to automatically upgrade multiple workstations from the Microsoft Client for NetWare Networks to Novell Client for Windows NT/2000/XP.

■ *Windows NT Network control panel*: Use this option if you want to use the Network control panel to install Novell Client for Windows NT/2000/XP as you would other services.

Using Other DOS and Windows 3.1x Installation Options

There are two additional network installation methods for installing the Novell Client for DOS and Windows 3.1x:

■ *Automatic Client Upgrade*: Use this option to set up and standardize the installation process. During installation, ACU automatically configures each workstation's client settings, thus virtually eliminating the need to configure individual workstations.

■ *User-Initiated Installation*: Use this option to set up an installation procedure with little or no user intervention. Once users are notified of the installation procedure, they can begin installing whenever it is convenient. For more information, see the online documentation.

Basic Functions of Novell NetWare

Resource Management

NDS, Novell's directory services software, is a distributed, replicated naming service that maintains information about and provides access to every resource on the network. (It's a sort of yellow pages or road atlas for the network.)

During the installation of a Novell server, a minimal NDS framework is set up. The minimal framework consists of an NDS tree, a container object, a NetWare server object, and an Admin user object.

After installation, you can create additional NDS objects using the QuickStart utility, the NEAT utility, or the NetWare Administrator utility. NDS allows users with the proper access rights to log in to the network and view and access network resources.

NDS Trees

The *NDS tree* represents the entire network. Network resources such as servers and printers are presented hierarchically in the NDS tree. Users log in to the NDS tree with a single login name and password instead of logging in to individual servers.

Tree Name

The NDS tree is given a name during the first NetWare server installation. The name of the tree should represent your entire organization. It can be up to 64 characters long and can contain underscores and dashes. Although other special characters are permitted, Novell does not recommend using special characters in the NDS tree name.

Objects

NDS objects are used to represent network divisions or network resources such as an organization or a NetWare server. See Figure 7-8. Objects have properties that define their characteristics. You can create two types of objects: container objects and leaf objects.

FIGURE 7-8
Different objects

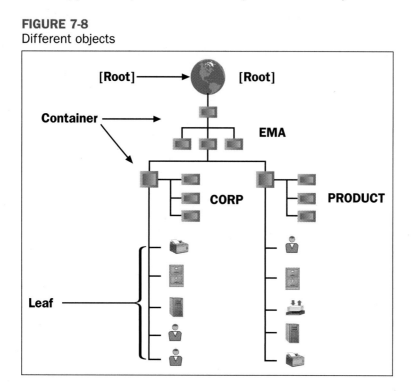

Container Objects

Container objects are used to organize the structure of the NDS tree. A container object can hold another container object, a leaf object, or both. See Figure 7-9. The two main kinds of container objects are Organization and Organizational Unit. However, all of the following container objects are available:

■ *[Root]* is the highest-level container object in the NDS tree. [Root] is created whenever a new NDS tree is created. [Root] cannot be renamed. All NDS objects exist in [Root]. A user with rights to the [Root] object has rights to the entire NDS tree. Only Country and Organization objects can be placed under [Root].

■ An *Organization* (O) object is a container object that represents the first level of grouping for most networks. Depending on the scope of your network, this level could represent a company, division, or department. At least one Organization object is required in an NDS tree. An Organization object can contain Organizational Unit (OU) objects or other NDS objects.

■ *Organizational Unit* (OU) objects are container objects that can be used to organize other objects in the NDS tree into subsets. For example, Organizational Unit objects might be departments or project groups. Organizational Unit objects are optional, but must exist below an Organization (O) object or another Organizational Unit (OU) object.

■ *Country* (C) objects are container objects that can be placed only directly off the [Root]. Although you can have as many Country objects as desired, they add a level of complexity to your NDS tree that might not be necessary. The Country container object is provided to comply with X.500 global naming specifications.

■ The *Locality* (L) container object is provided to distinguish the geographical location of an object.

When you create a new NDS tree, the container objects, such as Organization or Organizational Unit object, that will contain the NetWare Server object must be created immediately. The installation program for this product automatically creates the needed Organization object for you.

FIGURE 7-9
Different container objects

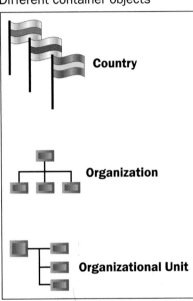

Country

Organization

Organizational Unit

Leaf Objects

Leaf objects represent information about network resources such as servers or printers. Unlike container objects, leaf objects cannot contain other NDS objects. Many types of leaf objects exist, such as Application, Computer, Printer, User, and NetWare Server objects. At least two leaf objects are created during the server installation.

■ The *NetWare Server* object is a leaf object that represents any server running any version of the NetWare operating system. The NetWare Server object is automatically created and placed into the NDS tree during server installation.

■ When a new NDS tree is created, an *ADMIN user* is automatically created. ADMIN has Supervisor rights to the entire NDS tree. Supervisor rights allow a user to create and manage all objects in the tree. For security reasons, you can rename user ADMIN after the installation using the NetWare Administrator utility, or the SETPASS command-line utility.

Other users can be assigned Supervisor rights to container objects and all their leaf objects. Having Supervisor rights to a container object allows the user to create and manage all objects in the container.

When installing a new server into an existing tree, you must have Supervisor rights in the container in which you are installing the new server.

NDS Context

NDS allows you to refer to objects according to their positions within a tree. The NDS context describes the full path (including container objects) of an object in the NDS tree structure. This is similar to giving a friend directions to your house.

The notation to describe the NDS context is the list of container objects, separated by periods, between the leaf object and [Root]. For example, the context of the NetWare Server object SERVER1 to be placed in the Organizational Unit (OU) container SALES in the Organization (O) container ACME would be noted as: SALES.ACME. The full NDS context name for this server would be SERVER1.SALES.ACME.

NDS context can also be noted using typeful names. Typeful names include the object abbreviation types. For example, the NDS context described above written in typeful notation would be CN=SERVER1.OU=SALES.O=ACME.

When reading a typeful name, the leftmost object is assumed to be a leaf object. Leaf objects have common names (CN) which are described in typeful notation with a CN= preceding the object name.

Unique Features of NetWare

Printing to a Network Printer

Printer setup can be automated so that users' workstations attach to the network printers they use each time users log in to the network. Users can use the network printers without manually connecting to the printer every time they want to print.

After connecting to a network printer, users can select the printer from any application that they are using.

A printer driver for each type of printer must be installed on the workstations.

Users can set up network printing on a workstation by specifying the name of the printer in any of the following programs:

- Windows Add Printer Wizard
- Novell Capture Printer Port

The following can automate printer connections so that the computer connects to network printers each time a user logs in:

- NetWare Login Script
- NT/2000/XP Restore Connections
- NT/2000/XP Logon Script

STEP-BY-STEP 7.6

1. Click **Start** and click **Printers and Faxes**. (These instructions are for use with WinXP.)

2. Click **Add Printer**. See Figure 7-10.

FIGURE 7-10
Add Printer dialog box

3. Click **Next** in the Add Printer Wizard. See Figure 7-11.

FIGURE 7-11
Add Printer Wizard

4. Click **Capture** and if necessary enter a network password for the printer.

STEP-BY-STEP 7.6 Continued

5. Click a Network printer, or a printer attached to another printer. See Figure 7-12.

FIGURE 7-12
Add a network printer

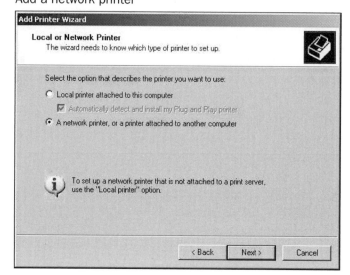

6. Select a printer you want to use from the Shared Printers box.

    a. For NetWare 4 or later networks, double-click **Novell Directory Services** and find the context for the printer. Then select a Printer object from the list.

    b. For NetWare 3.X and earlier, double-click **NetWare Servers**. Then, double-click the name of the server that supports the queues you want to use and select the queue.

7. Click **OK**.

8. (Conditional)

    a. If a dialog box prompts you to install a driver for the printer, click **OK** and install it.

    b. Select the name of the printer from the Driver box and then click **OK**.

    c. Enter the path to the printer driver and then click **OK**.

9. Run an application and select the network printer when you print.

Specifying Capture Settings with Windows Printing

Windows does not require captured printer ports to print to a network printer. Windows can use print devices that are associated with network printers. This allows applications to print directly to a network printer.

Use the Capture Settings dialog box to specify printer settings for print captures created with Windows. This can be useful if you want to use a DOS or Windows 3.x application that relies on print captures.

> **Note** ☑
>
> The Capture utility does not affect Windows printer devices. Captures are global. If you capture a printer port, the port is available for network printing from anywhere in Windows.

Step-by-Step 7.7

1. Right-click the **N** icon in the system tray. See Figure 7-13.

FIGURE 7-13
Novell icon in system tray

2. Click **Novell Capture Printer Port**.

3. Enter the correct information in the dialog box. See Figure 7-14.

FIGURE 7-14
Capture Printer Port dialog box

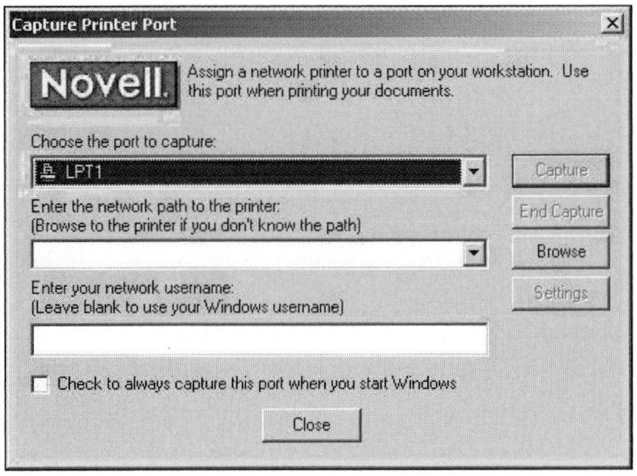

4. Click **Capture**.

5. Click **Close**.

6. Log off the network.

SUMMARY

In this lesson, you learned:

- In 1983, Novell realized the potential of connecting a company's desktop computing resources and sharing them. This was the beginning of the local area network (LAN).

- Simply stated, a network is a group of computers (workstations, sometimes called hosts) that can communicate with each other, share hardware resources (such as hard disks or printers), and access remote computers or other networks. Novell software requires a server, although peer-to-peer networks do not.

- Novell NetWare networks are used in many of the major corporations around the world.

- If your installation involves new client software installation or an upgrade from older client software, the software is installed or upgraded when users log in. The new software is copied to the client machines. The workstation must be restarted to make the changes active. Users might see system messages set up by the administrator as their workstations are upgraded, depending on how you set up the installation.

- NDS, Novell's directory services software, is a distributed, replicated naming service that maintains information about and provides access to every resource on the network.

- Users can set up a Novell printer by using the Add Printer Wizard in Windows.

VOCABULARY *Review*

Define the following terms:

Cabling	Leaf objects	Protocol
Container objects	NDS	Rights
Drivers	NDS tree	Router
Ethernet	Network	Token
FDDI	Network board	Token Ring
Gateway	Packets	Wide area network (WAN)
Local area network (LAN)	Print server	

REVIEW *Questions*

MULTIPLE CHOICE

Select the best response for the following statements.

1. NIC stands for:
   A. Network InterChange.
   B. the network administrator's title.
   C. Network Interface Console.
   D. Network Interface Card.

2. When speaking strictly about networking, media refers to
   A. the wiring used to connect the machines.
   B. the hard drives and floppy drives used to store information.
   C. the manuals or other documentation.
   D. sounds, images and text distributed across shared computers.

3. Online documentation refers to
   A. the manuals that are digitally stored on the installation CD(s).
   B. documentation kept on the Internet.
   C. calling tech support to help resolve your issue.
   D. documentation available as an automated phone service.

4. IPX stands for
   A. Internet Protocol Extension.
   B. Interconnected Printer Exchange.
   C. Independent Protocol Extension.
   D. Internet Protocol Exchange.

5. NetWare can be run across what cabling?
   A. Coaxial
   B. Ethernet, "ThinNet"
   C. ThickNet
   D. All of the above

6. Which of the following is Novell NetWare's transport protocol?
   A. TCP/IP
   B. IPX
   C. IP
   D. SLIP

7. Which of the following devices manages the communications on the network?
   A. Client
   B. Workstation
   C. Server
   D. Printer

8. Which of the following is a pre installation task?
   A. Check the server protocols and requirements.
   B. Check for a valid network connection.
   C. Check client workstation requirements.
   D. All of the above.

9. Which of the following network components is compatible with Novell Client for Windows 95/98?
   A. Microsoft Client
   B. Microsoft Service for NDS software
   C. Microsoft file and printer sharing for NetWare networks
   D. None of these network components is compatible with Novell Client for Windows 95/98.

10. Which of the following is a container object?
    A. Root
    B. Leaf
    C. Printer
    D. User

FILL IN THE BLANK

Complete the following sentences by writing the correct word or words in the blank provided.

1. A(n) _____ is a group of computers that can communicate with one another, share hardware resources, and access remote computers or other networks.

2. A(n) _____ is a set of rules that govern transmission between two machines or pieces of software.

3. _____ connects each device on the network.

4. A(n) _____ server is a computer that does nothing but pass print requests from the network to a printer attached to the computer.

5. _____ is Novell's directory services software.

CRITICAL *Thinking*

ACTIVITY 7-1

Novell has entered the open source market with a developer kit in which the code will be available to all, as opposed to the usual proprietary software that cannot be changed by anyone but Novell programmers. This will allow free distribution of the operating system and the ability to make user-specific changes to the operating system. Which practice do you think will benefit the customer more: open source code or proprietary software?

ACTIVITY 7-2

Novell, like Windows, has a variety of certifications available for its operating system. What are some of these certifications and what benefits do they provide?

LINUX

LESSON 8

OBJECTIVES

Upon completion of this lesson, you should be able to:

- Install the Linux operating system properly.

- Understand the basic functionalities of the Linux operating system.

- Work within the GNOME desktop environment.

- Work in a terminal emulation program using some of the more common shell commands.

- Describe the Linux file system.

- Describe the unique features that make Linux different from other operating systems.

- Obtain help through the Red Hat Help documentation, the man pages, or the info pages.

- Properly shut down the Linux operating system either through an XTerm window or through the GNOME interface.

Estimated Time: 6 hours

VOCABULARY

Daemons

Desktop environments

Disk Druid

Extended file system (EXT2)

GNOME

GNOME Panel

Graphical user interface (GUI)

Info pages

Man pages

Mount directory

Mount point

Open source code

Virtual display

Virtual File System (VFS)

XTerm

Introduction

If you have experience with the popular Microsoft Windows operating system, the first thing you are likely to notice about Linux (pronounced len-ix) is that it is very different from Windows. Linux is primarily a command-line operating system that requires the user to key commands on the keyboard. This gives Linux the performance and flexibility that many power users require. However, Linux also has a graphical interface called X Window, which operates similarly to Microsoft Windows. This makes Linux more accessible to the average user. With earlier versions, Linux tended to intimidate many potential users because it required that you understand a little more about how the computer operates. All in all, Linux was not for the timid. But many users wanted an operating system that allowed more control over their computer performance. The latest version of Linux provides the best of both worlds. It allows those who want more control over their computers to have it while also providing a nonintimidating, user-friendly graphical interface for those who simply want to use a reliable machine.

As we enter the new millennium, many users want their computers to be appliances, which they can turn on and use, rather than instruments that require some degree of knowledge to use effectively. Yet there are other users who primarily want high performance and system flexibility—and they are willing to invest the time and energy required to achieve these results. This latter group of users is primarily the one attracted to Linux.

Some of today's operating systems, such as Windows XP and Mac OS X, are relatively mature consumer products. Linux is rapidly joining this group of products for the general consumer, but it has traditionally been a system designed for more technical, hands-on computer users. The difference between the two types of users can be best understood through the following analogy. Using a prepackaged, ready-to-use operating system is like buying a toy car at a store. When you take the car out of the package, it's ready to use. But what happens when you get tired of the car's color or you want to modify it for off-road use? You can't. Linux and its parent, Unix, are different. Imagine that instead you went to the toy store and bought a box of building blocks. When you get home you cannot play with a car right away—first you have to build it from the parts. Then you can play with the car you just built. The box contains wheels and other things to make the building easier, but you still have to put some effort into it. The advantage here, however, is that when you get tired of it, you can take it apart and modify it. Which do you think is more fun? A toy car or a box of building blocks? Some people don't want the "hassle" of putting together the blocks and would prefer the ease of a premade car. Others would prefer the flexibility and customization available with building blocks.

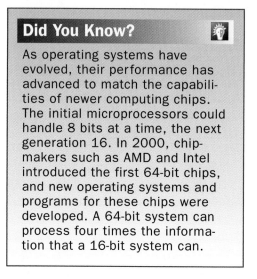

Did You Know?

As operating systems have evolved, their performance has advanced to match the capabilities of newer computing chips. The initial microprocessors could handle 8 bits at a time, the next generation 16. In 2000, chipmakers such as AMD and Intel introduced the first 64-bit chips, and new operating systems and programs for these chips were developed. A 64-bit system can process four times the information that a 16-bit system can.

Origins of Unix/Linux

In 1969, while working at AT&T's Bell Labs, Ken Thompson and Dennis Ritchie wrote Unix, a compact, time-sharing, multi-user operating system that ran on a Digital Equipment Corporation (DEC) computer. This initial version was written in assembly language. Although this operating system ran very quickly and efficiently, it was extremely difficult to modify. To increase the ease of modifying it, as well as to increase the number of mainframe and minicomputers that could run Unix, programmers rewrote it in the C programming language. Starting in 1974, Bell Labs licensed Unix to interested universities as a development tool. Later, Bell Labs continued to develop and market Unix itself.

Students at the colleges and universities that were licensed users of Unix quickly began to write utility programs—programs to perform small but important tasks. These were shared among all users and many of them are still part of the Unix kernel. (A *kernel* is the part of the operating system code that is closest to the machine and activates the hardware components, directly or through another software layer.)

Some licensed universities continued to develop Unix. The University of California at Berkeley is one such university. It developed the Berkeley System Distribution (BSD) version of Unix, and it continues to refine this version to meet the needs of the school and fully utilize the ever-changing hardware technology.

problems during the installation, don't despair. There are a number of ways to install—one of which will work on your machine. You can read about the various installation methods on the Red Hat Documentation CD or in the Installation Guide.

S TEP-BY-STEP 8.1

1. Insert the Linux installation CD into the CD-ROM, then restart the computer.

2. Turn on your computer. After a few moments, a screen containing the "boot:" prompt should appear. This screen also contains information on a variety of boot options and describes the function keys used to get help with those options. This initial screen will automatically start the installation program if you do nothing for one minute. (Or you can press **Enter** to continue.)

> **Note** ☑
>
> Your BIOS settings may need to be changed to allow booting from the CD-ROM. If your system does not support a bootable CD-ROM drive, you'll need to create a boot diskette to perform these steps. See the documentation that came with your software.

3. Press the **Enter** key. Watch the boot messages to see whether the Linux kernel properly detects your hardware. If it does not, you may need to restart the installation and choose Expert mode at the boot prompt screen. This is not usually required.

4. Next, you may be asked to select the installation method: CD-ROM, Hard Drive, NFS Image, FTP, or HTTP. Click **CD-ROM** and then click **OK**. (This selection may be made automatically.)

5. When prompted, insert the CD into your CD-ROM drive (if you did not boot from it), select **OK**, and then press **Enter**. The installation program will begin by looking for an IDE CD-ROM drive, the most common CD-ROM type. If it finds the drive the installation will continue. If it does not, you will see a screen that asks what type of drive you have: SCSI or Other. If necessary, choose one of these. Once the installation program has identified your CD-ROM drive, you will then be asked to insert the Linux CD.

6. Read over the text in the Welcome screen for instructions on registering your software. When you are finished reading, click **Next**.

STEP-BY-STEP 8.1 Continued

7. After the initial boot-up, the installation program begins by displaying the Language Selection dialog box as shown in Figure 8-1.

FIGURE 8-1
Language Selection dialog box

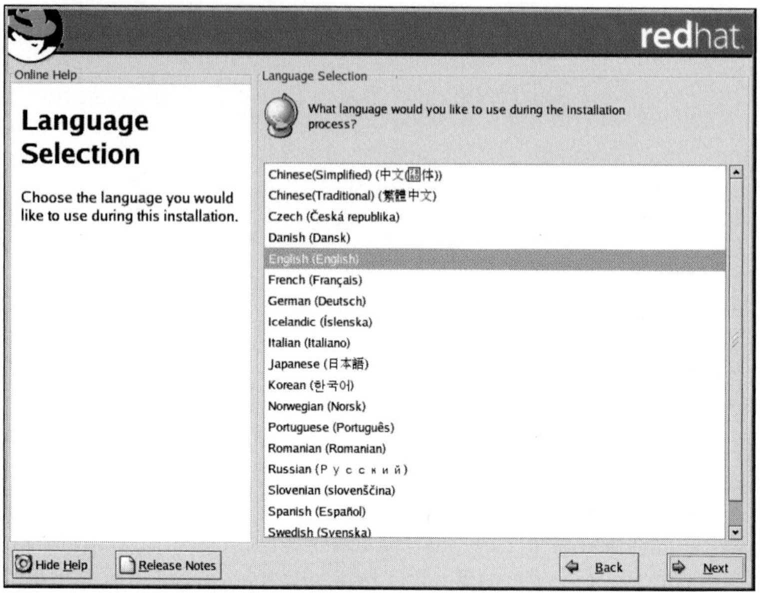

8. Use your mouse or the arrows on the keyboard to select the language to use during the installation process—this will also be the system default language. Then click the **Next** button.

STEP-BY-STEP 8.1 Continued

9. The installation program will display the Keyboard Configuration dialog box as shown in Figure 8-2. It will display the model and layout that it believes are correct for the language you have chosen. If these are correct, click the **Next** button and continue. If not, use the arrow keys on your keyboard or your mouse to select the correct items, and then click the **Next** button.

FIGURE 8-2
Keyboard Configuration dialog box

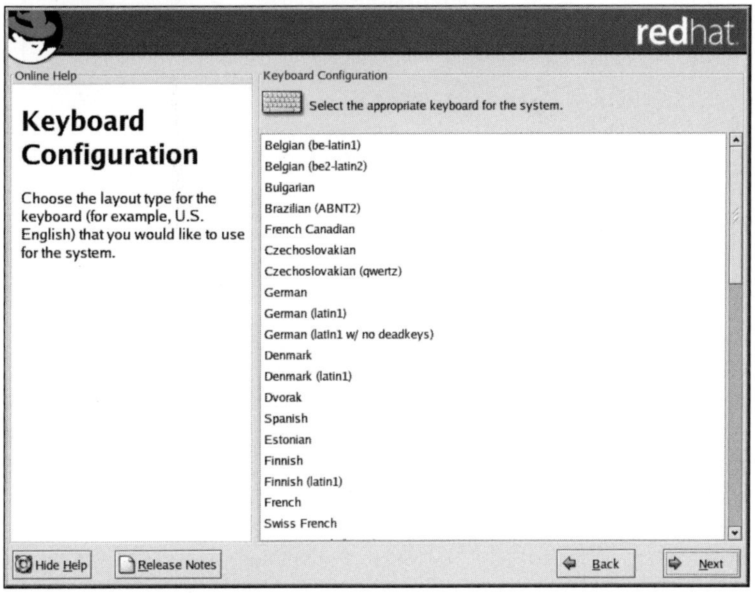

10. The next dialog box (shown in Figure 8-3) allows you to choose the correct Mouse Configuration for your system. Choose the correct mouse type for your system and click **Next**.

FIGURE 8-3
Mouse Configuration dialog box

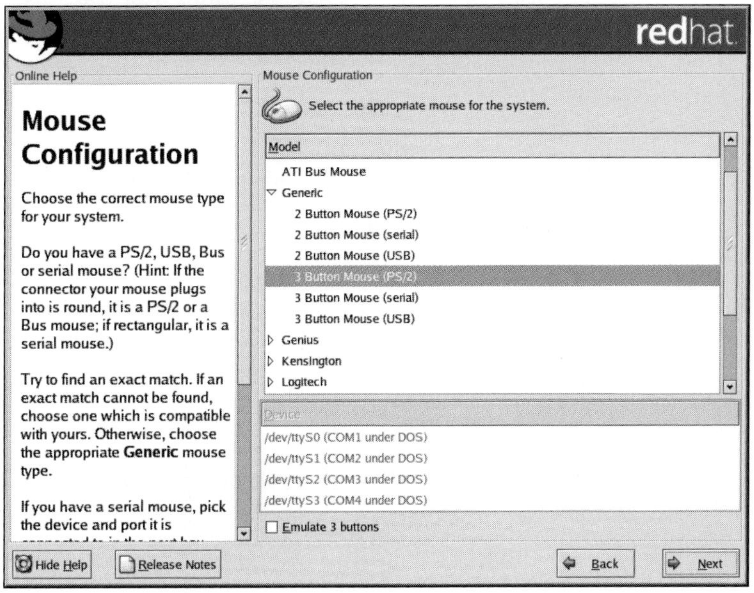

STEP-BY-STEP 8.1 Continued

11. From the Installation Type dialog box (shown in Figure 8-4) you can choose whether you would like to perform the full installation or an upgrade. For this example, you will choose to install.

FIGURE 8-4
Choose install or upgrade

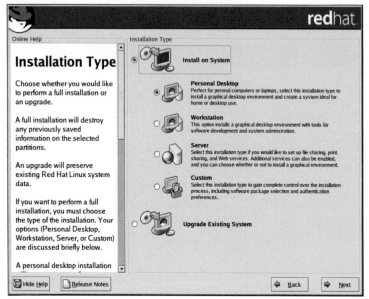

12. If necessary, click the radio button next to the Install on System option.

13. While still in the Installation Type dialog box, you must also choose the class of the installation. Your options include: Personal Desktop, Workstation, Server, or Custom. These options are discussed in the next sections. Leave this screen open for the next Step-by-Step while you read more about these options.

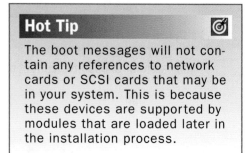

Hot Tip

The boot messages will not contain any references to network cards or SCSI cards that may be in your system. This is because these devices are supported by modules that are loaded later in the installation process.

Install to Personal Desktop

The Personal Desktop installation is the best choice if you are new to Linux and want to try it out. It will install a graphical desktop environment (the X Window System) and create a system that is ideal for home or desktop use.

The Personal Desktop option, if you choose automatic partitioning, installs three partitions. The three partitions are:

1. A swap partition with a fixed size determined by the amount of RAM in your system and the amount of available hard drive space.

2. A partition mounted under /boot in your root file system of fixed size (100 MB). This contains the Linux kernel and related files.

3. The root partition the size of which is determined by the available disk space.

Install to Workstation

A workstation is a computer that will not be supporting more than one user at a time. It will not serve files to others and may have limited RAM, hard drive space, and CPU speed. It also may not have a modem, network card, or other peripherals.

The Workstation option installs Linux with standard options and erases all previous partitions. Three partitions are created:

1. A swap partition with a fixed size determined by the amount of RAM in your system and the amount of available hard drive space.

2. A partition mounted under /boot in your root file system of fixed size (100 MB). This contains the Linux kernel and related files.

3. The root partition the size of which is determined by the available disk space.

Install to Server

A server is a computer that will be supporting more than one person. It will be serving files on a network. It should have lots of RAM as well as hard drive space. It should have a modem or a direct Internet connection via the network card. It may have more than one network interface card (NIC) used for routing between different networks and may have multiple CPUs working together. Generally the video card is of a lower quality than on a workstation machine, because users do not work directly on a server. Since all work is normally done through the network, a server may not even have a monitor, keyboard, or mouse attached.

The Server option installs Linux with server options and erases all previous partitions. Six partitions are created:

1. A swap partition of a fixed size determined by the amount of RAM in your system and the amount of available hard drive space.

2. A partition mounted under /home the exact size of which is dependent upon the disk space available.

3. A partition mounted under /usr the exact size of which is dependent upon the disk space available.

4. A partition mounted under /var of fixed size (256 MB).

5. A partition mounted under / (the root partition) of fixed size (384 MB).

6. A partition mounted under /boot in your root file system of fixed size (100 MB). This contains the Linux kernel and related files.

> **Did You Know?**
>
> *Mounting* means pretending that a directory on another disk or even on another computer is actually part of the directory system on your disk. This means that files stored in lots of different places can appear to be nicely organized into one tree-structure directory. You can mount local directories (local means on your own machine); this is useful if you want them to appear connected. You can also mount remote directories (on a disk or some other computer). This can be handy if you want to use two directories at the same time, but you don't want to have a navigational nightmare as you move back and forth between them. A mount point is a directory where one disk is logically attached to another.

Custom Installation

The Custom installation allows you the greatest flexibility during installation. You can choose the boot loader, which packages you do and do not want, and many other specific options. This installation does, however, require you to be familiar with Red Hat Linux installations.

The Custom option installs Linux with three partitions:

1. A swap partition with a fixed size determined by the amount of RAM in your system and the amount of available hard drive space.

2. A partition mounted under /boot in your root file system of fixed size (100 MB). This contains the Linux kernel and related files.

3. The root partition the size of which is determined by the available disk space.

Partitioning Your Disk

We'll use automatic partitioning in our installation. You could, however, choose to manually partition your hard drive using either FDISK or Disk Druid.

FDISK

FDISK is included with every Linux distribution and is comparable to using FDISK with any other operating system. If you know FDISK, you will always know at least one way to modify the partitions on the drive. FDISK is a command-line driven program. To see a menu of options, you press the "M" key and then press Enter. To see preexisting partitions, you would press the "P" key and then press Enter.

Since it is likely that you will be in a situation where you want to add Linux to a system with a preexisting Windows installation, it may be useful for you to learn more about this process. If you are installing on a "fresh" system the screens may appear slightly different, but the basic process remains the same.

If you add partitions using the free space on your hard drive, then you can set up a multiple boot menu so you can boot your machine into Windows or Linux at any time. Once up and running, you will be able to access the Windows partition from Linux, but not the other way around. It is fine to reuse a preexisting Linux partition if you are reinstalling. Please note that, due to the design of Windows, if you corrupt Windows and need to reinstall you will have to archive everything on the Linux installation. This is because the Windows installation will not recognize the Linux partition; Windows will just install on top of it as if it weren't there. You will lose all Linux data in the process.

If you need to delete partitions, do so using the "d" option in FDISK. Doing this will cause the system to ask which partition number to delete. It is generally good to start with the lowest number and work up, skipping over partitions you want to keep. Please note that you will have to delete all logical drives before deleting extended partitions. The partition number is the number listed in the device name. So, /dev/hda3 is the third partition.

Did You Know?

Hard drives can have a maximum of four primary partitions, but any number of logical partitions. The difference is that primary partitions are bootable and, for most operating systems, logical partitions are not. Logical partitions surrender bootability to gain extra configurability. Linux does not have this problem, so you can have several different Linux installations on one drive. There are advantages to doing this. For instance, it is common to have a server and many dumb terminals or clients that boot from the network. In this scenario it is possible that not all the machines will be the same. And many may have hardware that is incompatible—such as Macs on one part of the network, PCs on another, and dumb terminals on another. It is easy and efficient to create a partition for each set. This keeps the files separate, ensuring that a change for one set of machines doesn't affect the other sets. It also means that the machines can all communicate using the same network.

Disk Druid

Disk Druid has a slightly friendlier interface than FDISK, although it is not a true graphical user interface (GUI): you don't use the mouse, just the keyboard. As you may have noticed, Linux has a particular convention for naming disks. Each IDE device has the name /dev/hdx. Each SCSI device has the name /dev/sdx. The valid name for the third IDE hard drive in the system is /dev/hdc. Each partition is accessed by appending the partition number to the device's name. (For example, the second partition of the third IDE device is /dev/hdc2.) Using this nomenclature, you can locate the existing Windows partition: its device name should be /dev/hda1.

Sizing the Swap Partition

When you select either Server or Workstation, the installer can automatically partition the hard drive as needed. The Linux swap partition is the area the computer will use to store information temporarily. It uses it in much the same way you would use a scratch pad. Linux swap partitions should never go above 128 MB. Most kernels won't support swap files above 128 MB, but you can have multiple swap partitions and the computer will use all of them as if they were one big swap file. A good rule of thumb is to create a swap partition that is twice the physical RAM in your system. For example, a machine with 32 MB of physical RAM would want a swap partition of 64 MB. You could make it 70 MB or 90 MB but in all likelihood it won't be used, so it is a waste of hard drive resources. You could also make a smaller swap partition but you would probably find the machine running slower than it should.

Continuing the Installation

As you will see, the Linux installation gives you many opportunities to customize your system to exactly meet your needs. We will discuss these options so that you can see what is available to you. If you are already comfortable with computer hardware and software and consider yourself an advanced user, you may want to take advantage of these opportunities for customization. If, on the other hand, you are a novice user, then you will want to avoid attempting to make these sorts of changes until you have more experience and knowledge.

Computer Concepts

Heads, cylinders, and sectors are the units that describe where data is located on your hard drive. The hard drive is composed of platters, which, just like old-fashioned LP records, have two sides. There is one head for each side. Each side is divided into concentric rings called cylinders. Each cylinder is divided into identical sectors.

S TEP-BY-STEP 8.2

1. In the Installation Type dialog box, select the **Workstation** option and then click the **Next** button. The Disk Partitioning Setup dialog box will appear as shown in Figure 8-5.

FIGURE 8-5
Disk Partitioning Setup dialog box

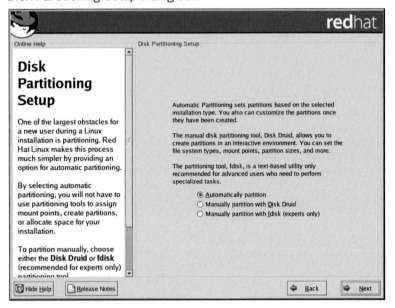

2. Automatic partitioning enables you to perform an installation without having to partition the hard drive(s) yourself. This is the recommended procedure if you are not familiar with drive partitioning. Note that with automatic partitioning, all data on the hard drive will be removed. (If you do not want to perform this sort of installation, then you could choose one of the *Manually partition* options.) If necessary, select **Automatically partition** and then click **Next**. See Figure 8-6.

FIGURE 8-6
Automatic Partitioning dialog box

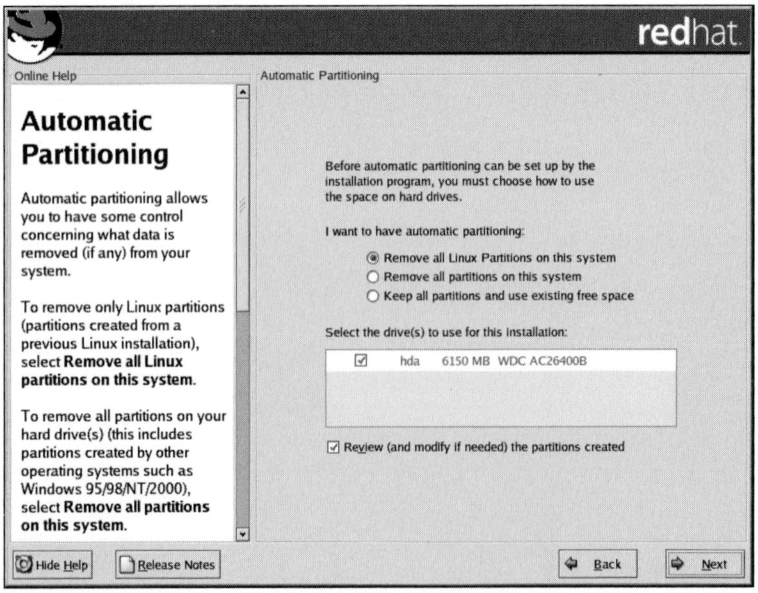

STEP-BY-STEP 8.2 Continued

3. Select the **Remove all Linux Partitions on this system** option. This will remove Linux partitions created from a previous Linux installation but not remove other partitions on your hard drive (i.e., VFAT or FAT32 partitions).

4. Select the hard drive on which you want Red Hat Linux installed.

5. If necessary, deselect the option to review the partitioning of the disk drive. (If you select this option, you will see the partitions created in Disk Druid and be able to make modifications to the partitioning.) Click **Next**. Click **Yes** if you see the Warning dialog box, then click **Next** in the Boot Loader Configuration window. If you are connected to a network, the dialog box shown in Figure 8-7 will appear. If you are not connected to a network, skip to Step 7.

FIGURE 8-7
Network Configuration dialog box

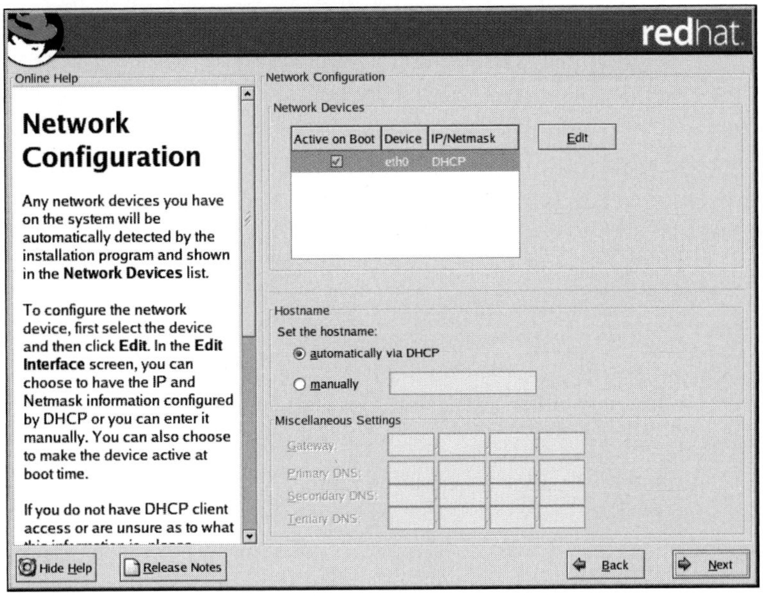

STEP-BY-STEP 8.2 Continued

6. The Network Configuration dialog box allows you the opportunity to configure your networking. If this is required for your installation, ask your instructor or computer lab technician for the information to be filled in on this screen. Even if your computer is not part of a network, you can still enter a Hostname for your system. If you do not, the default hostname "localhost" will be applied. Enter the required information and then click the **Next** button. The Firewall Configuration dialog box appears as shown in Figure 8-8.

FIGURE 8-8
Firewall Configuration dialog box

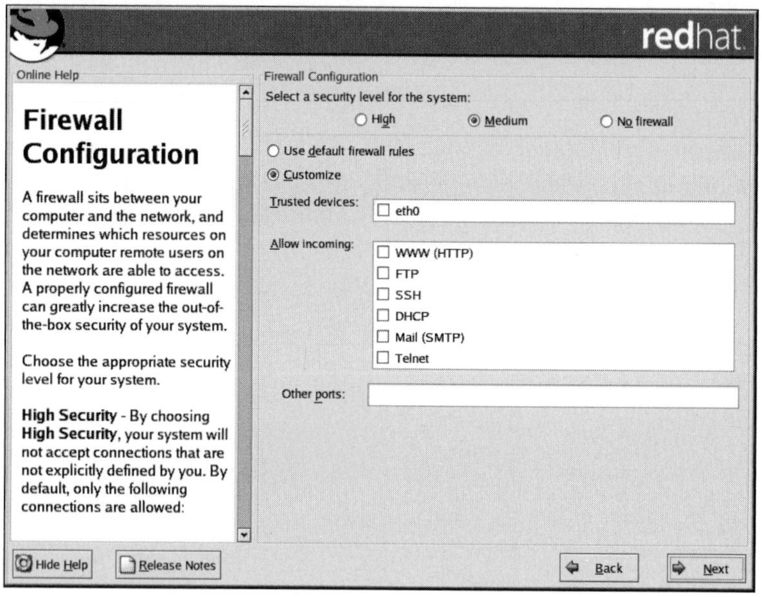

STEP-BY-STEP 8.2 Continued

7. The firewall exists between your computer and the network. It determines what resources on your computer remote users can access. Choose **High** to ensure that your system does not accept connections other than those specifically defined by you. Choose **Medium** to limit remote users to only certain resources on your computer. **No firewall** provides complete access to your system. This should only be chosen if you are on a trusted network. Ask your instructor or computer lab technician which option you should select. Click **Next**. The Additional Language Support dialog box appears as shown in Figure 8-9.

FIGURE 8-9
Additional Language Support dialog box

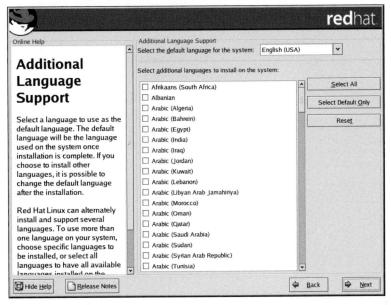

8. Select a language to use as the default language and any additional languages you want the system to support. Click **Next**. The Time Zone Selection dialog box appears as shown in Figure 8-10.

FIGURE 8-10
Time Zone Selection dialog box

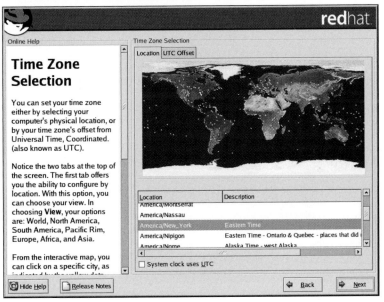

STEP-BY-STEP 8.2 Continued

9. There are two tabs on this display. The first (Location) allows you to configure your time zone, based on the physical location of the computer. On this tab, you can select by pointing and clicking on a specific location on the map or by selecting the appropriate text in the list box. Alternatively, you can choose your time zone as an offset from the Universal Coordinated Time (UTC) by selecting the UTC Offset tab. Make your time zone selection and then click the **Next** button. Leave the installation dialog box open for the next Step-by-Step.

Creating Users

Much like other operating systems, Linux requires you to create users and passwords. The first users will be general unprivileged users. You might want to call the first user "joeuser" and give him the password of "tester." You can then use this account to test your user configurations. Sometimes things work for root, but not for a user, because the user's permissions restrict them from doing something. It is always best to test a configuration before assigning it.

As a rule, a root account is generated automatically and you should be asked for a root password. If you are new to Linux, remember that the /root account is able to access everything and therefore can be dangerous if misused. The /root account is generally the system administrator and usually the installer as well. It is possible for other users to have some or all of root's powers. This comes by adding permissions to the account. Be careful: Some permissions are restricted to keep you from doing something accidental like unmounting a hard drive, thus making it inaccessible. It is easy to remount, but impossible if you don't have the permissions. And since resources are shared, this means unmounting the drive could destroy what another user is doing with the drive.

STEP-BY-STEP 8.3

1. After you have established your time zone and pressed the Next button, the Account Configuration dialog box displays as shown in Figure 8-11.

FIGURE 8-11
Account Configuration dialog box

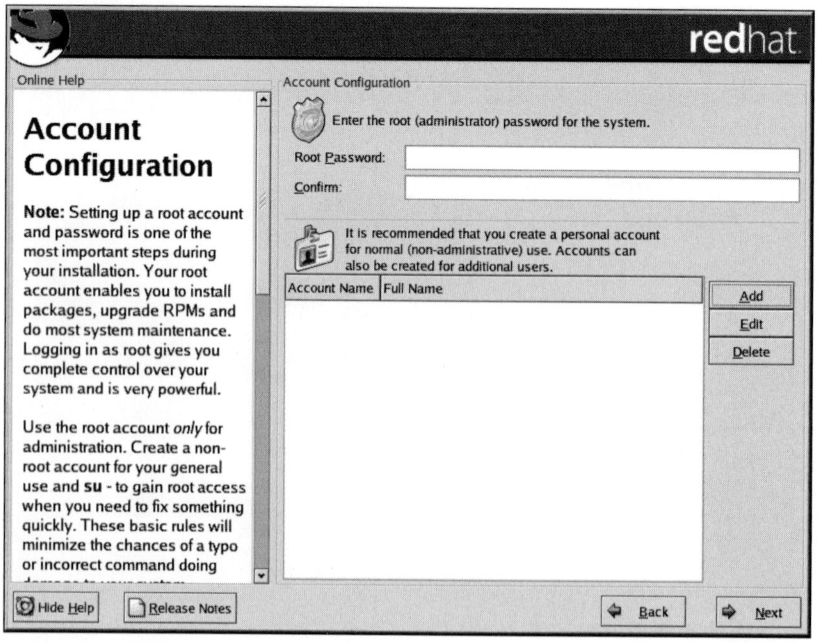

STEP-BY-STEP 8.3 Continued

2. The Account Configuration dialog box allows you to set your root password. You can also set up other user accounts to be used after you complete the installation. In the Root Password text box, key your root password and then key it again in the Confirm text box.

3. You can at this time, set up other user accounts by using the **Add** key. This will open the Add a User Account dialog box. In this dialog box, enter the username, password, confirmation of password, and the user's full name. Click **OK**. Repeat this step for as many users as necessary or as indicated by your instructor.

4. When finished, click the **Next** button in the Account Configuration screen. Remain in this screen for the next Step-by-Step.

Hot Tip

The root password must be at least six characters long. You should avoid using your name, your birth date, or other obvious words or numbers. The best passwords (the ones hardest to guess) are those that combine words and numbers. Also remember that the password is case-sensitive. Once you establish your password, you should write it down and keep it in a secure location.

Selecting Your Package Group

After you have set up the partitions for your installation, it is time to choose the packages you want to install. GNOME, KDE, and X Window are graphical desktop environments (much like those you may be familiar with from other operating systems) that control the look and feel of your system. You must choose one of these as the default graphical interface, but you can also choose to install all of them and determine for yourself which you prefer. We will discuss these interfaces later in this lesson.

Also during this next phase of the installation, you can choose which components or individual packages you want to install. Unless you choose the custom installation, the installation program will automatically select most packages for you. You can select components, which group packages together according to function, individual packages, or a combination of the two.

If you wanted to install all components you could select the Everything check box, which is located at the end of the list of components. This complete installation would require approximately 3.7 GB of disk space.

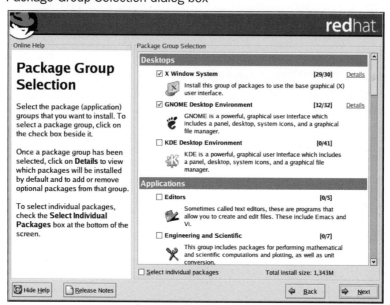

STEP-BY-STEP 8.4

1. After you click Next in the Account Configuration dialog box, the Workstation Defaults dialog box appears. Select **Customize the set of packages to be installed**, then click **Next** to open the Package Group Selection dialog box, as shown in Figure 8-12.

FIGURE 8-12
Package Group Selection dialog box

2. Some items are already selected. Accept these default selections but also verify that the following are checked: **GNOME Desktop Environment**, **KDE Desktop Environment**, and **X Window System**.

3. Check with your instructor to determine if there are any other components that you should or should not install.

4. If necessary, deselect the **Select individual packages** checkbox.

5. Click **Next**. Remain in this screen for the next Step-by-Step.

Configuring the Video Card

Once you have completed the package selection, Xconfigurator (the X Window System configuration tool) will run to test and set up your video card. Video card setup is typically done by someone with computer experience because it requires some knowledge of exactly what video card you have and how much RAM it has. (If you are not knowledgeable about these items, then you should *not* attempt to perform the video card setup.) If your video card is shown in the list of video cards, just enter the required information. If you aren't comfortable with this part of the installation or can't manage to get a working card, then just skip it at this time. To do so, select the Skip X Configuration at the bottom of the dialog box.

Once the relevant card has been set up, the correct server for X Window will be installed on your hard disk. Later in the installation process, you will need to identify your monitor type, which you can select from the list.

STEP-BY-STEP 8.5

1. After you complete the Package Group Selection dialog box, you may see the Graphical Interface (X) Configuration dialog box opens. (This does not appear for all video cards. If you do not see this screen, skip this Step-by-Step.)

2. Xconfigurator probed your system for any video hardware. If you have hardware that is recognized by Linux, then the defaults for this hardware will appear in the X Configuration dialog box. If not, it will present a list of video cards from which you can select. If your video card is not in this list, it may not be supported. If this is the case, you could choose "Unlisted Card" and manually configure it, but this is only recommended for the knowledgeable user.

3. Select the amount of video memory installed on your video card from the Video card RAM drop-down list. Consult your video card documentation if you are not sure of this number (or ask your instructor). You will not damage your card by selecting more memory than what is available, but it may not start correctly.

4. Click the **Next** button. You should see a screen preparing for the installation of Red Hat Linux. Remain in this screen for the next Step-by-Step.

Completing the Installation

The final step is where the actual installation begins. Up until now, no permanent changes have been made to your computer. If you do not want to perform the installation you may reboot your system to return to whatever operating system and software you had already established on your machine. Once you click the Next button from the About to Install dialog box, partitions will be written and packages will be installed.

Part of this final step in the installation is creating a boot disk. The boot disk is a bootable floppy you can use to reboot the system in the event of a failure. It enables you to access the system when it isn't working. Since this is your first time performing an installation, it is in your best interest to make a boot disk. But bear in mind that the ultimate goal is to configure the system so that if it crashes it is easier and faster to just reinstall from scratch. If you are the "administrator" for this computer system, then you should take responsibility and back up everything that you cannot live without. That way, if your system does fail, you always have the backups to rebuild from. If you do lose something, it will only be a small amount and easy to replace. This philosophy accounts for the fact that hard drive failures will happen. (There's a saying among computer programmers: "It's not a matter of if the hard drive will fail—it's a matter of when.") If you choose not to create the boot floppy you can always make one at a later time using the bootdisk command, or create it from the installation CD. During this installation, you will take advantage of the opportunity to create a boot disk.

Another part of this final step in the installation is selecting your monitor. Earlier, in the installation setup, you selected your video card. In this part of the installation you will need to select and configure your monitor. If you can't find yours, then you can choose Custom and supply your own setting. The program will need to know the vertical and horizontal sync rates.

> ### Hot Tip
> If you don't know the sync frequencies of your monitor you can ask your instructor or lab assistant, but don't guess. It is very easy to exceed the ratings of your monitor and cause permanent damage. If you have any doubts about this procedure, do not perform it.

Once the monitor is configured, it is very easy to switch display resolutions. This is done with the Ctrl-Alt and "+" or "-" keys. The plus key takes you to the next higher display resolution. If you are already at the highest, then it loops back to the lowest and continues. The reverse is true of the minus key.

S TEP-BY-STEP 8.6

1. If you are ready to install, click the **Next** button in the About to Install dialog box.

   At this point the installation process begins. How long it takes depends upon the number of operations that the installation has to complete and your computer's speed. When prompted, insert the Red Hat Installation CD number 2, then click **OK**.

   The next input required from you will be to indicate if you want to create a boot disk.

2. Insert a blank, formatted diskette into your floppy drive. Click the **Next** button. Click **Make boot disk** in the Insert a floppy disk dialog box.

3. After a moment, the boot disk creation will be complete. Remove the diskette from the drive and clearly label it. Store it in a safe, well-maintained location.

   In order to complete the X configuration, you must customize your X settings and configure your monitor at this point.

4. You can either choose the monitor that was auto-detected or you can choose another monitor. If your monitor is not in the list, select the most appropriate generic model and then manually enter the Horizontal and Vertical Sync values—but you must have the monitor documentation in order to enter these values correctly. Make your monitor selection, heeding the warnings given previously. Click **Next**.

5. In the Customize Graphics Configuration dialog box select the correct color depth and resolution for your X configuration.

6. Click the **Test Setting** button and confirm that the colors and resolution are accurate.

7. Once you have verified your monitor settings, click **Next**.

   The installation process is complete. You now have a computer running the Linux operating system (often referred to as a "Linux box").

8. The program will instruct you to remove any diskettes in preparation for rebooting. Then click the **Exit** button (or press the **Enter** key).

9. The system will shut down and restart. Click **Quit** in the Welcome screen. After a moment, you will see the GUI login screen, where you can enter your username and password. Remain in this screen for the next Step-by-Step.

Basic Functionalities

There are two basic ways to work with Linux—or two basic "user environments." The older environment is working from the command (or shell) prompt where the user must know particular commands to accomplish a given task. In this environment, there are no clues regarding what you need to enter to accomplish these tasks. The command prompt is considered a "user-unfriendly" environment. The newer environment is X Window System. X Window, often called simply X, establishes a graphical interface between the user and the set of Unix/Linux tasks that makes navigation simple and user-friendly. We will discuss these two environments below.

Graphical User Interface (GUI)

The X Window environment mentioned above is a *graphical user interface (GUI)*. This environment is much like the Microsoft Windows, Apple Macintosh, or IBM OS/2 environments where you can choose a task using the pointing device. Unlike these other environments, however, X allows you to select one of four desktop configurations, commonly called *desktop environments*. Depending on how your system was installed, you may or may not have all the desktop environment choices. A desktop environment includes, among other things, graphical elements visible on the screen and mechanisms allowing the user to launch various applications. An X server allows the user to manage the elements of the window using a window manager.

GNOME is an acronym for GNU Network object model environment and is available in many languages for worldwide use. GNOME is a desktop environment, written in X, which allows you to use and configure your computer more easily. The GNOME Desktop environment is highly customizable and allows you to open multiple workspace areas.

The KDE (K development environment) is considered to be more familiar than GNOME to Windows users. It provides a complete desktop environment, including a file manager, window manager, an integrated help system, configuration tools, and many other tools and utilities, as well as many useful applications.

The failsafe desktop environment produces an XTerm window in the lower-right corner of the screen. The XTerm program provides a command-prompt window that is integrated fully into the X Window System environment, allowing the user to access the most powerful and flexible features of Linux while retaining the graphical interface on the screen. We will discuss the XTerm window a little later in this lesson.

We have chosen to illustrate the GNOME Desktop environment because it provides the new Linux user with an easy-to-learn and configurable graphical user interface. The Red Hat distribution uses the GNOME Desktop environment as its default. If, however, a previous user selected another desktop environment, you will need to select the GNOME Desktop in order to follow along with this example. To log in and select the GNOME Desktop or to verify that it is the default desktop environment, perform the following steps.

STEP-BY-STEP 8.7

1. After you have installed Red Hat Linux, your system will automatically take you to the Login screen whenever it starts. If necessary, start (or reboot) your system now.

2. On the login screen, position the mouse pointer over the word **Session** in the menu bar at the bottom of the screen and then click the left mouse button once.

STEP-BY-STEP 8.7 Continued

3. Position the mouse pointer over the **GNOME** option and click the left mouse button once. Click **OK**. The GNOME session manager is selected.

4. Key your username in the Login text box and then press the **Enter** key. (If you did not perform the installation or you do not know what the username is, ask your instructor.)

5. Enter your password in the Password text box and then press the **Enter** key. If you have properly entered your password, the GNOME Desktop displays as shown in Figure 8-13. If you incorrectly entered your password, the password screen will be redisplayed and you can enter the correct password. You do not need to select the desktop environment again.

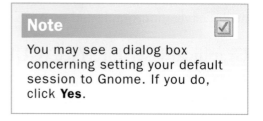

> **Note** ☑
>
> You may see a dialog box concerning setting your default session to Gnome. If you do, click **Yes**.

FIGURE 8-13
The GNOME Desktop

GNOME Desktop Basics

The coordination of hardware and software including workspace icons, the keyboard, and the mouse are referred to as a graphical user interface or GUI. In computer terminology, an icon is a pictorial representation of a program or an action to be performed. Icons display on the workspace (the computer screen) and you select them by clicking them with the mouse. When you double-click an icon, a window opens on the screen and the selected program runs in that window. The GNOME Desktop consists of icons, foreground and background windows, and the GNOME Panel.

Active and Inactive Windows

Within GNOME, like many other graphical user interfaces, windows are displayed in either the foreground or the background. The most recently opened windows are in the foreground and those that were opened earlier are in the background. These windows, and any others that are open on the workspace, can be moved from a background position to a foreground position by clicking anywhere in the window. When you click in a background window, the window that was in the foreground moves to a background position and the chosen window moves to the foreground. This is then the active window. All other windows are said to be inactive. You also can choose the foreground window through the GNOME Panel, as explained in the following section. Whenever a new program (and hence a new window) is opened, it automatically becomes the foreground window.

The GNOME Panel

At the bottom of the workspace you will see something that, if you are familiar with the Microsoft Windows operating systems, will remind you of the taskbar. It performs the same functions as the taskbar and more. This is the *GNOME Panel*, a configurable display (see Figure 8-14).

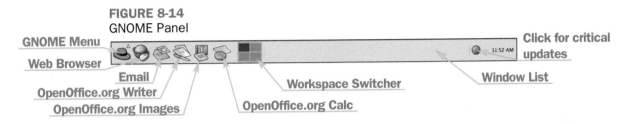

FIGURE 8-14
GNOME Panel

GNOME Menu

Web Browser

Email

OpenOffice.org Writer

OpenOffice.org Images

Workspace Switcher

OpenOffice.org Calc

Click for critical updates

Window List

In the lower-left corner of the panel is a red hat that serves as the GNOME Menu (main menu) button, which provides access to program menus. This is comparable to the Start button in Microsoft Windows. Additional program launchers display to the right of the GNOME Menu button. Exactly what buttons appear here will depend upon the selections you made when you installed Red Hat Linux. If you accepted the default selections, you will likely see the OpenOffice applications that are shown in Figure 8-14 as well as a couple of others. These buttons provide shortcuts to the most commonly used applications including a Web browser and Evolution e-mail and calendaring. The Open Office applications include OpenOffice.org Writer (a word processor), OpenOffice.org Impress (for creating presentations), and OpenOffice.org Calc (a spreadsheet program). To the right of the program launchers is the GNOME Pager that contains two main areas—the Workspace Switcher, which shows your four work areas, and Window List, which lists open applications on the current workspace. In the Workspace Switcher, each of your workspaces is represented as a small rectangle, or pane. If there are any programs on the workspace, they display as small outlines according to their positions on the workspace. The Window List displays the programs on your active workspace in a list view. The programs display as buttons. If the program window is open and in the foreground, then the button will display as recessed (shaded). If the program window is open but in the background, the button will not be recessed. If the window has been minimized (if it is not on the workspace), then the text on the button appears in brackets.

Virtual Consoles

Red Hat provides you with five virtual consoles available during any Linux session. A *console* is an area within the operating system that recognizes only commands entered from the keyboard. Instead of displaying icons on a workspace, you must respond to a command (shell) prompt. Each virtual (meaning that it appears limitless) console works independently of the next. In effect, on one Linux workstation you can have X running on your workspace, and also operate each of five virtual consoles—simultaneously. A virtual console may be used by a Linux user to run diagnostic programs if X does not load correctly, or to perform an administrative task not available as an icon on the X desktop. You must log in to each virtual console separately. Table 8-1 illustrates the keyboard shortcuts that enable you to enter various virtual consoles or to return to the X Window System environment if X loads correctly.

TABLE 8-1
Keyboard shortcuts to the Virtual Consoles

KEYBOARD SHORTCUTS	VIRTUAL CONSOLE
Alt+CTRL+F1	Virtual console #1
Alt+CTRL+F2	Virtual console #2
Alt+CTRL+F3	Virtual console #3
Alt+CTRL+F4	Virtual console #4
Alt+CTRL+F5	Virtual console #5
Alt+CTRL+F7	Return to X Window System

Managing the GNOME Desktop

When activated, the GNOME Desktop occupies the entire screen. On the workspace there are any windows you open, and a number of icons. You may find that the workspace is not arranged exactly the way that you would like. Problems could develop, such as:

■ The window or icon you want to use is behind another window.

■ The window where you currently are working needs to be larger.

■ When you have finished working with a program, you would like to close its window.

■ You find that looking at several windows at one time is proving difficult.

All of these problems can be resolved by learning to manage your workspace areas and the respective windows.

For the most part, the operations on the GNOME Desktop are the same as what you are probably already familiar with from working with Microsoft Windows or other operating systems. Minimizing, maximizing, restoring, dragging, sizing, opening, and closing are all performed in essentially the same manner. One feature that is different, however, is the ability to open other workspace areas. The GNOME Desktop allows the user to access different workspaces in the computer's memory. By default, there are four workspace areas, or desktop views, available to you; they are all accessible from the GNOME Panel. Each of these four workspace areas is represented as a pane in the Workspace Switcher on the GNOME Panel. To open windows in different workspace areas, complete the following steps.

S TEP-BY-STEP 8.8

1. Click on the **GNOME Menu**, point to **Accessories**, and then click **Text Editor**. This will open a simple text editor.

2. Click on the **GNOME Menu**, point to **Accessories**, and then click **Calculator**. This opens a calculator application. Note that the upper-left pane (#1) in the Workspace Switcher shows that it is currently selected and there are two rectangles shown to represent the two applications you are currently running. See Figure 8-15.

FIGURE 8-15
Workspace Switcher illustrating two applications in workspace #1

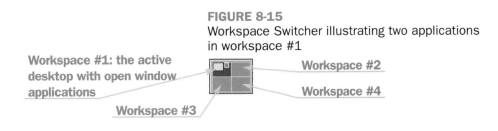

Workspace #1: the active desktop with open window applications

Workspace #2

Workspace #4

Workspace #3

3. Move the mouse pointer to the upper-right pane (#2) in the Workspace Switcher and click. That pane now indicates that it is selected, and it shows the current workspace (Figure 8-16), which is blank.

FIGURE 8-16
Active GNOME workspace

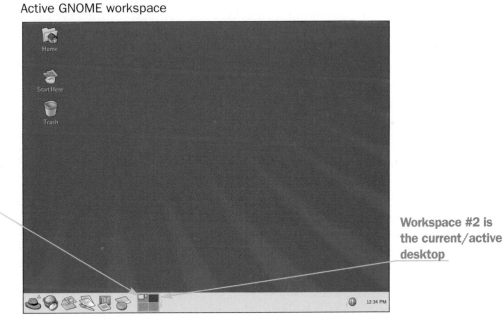

Workspace #1 has open applications

Workspace #2 is the current/active desktop

STEP-BY-STEP 8.8 Continued

4. Click the **GNOME Menu** button. Point to **Sound & Video** and click **CD Player** to open the Gnome CD Player window. A small rectangle displays in pane #2 in the Workspace Switcher. (Note that this rectangle displays in the same relative location—and approximately the same size—on the pane as the Gnome CD Player window displays on the workspace.) Figure 8-17 is an example of how the Workspace Switcher may appear.

FIGURE 8-17
Workspace Switcher with active application in workspace #2

The active window 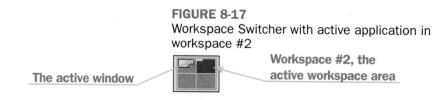 Workspace #2, the active workspace area

5. Close the Gnome CD Player by clicking the **X** button in the upper-right corner of the window.

You can see how these different workspaces can come in very handy when you are working with a number of files or programs and need to have several things open and visible at the same time.

Obviously, there is a good deal more that can be said (and learned) about the GNOME user environment as well as the other GUI environments available with Linux. This was only a brief introduction. However, much of this can be learned through exploration and by reading the online help and documentation that comes with the software. Since a GUI interface is inherently intuitive, we will not devote any more time to explaining the use of these environments. Instead, we will turn our attention to the features that are less intuitive, but certainly very important if you want full use of your Linux system.

XTerm Program

In the early years of Unix the typical input/output device was a dumb terminal. A dumb terminal was a CRT combined with a keyboard that had no processing capabilities of its own. Today, a terminal emulator makes your computer behave like a dumb terminal. *XTerm* (short for x terminal) is one of these emulators. When working under X, the XTerm program allows the Linux user to execute shell commands. In addition to entering commands interactively, XTerm allows you to execute a batch script in the background that you created earlier during an XTerm session.

Did You Know?

Regardless of which Linux distribution you have installed, once you enter a terminal session (i.e., XTerm—also referred to as a virtual console or a shell) the commands used are the same.

You can open a terminal emulator (through the GNOME or KDE interface) and use it to access all of the powerful shell commands available to Linux, while still maintaining the convenience of a GUI interface.

STEP-BY-STEP 8.9

1. Open the **GNOME Menu** and select **System Tools**.

2. Click **Terminal** option on the System Tools menu. The Terminal emulation screen appears on the workspace similar to that shown in Figure 8-18. Leave this window open for the next Step-by-Step.

FIGURE 8-18
Terminal emulation window

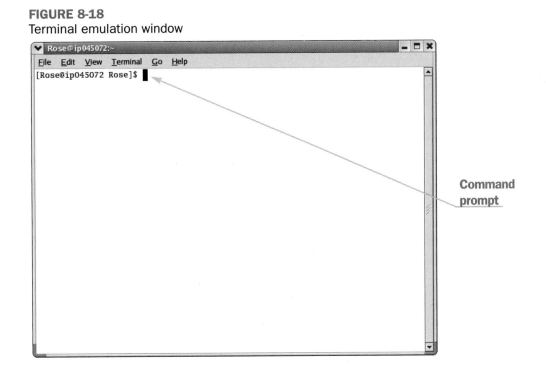

Command prompt

Since some of the most powerful features of Linux are the ones that are accessible from the command prompt within the terminal emulation window, the rest of this section describes the use of the command prompt window. While this program is less "friendly" than the GUI, it is important if you want to gain a full understanding of the Linux system's advantages over another operating system.

Using the Keyboard to Maneuver in Linux

Since Linux was originally designed to be used without a mouse, you can do most things by keying—especially when you are not using one of the GUI interfaces available with Linux. Many users do not have strong keyboarding skills. So, certain tools have been included to speed things up and make keying easier.

Command Completion

One of the most helpful features available when working with the command line is the command completion. Command completion enables the computer to match the command or program to what you are keying. You just press the Tab key, and the computer finishes the command for you. You just need to make sure you enter enough characters of the command so that it is obvious that you could mean no other command.

STEP-BY-STEP 8.10

1. At the command prompt, key **cd /e**.

2. Press the **Tab** key. The computer will finish the line with `tc/`. (The whole line should read `cd /etc/`.)

   If you were to press Enter you would go to the `/etc` directory. Of course, this particular example didn't save you many keystrokes. But many of the files you work with will have long filenames (Linux allows up to 255 characters). In order to make the filename more descriptive, many filenames contain not only the program name, but the version or boot as well. This lets you have several versions of a file in one spot. For instance, the `dmesg` file contains most of the boot information. You want to inspect it at least once after an install or hardware upgrade because this file provides important feedback for problem resolution. You know to start looking for `dmesg` in the `/var` directory but forget the rest of the path from there.

3. Press the **Backspace** key repeatedly to erase the text entered above.

4. Key **cd /v** and press the **Tab** key. (Remember that V and v are different.) Linux will finish the line with `ar/` because there isn't another subdirectory that begins with `v`.

5. Now you think that the `dmesg` file is in the log directory. Key the letter **l** and press **Tab**. The computer should beep at you this time and appear to do nothing. This is because there are several subdirectories in `/var` that begin with `l`.

6. Press the **Tab** key again and you will get a listing of all subdirectories that match what you have keyed so far.

   This procedure is very useful for trying to remember long filenames that are automatically generated. It also works with finding commands. If you don't remember the spelling of a command, enter the first couple of characters (or whatever you know) at the command prompt and press **Tab** twice. This brings up a listing of all known commands that match the pattern. In some cases the list will be several pages long and the system will ask you if it should display all the listings. Say Yes (**Y**). Then use the scroll bar to scan up and down the display.

7. Press the **Backspace** key repeatedly to erase the text that has been entered thus far.

8. Key **x** and press the **Tab** key twice. You will be asked if you want to display more than a hundred possibilities.

9. Key **Y**. The list of commands should fill the screen and you will see a —More— option at the bottom of the list. Press **Enter** as many times as necessary to view more files, until you see the command prompt.

10. Use the scroll bar to scan up the list. (You can also resize the window to see all of the information.) On most systems you will get to go back about five screens. The actual number may be more or less, depending on your installation. Leave the terminal emulation program open for the next Step-by-Step.

Command History

Another timesaving feature is the command history, which allows you to retrieve a previously entered command from the history file. This is accomplished by pressing the up arrow key. Pressing this key causes the most recent command to be taken from the top of the previously stored commands. This command then appears at the command prompt. If you continue to press the up arrow, you will cycle through all of the previously stored commands in the history file. If you go back too far, you can use the down arrow key to step forward through the command history file.

File Management

Each file in a file system is a collection of data. A file system not only holds the data that is contained within the files, but also the structure of the file system itself. It holds all of the information that Linux users and processes see as files, directory soft links, file protection information, and so on. Moreover, it must hold that information safely and securely; the basic integrity of the operating system depends upon its file systems. Nobody would use an operating system that randomly lost data and files.

One of the most important features of Linux is its support for many different file systems. This makes it very flexible and able to coexist with many other operating systems. At the time of writing, Linux supported 15 file systems: ext, ext2, xia, minix, umsdos, msdos, vfat, proc, smb, ncp, iso9660, sysv, hpfs, affs, and ufs. Over time, no doubt, more will be added. These file systems are from different operating systems.

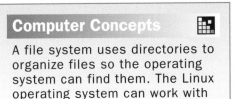

Computer Concepts

A file system uses directories to organize files so the operating system can find them. The Linux operating system can work with files from a variety of operating systems.

In Linux, as in Unix, the separate file systems your computer may use are not accessed by device identifiers (such as a drive number or a drive name) but instead they are combined into a single hierarchical tree structure that represents the file system as a single entity. Linux adds each new file system into this single file system tree as the file system is mounted. As mentioned earlier, mounting is the act of connecting a device or file system to the operating system. In this way you are creating the links that allow communication to occur. All file systems, of whatever type, are mounted onto a directory. This directory is known as the *mount directory* or *mount point*. Think of the mount point as the location where you can find the device or file system. The files of the mounted file system cover up the existing contents of the mount directory.

When disks are initialized (say, using FDISK or Disk Druid) they have a partition structure imposed on them that divides the physical disk into a number of logical partitions. Each partition may hold a single file system—for example, an EXT2 file system (see details below, under *Linux File System History*). File systems organize files into logical hierarchical structures with directories. Devices that can contain file systems are known as block devices. The Linux file system regards these block devices as linear collections of blocks; they do not know or care about the geometry of the underlying physical disk. An IDE drive is treated the same as a SCSI drive, even though they operate differently. Moreover, using Linux's file systems, it does not matter (at least to the systems user) that these different file systems are on various physical media controlled by separate hardware controllers. The file system might not even be on the local system; it could just as well be a disk remotely mounted over a network link halfway around the world. Neither the users nor the programs that operate on the files themselves need know that /C is, in fact, a mounted VFAT (Windows-compatible) file system that is on the first IDE disk in the system. Neither does it matter that the first IDE controller is a PCI controller and that the second is an ISA controller, which also controls the IDE CD-ROM. The long and short of all this is that Linux makes any device attached to it look exactly like any other device. By way of comparison, Windows will restrict what you can do if a drive is connected through a network. It even restricts what you can do if the device is connected locally—such as a CD-ROM drive and a hard drive. Both store data, but they work differently. Windows shows you those differences, while Linux does not. Linux lets you access the two drives exactly the same way, thanks to the virtual file system (VFS).

Linux File System History

Minix, the first file system used by Linux, is rather restrictive and lacking in performance. In this file system, filenames cannot be longer than 14 characters (which is still three characters longer than the old DOS limit). The first file system designed specifically for Linux, the extended file system, or EXT, was introduced in April 1992 and cured many of the problems—but designers still felt it lacked performance.

The second *extended file system* (*EXT2*) was devised by Rèmy Card as an extensible and powerful file system for Linux. It is the most successful file system so far in the Linux community and is the basis for all Linux distributions that are currently shipping. The EXT2 file system, like a lot of the file systems, is built on the premise that the data held in files is kept in data blocks. The size of every file is rounded up to an integral number of blocks. If the block size is 1024 bytes, then a file of 1025 bytes will occupy two 1024-byte blocks. This means that 1023 bytes go wasted. Of course, you don't usually waste that much; on average you waste half a block per file. As always in computing, you trade off CPU usage for memory and disk space utilization.

Virtual File System

The *Virtual File System* (*VFS*) allows Linux to support many file systems—each presenting a common software interface to the VFS. All of the details of the Linux file systems are translated by software, so that all file systems appear identical to the rest of the Linux kernel and to programs running in the system. Linux's VFS layer allows you to transparently mount the many different file systems at the same time. The Linux VFS is implemented so that access to its files is as fast and efficient as possible.

To speed up access to commonly used directories, the VFS maintains a cache of directory entries. As the real file systems look up directories, the details of the directory are added to the directory cache. The next time the same directory is looked up—for example, to list it or open a file within it—it will be found in the directory cache. Only short directory entries (up to 15 characters long) are cached; this is reasonable, as the shorter directory names are the most commonly used ones.

The "/proc file system" really shows the power of the Linux VFS. Neither the /proc directory nor its subdirectories and files actually exist. The /proc file system, like a real file system, registers itself with the VFS. However, when the VFS makes calls to it, requesting inodes as its files and directories are opened, the /proc file system creates those files and directories from information within the kernel. For example, the kernel's /proc/devices file is generated from the kernel's data structures that describe its devices. The /proc file system presents a user-readable window into the kernel's inner workings. Several Linux subsystems create entries in the /proc file system.

Mounting a File System

As mentioned earlier, the mount command allows a physical device (such as a hard drive, a disk partition, a floppy disk, or a CD-ROM) to be addressed by the Linux software. In order to do this, you must be the root (or superuser). Normal users don't have this capability. (If you didn't log in as root, then key su root and press Enter. You will be asked for the root password. This will make you root and allow you to mount a drive.)

Once a device is mounted it can be read, written to, or called upon to perform its functions. Each particular device is, of course, limited by the file system table (i.e., you can't write to a standard CD-ROM drive).

To mount a file system, two things must be in place. First, a physical device must exist that you want to mount to the system. An example might be an IDE Zip drive or CD-ROM. Second, a point where this device is to be mounted must exist or be created in the existing file system tree. Examples of the command format to mount a floppy drive are shown in Table 8-2.

> **Did You Know?** 💡
>
> If you are using one of the graphical user interfaces, as soon as you insert a CD the /mnt/cdrom will automatically run. This mounts the CD, opens a directory of the CD, and places its icon on the workspace. If there is an autorun program on the CD, a message will appear asking if you want to run that program.

TABLE 8-2
Command formats to mount a floppy drive

COMMAND	FILE SYSTEM TYPE	DEVICE DRIVER	MOUNT POINT
mount	[-t ext2]	/dev/fd0	/mnt/floppy
mount	-t msdos	/dev/fd0	/mnt/msfloppy
mount	-t vfat	/dev/fd0	/mnt/winfloppy
mount	-t iso9660	/dev/cdrom	/mnt/cdrom

If we look at the last example, the CD-ROM, the -t option (known as the type or type switch) tells the mount command that you are specifying what type of file system is encoded on the CD-ROM. There could be several. The most common are iso9660, rockridge, and joliet. The –t is required if a file system type follows. The /dev/cdrom tells the mount command to take the physical device of /dev/cdrom and connect it in the file system tree and the point /mnt/cdrom.

> **Hot Tip** 🎯
>
> Remember that all commands in Linux are in lowercase; no uppercase is allowed.

This way you know where it is and from what type of file system to pull information. You could have just as easily told the mount command to connect the CD-ROM drive any other place we wanted. The only stipulation is that the mount point directory already exists and it is not already being used by something else. The name /mnt/cdrom is not set in stone. It is just as easy to call the mount point for the CD-ROM /home/ftp/henry. Linux doesn't care what we call it—the name is purely for our reference. It is best, however, to keep it as simple and descriptive as possible. The /mnt directory is the mount directory.

Let's use the CD-ROM as an example because you will be required to mount it each time you change the disk. For the CD-ROM there should already be a mount point in the /mnt directory. It should be called /cdrom.

S TEP-BY-STEP 8.11

1. First, you need to make sure that the /mnt directory already has a mount point for the CD-ROM. Key **cd /mnt** and press **Enter**. The cd command means to change directory. This will take you to the /mnt directory.

STEP-BY-STEP 8.11 Continued

2. List the directory by keying **ls** and pressing **Enter**. If the directory already exists, you should see cdrom listed. If not then create the directory, by keying the command **mkdir cdrom** (make directory) and pressing **Enter**.

3. Now, to mount the CD-ROM drive, key **mount -t iso9660 /dev/cdrom /mnt/cdrom**. Press **Enter**.

If this worked, you should see a message indicating that you are mounting a read-only cdrom and then you will get the command prompt back without an error message. If you get an error message, make sure that there is a CD-ROM in the drive. If there is, try keying the command again. If it still doesn't work, ask your instructor for assistance or work with a classmate for the rest of this exercise.

4. To verify that the disk is actually mounted simply key **cd /mnt/cdrom** and press **Enter**. This will take you to the CD-ROM drive.

5. Now, key **ls** and press **Enter** to look at the directory. Leave the terminal emulation program open for the next Step-by-Step.

To see what other devices are mounted, all you need to do is key the mount command and press Enter. This will show all devices currently mounted and where they reside. Don't worry if you have difficulty discerning this information. It will become easier as you become familiar with the system. You will also notice that you can't eject the CD-ROM as you used to. This is because the file system has locked the drive. Remember that it is assumed that all devices and resources in the computer will be shared. The system locks the CD-ROM so that the media can't be ejected just in case someone is using it. To eject the disk, you must make sure nothing is using the drive and thus, that you have the right to unmount it.

Unmounting a File System

The umount command is used to deselect, and then remove a file system. Unmounting a file system is more or less the reverse of mounting it. A file system cannot be unmounted if any part of the system is using one of its files. So, for example, you cannot umount /mnt/cdrom if a process is using that directory or any of its children. Notice the command to unmount the device is umount *not* unmount.

> **Did You Know?**
>
> If you are using one of the graphical user interfaces, you can right-click on the CD icon on the workspace and choose **Eject** from the shortcut menu. This will unmount the CD and automatically eject it.

STEP-BY-STEP 8.12

1. Make sure you are not in the /cdrom directory.

2. To unmount the drive key **umount /dev/cdrom** and press **Enter**.

If nothing is using the CD-ROM, then it should unmount without errors and give you the command prompt.

Leave the terminal emulation program open for the next Step-by-Step.

The FAT Table

The FAT table is kind of like a phonebook for files. If everyone in your life had a number instead of name, it would be very hard to remember everyone's number. But numbers are much more useful to a computer than alphabetical names. So, engineers had a problem: how to bridge the gap between what is easy for humans and what can be done with a machine. The answer is the FAT table (short for file allocation table). If you give it a name like quake or WordPerfect, the computer looks up the corresponding numeric code on the FAT table. Then it knows how to load the program.

Operating systems take great care that nothing corrupts the information in the FAT table. Most of this is to ensure that all information is kept to the correct format when writing to the FAT. This includes filenames, which must be less than 255 characters. Names can include spaces, hyphens, punctuation marks, and numbers. Subdirectories are just a special type of file capable of holding other files. Files are divided into executable and nonexecutable.

Linux Shell Commands

Many of the commands that you can enter at the command prompt of the Linux terminal are commands used for file creation and system maintenance. You've already used a couple of these in the exercises above: `cd` and `ls`. In addition, several others are used commonly and would be useful to know.

Print Working Directory Command

The print working directory command (`pwd`) shows your location in the directory tree. The working directory is the location where any files created will reside, unless you intentionally place them elsewhere. The working directory is sometimes called the *default directory*.

S TEP-BY-STEP 8.13

1. At the command prompt, key **pwd**.

2. Press the **Enter** key. The working directory (the default directory) is displayed on the line below your `pwd` command. Notice that the command prompt has also returned. Leave the terminal emulation program open for the next Step-by-Step.

Change Directory Command

The change directory (`cd`) command is one of the most frequently used commands in Linux. The command is the same for Linux as it is for DOS. This command establishes a path to the new working directory. By keying the command `cd` and a subdirectory (i.e., `cd /etc`) you will be transferred to that subdirectory if it exists. By starting the name of the subdirectory with / you are implying the name is absolutely referenced from the root directory. If / isn't leading the directory name then the path is relative to your current position. For instance, `/etc` and `etc` are not the same thing. `/etc` means start at the root directory, which is indicated in Linux by the forward slash (/). Then, continuing from there, transfer to the subdirectory `etc`. If / is not included, it is assumed you mean to look at the subdirectories in the directory you are in, find the subdirectory called etc, and transfer to it. Table 8-3 shows some different uses of the change directory command.

TABLE 8-3
Change directory command

COMMAND	PARAMETER	RESULT
cd	[/] directoryname	Switches to the directory specified
cd	/	Returns to the root directory
cd	..	Returns to the parent directory
cd	-	Returns to your last directory
cd		Returns to your home directory

List Command

The list command (ls) lists the contents of a directory. This command can be used with or without a parameter following it and with or without an argument. The argument is just the name of the directory that you want to list. If the ls command is issued alone, the screen displays the current contents of the current directory. If an argument follows the ls command, the contents of the specified directory are listed, as in ls /etc/rc.d/init.d. As Table 8-4 shows, the ls command has several parameters that enable you to view your file list in different ways, which allows you to see precisely what you want to see.

TABLE 8-4
List command

PARAMETER	FUNCTION
pathname	Lists the files in that path
-a	Lists all files and directories (including hidden files)
-l	Lists the details on the file (i.e., size, date, owner, etc.)
-p	Puts the forward slash (/) after each directory name
-r	Lists files and directories in reverse order
-R	Lists filenames by subdirectory
-t	Lists files ordered by their last modification date
-x	Lists files using the full width of the display

S TEP-BY-STEP 8.14

1. Key **cd /** and press **Enter**. This will take you to the top of the directory tree.

2. At the command prompt, to display a directory list, key **ls** and press **Enter**. You should see one directory called etc.

3. Key **cd etc** and press **Enter** to transfer to that directory.

4. Key **ls** and press **Enter** to list the etc directory. You will notice it is different from the list you saw before. This is the contents of the subdirectory /etc.

STEP-BY-STEP 8.14 Continued

5. Key **cd rc.d/init.d** and press **Enter** to change to that directory.

6. Key **ls** and press **Enter** to list the contents of the directory to which you just changed.

7. Key **cd etc**. (Intentionally omit the leading /.) Press **Enter**. You will get the following message: `bash: cd: etc: no such file or directory`. This means that the subdirectory does not exist. Generally this means that you need to check the spelling of the directory or its location relative to your current position.

8. Key **cd /etc** and press **Enter**. This will let you jump up two directory levels. Leave the terminal emulation program open for the next Step-by-Step.

Make Directory Command

The make directory command (`mkdir`) is used to create directories. A valid filename must be used for the directory name.

STEP-BY-STEP 8.15

1. At the command prompt, key **mkdir /tmp/quake**.

2. Press the **Enter** key. You have just created a directory called `quake` beneath the `tmp` directory. Leave the terminal emulation program open for the next Step-by-Step.

Remove Directory Command

The remove directory command (`rmdir`) deletes the directory from the file system. Before you can remove a directory, it has to be empty of all files and you cannot be inside of that directory (i.e., it cannot be the current working directory). You should remove directories when they are obsolete or no longer used.

Remove File/Directory Command

The remove file/directory (`rm`) command is a relative of `rmdir`, which is used only to delete empty directories. Like `rmdir`, this command requires that a filename be specified. If the `-rf` parameter is used, this command will delete files and subdirectories recursively and will not ask you if it is OK to do so. This is called *forced mode*.

STEP-BY-STEP 8.16

1. At the command prompt, key **cd /tmp** and press **Enter**. This will change your location to the `tmp` directory.

2. Key **ls** and press **Enter**. You should see the name of the directory you created in the previous exercise (quake). Since you are not in that directory and since you have added no files to it, it can be deleted.

3. Key **rm -rf quake** and press **Enter**. The directory quake will be removed. Because you added the parameter `-rf`, the removal was "forced"—there was no confirmation to verify that you wanted to remove that directory. Leave the terminal emulation program open for the next Step-by-Step.

Move Command

The move command (mv) moves a file or directory to another position in your file system tree or renames a file. It does so by rewriting the path to each file. The mv command is extremely useful. After the command is completed, the file resides only in its new location (or under its new name). The syntax for use is `mv oldposition/and_files newposition/`. Notice that if you omit the files at the new position, the old filenames will be used. You may also use the command to rename a file. The syntax for renaming is `mv oldname newname`.

Copy Command

The copy command (cp) takes the contents of one or more files and copies them to a secondary location. The syntax is `cp source_files destination_files`. This command is useful when you want to modify an original file or use it for a second time. As Table 8-5 shows, there are two possible parameters for the copy command.

TABLE 8-5

PARAMETER	FUNCTION
-i	Inquiry copy. This will instruct the system to ask before overwriting a file.
-r	Recursive copy. Copies the files in the directory and subdirectory.

Wild Cards

Wild cards (* and ?) are special characters used to specify whole groups instead of individual items. The * means to take any grouping of characters and substitute here. If you want to copy several files with different names, but all of them end with ".re", you could use the wild card to specify which files you wanted to copy. The command would be `cp *.re`. The asterisk is used to find any file that has any filename for a beginning, but only `re` as an extension. The opposite would be true for `re*`, which means find all files that begin with "re," no matter what the extension. It is easy to mix and match. You can use the wild cards with the other shell commands as well. To list all the files in your current directory that begin with "s," key `ls s*`. This will list only files that begin with "s." To limit the list a bit, try using `ls se*`. This will only list files beginning with "se." Remember that the asterisk can stand for one or more characters. Adding more asterisks to the list does nothing. Therefore, `ls se*` is the same as `ls se****`.

The ? works much like the asterisk, except it stands for only one character. Here `ls se?` and `ls se??` mean different things. If `??` is used, the computer will try to find any name that has two or fewer characters after "se." The single ? means to only find names with one character after the "se." This can be used to find a group of names while excluding others.

Mtools

If you are a user who is already familiar with MSDOS and the commands used within a DOS window, you may find the mtools useful. mtools is a set of commands that allows you to access and manipulate DOS on a Linux machine. Most Linux distributions automatically install the mtools package on your computer. The mtools commands are identical to DOS commands except that in each case the letter "m" is placed in front of the command. Some examples are given in Table 8-6.

TABLE 8-6

DOS COMMAND	MTOOL	FUNCTION
cd	mcd	Changes directory
copy	mcopy	Copies a file
md	mmd	Makes a new directory
rd	mrd	Removes a directory
del	mdel	Deletes a file

Special Linux Files

Devices

Linux, like all versions of Unix, presents its hardware devices as special files. So, for example, /dev/null is the null device. Consider this device a black hole. Anything that is dropped into it disappears forever. A device file does not use any data space in the file system; it is only an access point to the device driver. The EXT2 file system and the Linux VFS both implement device files as special types of inodes. There are two types of device files: character and block special files. Within the kernel itself, the device drivers implement file semantics: You can open them, close them, and so on. Character devices allow I/O operations in character mode and block devices require that all I/O is via the buffer cache. When an I/O request is made to a device file, it is forwarded to the appropriate device driver within the system. Often this is not a real device driver but a pretend device driver for some subsystem, such as the SCSI device driver layer.

S TEP-BY-STEP 8.17

1. At the command prompt, key **cd /dev**.

2. Press the **Enter** key. This will change your location to the devices directory.

3. Key **ls** to list all of the files within that directory.

4. Press the **Enter** key. You will see several pages of devices scroll by. You can use the scroll bar to page up through the list. Remember that this does not represent everything that is actually connected to your computer. Instead it shows you all the things that can be connected to your machine. Try guessing what some of the devices are by looking at their names. Don't worry if they seem cryptic. It will become clearer as you use the system.

> **Note** ☑️
>
> Notice the color scheme that is applied to the files listed. Each color or highlighting indicates different types of files.

5. Look for the "zero" device in your list of devices. It is a special device that only produces zeros. It doesn't actually exist. It is a virtual device. This device is useful for generating test files that contain only zeros. You would use this file because it is often unimportant what the data is, just that a program can read the file or move it from place to place.

6. Close the terminal emulation program.

Daemons

Daemons are a key part of the Linux operating system. A daemon is a very special program. There are many of them running on your system. Learning to use them can be extremely helpful in getting the most use out of your Linux system. Most are actually part of a much bigger program or suite of programs. A daemon is a process that runs all the time in the background looking for certain events to happen. When those events happen, the daemon is triggered into action. Daemons make your life easier and convenient—and they are easy to recognize. The Linux standard for naming them is to use the name of the program and tack a "d" on the end. The atd is the daemon for the "AT" utility. The crond is the daemon for "cron."

To understand why daemons are needed and why they work, let's take a common example, the printing spooler. The spooler is a daemon associated with printing. Or more precisely, the printing process has a daemon called lpd. The printing process is not just one thing or application generating the hard copy. It is produced by several programs working in conjunction. It takes the lpd daemon, the spooler, any filters, and the operating system (for the I/O) to work.

■ lpd—A small program or daemon that runs in the background looking in the spooler queues for jobs to print. When a user submits a job to these queues, the daemon finds the file, starts the spooler program and tells it to take the file/print job and serve it to the appropriate printer for that queue.

■ Spooler—A program that takes a file from a specific directory and oversees the transmission of the file. This program does not require a daemon to work correctly. It must be considered one way when the daemon is running and considered another way when it isn't. This gives the program a sort of dual personality. Either way, if this program is not installed or working, then your print jobs will not make it to the printer—even if everything else is OK.

■ Filter—A filter is a set of instructions used to make sure the print job is correctly structured for the printer. In general, filters make it possible to convert from one printer type to another, including language changes, or to remove unwanted information and add needed information. This is not limited to converting from one printer language to another or simply image scaling so multiple pages will fit on one sheet. Filters are also conversion tools.

■ Spooler queue—A set of directories kept in a common spot, usually /var/spool/lpd/xxx, where xxx is the name of the printer. When users want to print a file, they print to a file at this directory. When the lpd daemon next passes the directory, it will see there is a file and automatically try to spool it to the printer. If there are multiple files, the daemon will try to spool them each in turn. If there is a job that can't be printed, the system administrator will receive mail reporting that it failed.

On the surface, this may seem overly complicated. If you were just setting up the printer for one user you may be right. But remember that Linux is a network operating system. That means it expects to be connected to a network. And in a network setting all users don't have their own printers. The machine the printer is connected to is called a print server. Sending a print job across the network is called submitting the print job. When the job is finally printed, it is said that the print job has been served. If the printer goes down for any reason, the print spooler will continue to collect jobs until the printer comes back online or it runs out of drive space. For this reason alone, this method is far more reliable than just keeping the job in memory until it is printed. For instance, if power is lost, you just need to reboot and the print spooler will pick up where it left off. All the unprinted jobs are still on the hard drive as files. Even if the print server goes down, print jobs will collect on your local machine until you run out of drive space or the server comes back up and printing resumes.

All that is needed to print across a Linux/Unix network is the IP address of the machine with the printer, the local directory on the printer machine for the spooler, usually `/var/spool/lpd/xxx`, and the name of the printer, xxx. The `lpd` daemon will take the print job generated by your machine and pass it along the network to the print server. From there the local printer daemon will see that the job gets printed.

Each Linux daemon should have its own suite of utilities or command-line options to control how it behaves. The following daemons are part of `lpd`:

- `lpr`—Offline print; the actual print command issued from the command prompt. This printer facility is very flexible and fast. As a result, many applications just redirect their output to this function and let the system manage the print job.

- `lpc`—Line printer control program. This small utility shows what printers and queues are enabled, allows rearrangement of jobs, and reports printer status.

- `lpq`—Spool queue examination program. This utility is used to manage, delete, and view the printer queues.

Unique Features

Some of the unique features of Linux are the things you don't see or know about unless you become a "power user" as discussed in the introduction to this lesson. The GUI (whether it be GNOME, KDE, or some other) makes Linux appear much like other operating systems that are currently available, and it also makes Linux much more accessible to the average user. However, we have not spent much time discussing the interfaces; although they do have some options and features that are not available in other operating systems (such as MacOs or Microsoft Windows), they are relatively intuitive. And they are not really what make Linux special.

In the previous sections, we have described a few of the things that give Linux its special power. And we have scratched the surface of what can be achieved through the command-line interface. In this last section, we will explore a few more features that are unique to Linux.

Modules

Linux is a monolithic kernel—in other words, it is a single, large program where all the functional components of the kernel have access to all of its internal data structures and routines. Because of this, Linux allows you to dynamically load and unload components of the operating system as you need them. Linux modules are lumps of code that can be dynamically linked into the kernel at any point after the system has booted. They can be unlinked from the kernel and removed when they are no longer needed. Most Linux kernel modules are device drivers, pseudo-device drivers such as network drivers, or file systems.

You can either load and unload Linux kernel modules explicitly using the `insmod` (install module) and `rmmod` (remove module) commands, or the kernel itself can demand that the kernel daemon (`kerneld`) load and unload the modules as they are needed.

This process of dynamically loading code as it is needed is attractive, because it keeps the kernel size to a minimum and makes the kernel very flexible. Modules can also be useful for trying out new kernel code without having to rebuild and reboot the kernel every time you try it out. However, nothing is for free and there is a slight performance and memory penalty associated with kernel modules. A loadable module must provide a little more code; this and the extra data structures take a little more memory. This process also introduces a level of indirection, which gives modules a slightly less efficient access to kernel resources.

Once a Linux module has been loaded, it is as much a part of the kernel as any normal kernel code. It has the same rights and responsibilities as any kernel code. In other words, Linux kernel modules can use the kernel just like all kernel code or device drivers can.

Modules must be able to find the kernel resources in order to use them. The kernel keeps a list of all of the kernel's resources in the kernel symbol table so that it can resolve references to those resources from the modules as they are loaded. Linux also allows module stacking, where one module requires the services of another module. One module requiring services or resources from another module is very similar to the situation where a module requires services and resources from the kernel itself. However, in this case, the required services are in a previously loaded module. As each module is loaded, the kernel modifies the kernel symbol table, adding to it all of the resources or symbols exported by the newly loaded module. This means that when the next module is loaded, it has access to the services of the modules loaded previously.

When an attempt is made to unload a module, the kernel needs to know that the module is unused and it also needs some way of notifying the module that it is about to be unloaded. That will enable the module to free up any system resources that it has allocated (for example, kernel memory or interrupts) before the module is removed from the kernel. When the module is unloaded, the kernel removes any symbols that the module exported into the kernel symbol table.

Virtual Consoles and Displays

When you boot your computer, you are brought to a console. This is where the computer asks for your login name and password. Think of the console as a physical computer. You have six consoles. Each behaves like a separate computer: It's as if you have six computers in one. The consoles, which are numbered 0 to 5, can be accessed from X Window by pressing the Ctrl and Alt keys and the appropriate function key, Vex. If you are already at a console, you switch consoles by pressing Alt and the appropriate function key, Fx. One major difference is that you must start the *virtual display* (X Window) using a console. You can't start a console from X Window. However, you can start the virtual display by starting a virtual terminal, which behaves exactly like a console.

Your computer has six virtual consoles and as many virtual displays as you want. The two are slightly different. In hardware terms, the *display* is the actual monitor. In operating system terms, it is what you see on the screen. The display can have several virtual terminals. You start a virtual terminal by clicking on the icon of a monitor on your workspace. Each one acts like a console, as if it were a completely separate machine. The virtual display can hold as many of these as you like. Remember that each time you open another virtual terminal, you are creating another job for the computer. It will run slightly slower for each one you open. The display is virtual in terms that it may be logically larger than the physical size of your monitor. This means that the computer will only be able to display part of the workspace. There will always be a part of the workspace it can't display. You end up with a window that floats across the workspace. To see different parts of the workspace, you move the frame using your mouse.

CRON

CRON is a powerful daemon that loads at boot time. From then on it is always running until you, as the superuser, disable it. It works like this: The CRON daemon loads and periodically checks the /etc/crontab file. In it is a listing of all the files it is supposed to run and when. Part of the listing is five special directories: /etc/cron.d, /etc/cron.hourly, /etc/cron.daily, /etc/cron.weekly, and /etc/cron.monthly. CRON treats each of these slightly differently. Whatever files it finds in these directories it tries to run. Every program that CRON tries to run is called a *job*. If it can't run a job, it will generate an e-mail message and try to send it using whatever mail service daemon is loaded to the root directory. (If a mail server isn't loaded, the message disappears into NULL.) The significance of the five directories is that you can just copy a program into the directory and it will run. There isn't any special configuration. The only stipulation is that the directories are run at different times. For instance, the cron.monthly directory is run only once a month. The cron.weekly is run only once a week.

All the files placed in the cron.hourly directory will be run once every hour. All the files placed in the cron.daily will be run once a day. All the files placed in the cron.weekly will be run once a week, and so on. The /etc/crontab file contains the settings that tell when these events are supposed to take place.

The crontab file lists data by columns. The leftmost column represents at what minute to start each job. Next is what hour to run, then on what week to run, then on what month to run. Next is on what day of the week to run. Days are numbered 0–6 for Sunday through Saturday, respectively. The last column is the description. On the surface this may seem very complicated—having to write one file and put it in spot A, then editing a different file in spot B—which, in turn is run by program C. Remember, though, that Linux was developed specifically as an open-ended system. That means it takes a building-block approach to things. There are a million little "widgets" that don't do much by themselves. But if you arrange them properly they are very powerful and act as a whole.

The different directories allow you to quickly save a job file to a different directory without doing any configuration specific to that file. Most people don't care what part of the day their daily jobs are run as long as they get done. And for most things this works fine. But for important things you can adjust the /etc/crontab for specific times and dates.

Processes

Processes perform tasks within the operating system. A computer program is a set of machine code instructions and data stored in an executable image on disk and is, as such, a passive entity; a process can be thought of as a computer program in action. Pretty much any command you run is a process.

A process is a dynamic entity, constantly changing as the processor executes the machine code instructions. The process also includes the program counter and all of the CPU's registers, as well as the process stacks containing temporary data such as routine parameters, return addresses, and saved variables. The currently executing program, or process, includes all of the current activity in the microprocessor. Linux is a multiprocessing operating system. Processes are separate tasks—each with its own rights and responsibilities.

If one process crashes, it will not cause another process in the system to crash. Each individual process runs in its own virtual address space and is not capable of interacting with another process except through secure, kernel-managed mechanisms.

A process uses many system resources during its lifetime. It uses the CPUs in the system to run its instructions, and it uses the system's physical memory to hold the process and its data. It opens and uses files within the file systems, and it may directly or indirectly use the physical devices in the system. Linux must keep track of the process itself and of the system resources that it is using, so that it can manage it and the other processes in the system fairly. It would not be fair to the other processes in the system if one process monopolized most of the system's physical memory or its CPUs.

The CPU is the most precious resource in the system; most workstations contain only one CPU. Linux is a multiprocessing operating system, whose objective is to have a process running on each CPU in the system at all times, to maximize CPU utilization. If there are more processes than CPUs (and there almost always are), the rest of the processes must wait until a CPU becomes free so that they can be run. Multiprocessing is a simple idea: A process is executed until it must wait, usually for some system resource; when it has this resource, it may run again. In a uniprocessing system (such as DOS) the CPU would simply sit idle and waste time while waiting. In a multiprocessing system, many processes are kept in memory at the same time. Whenever a process has to wait, the operating system takes the CPU away from that process and gives it to another, more deserving process. It is the scheduler that chooses which is the most appropriate process to run next. Linux uses a number of scheduling strategies to ensure fairness.

As a process executes it changes state according to its circumstances. Linux processes have the following states:

- Running—The process is either running (it is the current process in the system) or it is ready to run (it is waiting to be assigned to one of the system's CPUs).

- Waiting—The process is waiting for an event or a resource. Linux differentiates between two types of waiting process: interruptible and uninterruptible. Interruptible waiting processes can be interrupted by signals, whereas uninterruptible waiting processes are waiting directly on hardware conditions and cannot be interrupted under any circumstances.

- Stopped—The process has been stopped, usually by receiving a signal. A process that is being debugged can be in a stopped state.

- Zombie—This is a halted process, which, for some reason, still has a `task_struct` data structure in the task vector. It is what it sounds like, a dead process.

Each process within Linux also contains the information listed below which aids in decision-making processes:

- Scheduling Information—The scheduler needs this information in order to fairly decide which process in the system most deserves to run.

- Identifiers—Every process in the system has a process identifier. The process identifier is not an index into the task vector, it is simply a number. Each process also has user and group identifiers; these are used to control this process's access to the files and devices in the system,

- Inter-Process Communication (IPC)—Linux supports the classic Unix IPC mechanisms of signals, pipes, and semaphores and also the System V IPC mechanisms of shared memory, semaphores, and message queues.

Identifiers

Linux, like classic Unix, asks user and group identifiers to check for access rights to files and images in the system. All of the files in a Linux system have ownerships and permissions; these permissions describe what access the system's users have to that file or directory. Basic permissions are read, write, and execute. They are assigned to three classes of user: the owner of the file, processes belonging to a particular group, and all of the processes in the system. Each class of user can have different permissions. For example, a file could have permissions that allow its owner to read and write it, the file's group to read it, and all other processes in the system to have no access at all.

Groups are Linux's way of assigning privileges to files and directories for a group of users rather than to a single user or to all processes in the system. You might, for example, create a group for all of the users in a software project and arrange it so that only they could read and write the source code for the project. A process can belong to several groups (a maximum of 32 is the default) and these are held in the groups vector in the `task_struct` for each process. As long as a file has access rights for one of the groups that a process belongs to, that process will have appropriate group access rights to that file.

User Manual

Most of the documentation you will need is contained right on your hard drive in manual pages and information pages that are part of Linux. Most distributions (Red Hat included) have their own documentation as well. You can use the Help button on the GNOME Menu to access the Red Hat documentation as well as the manual and information pages.

Man Pages

The man pages are accessible through the command-line prompt. The manual is a simple program used to view the operating system manual pages. Each program or set of programs has a man page associated with it. When you install the program, the man pages are installed with it and your system is updated.

To use the man pages from the command prompt, you enter the word `man` and then the topic on which you want information. There is a catch, however. If your spelling does not match known topics, `man` will return `No manual entry for ____`. Many new users are discouraged by this idea because it can take several guesses to get the information you are seeking. But even in Windows, you have to look through the table of contents to find what you want.

The secret to using man effectively is to treat it like a search engine on the Internet. Try searching for several different variations on a single topic. The man[ual] pages will provide you with a complete online description of each command, followed by all of the command options.

If you access the man pages through the Help program, you will be provided an alphabetical listing of all of the man topics. You can then scroll through this list to view information.

> **Did You Know?**
>
> You can also access the help documentation for specific applications by selecting the Help menu option.

Info Pages

Another program that is also popular is called `info`. The *info page* provides a list of the most frequently used commands in Linux/Unix. You use it in much the same way as the man command. Just key `info` and the topic of interest and it will display the relevant topic. If no matching topics are found, it will list any that are available. Use the commands shown in Table 8-7 to navigate the info pages in the terminal emulator.

TABLE 8-7

COMMAND	RESULT
q	Quits
d	Directory of commands
h	Help tutorial
n	Next screen
p	Previous screen

Just like the man pages, the info pages are also integrated into the Red Hat user documentation so, if you are using this distribution, you can access all of your online help in one location.

STEP-BY-STEP 8.18

1. Open the **GNOME Menu** and click **Help**. The GNOME User Guide is displayed similar to Figure 8-19.

FIGURE 8-19
The Help Contents page

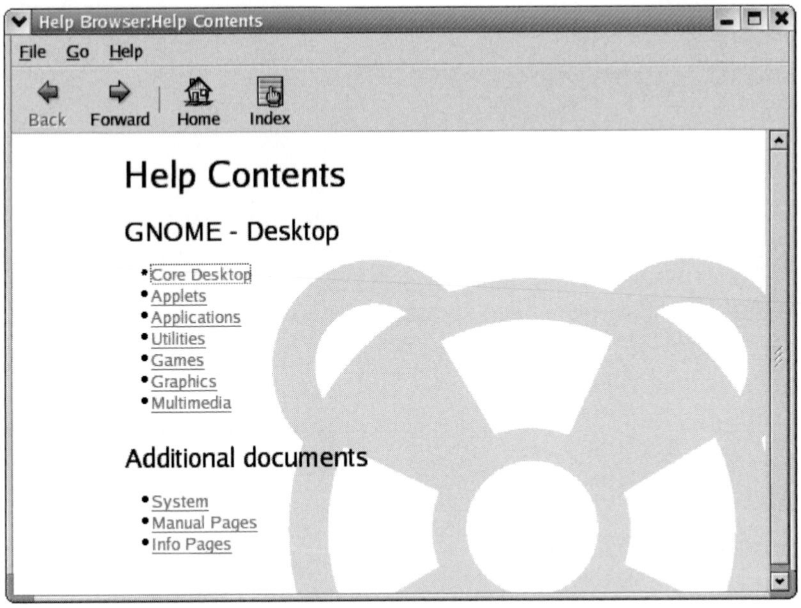

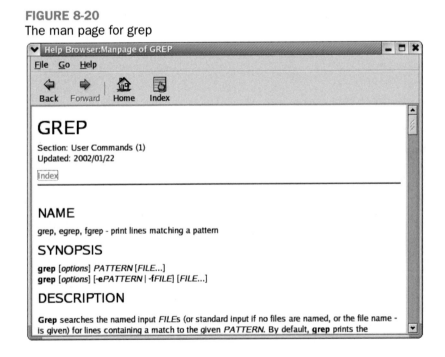

2. Click the **Manual Pages** link and then click the **Applications** link.

3. Scroll down and double-click the topic **grep (1)**. The manual page for grep is displayed as shown in Figure 8-20.

FIGURE 8-20
The man page for grep

STEP-BY-STEP 8.18 Continued

4. Read through the information on grep, scrolling down as necessary.

5. Click the **Home** button to return to the Help Contents page.

6. Click the **Info Pages** link.

7. Scroll down and click **find (info)**. The info page for the find command is displayed as shown in Figure 8-21.

FIGURE 8-21
The info page for find

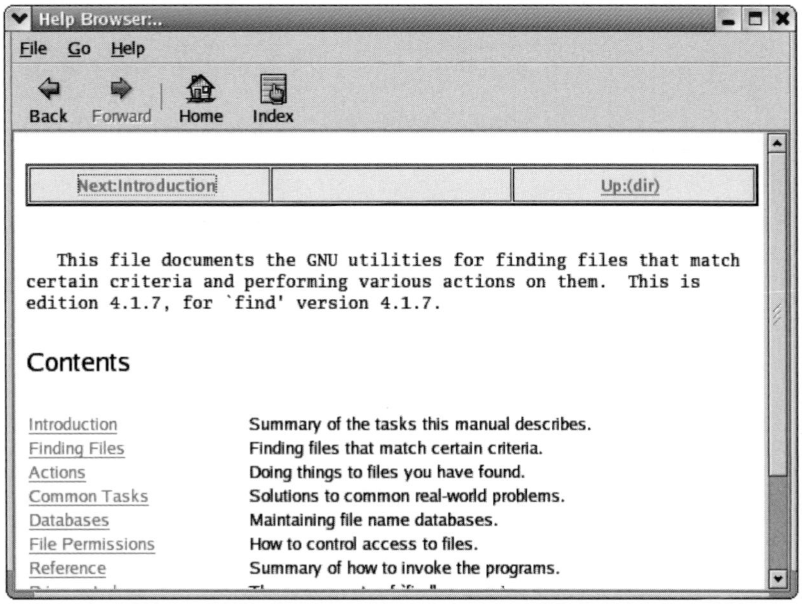

8. Read through the information on the find command, scrolling down as necessary.

9. When you have finished reading the information on find, close the help window.

Grep

Grep is the global regular expression parser. Given a source, it finds patterns of words that match what you supply. Grep will use any source that has been redirected to it. This could be anything from a text file to a microwave data stream. The pattern to match can be as simple as a single letter or as complex as a Shakespeare sonnet.

For example, if you are a crossword enthusiast you could use it to help you find a word you don't know. Let's say the word is 16 letters long and means *to sneeze*. You could tell grep to look for all 16-letter words using the *American Heritage Dictionary* as a source. You would specify the number of letters by using the ? wildcard. If there were any hits, they would be sent back to you for your inspection. If none were found you could always try another source. If you did know some of the letters, such as hy_ _ _ _ _ _ _ _ _ _ _ _ _ n, you could narrow the search. (The answer, by the way, is *hystoblogination*.) You can also use numbers in a grep search.

Pico

In Unix and Linux, `pico` is a small, simple-to-use text editor. It is useful in creating and changing text-based files. You can also use it when you need a quick-and-dirty edit (something like Notepad in Windows). Commands are listed across the bottom of the `pico` screen. They are the usual two-key shortcuts found in many programs. Ctrl-x exits the program. Usage is:

```
pico/path/filename
```

Package Management

A package is just another term for a Linux installation program. The package manager will install all the files in the proper places for the program you want to install. Using the package manager is not the only way to install a program—but it is the easiest.

It works this way: All packages have filenames that end in "rpm," or "rpms." (Generally you will only see "rpm.") Download the package on your hard drive. Then install it using this command:

```
rpm -Uhv packagename.rpm
```

The U must be capitalized and the hv must be lowercase. (If you want to try a few yourself, insert the Red Hat Installation CD number 2 and mount the drive. Remember that you use the command: `mount -t iso9660 /dev/cdrom /mnt/cdrom` to mount the drive.) Then, change into the `/mnt/cdrom/RedHat/RPMS` directory. This directory contains all the packages that come with Red Hat. Try a few if you wish. Most will already be installed on your computer, so don't worry if you get a message that they are already installed.

Shut Down the Linux System

When using Linux, it is important (just as it is with Windows or any operating system) that you shut the machine down in an orderly fashion. Don't turn it off without doing a formal shut-down. Your files are kept in cache (temporary) memory. The act of shutting down writes any file changes to your hard drive. If you turn off the computer without shutting down properly, you'll lose these changes. You could also lose part of your operating system—a situation you definitely want to avoid.

You can shut down Linux either through the command prompt or the more familiar GNOME Panel.

If you shut down through the command prompt, there are two possible parameters: The -r switch that causes Linux to shut down and reboot (returning to the login prompt); and the -h switch that causes Linux to shut down and halt (telling you to turn off the computer). You can also add a timeframe parameter after the switch, which specifies the number of minutes to wait before the switch takes effect. If you want the command to go into effect immediately, you enter "now" instead of a number.

We will instead use the shutdown method accessible through the GNOME Panel.

S TEP-BY-STEP 8.19

1. Click the **GNOME Menu** button on the GNOME Panel.

2. Click the **Log Out** command as shown in Figure 8-22.

FIGURE 8-22
The Log Out command on the GNOME Menu

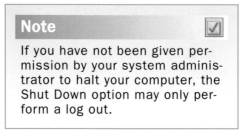

Select to log out

3. A confirmation dialog box asks if you really want to log out and gives you a choice of actions. The Log Out action logs out the current user and presents you with a new login screen. The Shut Down option stops all processes and unmounts all file systems. The Restart the computer action performs a shutdown, and then loads a clean version of the kernel.

Note ☑

If you have not been given permission by your system administrator to halt your computer, the Shut Down option may only perform a log out.

4. Select **Shut Down** and then click the **OK** button. The system then shuts down, leaving the Power Down message on the screen.

5. Turn off the power to the system.

While this brief lesson cannot tell you all there is to know about a Linux operating system, it should give you a basic understanding of it and help you appreciate what makes it different from other operating systems. If you want to learn more, please read the documentation provided with Linux, or visit one of the many Web sites devoted to Linux or sponsored by one of the Linux distributors.

SUMMARY

In this lesson, you learned:

■ The installation used the Red Hat 8.0 distribution. If you don't have it available don't worry. Most distributions (there are more than 40 of them) use the same or similar installation. You can modify the base installation to fit your needs and you can tweak the installation to improve performance and add neat features. Linux can be installed on a hard drive that also contains other operating systems.

■ You can work with your Linux system through the user-friendly GNOME interface or one of the other GUI environments available. Working in these environments is much the same as working in the environments with which you are already familiar—with some added benefits.

■ Linux was originally designed to be used without a mouse. You can still easily access this command-line environment, in which you do most things by keying. Since many users do not have strong keyboarding skills, certain tools have been included to speed things up and make it easier for the person keying.

■ The Linux kernel is the core of the operating system. It maintains the files in the file systems that it supports.

■ Linux, like all versions of Unix, presents its hardware devices as special files. The EXT2 file system and the Linux VFS (virtual file system) both implement device files as special types of inode. There are two types of device files: character and block special files. The device drivers implement file semantics within the kernel itself: You can open them, close them, and so on.

■ When using Linux it is most important that you always shut the machine down properly. Don't turn it off without doing a shutdown. The act of shutting down writes any changes to your hard disk drive. If you turn off the computer without shutting down, you lose any changes to your files—and you might also lose part of your operating system.

VOCABULARY *Review*

Define the following terms:

Daemons	GNOME Panel	Mount point
Desktop environments	Graphical user interface (GUI)	Open source code
Disk Druid	Info pages	Virtual display
Extended file system (EXT2)	Man pages	Virtual File System (VFS)
GNOME	Mount directory	XTerm

REVIEW *Questions*

MULTIPLE CHOICE

Select the best response for the following statements.

1. The Linux man pages
   A. refer the user to a specific page number in the Linux manual.
   B. provide a complete online description of each command, followed by all of the command options.
   C. were named after their creator, Humphrey Mandrake.
   D. None of the above.

2. In addition to the GNOME desktop environment, at startup the user can
   A. select the KDE and Default desktop environments.
   B. select the Failsafe desktop environment.
   C. elect to log off the Linux system.
   D. All of the above.

3. You know that you have a second workspace area opened when
   A. the words "a second workspace is open" appear at the top of your display.
   B. the second pane in the Workspace Switcher appears to be depressed.
   C. circles appear in the Workspace Switcher's indicators.
   D. the Workspace Switcher's indicator flashes.

4. The command used to deselect and then remove a file system is:
   A. `unmount`
   B. `dismount`
   C. `umount`
   D. `remove`

5. To change the directory, key:
   A. `chgdir`
   B. `change`
   C. `chdir`
   D. `cd`

TRUE/FALSE

Circle T if the statement is true or F if the statement is false.

T   F   1. The command `cd root` performs the same function as `cd /root`.

T   F   2. To use Linux, you must pay royalties to Linus Torvalds.

T   F   3. You can mount a hard drive wherever you want in the file system.

T   F   4. Linux is considered a single-user operating system.

T   F   5. A Linux distribution makes the Linux operating system available for free to anyone who wants it.

MATCHING

Match the correct term in Column 1 to its description in Column 2.

Column 1	Column 2
___ 1. cd	A. list command
___ 2. md	B. print working directory
___ 3. pwd	C. copy command
___ 4. ls	D. make directory
___ 5. cp	E. change directory

WRITTEN QUESTIONS

Write a brief answer to each of the following questions.

1. What is the difference between a virtual console and a virtual desktop?

2. How do you access the Linux manual?

3. What is the kernel?

4. What does LILO stand for? What does it do?

5. What are some of the commands that you can use in a terminal emulation window and what can they do?

PROJECTS

PROJECT 8-1

1. Start the text editor gedit or pico.

2. Create a new text file that lists the names of five of your friends and their phone numbers.

3. Save the new file as **myfile**.

4. Use grep to locate one of your friends (search for the name) in myfile.

5. Using the man pages, find out how you would send this job to print in 10 minutes using the AT utility.

6. Try using the AT utility again—this time setting the job to occur in a short amount of time.

PROJECT 8-2

1. From the GNOME Menu, launch the following applications—one in each of the four workspace areas.
   - The terminal emulation program in workspace area #1.
   - A Web browser in workspace area #2.
   - The Help documentation in workspace area #3
   - A simple text editor in workspace area #4.

2. Close each application.

CRITICAL *Thinking*

ACTIVITY 8-1

Name some of the major companies worldwide that now use Linux as their primary operating system. Why do you think they have switched from other commercial operating systems such as Windows NT or Windows 98 to Linux?

ACTIVITY 8-2

Linux is developed under the GNU General Public License and its source code is freely available to everyone. How is it, then, that companies and developers may charge money for the source code? Is this an ethical practice on their part?

Glossary

A

Administrator A person with special rights and privileges. This person has a better-than-average knowledge of computers. He or she runs, upgrades, and troubleshoots the network.

Alias A copy of the icon representing a pointer to an original file. Aliases have italicized text and a small bent arrow added to their icon.

Application A program that does work or processes information. Different applications perform different tasks. Drawing programs create pictures, word processors create documents, and so on.

Aqua The user interface that Apple has placed over Darwin to make it more useful.

B

Basic input-output system (BIOS) The ROM chip that has been programmed with the instructions needed to begin the boot process. It contains the necessary code to enable the CPU to talk to the other hardware in the system.

Booting up The initial startup procedure of a computer.

C

Cabling The physical wire used to carry the networking electrical impulses. It includes twisted-pair, coaxial, ThickNet, ThinNet, fiber-optic, and mixed-media cable.

CD Changes the directory.

Central processing unit (CPU) The microprocessor that is the "brain" of a microcomputer. See *microprocessor*.

Check Disk A utility that will locate problem areas of the hard disk, attempt to repair them, and, if not repairable, mark them as bad so that no data will be stored there in the future.

Classic A kind of emulation mode to accommodate programs written for the older Macintosh systems. It is identical to Mac OS 9.

Click A mouse gesture whereby the user positions the mouse cursor over an object and then presses and releases the mouse button quickly. Used to select items on the screen.

ClickLock A feature of your mouse that allows you to lock a mouse button to select text without continuously holding it down.

Close box A small square button at the upper-right corner of a window, in the title bar, that closes the window when clicked (reduces it to its icon).

ColorSync Apple's system for making sure that colors match between devices. It uses a set of standardized profiles based on color space and intended input or output.

Command key A key on Macintosh keyboards, often located next to the spacebar, with an open apple and "propeller" symbol. Used to perform keyboard shortcut commands. See *control key* and *option key*.

Command-line user interface An interface in which the user types a command to get the computer to do something.

Compression The coding of data to save storage space.

Container A method of organizing computer files. Usually called folders or subdirectories, among other things.

Container objects Containers are used to organize the network. Think of a container as a drawer in a filing cabinet.

Context menu Shortcut menu, activated by the right mouse button, which displays several tasks that are commonly performed with an item.

Control key   A key, usually located in the bottom corner of the keyboard, that allows the typing of control characters. It is also sometimes used as a command key. See *option key* and *command key*.

Control Panel   A utility which contains accessory programs and tools for configuring and customizing the Windows operating system and your hardware.

Copy   Copying information (text, pictures, sounds, etc.) from a document to a temporary file (called the Clipboard) for "pasting" somewhere else. See *paste*.

COPY   Duplicates a file.

CPU   Central processing unit. The microprocessor chip or card that is the main "brain" of the computer.

Cut   Cutting information (text, pictures, sounds, etc.) from a document to a temporary file (called the Clipboard) for "pasting" somewhere else. See *paste*.

D

Daemon   A process that runs continuously in the background looking for certain events to happen.

Darwin   Apple's open-source version of BSD Unix. It is invisible to the user.

DEL   Deletes a file.

Desktop   Generally, when people refer to the desktop, they mean what is on the monitor. For all practical purposes, treat this just as you would your desktop in your office.

Desktop environment   One of four desktop configurations allowed in Linux by X Window. Depending on how your system was installed, you may or may not have all the desktop environment choices. A desktop environment includes, among other things, graphical elements visible on the screen and mechanisms allowing the user to launch various applications.

Devices   Physical components attached to your computer (examples: printer, modem, scanner, mouse).

DIR   Displays a directory listing.

Disk   A circular piece of plastic or metal coated with magnetic material, used for storing computer data. Also, the hardware device used to read from and write to a disk.

Disk Cleanup   A utility that helps you remove unnecessary files safely from your machine.

Disk Druid   A program, like FDISK, that is used to format diskettes. It has a slightly friendlier interface than FDISK.

DISKCOPY   Copies the contents of a disk.

Dock   Found on the bottom of the Macintosh screen by default, but you can change its location. The Dock can contain application icons and folders and always contains the Trash.

Document   A type of computer file that contains information. Documents are created and read by programs. Sometimes called a data file.

Domain   A group of computers and devices on a network that are administered as a unit with common rules and procedures. A domain is found in server-based networks.

DOS   Acronym for disk operating system. The generic term for early microcomputer operating systems. Especially used to refer to MS-DOS from Microsoft.

Double-click   A mouse gesture whereby the user positions the mouse cursor over an object, then presses and releases the mouse button twice in quick succession. Used to open items on the screen.

Drag   A mouse gesture whereby the user sets the starting position by moving the mouse cursor on the screen, then holds the mouse button down while moving the mouse. Used to select multiple items or to move items from one place to another.

Drivers   Programs that tell the computer how to access a network or another component.

E

Edit   Opens the text editor to create files.

Ethernet   Used to describe a type of networking. It is so common that it has become a de facto standard. You may not see any other type.

EXT2   The second extended file system (EXT2) was devised by Rémy Card as an extensible and powerful file system for Linux. It is the most successful file system so far in the Linux community and is the basis for all of the Linux distributions that are currently shipping.

F

FAT   File allocation table.

FDDI Fiber Distributed Data Interface. This fiber-optic technology is a high-speed method of networking. It is composed of two concentric rings of fiber-optic cable. The transmission distance is measured in kilometers, as opposed to meters for other technologies. It is very expensive and therefore only used to connect large offices together or in locations where high traffic necessitates it.

FDISK A fixed disk utility. Its purpose is to partition a hard disk drive.

File A named collection of data that is stored in a specific location.

Finder The actual name of the user interface portion of MacOS.

Floppy disk A 3.5-inch disk used to store data.

Folder An icon that looks like a folder. In actuality, it is a subdirectory on your hard drive. It is capable of holding other folders, icons, documents, programs, and files.

Format A utility which configures a disk so that it can accept and hold data.

G

Gateway A computer used as a portal to everything outside of the network. All traffic is passed through this point on the network. Think of it as the only road off an island.

Get info A command that allows you to find out how big a file is, when it was created, or the access privileges.

GNOME An acronym for GNU Network object model environment and is available in many languages for worldwide use. GNOME is a desktop environment written in X, which allows you to use and configure your computer easily.

GNOME Panel A configurable display at the bottom of the desktop in Linux that should remind you of the taskbar in Windows. It performs the same functions as the taskbar and more.

Graphical user interface (GUI) An interface in which the user interacts with the computer through a screen pointing device (usually a mouse), with graphical representations of the files on the computer screen.

H

Hard drive Also called "hard disk." It is the physical storage device for all data on your computer.

Hardware The physical parts of a computer, usually consisting of a box that contains the microprocessor, memory, and other components, a monitor, and attached devices.

Hardware compatibility list (HCL) A list available from Microsoft that shows which hardware devices are compatible with Windows software.

I

Icon A small picture that represents a file, disk, menu, option, or program.

Icon view When in this view, items within the window will be represented by small pictures called icons. These icons can be moved around by dragging them.

Info pages Short for information pages. Part of the Linux help system.

IP Internet Protocol. The common language spoken by every machine on the Internet.

K

Kernel The heart of an operating system. Usually used in reference to Unix, it is the part of the OS code that does not change between different kinds of hardware.

Keyboard A standard input device consisting of several rows of spring-loaded switches, each representing a letter of the alphabet, a number, or symbol and so on, which users can press sequentially to input text into a computer. Modern keyboards are usually arranged in a QWERTY arrangement. See *QWERTY*.

L

Leaf objects Leaf objects contain information about the different components/computers on the network. Think of these as the file folders you put in a filing cabinet drawer.

Left-click The act of pressing the left mouse button once. The left mouse button is the default button for selecting an item or making an item active.

Left-drag The act of positioning the mouse pointer over an icon or option, pressing and holding down the left mouse button, and then moving the mouse to a new position. The icon will follow the mouse pointer. When the button is released, the icon is released and dropped to its new position.

Linux A version of Unix created by Linus Torvalds. Linux is unique because it is an "open source," which means that it is available for change by any programmer.

List view This view allows items to be represented as icons, although the icons are much smaller (and sometimes less detailed), with information to the right of the icon.

Local area network (LAN) A network of interconnected workstations sharing the resources of a single processor or server within a relatively small geographic area.

M

Macintosh A PC from Apple Computer. The first company to make a commercially viable GUI.

MacOS The Macintosh operating system from Apple Computer. See *Macintosh*.

Mainframe computer A large computer, originally handmade, built on a hardware frame (hence the name).

Man pages Short for manual pages. This is the Linux help system. By typing man and then a keyword, you can receive help about the keyword.

MB An abbreviation for megabyte.

MD Makes a directory.

Media See *cabling*.

Menu bar The top edge of a screen that has all the menus in it.

Menu-based user interface A computer user interface whereby the user selects options from a menu to get the computer to do something.

Microcomputer An early name for a personal computer. Usually built around a microprocessor such as the Intel 4004, 8008, 8086, or the Motorola 68000, etc.

Microprocessor A microscopic circuit on a small chip of silicon or similar material. A typical microchip consists of hundreds and thousands of transistors. Sometimes called the CPU or central processing unit. See *central processing unit* and *microcomputer*.

Minicomputers Manufactured computers that are more powerful than microcomputers, but less powerful than mainframe computers.

Monitor A CRT (cathode-ray tube) or other display device connected to a computer to provide principal output.

Mount directory See *Mount point*.

Mount point The location where you can find the device or file system. The files of the mounted file system cover up the existing contents of the mounted directory.

Mouse A motion-sensitive device whose actions are replicated on the computer screen; usually has one or more buttons to effect actions on the computer.

Mouse keys Using mouse gestures in combination with control, option, shift, or command keys. The most common are shift-click (used to select multiple items on the screen) and control-click (used to replicate the function of the alternate mouse key; brings up pop-up contextual menus).

Multitasking The ability of a computer to appear to do more than one thing (run more than one program) at a time by sharing the memory and CPU.

My Computer A utility that gives you access to all of the storage devices attached to your computer.

N

NDS Novell Directory Services. This is Novell's method of keeping track of all computers and other resources on the network.

NDS tree Novell Directory Services tree. This is the representation of how all the computers, printers, and so on are attached to the network. It looks like a tree with one computer, usually the corporate office, as the root or control of the entire network.

NetWare A network scheme developed by Novell, Inc. It is an extension of IP, Internet Protocol. It was one of the first non-mainframe methods of creating large networks and connecting two or more networks into a wide area network, or WAN.

Network The connecting of two or more computers to share files or other services (such as printers).

Network board Also referred to as LAN cards, network adaptors, and network interface cards (NICs). This device provides an interface or access to the physical network. It allows the user to send and receive information across the network.

NIC See *network board*.

NTFS New Technology File System.

O

Online This term is used to describe any device or software that is accessible by the computer. A printer is considered online if it is turned on and you can print to it. If it is turned off, then the printer is offline.

Open source code Open source code means that the operating system code has no proprietary restrictions. Anyone may alter the code to meet his or her own needs without having to seek permission from the "owner."

Operating system (OS) A program that acts as an intermediary between the user or programs and the computer hardware.

Option key A key, often located next to the command key, with the word "Option" or "Alt" on it. Used to type additional characters from the keyboard. It is rarely used as a command key. See *control key* and *command key*.

OS See *operating system*.

P

Packets Small chucks of data translated into protocol and sent across the network.

Panels view In this view, the window divides itself into columns. Each column represents the contents of a folder. Within those contents, you may find other folders. Each time you click a folder, its contents are shown in the panel to its immediate right. If a file other than a folder is clicked, the panel to its right shows an enlarged view of the icon, with some extra details about the file. Clicking certain types of files may even bring up a short preview of the contents of the file in the new panel.

Partition A logical division of a disk drive.

Paste Moving information (text, pictures, sounds, etc.) from a temporary file (called the Clipboard) to the position of the cursor in a program. See *copy* and *cut*.

PC An acronym for "Personal Computer." Originally a brand name from IBM. Now generally used for all microcomputers intended for personal use.

Permissions Authorizations allowing a user to access certain files and folders on another machine in the network.

Primary partition This is the partition on which the bootable operating system will reside. The bootable operating system is the one your system will always boot to first. You can only have one primary partition.

Print server A dedicated computer or device that interfaces the printer to the network. It allows users to print from a remote location.

Printer A device that produces a hardcopy output of information, usually on paper.

Protocol An agreed-upon format for exchanging information. It is very easy to pass the same information using different protocols. Various protocols have different strengths. Think of protocols as being like human languages.

Q

QWERTY The name of the standard arrangement of the keys on a keyboard. Named for the first six letters of the arrangement at the top left. See *keyboard*.

R

RAM Random access memory; the native workspace memory of a computer. Found in memory chips on the computer.

Recycle Bin An area on the hard drive that holds files and folders deleted from your local hard drive(s) until you are absolutely sure you want to remove them.

Registry A system file where all configuration changes to Windows NT are recorded.

REN Renames a file.

Resize button A small button located at the bottom-right corner of a window used to change the size of a window by dragging it.

Right-click   The act of pressing the right mouse button. This causes a menu, which varies according to the item you clicked, to pop up. From there, you can use the left mouse button to make your selection. The right mouse button also causes contextual help to appear.

Right-drag   The act of positioning the mouse pointer over an icon, pressing and holding the right mouse button down, and then moving the mouse to a new position. The icon will follow the mouse pointer. Normally, this causes a copy of the icon to be made at the new position. It can also create a shortcut. Depending on what item is being right-dragged, the end result may be different.

Rights   The network's way of controlling who has access to what. They also guarantee that new users automatically get the basic utilities they need to do their job. They are an impartial system of controlling access, which are assigned by the system administrator, then managed by the network.

Router   A device used to physically connect two or more networks together. It provides a high degree of security and traffic control. It is much more than simply twisting two wires together.

S

Scanner   A device used to input graphics into a computer.

Scroll bar   A graphic method for moving the contents of a window into the viewable area of the window. It usually consists of a gray bar with a small button in it that moves relative to the contents of the window. It also has arrow buttons to move the button smoothly through the gray bar (and hence, the window's contents through the viewable area of the window).

SCSI   Small Computer System Interface. A way to connect high-speed devices to a computer.

Server   A powerful computer that is not used directly by users on the network. It controls the network and holds common programs/data that need to be accessed by everyone. It also manages printer requests, mail, chat, and other functions of the network.

Shortcut   A quick way to open a file or program without having to go to its original location. Shortcuts look like the original icons that they represent, except they have small arrows at the bottom indicating that they are shortcuts. They help save time and increase productivity by making your most commonly used programs and documents easily accessible from your desktop.

Snap to   This feature automatically snaps your mouse pointer to the default button in a dialog box.

Soft boot   Using Ctrl+Alt+Del to restart your system or using the reset button on the front of your computer system to do so.

Start button   This button is in the lower-left corner of your monitor and is used to access all features of Windows. Using the mouse, you click on it. This causes a series of menus to be displayed. From there, you can select any program or utility installed on your computer.

Start menu   The Windows menu used to access your favorites folder, documents, programs, files, and utilities and to shut down your computer.

Startup disk   A floppy disk used to recover your system in the event of operating system failure.

Subfolder   A folder within another folder which is used to further organize files.

System Folder   The folder containing all the files (control panels, extensions, etc.) used by the operating system to function.

System Preferences   An application in Mac OS X in which the Control Panels are located.

T

Tape   A lengthy strip of plastic, usually coiled onto a spool and often inside a plastic case. The strip is coated with magnetic material. Tape is then used as a storage medium for computer data.

Task Scheduler   A utility through which you can schedule certain tasks (Disk Cleanup, Check Disk, and Disk Defragmentation) which must be performed regularly for your computer to run efficiently.

Taskbar   A gray rectangular bar at the bottom of your desktop used to give quick access to programs, application windows, and system tools.

Terminal An early device for communicating with a mainframe or minicomputer. It usually consists of a keyboard and monitor, but has no CPU. Sometimes called a "dumb terminal" because of its lack of a CPU.

Title bar The bar across the top of the window that displays the name of the program you are using.

Token Not a physical object, but a special bit configuration used in a Token ring.

Token ring The predecessor to FDDI. This older and slower technology is slowly fading away because of its high price tag. It consists of a ring of computers that communicate by passing a token around the ring. Only the computer with the token is allowed to speak. This is a similar idea to raising your hand in class before speaking. It has a high effiency rate, usually around 86%. The downside is that, if one machine malfunctions, then the whole network stops working.

Trash An icon (on the Macintosh) representing the delete function. Files can be deleted by dragging them to the Trash icon.

Troubleshooter A tool available if you have problems with a hardware device. Among the problems that can be fixed are hardware problems and networking problems. You can also resolve issues with system setup, printing, and adding new hardware devices.

U

Unix An operating system that was initially used for larger minicomputers. See *Linux*.

USB port Universal System Bus; a high-speed, serial, daisy-chainable port in newer Macintosh computers, used to connect keyboards, mice, printers, and other input and output devices.

User The ordinary person who uses a computer.

User interface The part of an operating system (and all other programs) which provides a way for humans to communicate with the machine. Also called the human-computer interface.

User Manager A system utility for creating and managing user accounts.

V

Virtual display Your computer has six different virtual consoles and as many virtual displays as you want. The two are slightly different. In hardware terms, the display is the actual monitor. In operating system terms, it is what you see on the screen. The display can have several virtual terminals. You start a virtual terminal by clicking on the icon of a monitor on your desktop. Each one acts like a console—as if it were a completely separate machine.

Virtual File System (VFS) The Virtual File System allows Linux to support many, often very different, file systems—each presenting a common software interface to the VFS. All of the details of the Linux file systems are translated by the software, so that all file systems appear identical to the rest of the Linux kernel and to programs running in the system. Linux's VFS layer allows you to transparently mount the different file systems at the same time. The Linux VFS is implemented so that access to its files is fast and efficient as possible.

Virtual memory A method that uses disk space to substitute for RAM when the latter is unavailable.

W

Wide area network (WAN) Two or more local area networks connected together. An example of this is connecting all the regional offices in a company to the main office. Each office has its own network, but all of them connected together form a WAN.

Window The main functional object on the screen. A window contains icons that represent files and has a title bar, close box, zoom box, and other controls to change its look and function.

Windows The brand name for several GUI operating systems from Microsoft.

Workgroup A logical grouping of computers that shares resources such as files and printers. A workgroup is called a peer-to-peer network because all computers act as equals.

X

XTerm (short for x terminal) is a terminal emulator, which makes your computer behave like a dumb terminal (a CRT combined with a keyboard that has no processing capabilities of its own). When working under X, the XTerm program allows the Linux user to execute shell commands. In addition to entering commands interactively, XTerm allows you to execute a batch script in the background that you created during an earlier XTerm session.

Z

Zoom box A small square button in the upper-right corner of a window used to toggle the size of the window.

INDEX

A

Accounts system preference, 83–84

Add/Remove Hardware Wizard, 155

ADMIN user, 261

Administrators
Windows NT Workstation, 228
Windows XP, 146

Aliases, 66

AppleTalk tab, 81

Applications. *See* Programs

Aqua, 62–72

Arguments, 32

Automatic Client Upgrade, 258–259

B

Babbage, Charles, 13

Backslash, 32

Backup disk, creating, 46, 127

Backup utility, Windows 2000, 154

Basic input-output system (BIOS), 5, 8

Batch files, 45

Binary files, executing, in DOS, 35

Booting, from CD, 90

C

Cabling, 246

Capture Settings, specifying, with Windows printing, 264–265

Case sensitivity, in Linux, 272

CD-ROM, installing clients from, 250–253

Central processing unit (CPU), 4, 7, 9–10

Change directory command, 301–302

Check Disk utility
in Windows 2000, 200–201
in Windows XP, 143–144

Classic, 62–63

Classic preferences, 74

ClickLock feature, 106

Clients, installing, from CD-ROM, 250–253

Client workstations, 244, 249

Clipboard, 123, 183

ColorSync preferences, 75

Command completion, 295–296

Command functions, DOS, 44

Command history, 296–297

Command key, 59–60

Command-line user interfaces, 3–4

Command prompt, DOS, 32–33

Commands
Aqua, 70–72
DOS, 33–49
processing of, 2–3
Linux shell, 301–305
Windows XP, 123–126
See also File management

Compiler, 271

Compression, 223

Computers
early, 13–15
evolution of, 12–20
frozen, 112, 169

Configuration files, updating, in Novell Client, 256–258

Container objects, 260

Containers, 11

Contents, in Help, 116–117, 172

Context menus, 105

Control Panel
Windows NT Workstation, 225–228
Windows 2000, 196–198
Windows XP, 105, 138–140

Copy command, Linux, 304

Copying files
in Aqua, 70
in DOS, 40–42
to floppy disk, 127, 186–187

in Novell Client, 255
in Windows 2000, 182–183
in Windows XP, 123–124, 130–131

Country (C) objects, 260

CRON, 308–309

Custom installation, Linux, 277–288

D

Daemons, 306–307

Darwin, 62

Date, checking and changing, in DOS, 27

Default directory. *See* Working directory

Defragment disk, 46

Deleting files
in Aqua, 71–72
in Windows 2000, 184–186
in Windows XP, 125–126, 130–131

Desktop, 104
Aqua, 64
environments, 289
GNOME, 290, 292–294
Personal, installing Linux to, 276

Device icons, 219

Diagnostics, 46–48

Directory, 33–34
changing, 36
install, 31
making, 35–36, 303
mount, 297
remove, 303

root, 32
working, 301

Directory commands, DOS, 44

Disk(s), 7–8
automatic partitioning of, 278
checking and defragmenting, 46
copying files to, 127, 186–187
formatting, 119–120, 178–179
manually ejecting, 90
See also Hard disks

Disk Cleanup utility
in Windows 2000, 199–200
in Windows XP, 142–143

Disk Defragmenter utility
in Windows 2000, 154, 201–202
in Windows XP, 144

Disk Druid, 279

Disk operating system (DOS)
environment, 31–32
installing Novel Client from, 253–254
introduction to, 25–26
mtools and, 304–305
unique features of, 44–49
in Windows NT Workstation, 223–224

Disk partitions, 156

Disk Utility, 85–87

Displays preferences, 75–77

Dock, Mac OS X, 64, 69–70

Dock preferences, 77–78

Document icons, 219

Documents, 11

Domain, 157

Drivers, 242, 249

E

Editing, text files, in DOS, 40

Email tab, 82

Encrypting File System (EFS), 154

Environment, 1
desktop, 289
DOS, 31–32

Error messages, DOS, 49–51

Ethernet, 246

Extended file system (EXT2), 298

Extensions, in Windows NT Workstation, 221

F

FAT32, 154

FDISK, 26, 28–29, 278

Fiber distributed data interface (FDDI), 245

File allocation tables (FATs), 29, 100, 213, 301

File commands, DOS, 45

File management, 10–12
Aqua, 70–72
DOS, 34
Linux, 297–301
Windows Explorer, 129–131
Windows NT Workstation, 221–225

Windows 2000, 154, 175–188

Windows XP, 117–131

See also Resource management

Files

batch, 45

binary, 35

configuration, 256–258

copying, 11–12

in Aqua, 70

in DOS, 40–42

in Novell Client, 255

in Windows 2000, 182–183

in Windows XP, 123–124, 130–131

defined, 181

deleting, 12

in Aqua, 71–72

in Windows 2000, 184–186

in Windows XP, 125–126, 130–131

finding

in Windows 2000, 187–188

in Windows XP, 128

identifying, 11

moving, 11–12

in Aqua, 70

in DOS, 42–43

in Windows 2000, 182–183

in Windows XP, 123–124, 130–131

navigating and locating, 11

opening, in WordPad, 136, 193–194

printing, in WordPad, 135, 192–193

renaming

in Aqua, 70

in DOS, 43–44

in Windows 2000, 183–184

in Windows XP, 124–125, 130–131

saving, in WordPad, 134, 191–192

text, 39–40

types of, 10–11, 34–35

File systems

mounting and unmounting, in Linux, 298–300

for Windows 2000, 156–157

for Windows XP, 100–101

Finder, Windows and, 65–68

Floppy disk. *See* Disk

Folder icons, 219

Folders, 120–122, 180–181

creating

in Aqua, 70

in Novell Client, 255

See also Containers

Force Quit, 90–91

Formatting

floppy disk, 119–120, 178–179

hard drive, 30

Format and Unformat commands, 48

Format utility, 26

Function keys, 60

G

Gateway, 247

Get Info command, 70–71

GNOME, 289

GNOME Desktop, 290, 292–294

GNOME Panel, 291

Graphical user interface (GUI), 4, 216–221, 289

Grep, 313

H

Hard disk drive

formatting, 30

partitioning, 213

preparation for, 26–27

Hard disks, 7–8

storage space on, 222–223

Hardware, 4–8

classification of components, 5–8

Linux devices, 305

minimum requirments

for Windows NT Workstation, 212

for Windows 2000, 155

for Windows XP, 98–99

troubleshooters, 140–141

for use with Windows 2000, 155

Windows-based versus Macintosh, 58–62

Hardware compatibility list (HCL)

for Windows NT Workstation, 213

for Windows 2000, 156

for Windows XP, 99–100

Help, 48

Macintosh, 89–90

Windows 2000, 172–174
Windows XP, 116
See also Troubleshooting

I

Icon(s)
 changing name of, 172
 changing display of, 177–178
 Control Panel, 197
 in Finder, 66
 five basic types, in Windows NT Workstation, 219
 My Computer, 218–219
 Server, 227
 Tape Devices, 226
Icon view, 67
Identifiers, Linux, 310–311
Incompatibilities, with Novell Client, 249–250
Info page, 311–313
Input devices, 5–6
Installation
 DOS, 26–30
 Linux, 272–288
 network options, 258–259
 Novell Client, 247–259
 Windows 2000, 155–160
 Windows NT Workstation, 212–215
 Windows XP, 98–103
Install directory, changing, 31
Interfaces. *See* User interface
Internet Protocol Security, 154
Internet system preference, 81–83
iTools tab, 82

K

Keyboard, 5–6
 Macintosh, 59–62
 using, to maneuver in Linux, 295–297
Keyboard shortcuts
 to DOS menu functions, 38
 to Virtual Consoles, 292
Key Caps utility, 87

L

LAN cards. *See* Network boards
Leaf objects, 261–262
Linux
 basic functionalities of, 289–307
 file system history, 298
 installation of, 272–288
 introduction to, 269–272
 selecting package group for, 285–286
 shutting down system, 314–315
 special files, 305–307
 unique features of, 307–314
List command, 302–303
List view, 67
Local area network (LAN), 241
Locality (L) container object, 261
Logging on
 Windows NT Workstation, 215–216
 Windows 2000, 154
 Windows XP, 103

M

Mac OS X
 introduction to, 57–58
 managing options, 72–79
 three faces of, 62–63
 troubleshooting, 89–91
.mac tab. *See* iTools tab
Mainframes, 15–17
Make Alias command, 70
Make directory command, 303
Man pages, 272, 311
Memory management, 10
Menu bar, Aqua, 64–65
Menu-based interfaces, 4
Menus, context, 105
Minicomputers, 15–20
 See also Central processing unit (CPU), Computers
Modules, 307–308
Monitor, 6–7, 58
Motherboard, 5
Mount directory, 297
Mounting, 277
Mount point, 297
Mouse, 5–6
 Macintosh, 58–59
 using and configuring, 104–108, 161–165
Move command, Linux, 304
Moving files
 in Aqua, 70
 in DOS, 42–43
 in Windows 2000, 182–183
 in Windows XP, 123–124, 130–131
Moving folders, in Windows 2000, 181

Mtools, 304–305

Multitasking, 9–10

My Computer
icon, 218–219
moving folders around in, 122
Windows 2000, 175–178
Windows XP, 117–119

N

NDS, 259

NDS context, 262

NDS tree, 259

NetWare Server object, 261

Network, 243–247
checking for connection, 248
installing clients from, 254–255
managing, 79–85

Network boards, 245, 249

Network Neighborhood, 233–236

Network printer, printing to, 262–264

Network protocols, configuring, 253–255

New Technology File System (NTFS), 100–101, 154, 156–157, 213, 231–232

News tab, 82

NICs. *See* Network boards

Novell Client
installing, 247–259
introduction to, 241–247

Novell NetWare
basic functions of, 259–262
unique features of, 262–265

O

Objects, 260–262

Open Data-Link Interface (ODI) drivers, 249

Open source code, 271

Operating system (OS), 1–4
basic functionalities of, 8–12, 31–44
installing, 30–31
shutting down, 9
starting up, 8–9
See also Disk operating system (DOS)

Option key, 60

Organization (O), NDS tree, 260

Organizational Unit (OU), NDS tree, 260

Output devices, 6–7

P

Package management, Linux, 314

Panels view, 68

Partition, 213
with Linux installation, 278–279
Windows XP, 100

Password, changing, 216

Permissions, 231

Personal Desktop, installing Linux to, 276

Pico, 314

Plug and Play Support, 155

Pointing device, 5–6

PPPoE tab, 81

Preferences
Mac OS X, 72–79
Network system, 79–81

Print Center utility, 87–89

Printer, 6–7

Printing
Capture utility and, 264–265
list of files, 34
from network printer, 245, 262–264
text files, in DOS, 40
WordPad file, 135, 192–193

Print server, 247

Print working directory command, 301

Processes, Linux, 309–310

Program icons, 219

Programs, 10
word processing, 131–138, 189–194
Workstation versus Server, 211–212

Protocol, 244

Proxies tab, 81

R

Random access memory (RAM), 5

Read-only memory (ROM), 5

Rebooting, 29

Recycle Bin, 125–126, 184–186

Registry, Windows, 227–228

Remove directory command, 303

Remove file/directory command, 303

Renaming files
in DOS, 43–44
in Windows 2000, 183–184

Resource management, 8–10, 259–262

Rights, assigning, 256

[Root], 260

Root directory, 32

Router, 247

S

Saving, WordPad file, 134, 191–192

ScanDisk, 48

Scanner, 5–6

Scroll bars, 114–115, 170–171

Scrolling, in Mac OS X, 67

Search, Help, 173–174

Security
    Windows NT
        Workstation, 231–233
    Windows 2000, 154

Server(s), 244
    icon, 227
    installing Linux to, 277
    print, 247

Server protocols and requirements, checking, 248

Settings, MS–DOS, 30–31

Shared network driver, mapping, 234–236

Sharing system preference, 84–85

Shell commands, Linux, 301–305

Shortcuts
    creating, on Desktop, 137–140, 194–195
    to DOS menu functions, 38
    icons for, 219

keyboard, to Virtual Consoles, 292
    in Windows NT Workstation, 220–221

Shutting down
    operating system, 9
    when frozen, 112
    Windows NT Workstation, 224–225
    Windows 2000, 154
    See also Force Quit

Snap To feature, 107

Software Update preferences, 78–79

Start button, 110–113, 217–218

Start menu, 137–138, 154, 167–169, 195–196

Storage, 7–8
    checking and freeing space, 222–223
    devices for, in Windows NT Workstation, 221

Subfolders, 120

Swap partition, sizing, 279

System maintenance
    in Windows 2000, 198–205
    in Windows XP, 141–145

System Preferences, 72–73

T

Tape, 7–8

Tape Devices icon, 226

Task Scheduler utility
    in Windows 2000, 202–205
    in Windows XP, 145

Taskbar, 108–109, 165–167

Tasks, in Windows 2000, 154

TCP/IP tab, 79–81

Text
    keying and inserting, in WordPad, 190
    selecting and inserting, in WordPad, 133

Text editor, DOS, working with, 37–39

Text files, viewing, 39

Time, checking and changing, in DOS, 27

Title bar, 67, 113

Token, 246

Token ring, 246

Toolbar options, 109

Trackball, 5–6

Trash, 69–70

Tree name, NDS, 259

Troubleshooting
    Windows XP, 140–141
    Mac OS X, 89–91
    installation
        Windows 2000, 160
        Windows XP, 103

U

Unix, 270–271

Upgrade, versus clean install, Windows XP, 101–103

User accounts
    Windows NT Workstation, 228–231
    Windows XP, 146–147

User interface, types of, 3–4
    See also Aqua, Graphical user interface (GUI)

User Manager, 229–231

User manual, Linux, 311–313

Users
creating, in Linux, 284–285
managing, 79–85

Utilities
Backup, 154
Capture, and printing, 264–265
Check Disk, 143–144, 200–201
Disk Cleanup, 142–143, 199–200
Disk Defragmenter, 144, 154, 201–202
Format, 26
Mac OS X, 85–89
Task Scheduler, 145, 202–205

V

Video card, configuring, 286–287

Views, in Mac OS X, 67–68

Virtual Consoles, 291–292

Virtual consoles and displays, 308

Virtual File System (VFS), 298

Virtual memory, 10

Voice devices, 5–6

W

Web tab, 82

Wide area network (WAN), 242, 247

Wildcards, 45, 304

Windows, 113–114, 169–170
active and inactive, within GNOME, 290–291
and Finder, 65–68
versus Linux, 269–270
views, 67–68

Windows 95/98
incompatibilities with Novell Client, 249–250
installing Novell Client for, 258

Windows Explorer, 129–131

Windows NT Workstation
basic functionality of, 215–225
DOS in, 223–224
incompatibilities with Novell Client, 250
installing, 212–215
installing Novell Client for, 258
introduction to, 211–212
unique features of, 225–236

Windows registry, 227–228

Windows 2000
basic functions of, 161–174
changes to, from previous versions, 154–155
incompatibilities with Novell Client, 250
installing Novell Client for, 258
introduction to, 153
unique features of, 194–205

Windows XP
basic functions of, 103–117
incompatibilities with Novell Client, 250
installing, 98–103
installing Novell Client for, 258
introduction to, 97
unique features of, 137–147
upgrading versus clean install, 101–103

Word processing
Windows 2000, 189–194
Windows XP, 131–138

WordPad, 131–138, 189–194

Workgroup, 157

Working directory, 301

Workstation
installing Linux to, 277
New Location for, 79

Workstation versus Server software, Windows NT, 211–212

X

Xterm program, 294–295